The Logic of the Spirit in Human Thought and Experience

James E. Loder Jr. in Later Life

The Logic of the Spirit in Human Thought and Experience

Exploring the Vision of James E. Loder Jr.

Edited by
Dana R. Wright *and* Keith J. White

Foreword by John S. McClure

☙PICKWICK *Publications* · Eugene, Oregon

THE LOGIC OF THE SPIRIT IN HUMAN THOUGHT AND EXPERIENCE
Exploring the Vision of James E. Loder Jr.

Copyright © 2014 Wipf and Stock Publishers. All rights reserved. Except for brief quotations in critical publications or reviews, no part of this book may be reproduced in any manner without prior written permission from the publisher. Write: Permissions, Wipf and Stock Publishers, 199 W. 8th Ave., Suite 3, Eugene, OR 97401.

Pickwick Publications
An Imprint of Wipf and Stock Publishers
199 W. 8th Ave., Suite 3
Eugene, OR 97401

www.wipfandstock.com

ISBN 13: 978-1-62564-689-7

Cataloging-in-Publication data:

The logic of the spirit in human thought and experience: exploring the vision of James E. Loder Jr. / edited by Dana R. Wright and Keith J. White, with a foreword by John S. McClure.

xxvi + 358 p. ; 23 cm. Includes bibliographical references.

ISBN 13: 978-1-62564-689-7

1. Loder, James E. (James Edwin) 1931–2001. 2. Church work with children. 3. Christian education of children. 4. Children—Religious life. I. White, Keith J. II. McClure, John S., 1952–. III. Title.

BV4571.3 W33 2014

Manufactured in the U.S.A.

To and for all children of God everywhere

He called a little child to him,
and placed the child among them.

Matthew 18:2

Contents

List of Contributors ix
List of Illustrations xii
Foreword by John S. McClure xiii
Preface by Keith J. White xvii
Acknowledgements xxiii

Introduction: *Homo Testans*: The Life, Work, and Witness of James E. Loder Jr.—*Dana R. Wright* 1

PART ONE—The Child Theology Movement and James E. Loder in Dialogue

1. Child Theology, Loder, and Holistic Child Development —*Keith J. White* 33

2. Forgiving Constitutes the Person—*Haddon Willmer* 58

3. James E. Loder and Paul in Conversation: Discourses of Development and Disruption —*Elizabeth Waldron Barnett* 78

PART TWO—James E. Loder and Christian Education Theory and Practice

4. *The Transforming Moment* and Godly Play —*Jerome W. Berryman* 105

5. Baptizing John Dewey: James Loder's Pedagogy of Presence Theory and Practice—*Thomas John Hastings* 131

6. Pedagogical Implications of Loder's Theory of Transformation—*Lauren Sempsrott Foster* 143

7   *Educational Ministry in the Logic of the Spirit*: A Loder Legacy?—*Dana R. Wright*   155

PART THREE—**James E. Loder's Relevance to Psychology, Counseling, and Sociology**

8   The Healing of Memory as a Pathway to Transformation: A Case Study Presenting James Loder's Counsel —*Mark Koonz*   205

9   Transformation of the Ego: A Study via Sudhir Kakar and James E. Loder—*Ajit A. Prasadam*   243

10   Walking Alongside Children as They Form Compassion: Loder and Lerner in the Role of Relationships and Experience as Interactive Developmental Process —*Wendy Hinrichs Sanders*   268

PART FOUR—**James E. Loder and the Transformation of Christian Witness**

11   A Tactical Child-Like Way of Being Human Together: Implications from James Loder's Thought for Post-Colonial Christian Witness—*Dana R. Wright*   291

Loder Bibliography   333

Contributors

ELIZABETH WALDRON BARNETT is currently undertaking doctoral studies in the area of New Testament examining the constructs of maturity in the letters of Paul and harnessing Paul's theology as a critique of the developmentalist and progressivist assumptions of so much Western thinking, culture, and most tragically, theology.

JEROME W. BERRYMAN holds degrees from the University of Kansas and Princeton Theological Seminary (MDiv and DMin). He also earned a JD in law from The University of Tulsa, College of Law and holds honorary degrees (DD) from Virginia Theological Seminary and The General Theological Seminary in New York City. He is the creator of *Godly Play*, a comprehensive vision for enabling the spiritual life of children, and the author of many books

THOMAS JOHN HASTINGS is Senior Research Fellow in Science and Religion at the Japan International Christian University Foundation. He was formerly the Director of Research at the Center for Theological Inquiry in Princeton and Professor of Practical Theology at Tokyo Union Theological Seminary. He is the author of *Practical Theology and the One Body of Christ* (Eerdmans, 2007) and is working on a book on Kagawa Toyohiko's "scientific mysticism," having just finished editing and writing the introduction for the English translation of Kagawa's final work, *Cosmic Purpose* (Veritas Series, Cascade, 2014).

MARK KOONZ is Pastor of Emmanuel Lutheran Church in Walla Walla, Washington. He has written journal articles on T. F. Torrance, Karl Barth, George Sayer, and James Loder, especially focused on Loder's theory and practice of counseling.

AJIT A. PRASADAM is presently general secretary of the India Sunday School Union (ISSU), and director of the St. Andrew Centre for Human Resource Development and Counseling. He has facilitated a major curriculum based on the theories of James Loder, "Windows to Encounter," from pre-school to grade 11, available in Tamil, Hindi, Kannada, and English, and in translation into several more major languages of India. He has also taught in institutions of higher learning in the U.S., Sri Lanka, Myanmar, and India.

WENDY HINRICHS SANDERS is professor of early childhood education at College of the Desert in Palm Desert, California. She holds a doctorate in intercultural studies from Fuller Theological Seminary, having conducted her research on the formation of compassion within children. She holds degrees in elementary education and children's and family ministries from the University of Wisconsin and Bethel Seminary.

LAUREN SEMPSROTT FOSTER is a recent graduate of Wheaton College in the Christian Formation and Ministry program. She serves as the program director for the Glen Ellyn Children's Resource Center, Glen Ellyn, Illinois.

KEITH J. WHITE lives at Mill Grove, a Christian household and residential community that cares for children and families in the East End of London, UK. He founded and chairs the Child Theology Movement. His books include *A Place for Us* (1976); *In His Image* (1988); *The Art of Faith* (1997); *The Growth of Love* (2008); *Introducing Child Theology* (2012); *Entry Point* (with Haddon Willmer) (2013). He is editor of *The Bible Narrative and Illustrated* (2006).

HADDON WILLMER is Emeritus Professor of Theology at Leeds University of Leeds, England, where he taught for thirty years, publishing articles on theology, forgiving and politics. He also serves as a trustee of the Child Theology Movement and of Parents against Child Sexual Exploitation.

DANA R. WRIGHT is presently the Director of Christian Formation and Discipleship at the First Presbyterian Church, Everett, Washington, and serves as an adjunct faculty member for Trinity Lutheran College in Everett and for the St. Andrew Center in Coonoor, India, a division of the India Sunday School Union. He is the co-editor of *Redemptive Transformation in Practical Theology* (Eerdmans, 2004), a *Festschrift* in honor of James Loder.

Illustrations

Photo of James E. Loder Jr. in Later Life. Princeton Theological Seminary   ii

Child Theology Movement Logo   xvii

Photo of James E. Loder Jr. as a Young Scholar. Princeton Theological Seminary   10

Loder's Theological Interpretation of Talcott Parsons' Action Theory   182

Damasio's Emotional Thought Diagram   277

Foreword

I FIRST MET DANA Wright after he asked me to write a chapter in James E. Loder's Festschrift, *Redemptive Transformation in Practical Theology* (2004). I was impressed by several things. First, Dana is an earnest and exacting scholar. Second, he is one of the best and most comprehensive interpreters of Loder's complete body of work. Third, he is passionate about the *importance* of Loder's ideas for practical theology and the broader theology and science dialogue. Finally, and this is where this book comes into play, he is committed to sustaining and enhancing an international critical discussion in which Loder's ideas are brought into relation to key themes and issues in practical theology.

The book before you is a first rate academic work that focuses Loder's unique theological perspective onto one thought-provoking theological signifier: "the child." Without sentimentalizing or stereotyping either children or childhood, the authors you are about to read bring biblical, theological, and social scientific scholarship into conversation with Loder's consistently theological approach to epistemology, stage theory, and human formation.

Had he lived longer, James Loder would have found much to like about the Child Theology Movement (CTM). Loder had serious difficulties with many of the more "adult" proclivities within late modern society: socialization, achievement orientation, "normal" human development, and a host of other commitments and schemes devised by adult human beings seeking to secure themselves in the world. At the same time, much of his work was concerned with what it means to educate and form children in a way that embraces the creative power of the human spirit in relation to the transformative power of the Holy Spirit. He would find it very provocative, therefore, to see his ideas brought into dialogue with a host of international scholarship regarding "child theology."

As I read this book, I found myself in complete agreement with Dana Wright, who argues that scholars from many disciplines should begin to elevate the stature and importance of Loder's ideas to match the level of critical discussion surrounding another important theologically oriented theorist of faith development, James Fowler. Loder's work made use of some of Fowler's ideas, but Loder was deeply critical of the way that faith was normalized into stages in Fowler's work. For Loder, the creative power of the human spirit in relation to the Holy Spirit, at work *across* the developmental journey, was more important than the socialization of faith within stages. The reason for this difference in perspective is *theological*, and the essays in this book are quick to highlight this significant and pervasive theological element in Loder's work.

One of the great qualities of this book is that it makes Loder's work more accessible. One reason why Loder's work has not received as much critical discussion as Fowler's lies in its complexity and erudition. Without fail, each writer in this book breaks open, and breaks *down* (without dumbing down) Loder's ideas so that we can see how these ideas might help us to shape a huge variety of new perspectives on the child, childhood, and child development.

The scholarship in this book is also global and interdisciplinary, and we have the Child Theology Movement to thank for that. CTM is currently investing much of its time and energy encouraging scholarship in all parts of the world where the lives of children are at stake, and in which the biblical vision of the child can operate as an important metaphor for the Reign of God. From diverse cultural perspectives and situations, this book includes essays by a biblical scholar, sociologist, pastor, missiologist, Christian educator, public educator, theologian, and children's spirituality specialist. Loder was always concerned to discover new ways to understand the human spirit in its relation to the Holy Spirit across cultures and contexts. He would have found great value, therefore, in the global and interdisciplinary scope of this book.

Keith White, who directs the Child Theology Movement and who organized and led the convocation during which the essays in this book were first delivered, and Dana Wright, who edited the essays into a cohesive volume, are much to be thanked for seeing to it that this collection has come into being. In my experience, Loder was often misunderstood among his colleagues and academic peers. In part, this occurred because he was, as Wright points out, *homo testans*, a living human testimony to the transformative Spirit of Christ in his own life. His own personality, therefore, bore the marks of the liminal theology of the Spirit that he studied and taught. It is crucial, therefore, that those who know his work well, and believe in the value of his ideas, see to it that precisely *this* kind of critical engagement occurs in a variety of ways. One can only hope that more similar works, around a variety of topics, will follow soon.

John S. McClure
Charles G. Finney Professor of Preaching and Worship
Vanderbilt Divinity School

Preface

The Child Theology Movement (CTM) and Its Interest in the Work of James E. Loder

KEITH J. WHITE, CHAIR OF CTM

THE CHILD THEOLOGY MOVEMENT convened a small conference on the campus of Princeton Seminary in March of 2012. This event brought together members of CTM and several scholars who had studied with James E. Loder, Jr., who, for 40+ years until his death in 2001, served as the Mary Synnott Professor of the Philosophy of Christian Education at Princeton Seminary.[1] Both CTM members and Loder's former students delivered papers interacting with various aspects of Loder's work. Lively and frank discussions followed, and a special camaraderie developed among the participants. Hoping to share the experience with others, these papers were later revised, recollected and edited for inclusion in this collection. The purpose of this preface is to explain the brief history of CTM and why the directors committed the movement to a conference on the legacy of James E. Loder.

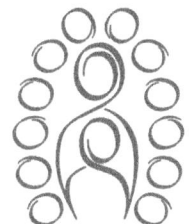

Child Theology Movement

---

1. See the survey of Loder's life and work in the introduction of this volume.

Child Theology

The putting together of the two words "child" and "theology" was done consciously for the first time as far as we know just a decade or so ago.[2] This close juxtaposition of terms does not mean that no one had thought of the relationship between child and theology, or theology and child, before that. There has been implicit attention to what we call Child Theology over the centuries, and this attentiveness continues today. For example, Jerome Berryman's *Children and the Theologians*[3] (which has a very full review on the Child Theology Movement website),[4] coupled with Marcia Bunge's *The Child in Christian Thought*,[5] provide ample evidence that others are at work in this general area.

So what, then, if anything, is distinctive about Child Theology as a contemporary movement? Let me begin by saying that history will be the judge. CTM comprises a small, but growing international network of theologians (of every hue) that seeks to explore what it means for followers of Jesus, whether as individuals or as church (including parachurch) communities, to change and become humble like little children. CTM pays close attention to the little child Jesus placed in the midst of the Gospel story as a call to welcome little ones in his name. We note particularly that in Matthew chapter 18 it is Jesus the Christ who acted by putting a little child in the midst of a theological argument among his disciples. Jesus spoke about what this act meant and how disciples of his should live in light of this act. Therefore his followers (historical and contemporary) cannot, and hopefully do not, wish to evade the implications of what we have called Child Theology. And it is precisely because it was not obvious to the disciples then, and has not been obvious to the church ever since—what this means, or how we should change—that there is important, possibly compelling and urgent, theological work to be done by all of us who call ourselves followers of Jesus.

Now in some parts of the world there are tighter categories of theology than in others, and so it may be asked which categories of theology

---

2. The first written record of their use is in an unpublished paper by Keith J. White, "Child Theology," given at the Annual Forum of the UK Christian Child Care Forum on 5th February 2002, in London.
3. Berryman, *Children*.
4. See www.childtheology.org
5. Bunge, *Child*.

those who are part of CTM are most interested in or committed to developing and living out. The answer is that we seek to live out whatever the action and teaching of Jesus commands of us. In order for us to follow this Jesus and live out his Gospel, we must mine the deepest levels of biblical, systematic, and historical theology. Yet our goal is always transformed practice. Those hundreds worldwide who have attended consultations and connected to the CTM network include perhaps a majority of Christians who seek what might be called transformational practical theology, including transformed Christian education (significantly enough for a Loder conference!) and a transformative mission and ministry with children as their focus.

So there is, and can be no neat answer to this question, "What is Child Theology?" Haddon Willmer (one of the contributors to this volume) and I have spent over ten years trying to work out what Child Theology—starting with Matthew 18—might look like.[6] By inclination and commitment we are both drawn to doing theology in real life situations, and therefore to practical theology. Yet ours is a practical theology that does not cease to wrestle with the very heart of biblical, systematic and historical theology—God in Jesus Christ, crucified, risen, and ascended. Some members of CTM come from different perspectives. Elizabeth Barnett, another contributor to this volume, concentrates her attention on Pauline theology. Others look through the lens of "children's spirituality," while still others from the standpoint of the history of Child Theology. CTM, therefore, is an ecumenical and inclusive movement that seeks to connect with all persons and groups who bow the knee before Jesus Christ as Savior and Lord.

It may help if we can hold on to the fact that the words "child" and "theology" do not in themselves, in English at least, define the relationship between them.[7] This fact is significant. CTM is not primarily about developing "theologies of children" (whatever they may look like). Neither is it about a child or children doing theology.[8] Nor is it intended to describe a form of liberation or contextual theology that

---

6. Willmer and White, *Entry Point*.

7. We have discovered over the past since 2002 that there are many languages, including Russian, German and Mandarin that have no way of conveying the open-ended nature of these two English nouns placed side by side, without one qualifying or being more prominent than the other.

8. An example of this interpretation would be Richards and Privett, *Through the Eyes*.

places children's concerns at the center of the theological task, as in say Feminist or Dalit theology. And it is certainly not to be equated with Holistic Child Development. Rather, the relationship between "child" and "theology" must be allowed to remain subtle and many faceted, as befits a venture that takes as its starting point a sign given by Jesus. By definition both signs and the kingdom of God are provisional—we see through a glass darkly on earth—and therefore so is the theological task that links "child" and "theology."

We have discovered, possibly at some cost to the integrity of their interrelation, that when one utters the two words "child" and "theology" together, it is always the former that trumps the latter. No matter whether you are talking with theologians in a seminary, or Christian child activists on the street, when the word "child" is heard loud and clear, the word "theology" quickly tends to get lost in the background noise or recede rapidly down the corridor. But if we take seriously Jesus' action of placing the child in the midst of our theological deliberations, we dare not make the child herself the primary focus of our attention and enterprise. This was not the purpose of Jesus, and it would be wayward of his followers to misconstrue his intentions! Rather, the child was a clue to the nature of the kingdom of God and a sign of how we can and should relate to Jesus. As we see it there is every reason to allow the child as sign to lead us into every area of theology. Right here CTM resonates with the work of James Loder, who, we will see, was not tied to any one area, doctrine or type of theology (perhaps his colleagues wished he was!). Loder offered insights applicable across the whole spectrum of theology, and indeed across the whole of human experience and the sciences that seek understanding of dimensions of experience, between what he himself called the little and big infinities.

The child placed by Jesus may well do the same: offering insights way beyond the particular context and conversation described in Matthew 18. So it is not about territory or putting boundaries around the limits of our interest, but rather seeking to follow where God in Christ through the transformational dynamic of the Holy Spirit leads. (The last phrase has been chosen to resonate with the work of Loder). And so, in the 2012 conference and throughout this book that resulted from our meeting together, we explore possible synergy, connections and insights between the concerns of CTM and those of James Loder. If it is anything, the Child Theology Movement sees itself as a response to an invitation by Jesus to follow Him, with no guarantee from Him where it will lead. The Child Theology Movement seeks to function in ways that respect and underline this Christological invitation, distinguishing Child Theology from other related enterprises described above, but without being doctrinaire in its diverse efforts.

So Why a Conference on the Work of James E. Loder?

The Child Theology Movement convened this Loder event, and did so by faith and at some financial risk, in part because of my personal intuition. I became convinced that the vitality of the development of Child Theology depended in particular on its ability to engage the deepest dimensions of practical theology. And this intuition (or hunch, if you will) developed in a particular crucible, called Mill Grove, where the world of children and the call of the Gospel of Jesus Christ become vivid for me.[9] All I knew of humanity through children, all I knew of theology, and all I knew of child development (in its broadest sense) came together in my book *The Growth of Love*.[10] And this book would not have been possible to write without the work of James Loder. Now *The Growth of Love* is not Child Theology: indeed it specifically points this out. It is, rather, an exploration on the theme of love always open to human experience, secular theory, and biblical theology.

In his book *The Logic of the Spirit*, James Loder seeks to understand human development (including of course, child development) in theological perspective. He does so, being acutely aware of the many challenges raised by those who seek to achieve a proper relationship among the disciplines, a relationship that does justice, for example, to theology ("the view from above") and socio-psychological theory ("the view from below"). Now Child Theology as we have already seen is not simply about this interdisciplinary issue: it has a far wider remit. But

---

9. Mill Grove is the name of the home of a unique extended family and residential community that began as an informal foster family in 1989. It is still a place of love and care where children and young people who cannot live with their own families may be fostered, or for families who need accommodation and support. In this home-like setting and atmosphere Christians share their lives, and many of these, now living in many different parts of the world, regard Mill Grove as their home. Hundreds more, though continuing to live with their own families, have found Mill Grove to be a place of acceptance, encouragement, and nurture.

10. White, *Growth*.

what Loder is doing is integral to any attempt to work at practical theology with children and young people. So it was and is that CTM decided to convene this event and to underwrite the publishing of the papers delivered in March 2012.

We were aware that Loder's legacy is known to a very loyal and enthusiastic band of former students and colleagues, but that his work is little quoted outside this coterie. And so we hope that the conference and this collection will bring his work to a wider international audience. Over time it has become clear to the directors of CTM that our calling is to find ways of identifying, connecting, nurturing and empowering a "Community of Scholars." Certainly universities were intended at the outset to be just such communities. This intention explains the architecture, design and philosophy of Princeton Theological Seminary, for example. The contemporary scholarly emphasis on specialization, autonomous disciplines, and insular routines makes true interdisciplinary conversation in community rare indeed. Now if that interdisciplinary conversation fails to happen when scholars have actually gathered in a single location, imagine how much more challenging it is to support a community of scholars drawn from every part of the planet! Our gathering together, and this modest collection of essays seeks to model a community of scholars that captures something of this need for international conviviality and trust. CTM has taken on this tall order as a central feature of its own sense of call. We trust that time will be a favorable judge of our efforts to enable a truly radical, worldwide, conversation.

Works Cited

Berryman, Jerome W. *Children and the Theologians: Clearing the Way for Grace*. New York: Morehouse, 2009.

Bunge, Marcia J. *The Child in Christian Thought*. Grand Rapids: Eerdmans, 2001.

Richards, Anne, and Peter Privett. *Through the Eyes of a Child: New Insights into Theology from a Child's Perspective*. London: Church House, 2009.

White, Keith J. "Child Theology is Born." Unpublished paper delivered at the Annual Meeting of the UK Christian Child Care Forum, London, February 5, 2002.

White, Keith J. *The Growth of Love*. Abingdon, Oxford: Barnabas, 2008.

Willmer, Haddon, and Keith J. White. *Entry Point: Towards a Child Theology with Matthew 18*. London: WTL, 2013.

Acknowledgements

THE EDITORS OF THIS volume would like to express our gratitude for all those who made both the March 2012 conference and the book that derives from it, possible. We thank, first of all, the directors of the Child Theology Movement for seeing the significance of the connection between CTM's own work and vision and the legacy of James E. Loder, and for being willing to support these efforts financially. In particular we thank John Collier, the Company Secretary of CTM for all the preparatory work he did for the conference, and Karissa Glanville, for so ably and joyfully taking on the responsibility of conference administrator (and on such short notice!). We thank those who helped make the practical arrangements of the conference such a joyous occasion: Amy Ehlin and her colleagues at PTS's Erdman Center for their warm welcome and efficient service, and Tom Hastings for serving as the host of the conference, organizing the many practical assignments that that task entailed.

We are, of course, greatly indebted to each of the contributors to this volume whose essays were first given orally and discussed among strangers who quickly became friends. We are grateful for their efforts to revise and re-revise the essays for publication. And whatever the liabilities of the digital age, we thank God for the internet, which makes such international collaborations possible with such speed. We also thank all of those who participated in the conference and who, though they may not have submitted papers, nonetheless contributed to this book through their passionate commitment to Christ and to children. They are: Marina Anderson, Ann-Charlotte, Karissa Glanville, Sandra Kuntz, Rune Oystese, and John Tiersma Watson.

We appreciate John McClure of the Vanderbilt Divinity School for his generous Forward. We also take note of the many scholars, pastors, and librarians who contributed to the bibliography that updates the one included in the Loder *Festschrift Redemptive Transformation in Practical Theology* (Eerdmans, 2004). We are also grateful to the staff at Pickwick

Publications and especially to our editor Justin Haskell, for their excellent guidance and expertize that made the conversation enshrined in these pages available to a wider audience.

Dana would also like to thank his congregation, the First Presbyterian Church of Everett, Washington, and its pastor, the Rev. Dr. Alan Dorway, for granting him study leave to attend the 2012 conference and for graciously allowing him to take the time necessary to write his essays and co-edit this volume. The connection between the local congregation and the academy is very important to all of us who contributed to this collection. Dana also thanks Judy, his wife of 38 years, for her continual support and encouragement. It's so nice to have someone be your biggest fan!

We wish to thank the following persons/publishers for granting permission to use copyrighted materials:

- From Mrs. Carol Browning, for her late husband Don Browning's unpublished essay "The Struggle over the Future of the Church: The Contribution of Practical Theology," delivered at the organizational meeting of the International Academy of Practical Theology, 1991. All rights reserved. Used by permission.

- From HarperCollins Publishers for C. S. Lewis' *The Last Battle*, copyright CS Lewis Pte Ltd 1956, reprinted in London: HarperCollins 1990. All rights reserved. Used by permission.

- From Helmers & Howard, for James E. Loder's *The Transforming Moment*, 2nd ed (1989) and *The Knight's Move: The Relational Logic of the Spirit in Theology and Science* (1994). All rights reserved. Used by permission.

- From Hope Publishing Company, for a stanza from the hymn "Remember, Lord, the World You Made," by Timothy Dudely Smith, Carol Stream, IL: Hope Publishing Co. 1981. All rights reserved. Used by permission.

- From Houghton Mifflin Harcourt for quotes from Robert Penn Warren's *All the King's Men* and from T. S. Eliot's poem "Little Gidding." All rights reserved. Used by permission.

- From John Wiley and Sons, Inc., for James E. Loder's *The Logic of the Spirit: Human Development in Theological Perspective* and from *Mind, Brain and Education*. All rights reserved. Used by permission.

- From John Wiley and Sons, Inc., for the diagram "Emotional Thought" from the essay "A Tale of Two Cases: Lessons for Education from the Study of Two Boys Living with Half Their Brains." All rights reserved. Used by permission.

- From the National Council of Churches for *New Revised Standard Version Bible* and *New Revised Standard Version Children's Bible*, copyright 1989. Division of Christian Education of the National Council of Churches of Christ in the United States of America. Used by Permission. All rights reserved.

- From Oxford University Press India for Sudhir Kakar, *Identity and Adulthood* (1979). All rights reserved. Used by permission.

- From Penguin Books India Pvt Ltd for Sudhir Kakar, *A Book of Memory: Confessions and Reflections* (2012) and Sudhir Kakar and Katharina Kakar, *The Indians—Portrait of a People* (2007). All rights reserved. Used by permission.

- From Princeton Theological Seminary for two photos of Dr. Loder. All rights reserved. Used by permission.

Last, but not least, we all thank James E. Loder Jr. for his extraordinary contributions to Practical Theology and Christian Education during the last half of the 20th century. He continues to inspire many of us—through his writings, his recorded interviews, and the vivid memories of his friendship and example—to bear witness to Jesus Christ with confidence and humility born of the fiduciary passion inspired by *Spirit Creator*.

Introduction

Homo Testans

The Life, Work, and Witness of James E. Loder Jr.

DANA R. WRIGHT

Insight happens to the well-prepared mind.
—ALBERT EINSTEIN

Love is non-possessive delight in the particularity of the other.
—JAMES LODER

Introduction: Theology, Science, Spirit? Of Course!

Theologian Brian Gerrish once voiced considerable skepticism, shared by many I am sure, regarding the legitimacy of the Christian Kerygma as a partner in academic or scientific discourse. He averred: "Anyone who believes that theology is possible and meaningful in the church alone, that it begins with God in his revelation in Jesus Christ, and that it is scientific just insofar as it corresponds to the word of God through obedience of faith, will need to come up with a quite different account of theology's credentials as a university discipline, or may prefer to pursue it somewhere else."[1] James E. Loder Jr.'s 40+ years of constructive work in practical theology dared to take up precisely this implausible challenge of rendering the Gospel intelligible to a scientific world.[2] He developed a "neo-Chalcedonian science of spirit" through which he sought to discern the hidden intelligibility underlying these two seemingly incommensurate realities. He argued that it is at the generative source of intelligibility—the human spirit and especially its potential for redemptive transformation by *Spiritus Creator*—that all human experience, religious and otherwise, becomes known at the deepest levels. His work remains a source of insight for some of us who labor to make our witness to Jesus Christ compelling in a postmodern setting. But it also remains a "hard sell" for many who might even appreciate aspects of Loder's work but who regard his project as a whole to be a highly irregular, irrelevant, or even illegitimate venture bordering on alchemic fancifulness.[3]

In April of 2001 I began a series of taped interviews with James Loder in the hope that one day I might write an essay summarizing his life and work for a Lilly-funded research project of Talbot Seminary—the *Christian Educators of the Twentieth Century* series. After Loder's death I ended up writing the essay for that series which is now complete and available on-line.[4] I also wrote two complementary essays on Loder's life and work, an introduction and an afterword for his *Festschrift* en-

---

1. Gerrish, *Continuing*, 273.

2. Loder was well aware of the dangers of giving priority to strong theological positions, especially in methodological considerations. See Loder, "Normativity," 359–81. Loder taught in the Practical Theology department of Princeton Seminary from 1962–2001.

3. Of the criticisms I heard about Loder's practical theology through the years, some of it focused on what was perceived to be his over-reliance on T. F. Torrance. One well-known scholar I interviewed for the *Festschrift* regarded this reliance on Torrance to be a failure of Loder's own intellectual integrity. Some African American students, feminists, and liberation theologians could not understand why Loder didn't say more about their causes. Others in practical theology did not appreciate his seemingly single-minded devotion to so-called outdated sources of interlocution he kept close—Freud, Piaget, Erikson, Jung, et al. Others lamented his theory dominant methodology.

4. See my overview "James E. Loder Jr." in this resource, which contains biographical essay, bibliography, annotated bibliography, reading guide and quotations from the Loder corpus, as well as an essay on the contribution of Loder to Christian education.

titled *Redemptive Transformation in Practical Theology*.[5] Toward the end of this set of interviews that stretched out over some weeks, I asked Loder if he was optimistic about the future of practical theology. His answer was a qualified yes, and relates directly to Gerrish's challenge and the conversation enshrined in this present book. According to Loder, in order to serve the Gospel and to be a generative force in both church and culture, practical theology had to be "reconceived according to the great themes of the 21st century, which are . . . science and . . . spirit."

> I think it is absolutely crucial that practical theology flourish. But I think it has to be somewhat reconceived according to the great themes of the 21st century, which are on the one hand "science" and on the other hand "spirit." And it is not my idea that the 21st century should emphasize these things. But the practical theology that is going to last is going to show the relevance of those two themes to what we want to talk about in the church and in the teaching of pastors, and in theological seminaries. There is so much to be done in the interplay of those two driving forces. So, I am hopeful because (a) we need it and (b) because I think it is possible for practical theology to adapt to these emerging needs of the church put on it by the changing of culture. And "science" of course applies to technology and "spirit" implies the Holy Spirit not just the human spirit. But I think we will adapt to that. I mean we'll adapt [practical theology] to the transforming work of the Spirit.[6]

Loder's comment struck me deeply when I heard it given so informally. Coming from most of us, the words "theology . . . science . . . and spirit" in the same sentence might have seemed fanciful indeed, even oxymoronic. But coming from the lips of James Loder they seemed completely natural and even deserving of a kind of "Amen!" Loder believed that practical theology needed to be considered a higher-order scientific pursuit, one that shows the inner connections among the Kingdom of God, inspired creative intelligence in a scientific world, and the human longing for meaning and purpose: theology, science, spirit? Of course! Loder argued continually that only through an enterprise that connects theology to science to spirit with their ultimate integrity revealed through the Presence of Christ can we hope to experience the redemptive transformation to which the Gospel calls us and to testify of Christ

---

5. Wright, "Are You There?," 1–42 and idem, "Afterword," 401–31.
6. Loder, Interview by Dana R. Wright, quoted in Wright, *Redemptive*, 402.

with integrity in a scientific world. What I believe Loder had in mind for practical theological science was the integration of the kerymatic and apologetic tasks of the Church in the world, the uniting of proclamation *to* the world and dialogue *with* the world, in the service of the redemptive transformation *of* the world.[7] Of course!

The *Festschrift* itself came out of those same interviews.[8] After the manuscript was submitted to the publisher, but before the proofs were issued for final editing, I came under the growing suspicion that the connection among theology, science, and spirit so close to Loder's neo-Chalcedonian scientific vision had been somewhat eclipsed in the book. I thought perhaps Loder's own response to the *Festschrift*, had he lived to write it, might have focused on making practical theology's connections to science and spirit more explicit than was evident in the essays themselves. So I decided to submit an afterword in the hope that it might capture this crucial concern for readers.[9] What amazed me over and over again as I wrote the afterword (rather feverishly, as I recall) was just how the themes of science and spirit, creative intelligence and meaning, generative insight and purpose—and theology—were so evident at every stage of Loder's life and work. It was as if through his lifetime he had become more and more deeply prepared to make precisely this eccentric connection, like a modern-day Paul who had been called to make the wisdom of Jerusalem understandable to the Athenians on Mars Hill.[10]

---

7. I tried to survey the history of practical theology in the United States using these two concerns, the kerygmatic and the apologetic, as two complementary forms of practical theology that had never really been integrated. See Wright, "Contemporary," 289–320. See also chapter 7 of this present work, where I revisit this concern in relation to Loder's unpublished book *Education Ministry in the Logic of the Spirit* (hereafter *EMLOS*).

8. In the course of those interviews I had also asked Loder if any of his colleagues or students had ever proposed a *Festschrift* in his honor. He advised me to take the matter up with President Thomas Gillespie, who immediately responded to my suggestion by throwing the seminary's support behind the project. *Redemptive Transformation* was the result. This book was a joy to bring to life, except for the disappointment we all shared that Loder himself did not live to see the results nor write his own planned response to the essays.

9. Wright, "Afterword," 401–31.

10. On the themes of "Athens" and "Jerusalem" see Loder, "Normativity," 359–381. Loder argued that there are at least five "ethos" that tacitly fund practical theological imagination today: empirical science ("Manchester"→Seward Hiltner), humanist ("Athens"→Edward Farley), ethical-scientific ("Berlin"→Pannenberg), experiential ("Delphi"→Mud Flower Collective), and neo-Chalcedonian science

Loder became more deeply self-aware and more thoroughly articulate about the Gospel's power to "cut the world open at its joints" in order to inspire scientific and theological insight into the nature of provident-contingent relations. He sought to convince us of the integrity of those relations and to empower us to live in them in the midst of a broken world. Loder had lived and died to give just this kind of faithful witness. I wanted the *Festschrift* in his honor to give witness to this passionate concern. That is my same goal for this introductory essay as well some 10 years later.

Science and Spirit in the Early Years

Creative intelligence and the search for meaning were evident in Loder's childhood. At his memorial service his daughter Tami told the story of "little Jimmy," whose kindergarten teacher recognized a special quality of mind that set him apart. "Every day we read a story, and after the story is over, Jimmy gets up and wants to tell us what the story means."[11] Science and spirit were powerfully present in Loder as a young college student. At the suggestion of an uncle, Loder attended Carleton College in Northfield, Minnesota in 1949, majoring in physics. But soon his professors realized what his kindergarten teacher knew so well, that Loder's intelligent search for learning the "How?" of things was inseparably linked to his equally insatiable curiosity for understanding the "Why?" of things. They suggested he might well turn his attention to *meta*physics. Loder took their advice and graduated with a BA in philosophy in 1953.

Loder enrolled in Princeton Seminary the next year. The connection of science and spirit to theology became explicit during Loder's Princeton years, but not in the classroom. During his second year his father took gravely ill and Loder went home to be with him. His father died. While in mourning, Loder was stricken with a glandular infection. Thoroughly frustrated and in despair, he grew increasingly desperate to find any meaning in the tragedy. Bedridden, he finally struck his pillow and shouted to the heavens to "Do something!" And something happened! Loder was met from the other side with a palpable sense of the presence of God that threw him out of bed and filled his spirit with hope

("Jerusalem"→Loder).

11. Tiss, "James Loder," 72.

and meaning right at the point of unfathomable darkness (he described it as his being enveloped in liquid heat). Initial articulations of the meaning of this experience came to him from hymnology (he burst forth in a rendition of "Blessed Assurance Jesus is Mine"!) and neo-orthodox theology (he picked up Emil Brunner's *The Scandal of Christianity* and did not so much read it as recognize the truth toward which it pointed).[12] Significantly, this experience fueled the intensity of what would become Loder's life-long search for higher-order intellectual explanations for convictional experiences that would make sense in a scientific culture. Theological experience had elevated the creative passion generative of Loder's search for intelligibility. That is, the spirit of Loder's intelligence was now reset and expanded in theological dimensions in order to make realistic sense of his traumatic and yet liberative experience.[13]

When he returned to Princeton Loder contacted the Swiss theologian Hans Hofmann, Professor of Theology and Psychology, who had studied with Brunner at Basel, and also with Karl Jung. He trusted that Hoffman would take his experience seriously, both psychologically and theologically. Hofmann introduced the young prodigy to the importance of Kierkegaard for understanding his spiritual experience. Kierkegaard, in turn, became Loder's preeminent and life-long interlocutor. Kierkegaard's own saving experience of Christ in the midst of familial chaos, and his extraordinary articulation of the significance of Christ within Christendom offered Loder a way to make sense of his own experience theologically, philosophically, and psychologically.[14] Loder immersed himself in the works of Kierkegaard, whom he testified provided "language for my head." He continued learning Kierkegaard during his time at Harvard, following his graduation from Princeton, and, of course, for the rest of his life.[15]

---

12. For details of this experience see Wright, "Are You There?," 13 and "Ruination," 77f.

13. Loder later argued that good science requires "fiduciary passion" that depends on what M. Polanyi called *prolepsis*, an "anticipatory glimpse" or "proleptic conception" that is "imprinted upon the informed mind because the internal structure of the phenomenon bears a kinship to our knowing and what we can know as we allow ourselves to indwell the phenomenon" (Loder, "Place of Science," 28–29).

14. In virtually all of his major writings Loder called attention to the conversion experience of Kierkegaard after the reconciliation with, and the death of, his father as a paradigm of convictional knowing events. For his discussions see *Religious*, 104–7; *Transforming*, 1–8; *Knight's Move*, 250–53; *Logic*, 234–38.

15. Loder told me in the aforementioned interview of his desire to write a major

But before he graduated, Loder's embrace of science and spirit showed itself to be quite aggressive when, during his senior year, he and some other students refused to take D. Campbell Wyckoff's required course in Christian education. They told the seasoned professor that his course lacked the rigorous intellectual depth and breadth that they all craved.[16] They asked him if they could redesign his course to address the deeper intelligible structures of the discipline itself. So Wyckoff in his wisdom gave them permission to redesign the course under his supervision in a way that satisfied both themselves and the course requirements. This effort to reconstruct the course at a level of intellectual depth proved to be a foreshadowing of the lifelong vocation that Loder would embrace—i.e., his quest to reconstruct the conceptual dimensions of what he considered to be a vastly underdeveloped interdisciplinary venture.[17] Wyckoff was so impressed by Loder's extraordinary conceptual abilities that this episode stayed with him and informed his own decision some years later to support hiring Loder to be his colleague in the Christian education department at Princeton Seminary teaching primarily (what else?) courses on the philosophy of Christian education.

After his graduation in 1957, Hofmann took Loder and three other gifted students with him to Harvard as his research assistants.[18] From 1958–1962 Loder earned two more advanced academic degrees as a Harvard Fellow—a ThM from Harvard Divinity School (1958, with distinction) and a PhD in the History and Philosophy of Religion from Harvard University Graduate School in Arts and Sciences (1962). Loder's

---

work on Kierkegaard. He taught seminars on Kierkegaard and supervised doctoral dissertations focused on Kierkegaard. Kierkegaard appears in all of his major writings, starting with his own dissertation.

16. The problem was not with Wyckoff per se, whose knowledge of the practice of Christian education was unparalleled. The problem was with the "applied disciplinary" status of the field as a whole. Christian education, like the other subdisciplines in practical theology, had little understanding of itself as a constructive theological enterprise in its own right, although voices for reconceiving the field in constructive terms were beginning to be heard.

17. Wyckoff recalled in a 2002 interview that the well-known religious educator Jerome Berryman was one of the other students! For the influence of Loder on Berryman's lifelong work see chapter 4 in this present volume.

18. Hofmann had received an appointment as Director of Harvard University's Project on Religion and Mental Health under a grant from the National Institute of Mental Health, See Ken Kovacs, "Relational," 20 and *Relational*, 15. See also Homrighausen, "Study," 544–45.

8   The Logic of the Spirit in Human Thought and Experience

Harvard dissertation, "The Nature of Religious Consciousness in the Writings of Sigmund Freud and Søren Kierkegaard," again manifested the connection of science and spirit to theology. In this study he sought "to work toward a sounder integration between theoretical points of view in the fields of religion and psychiatry," one that overcame Freud's unnecessary identification of all religious experience with pathology. Indeed, healthy religious experience (described in Kierkegaard) follows similar reality-restoring dynamics as therapeutic healing in Freud, according to Loder's thesis. That is, the dynamics of creative religious transformation and the dynamics of effective therapy are analogous and reality-restoring in impact.[19] Theology, science, spirit? Of course!

Science and Spirit Transformed

Loder finished his dissertation while serving as a Fellow at the Menninger Foundation in Topeka, Kansas. He was now in a position to develop this correlation of the generic patterns of scientific and religious knowing in his vocation as an academic practical theologian. As was noted earlier, Loder was called back to Princeton Seminary as Associate Professor of the Philosophy of Christian Education. His creative and radical approach gained a considerable hearing from the many students who flocked to his exciting courses centered on conflict learning.[20] But by his own admission he lost touch during the first 10 years on the faculty with the larger questions of meaning and purpose that his theological experience at the death of his father had opened up for him. Creative intelligence continued, but the larger theological meaning and purpose of his work became diminished and secondary. This intellectual and creative reductionism, however, was challenged again through another redemptive transforming moment. Loder suffered a serious accident in 1970 while on vacation with his family in upstate New York.[21] This accident

---

19. Batson, "Creativity," 84 n. 138f. Loder worked out an analogy between creativity and religious development to provoke healthy personal and social functioning as liberation. He called the underlying reality-restoring dynamism of the human spirit the "hypnagogic paradigm." See Loder, *Religious*, 180–229.

20. Also important was Loder's counseling ministry in the days when the seminary had no chaplain to serve students. Indeed, scores of them came to Loder for help in those early years and throughout his 40+ year tenure. For a glimpse into aspects of Loder's counsel, see the essay by Mark Koonz in this present volume, chapter 8.

21. Loder articulated the experience of "the accident" throughout his writings and

permanently re-opened for Loder the larger theological dimensions of Spirit through which his creative intelligence was transformed into faith seeking understanding. When asked in the 2001 interview, "What changed in your understanding and practice of Christian education after 1970?" he responded with this testimony:

> That's a good question, because before 1970 I was doing all of my teaching within a basic psychoanalytic model, that conflict learning is basic to psychoanalysis. So I was upgrading psychoanalysis a little bit. But that was the basic shape of my understanding. After 1970 I realized it was the Spirit of God who creates the problem and guides us into truth. And the whole convictional picture in four dimensions began to become a way for me to talk about what I know had happened, and what could happen. And so, it was still conflictual but now it had shifted into a much bigger perspective. And the dynamics involved were not just limited to the human spirit but also to divine redemption in action.[22]

Loder's awakening to the reality-affirming, reality-restoring, reality-transforming power of God in his first transforming moment had fallen under the spell of an unredeemed scientific reductionism of the theological. His creative intelligence had been constricted into a two-dimensional framework that obfuscated the larger spiritual and scientific integration toward which an experience of Christ ultimately points. What this second experience of Christ did for Loder, therefore, was to re-open the generative potential of his creative intellect to this larger framework of the Holy Spirit and permanently reset the theological dimensions of his science of spirit. Wising up to the Spirit's work he could no longer wise down. And now he felt compelled to make the connection among theology, science, and spirit explicit so as to witness to Christ in a scientific culture. Loder set out to restore the integrity of science and spirit in human experience by connecting them to their generative origins in the Spiritual presence of Christ, revealed in and through convictional experiences.[23] As he would later aver: "Transforming moments need to be recognized as sources of new knowledge about God, self, and the world... Moments of transforming significance radically reopen the

---

in many of his classes. See *Moment*, 9–13 for his written account. See also Wright, "Are You There?," 15f. and "Ruination," 80f., and Moorhead, "Princeton," 481–84.

22. Loder, Interview by Dana Wright.
23. Wright, "Prophetic," 20.

question of reality for the persons who experience them."[24] Theology, science, spirit? Of course!

James E. Loder as a Young Scholar.
Princeton Theological Seminary

Initially Loder sought to connect theology, science and spirit by immersing himself in pneumatology. He believed that the work of the Holy Spirit was the key to the integrity of both spiritual and intellectual power to restore human beings to sanity, so to speak. His immersion in the Church's teachings on the work of the Holy Spirit in relation to the human spirit suggested that reality-affirming, reality-restoring, reality-transforming insight ultimately come from the initiative of the Holy Spirit and not from the autonomous transformational capacities of the human spirit alone, nor from culture.[25] Loder also discerned that

24. Loder, *Transforming*, xi.
25. Loder found particular help from Regin Prenter's study *Spiritus Creator* and from George Hendry's book *The Holy Spirit*, especially chapter 5, "The Holy Spirit and the Human Spirit," 96–117.

our human participation in the work of the Spirit is actualized through the conviction-generated, reality-restoring experiences initiated by the Spirit that can be articulated intelligibly to a scientific culture.

After several years of wrestling with the Holy Spirit's connection to the creative human spirit through the relational dynamics of convictional experience, his ground-breaking book *The Transforming Moment* was released in 1981.[26] This carefully crafted work laid out Loder's pneumatological reconstruction of his earlier emphasis on the transformational dynamics of science and religious experience. Loder now gave conceptual clarity to how we might understand the Holy Spirit's convictional interaction with the human spirit in redemptive experience. He wanted to forge "a new understanding of knowing commensurate with the nature of convictional experience" (21) as the key to restoring the full creative intelligence of the human spirit. He argued: "Convictional knowing is a patterned process by which the Holy Spirit transforms all transformations of the human spirit . . . a four-dimensional knowing event initiated, mediated, and concluded by Christ" (93).[27] The paradigm of four-dimensional redemptive transformation is the Eucharist, theologically understood.

> . . . the four-dimensional transformation of the Eucharist requires that one be inside what is believed in order to "see" whatever is out there, in here, and everywhere in terms of Christ's intention for all creation, from the commonest bread crumbs to the Kingdom of God. Everyday Christian experience badly needs what the transforming moment does to place people inside their convictions, just as the transforming moment needs everyday Christian experience as its substantive content (119).

For Loder, convictional experiences are generative of scientific insight into the very nature of reality. They are reality-affirming, reality-restoring, reality-transforming events that penetrate beneath the social constructions of reality where the Holy Spirit works toward a deeper integrity for the human spirit. For example, a scientific understanding of human development generated out of convictional experience would include a full accounting of the powerful hold death has upon us throughout our lifetime. Citing Luther's experience of convictional

---

26. Loder, *Transforming* (pagination noted in the text).

27. For discussions of Loder's understanding of transformational processes and four-dimensional knowing events that open up the world, see several of the essays in this present volume as well as *Transforming*.

transformation Loder held that a truly scientific explanation of development would attend to its ultimate meaning by knowing it transformationally "in reverse." "In reverse" means that

> . . . the final stage in the ordinary course of human development, namely confronting one's own death and the ultimate meaning of life in light of that death, is inextricably tied to the ongoing sense of void at every stage in one's life. Thus, the final crisis in normal people is the lifelong crisis for the religious personality, and the scale of normal development cannot contain, much less explain, a person who brings his or her solution to life's final stage into every intervening stage. In effect, this is to reverse development from a standpoint implicitly outside it (140).

Furthermore, convictional experiences not only generate higher-order, reality-restoring intelligence that takes death and negation in human development seriously. Conviction also engenders an ontological realignment of all relations, which Loder argued was the restoration of power to love (*agape*) at the center of the personality. Convictional experiences "negate the negation" riven through human development so that the Spirit of Christ becomes "the ground of the self without absorbing the self, the living center of the personality displacing but not destroying the ego" (144), leading to the primacy of a dialectical identity, "*I yet not I but Christ.*" "*Spiritus Creator* acts from outside the stage sequence frame of human development" while at the same time She "follows the pattern of transformational logic that is so deeply ingrained in the dynamics of human development" (145). From this convictional standpoint Loder argued that normal human development under the "triumph of negation" ("negation incorporated") must be redemptively transformed by and through the Spirit of Christ, freeing human beings and communities to take up the way of love. The Spirit integrates higher-order intelligence with Her own relational nature as love, which is, in Loder's memorable phrase, "non-possessive delight in the particularity of the other." The true spirit of intelligence is non-coercive, joyous, Christo-qualitative relationality revealed as love, the relational integrity of persons and communities restored into the image of God through Christ (*imago Christi*).[28]

---

28. Here is a true point of contact between Loder's work and the concerns of the Child Theology Movement, in my judgment. Loder's theories, while academic in tone, are nonetheless oriented toward the restoration of the human spirit to love. Love is an expression of intellectual integrity and intellectual integrity fosters the ability to love.

Loder's efforts to describe the source and structure of the relational integrity of the human spirit in Christ, awakened through convictional experiences, developed further through the 1980s into what I have called his neo-Chalcedonian science.[29] In *The Knight's Move*, Loder in tandem with physicist James Neidhardt (a collaboration both men regarded as the richest of their lives) developed a generic model of spirit called "the strange loop." Patterned after the image of the Mobius strip, this disclosure model promised to engender insight into the relational structure of reality underlying both science and theology. In the forward, T. F. Torrance wrote: "One of the distinctive features of this work, written by a theologian and a physicist in intellectual and spiritual harness, is the brilliant way in which basic forms of thought, taken and developed from theological and scientific thinkers like Kierkegaard and Einstein, are allowed to interpenetrate one another with a creative feedback fruitful for both theology and science."[30] Loder and Neidhardt argued that relationality in theology and higher-order science (physics) becomes most fully intelligible through Jesus Christ, a claim that needed to be made with great care in order to convince a scientific culture. They wrote that

> . . . theology and science qua science need to find new grounds for dialogue that will reach into their common epistemological concerns and restore what once was, contrary to popular opinion, a profoundly rich reciprocity between theological concepts of creation and the scientific study of nature . . . the underlying theological premise of this entire study [is] . . . that relationality is revealed to us definitively in the inner nature of Jesus Christ. In Christ's nature as fully God and fully human, we have the definition of relationship through which all other expressions of personal, social, and cultural relatedness are to be viewed. This applies as well to the model we are using in the methodology of this study; the inner nature of Jesus Christ ultimately defines the scope and limits of the relational model; not the reverse. Our use of the model is intended to reveal the illuminative and explanatory significance of viewing all creation through the eyes of faith in Jesus Christ.[31]

---

29. See my "Introduction" and "Afterword" in *Redemptive* for this general rendering of Loder's work as "neo-Chalcedonian science."

30. Torrance. "Forward," xi–xii.

31. Loder and Neidhardt, *Knight's Move*, 7 and 13. The authors drew on insights from the natural sciences, i.e. James Clerk Maxwell, Michael Polanyi, Albert Einstein, Nels Bohr, Werner Heisenberg and Illya Prigogine; from the human sciences, i.e. Sigmund

In essence Loder and Neidhardt argued that the closer one gets to the mystery of God-in-the-flesh revealed through the Spirit the closer one gets to discerning and elaborating scientifically the nature of human reality as a contingent and unfolding order of meaning and purpose that renders the natural world as *creation*. This knowledge is scientific and confessional, and no less, but rather, more scientific because it is confessional. "*The Knight's Move* bore testimony to Loder's conviction that the two-fold crisis of . . . postmodernity—the crisis of science (discerning the nature and limits of human knowing) and the crisis of spirit (reaffirming the importance of human participation in scientific knowing)—was profoundly addressed in the reality of Jesus Christ."[32] This confessional priority was articulated in the 2001 interview during which Loder responded to a question about his critique of Christian education theories.

> Question: "Did you have any sense that something was at stake in the discipline of Christian education itself? Did you have a concern that the developmental paradigm would lead us into error or a loss of something vital?"
>
> Answer: "Yes. Well, the concern that I had that came more and more into focus was, . . . that the definitive discipline is theology, and not anything else. The point is that we are not trying to work theology into our behavioral sciences or our philosophy. And *that* shift was definitive for me. The Spirit made that definitive for me . . . I continued to learn more profoundly from Torrance [that] you have to start with the answer. You *know* the answer. Don't try to work up to it. Go from the answer. Start there. And then do the rest ... You always think it's not legitimate to start with the answer. [You think] you have to get *to* it from somewhere. No. Start with the answer. And unpack it so that it can be appropriated. Because you can't get from nature to grace. So if you start from grace as the only theological premise that you can work with, then everything is continuity in reverse. And about the Chalcedonian model. When I began to try to work out the interdisciplinary thing theologically, obviously, that's already

---

Freud and Jean Piaget, and from theologians like Karl Barth, T. F. Torrance, Wolfhart Pannenberg, the early Church fathers, and especially the ever-present Kierkegaard, to develop "the strange loop model," a generic, asymmetrical version of complementarity they hoped would enrich the theology/science dialogue and testify to the nature of reality as relational, according to the definitive revelation of relationality in Jesus Christ.

32. Wright, "Are You There?," 21.

worked out. The nature of Jesus Christ, the relationship [of divine to human action] is already established. You don't get into that [from somewhere else]. That's the power of the Spirit. So it all began to unfold, and the significance of the Spirit into the testimony of the Spirit through Christ, and the interdisciplinary material is already given to us. That's again starting from the answer."[33]

Loder and Neidhardt developed an interdisciplinary basis for a science of Spirit-to-spirit relations that "preached Christ" and was no less, but more scientific, for doing so. Theology, science, spirit? Of course!

Science and Spirit in Human Development and Christian Education

In the decade following the release of *The Knight's Move* (1992) and the re-release of *The Transforming Moment* (1989), Loder turned his neo-Chalcedonian scientific lens toward explaining the hidden orders of intelligibility underlying both (1) human development and (2) Christian education as a practical theological discipline. In regard to the former subject, Loder's *The Logic of the Spirit* took his analysis of the power of convictional experience and the ground of conviction in the Spirit of Christ to develop a theological and interdisciplinary scientific explanation of human development.[34] Loder argued that Chalcedonian insight discerns that our profound longing to understand *what* human life is (the *science* quest) and *why* human beings take up the courage to live it (the *spirit* quest) gets distorted under the "reality-diminishing" powers of "normal" human development governed by ego and socialization. He constructed a practical theology of human development that reconsidered the question of "normal" human development in Chalcedonian dimensions. He wrote: "the larger aim of my inquiry is to demonstrate the overall context that a Christian theology of the Spirit provides for the study of human nature, and especially for issues of purpose and meaning implicit in and often insufficiently articulated through the facts and theories of human development" (xiii). Thus, "the human spirit makes

---

33. Loder, Interview by Dana Wright. See also Loder, "Place of Science," 22–44, in which he speaks of the relevance of "Jerusalem" for engaging in postmodern scientific discourse.

34. Loder, *Logic* (pagination noted in the text).

all acts of human intelligence self-transcendent and self-relational," but "[w]hen God acts, Spirit-to-spirit, then human intelligence is transformed into a 'faith seeking understanding' of God's self-revelation— that is, the disclosure of God's mind in the Face of God in Jesus Christ" (12). Loder carefully delineated how the Holy Spirit, working according to the dynamism of the God-Human structure of relational reality, (a) *affirms* the human spirit's ability to reconstruct itself through the life span, and (b) *crucifies* the human spirit's futile efforts to order and reorder ultimate meaning and purpose according to its constructive capacities alone. This affirmation-crucifixion movement through which the Spirit reveals to the human spirit its destiny in death (the "triumph of negation") at the same time also reveals its power to (c) *liberate (resurrect)* the human spirit out of death in order to live kinetically in the Spirit, making love with integrity possible. That is, Loder showed how the Spirit negates the negation in human development and reconstitutes the relational dynamism of the divine life acting in human experience to redeem us as spirit. He argued for the restoration of the *imago Dei* in human experience at every stage of the life span—human beings fully alive and flourishing in the power to give and receive love—which is the glory of God manifest in human experience.[35]

In regard to Christian education theory, Loder had taught for many years a popular class on education known as ED105. His follow up to *The Logic of the Spirit* was to be *Educational Ministry in the Logic of the Spirit* based on this course.[36] This book, which has never been published, outlined his scientific understanding of the underlying relational meaning and structure of the theory and practice of Christian education.[37] Loder began this study with a programmatic chapter entitled "The Crux of Christian Education: Introductory Dilemmas and

---

35. See my discussions of these transformational dynamics in chapters 7 and 11 of this book.

36. Hereafter *EMLOS* (chapter and page numbers noted in the text). See my lengthy discussion of this manuscript and its potential place as a significant legacy to practical theology and Christian education in chapter 7 of this book.

37. There are several different copies of this manuscript. I am using the copy Loder gave me in the week before he died in Nov. 2001, a copy of the text he had hoped to get published at that time. In conversations with others and through my own readings this last manuscript may not contain his most articulate work. For a good survey of this book see Haitch, "Summary," 298–324. See also my essay in this present volume, chapter 7.

a Critical Perspective." First he argued for the priority of theory over practice in scientific discourse, based on his neo-Chalcedonian perspective. Through his Chalcedonian lens Loder discerned that two contradictory dynamic forces in potentially creative tension underlie Christian education—socialization and transformation. He created a theological reinterpretation of Talcott Parsons' model of human action theory that can be considered his ingenious, theoretical and scientific description of what Scripture means by the conforming powers of "the world."[38] That is, the model describes scientifically and theologically what it means for the church to be held captive to the principalities and powers that ultimately work at cross purposes with the Reign of God.[39] Loder defined socialization as "*a tension-reduction, pattern-maintenance process* designed to serve the purposes of adaptation and incorporation into larger and more complex social milieu."[40] Transformation, on the other hand, was "*a patterned process whereby in any given frame of knowledge or experience, a hidden order of meaning emerges with the power to redefine and/or reconstruct the original frame of reference.*"[41] These contradictory dynamics are at work in four dimensions of human action—bodily, psychic, social and cultural—that make up the relational matrices of the social construction of reality, from human development in context, to family dynamics, to national and international relations, etc.

In Loder's understanding, the power of unredeemed socialization-transformation dynamics is entropic. Ultimately, therefore, socialization's concern for survival generally dominates transformation as death dominates or haunts life. The creativity of the unredeemed human spirit

---

38. Loder studied under Parsons at Harvard. He later reconceived Parsons' comprehensive theory of human action theologically and used it as a kind of organizing principle for *EMLOS*. For an introduction to Parsons' thought, see Hamilton, *Talcott Parsons*.

39. For Loder, the power of the "world" lies not just in its "products" (ideology, pornography, economic disparities, *ad nauseum*), but more importantly must be discerned in how the transformational dynamics of the human spirit that generate these "products" are themselves inevitably distorted and held captive to the dynamics of socialization. These distorted dynamics generate these dehumanizing and dis-relating "products" until and unless they are redeemed by the Spirit of Christ. Thus, the transformation-socialization dynamics must themselves be transformed by the Spirit if human beings and communities are to be liberated from the powers of death and disrelation.

40. *EMLOS*, ch. 1, 12 (emphasis added).

41. Ibid., 14 (emphasis added).

may, on the one hand, be domesticated by being placed in the service of pattern maintenance, tension-reduction, spirit-distorting adaptation to socialized interests for the purpose of survival and control. On the other hand, that same unredeemed creativity may seek liberation from the entropic power of socialization through non-conformity in search of authenticity or self-actualization. Either way, the power of unredeemed socialization-transformation dynamics is essentially tragic in that neither culture nor the creativity that gives rise to it can overcome the entropic movement toward death. Loder calls this inevitable failure of spirit "the triumph of negation" in human experience. Apart from the power of the Spirit, unredeemed transformation has no final power against socialization and no true ground for its ultimate purpose. Under the conditions of sin and the power of death, socialization almost always dominates the socialization-transformation relational matrix, placing even scientific creativity under the power of ego and in service to forms of disrelation endemic in the unredeemed world.[42] Socialization domesticates the impetus toward transformation and distorts relations that transformation seeks to regenerate and vivify. Furthermore, efforts of persons or communities to escape the conforming hold of socialization through unrestrained spiritual experience or non-conformity renders transformation "gnostic," or reality-denying. Transformation needs socialization to keep the human spirit from being disconnected from the limitations of human nature. Thus, Loder argued that the distorted spiritual relations embodied in these two contradictory forces must be redemptively transformed though the power of the Spirit of Christ. The Spirit negates the negation underlying the entropic power of socialization and the gnostic flights of fancy and places socialization-transformation dynamics in the service of the redemptively transforming power of the Reign of God.

After this programmatic introduction, Loder traced the history of Christian education in America through the lens of transformation-socialization and the socialization-dominant theory of C. E. Nelson in particular (chapter 2).[43] He wrote, "My basic objection to Nelson's ap-

---

42. For a powerful study of two creative geniuses, Pablo Picasso and Albert Einstein, who ultimately could not escape the power of negation in their personal and professional lives, see Miller, *Picasso*. Miller was Professor of the History and Philosophy of Science and University College London from 1991–2005. He is now a writer, commentator, and consultant on cognitive theory and creativity.

43. Loder here gives an in-depth analysis of C. E. Nelson's theory of Christian education articulated in *Where Faith Begins*.

proach is that it seeks to socialize the transforming work of God's Spirit. It needs to be the other way around since God's Spirit is much larger than society and socialization."[44] In chapter 3, "Lifestyles: Taking Social Reality Seriously," Loder acknowledged Nelson's proper emphasis on "life style" as the "fashioning of power." But he goes on to show how such power operating through socialization permeates communities of faith as well as American culture to fundamentally authorize destructive and distortive life-styles in the name of Christ: *achievement* (distorting love relations), *protean* (distorting the longing for freedom), *authoritarian* (distorting power relations), and *oppressive* (distorting justice). In chapter 4, "Human Development and Personality Formation," Loder showed how the same relational distortions he described in society and culture are relevant to understanding the negation riven into "normal" human development based on ego's unredeemed executive function.[45]

How the Holy Spirit redemptively transforms the socialization-transformation captivity of unredeemed human agency is the subject of the middle section of *EMLOS*, "The Holy Spirit and Human Transformation." Chapter 5, "Transformation in Theology: Analogy of the Spirit," rehearsed the argument of *The Transforming Moment* for its generative insights into the transformation of the human spirit by the Holy Spirit. The Spirit of Christ reveals to us the deeper dimensions of human existence underlying the social construction of reality through convictional experiences that call us to embrace reality fully in the Presence of God. In this way "the ordinary world becomes the bearer of the extraordinary" as we come to know it through the Mind of Christ.

In chapters 6 through 8, Loder described the impact of the Holy Spirit in more detail in terms of the four dimensions of human action: organic, psychic, social, and culture. His brief discussion of the organic dimension focused on the transformation of bodily concerns for satisfaction and safety into a profound love of life. In relation to ego development (chapter 6), the Spirit's intimacy with the human spirit transforms the defensiveness and control sought by unredeemed ego by placing ego in the service of the relational integrity of Christ—*I yet not I but Christ*. In relation to social reality (chapter 7), Loder showed how the search for

---

44. *EMLOS* ch. 2, 53.

45. Essentially this chapter reviews his argument in *Logic*, focusing especially on the work of James Fowler. Loder shows how "normal" human development under the unredeemed ego tends to deepen the "captivity" of the human spirit to the power of death.

conviviality—for a non-coercive and intimate relational context of rapport—is found in the *koinonia*, the communion-creating reality of Jesus Christ. The Spirit transforms socialized role structures and makes them reversible so that they are placed in the serve of a deeper intimacy that makes genuine community possible. And in relation to culture (chapter 8), the power of the Spirit works to render language, images, and symbols transparent to the Reality to which they tacitly or explicitly refer, negating the negation of their tendency to lie.[46] When the Spirit works transformationally in relation to culture, She negates the negation inevitably residing in the "static" image, allowing the human knower to look "through" the image to behold its true power resident in the "imageless" Presence of Jesus Christ—i.e., the Living Presence beyond the cultural construction of reality through which all cultural images find their ultimate meaning. "The transformation of culture . . . does not eliminate culture but makes it iconic, a visible and tangible occasion for entering into the invisible and intangible presence of God."[47]

In the final section of this book entitled "Human Participation in Divine Action: The Claims of the Theory," Loder outlined the practical implications of his theory for the practice of Christian education. In chapter 9, "Structuring the Vision," Loder used a version of the "reporter's interrogative hermeneutic" to demonstrate how his neo-Chalcedonian lens illuminates the purpose (why?), scope (what?), context (where?), process (how?) personnel (who?), and timing (when?) of educational praxis. In chapter 10, "Climax in Worship," Loder summarized how the relational reality celebrated in worship becomes the paradigm of redemptive transformation for the whole of the believing community and, by extension, for the whole world. Worship in the Spirit demonstrates and embodies again and again the proper relational integrity of human experience under the transformation of transformation-socialization dynamics governed by the Spirit of Christ.[48]

In the final years of his life, Loder encouraged the practical theological guild to recognize the need for a richer theological and scientific approach to the discipline. In "Normativity and Context in Practical

---

46. "From the Cynics to the Epicureans, from Nietzsche to Freud, from existentialism to deconstructionism, the point is made again and again: it is extremely difficult, if not impossible, for language to tell the truth" (*EMLOS*, ch. 8, 1).

47. *EMLOS*, ch.8, 40.

48. For an extensive interpretation of *EMLOS*, see chapter 7 of this present volume, a chapter requested by the participants in the CTM/Loder consultation.

Theology: The 'Interdisciplinary Issue'" (1999) Loder argued that practical theology must "establish systematic procedures for remaining accountable to the phenomenon [it investigates] as well as to the disciplines involved in disclosing the inner substance, structure, and dynamics of that phenomenon."[49] He argued that practical theology "requires an inclusive theory of action" that "combines two incongruent, qualitatively distinct realities, the divine and the human, in apparently congruent forms of action."[50] He also averred that his own critical model for practical theology "calls forth *a transformational dynamic* which is repeatedly awakening us to contradictions between theology and the human sciences, intensifying oppositions until there is a new insight, finally bringing about a reappropriation of the original situation as parabolic of the new relationality in Christ."[51]

In a second essay "The Place of Science in Practical Theology: The Human Factor" (2000), Loder again addressed the core problematic in practical theology but this time focused upon the self-involvement of the knower.[52] The fundamental claim of the essay was stated in this way:

> In the theology-science dialogue, science, as distinct from technology, is the primary dialogue partner with theology. However, no view of science is adequate that fails to recognize that all knowledge of the universe is incomplete and probably misleading until it includes the person, the knower himself or herself. Indeed, it is precisely through persons that the universe becomes conscious of itself.[53]

Loder contended that just as human rationality reaches its logical limits in postmodern science, so in the Church's confrontation with the reality of the God-Human, her ability to know reaches its logical limits and compels her to reconfigure theological rationality accordingly. He wanted practical theology, like good science, to "press toward the infi-

---

49. Loder, "Normativity," 359–81.
50. Ibid., 2 note 2 (pre-publication draft).
51. Ibid., 11 (pre-publication draft).
52. Loder, "Place of Science," 22–44 (pre-publication draft).
53. Loder, "Place of Science," 26. I engage these two essays of Loder in the first part of my discussion of *EMLOS*, chapter 7 of this book, to help us understand how Loder sought to witness to the Gospel in the church and in the world through a redemptively transformed practical theology.

nite in all directions" by recognizing the priority of relationality and the knower's self-involvement in all rational discourse.[54]

Conclusion: The Witness of James E. Loder—*Homo Testans*

James Fowler, in his book *Stages of Faith*, once described persons who had reached Stage 6 (universalizing faith) as martyrs.[55] Fowler, however, had trouble explaining how Stage 6 came about through an unfolding of the native capacities of the ego (especially if we consider the conforming power of unredeemed socialization-transformation on all knowing). He argued that something like radical Grace appeared to intervene in those who embodied such faith, transforming the human knower (*Homo Sapiens*) or meaning maker (*Homo Poeta*) into the human witness (*Homo Testans*) to Grace. For Loder, too, this radical transformation of the human knower through redeeming Grace could not be explained as an unfolding of developmental potentials. Neither could the developmental paradigm explain how children bear authentic witness to Christ in powerful ways even when their cognitive and emotional capacities are quite "immature" on the developmental scale.[56] Rather, Loder argued that the transforming work of the Spirit took place at a deeper level than cognitive or emotional development, the level of spirit, where children may enjoy a distinct advantage over hyper-socialized adults. The crucial issue, then, is not development or cognition *per se* but the transformational dynamics of spirit-to-Spirit relations reconstituting the human knower as intimate witness. Ironically, Loder argued that such transformation of the knower is surprisingly relevant to the postmodern scientific emphasis on self-involved knowing.

---

54. In his essay "Philosophical Turn," LeRon Shults noted Loder's sensitivity to the postmodern "turn to relationality" in philosophy and science. "The theme of 'relationality' pervaded James Loder's writings, as well as his pedagogical and therapeutic practice. His passion was to lead others into a deeper understanding of the illuminative and transformative power of the ultimate relationality between God and humanity revealed in Jesus Christ" (325).

55. Fowler, *Stages*, 200.

56. Loder's "test case" of such transformation-unto-witness in children was Ruby Bridges, whom Robert Coles described in his work *Spiritual Life of Children*. Ruby testified to Christ in her response to those who violently protested her integration into the public school in Mississippi with threats of death. Coles could not appreciate Ruby's act of forgiving her abusers, because she was supposedly not old enough developmentally to embody such an ethic. Coles later changed his mind. See Coles, *Spiritual Life*, xi–xiii.

> In the exercise of reason there is always a self doing the reasoning—but that self is a blind spot, even to self-awareness. The observing self will always elude the attempt at self-observation, but that blind spot is where reason connects to the selfhood of the thinker. Cut that nerve, and reason is blind ... [This is] indicative of reason's own solution to one of its deepest dilemmas. When in any given frame of knowledge reason reaches its intrinsic limit, not just for this or that problem but the limit in itself with respect to its object of investigation, it is not just a matter of too little information or insufficient technology. It is finally because reason has ignored the reasoner. When this is accounted for, then, a wider frame of knowing must be conceived which includes both reason and the reasoner in a relationality that is pertinent to the field of inquiry involved ... Thus, in our knowing of physical nature, human nature, and divine nature, when reason encounters its own "invisible ignorance," as physicist A. B. Pippard puts it, it reconstructs the grounds of intelligibility in a frame of reference that ultimately must be comprehensive enough to include the knower.[57]

The neologism that I believe best describes the impact of the Spirit of Christ on the life and work of James E. Loder Jr. (and anyone awakened in spirit to the Spirit) is *Homo Testans*, the human being as *martyr* (*witness*). *Homo Testans* speaks to the theological transformation of *Homo Sapien* or *Homo Poeta*—a transformed life that reflects through the spirit of the knower, imperfectly yet truly, the True Self-witness of Jesus Christ (Rev. 1) and the witness of the Holy Spirit to the human spirit (Rom. 8). In terms of scientific knowing, *Homo Testans* describes the transformed human knower's self-involved spiritual knowing of reality that the Spirit enables through convictional experience—scientific inquiry redeemed as "faith seeking understanding."

If we are to appreciate Loder's achievement and its relevance to both the church and the world, we must learn to hear the totality of his *oeuvres* and his life as reality-affirming, reality-restoring, reality-redeeming testimony, one that discerned a Trinitarian achievement in the making at the heart of human experience and history. Loder's attunement to the complementary scientific and spiritual meaning of the postmodern world, and his experiences of redemptive transformation through the Spirit of Christ, made his testimony exemplary (faithful yet fallible) for

---

57. Loder and Neidhardt, *Knight's Move*, 62.

a scientific culture. Those of us who have participated in this consultation have heard the potentially revolutionary cadences in Loder's witness as a challenge to deepen our own fallible witness to Christ in the post-modern world.[58] We wish to invite others into a conversation that really matters about how we all might better bear witness to the Gospel in a world desperately in need of redemptive transformation unto non-possessive love at every level of human experience.

A Word about the Organization and Content of the Book

In August of 2011 Keith J. White, the executive director of the Child Theology Movement, contacted me and asked me to give an introduction to the life and work of James E. Loder Jr. at a conference sponsored by CTM in March of 2012. I had not heard of CTM, but the opportunity to help make the legacy of James Loder better known to scholars and practical theologians from around the world was something I could not pass up. So I joyfully accepted the invitation and created a version of this (now partially revised) introduction to deliver at the conference. About twenty of us gathered together, friends of CTM and friends who had studied with Dr. Loder, on the campus of Princeton Seminary where he taught. We seemed to find unusual rapport as we learned of each other's passion for the kingdom of God and for the most vulnerable of persons whom Jesus declared have a special place in God's heart. Various papers, engaging aspects of Loder's work from a variety of angles and contexts, were delivered, and responses were made and further questions were asked. Many of us felt that something special was emerging through our dialogue together. As time progressed, we decided to produce a book based on our interchange, one that might reveal the importance of Loder's legacy for the work of CTM and show the fruitfulness of such an engagement for CTM and for others. I was asked by the group to edit the volume. I received revisions of the papers in the following months.

As the revisions returned to me, four thematic categories emerged to give the book its present order. First, Part One, "Child Theology Movement and James E. Loder in Dialogue," consists of three chapters that give established members of CTM a chance to critically engage por-

---

58. I try to articulate how I understand dimensions of the Spirit's redemptive transformation of human nature itself into faithful testimony (*homo testans*) in light of Loder's work in chapter 11 of this book.

tions of Loder's work from diverse perspectives. In the opening chapter, Dr. White discusses what he believes to be the relevance of Loder's work to both CTM and to the Holistic Child Development efforts in England and around the world. White's "exploratory and tentative" reflections on what he believes Loder's potential contributions to CTM could be is offered as a means to revitalizing what White regards is an underdeveloped theological approach within the Holistic Child Development constituency. White's colleague, theologian Haddon Willmer, then reports on a "family resemblance" he discerns between Loder's theological reconstruction of human development and Willmer's own mature ruminations on the notion of forgiveness as constitutive of human nature (chapter 2). Willmer notes that Loder's description of the "uncanny capacity" of an infant to construct the world and create a future that "is indebted to but not controlled by the past" connects to Willmer's account of a forgiving integral to the very being of human creatures. I remember the excitement this essay generated as it was read at our gathering.

In chapter 3, New Testament scholar Elizabeth Waldron Barnett brings to her acute critical reading of Loder her artistic and imaginative appreciation of the radicalness of Pauline theology. Barnett notices certain parallels in how Loder's theological understanding of the Spirit's redemptive transformation of human experience opens up a penetrating critique of human development and progressive scientism in modernity that resonates to Barnett's own sensibility that this same modern bias continues to infect and distort our readings of Paul. Barnett makes a truly original interpretation of Paul's ode to love in 1 Corinthians 13, challenging us to overcome our Western obsessions with development and progress that often blind us to recognizing the in-breaking power of the Spirit of God. She also suggests that readers of Loder must become more fully aware of his own intellectual shaping in the Western intellectual tradition he criticizes.

In Part Two, "James E. Loder and Christian Education Theory and Practice," four essayists discuss important elements in Loder's work they believe to be relevant to this discipline. Jerome Berryman, who knew James Loder at Princeton Seminary, shows in chapter 4 some of the indirect but powerful influence Loder's vision had for Berryman's own well-known *Godly Play* paradigm. Berryman recounts in some detail the various ways in which the theory and practice of *Godly Play* supports important insights that continue to emerge in such scientific fields such as cognition, consciousness studies, and neurobiology, areas that also informed Loder's work. This essay supports the theology-science dialogue so crucial to both Loder and to Berryman. In chapter 5, Tom Hastings gives a brief but provocative interpretation of Loder's interaction with educator-philosopher John Dewey. Hastings argues that Loder's transformational model may be read as a theological commentary and epistemological expansion of Dewey's philosophy of experience. Loder believed that Dewey's pragmatism, which dominated American educational theory and practice in the twentieth century, needed itself to be transformed by a broader epistemology that more accurately accounts for actual cases of scientific discovery and spiritual awakening. In an attempt to gesture at such a broader epistemology, Hastings breaks with academic tradition by concluding his piece with a first person tribute to Loder's personal influence on his own life and work.

Lauren Sempsrott Foster (chapter 6) interacts with Loder's central paradigm of transformation to uncover practical implications for the practice in education, especially focused on learning theory and practice. She mines valuable insights from Loder's early articulation of the pattern of transformation for the classroom in which transformation of persons becomes the central focus of learning. She connects this dynamic understanding with other important and perhaps better known theorists of educational practice like Paulo Freire, Parker Palmer, and Thomas Groome. Sempsprott-Foser is one of a large evangelical constituency who has appreciated Loder's work through the years for its insights into the impact of conversion on learning theory and practice.[59]

In chapter 7, Dana Wright, at the request of the conferees, discusses the possible legacy of Loder's unpublished work on Christian education, *Educational Ministry in the Logic of the Spirit*. Wright first contextualizes Loder's *oeuvre* within the 100+ history of Christian education as a scholarly and interdisciplinary venture in the United States. He argues that Loder sought to transfigure this conversation and the polarities that dominated it—i.e., theory-practice, liberal-conservative, religious-Christian, theology-human sciences, Barthian-Niebuhrian, etc.—by grounding Christian education thought and practice in the power of the

---

59. Theorist such as Ray Anderson and Andrew Root make extensive use of Loder's understanding for articulating their own perspectives. Root, for example, sees Loder as a representative of Root's own Kierkegaardian approach to practical theological method. See Root, "Postscript."

Holy Spirit, which gives priority to the Christ-determined relationality that constitutes those polarities. Wright then discusses Loder's theory of education in detail. He avers that Loder offers a unique and even compelling vision for how the pedagogy of the Spirit redemptively transforms human beings and communities in every dimension of human action—survival instincts, egos, social roles, and cultural constructs—reconstituting all human experience as liberation unto worship in the Spirit—the true end of human history.

In Part Three, "James E. Loder's Relevance to Psychology, Counseling and Sociology," three essays break some new ground for discerning aspects of Loder's thought that complemented his primary professional concern for education *per se*. Pastor Mark Koonz skillfully orients his essay (chapter 8) around his conversations with Loder when, as a seminary student, he was confronted with a very difficult counseling situation with a teenage boy in crisis. Koonz transcribes portions of his remarkable taped conversations with Loder to parse out how Loder (and others) guided him to discern the "logic" of the Spirit in relation to this young man. Through this essay we are brought into Loder's study to overhear Koonz's conversation with his mentor. This essay puts some flesh on Loder's own accounts of counselling in his books and classes and makes us vicarious witnesses to practical theology in the making!

Then, in chapter 9, Ajit A. Prasadam, the General Secretary of the India Sunday School Union, effectively places Loder's understanding of transformation into relationship with one of India's primary theorists in human development, Sudhir Kakar, and pinpoints the parallels and distinctiveness of Loder's work to Kakar's. Kakar himself integrated Hinduism and the Western psychological tradition in his own magisterial work and therefore provides a fascinating dialogue partner with Loder on this important theme. Prasadam, who studied with Loder at Princeton and who shares Loder's strong Christological convictions and focus, effectively shows the promise of Loder's work for affirming and critiquing—and being affirmed and critiqued by—other faith traditions in a non-Western context. Indeed, Prasadam had the rare privilege of being Loder's travelling companion for a 15-day venture across India when he organized five one-day lecture events featuring Loder. This experience well-equipped Prasadam to appreciate the importance of bringing about this kind of international and interfaith conversation.

The final essay in this section (chapter 10) is by Wendy Sanders, who brings her expertise in the moral development of young persons and her appreciation of Loder together to give insight into the deep spiritual power children demonstrate for compassionate behavior. Sanders analyses some original research she did on expressions of compassion in children and shows how this research confirms a growing consensus in science generally about the spiritual vitality of children. Sanders encourages us to celebrate and be amazed by the power of the human spirit manifest in children, something very close to the heart of James Loder and to the work of CTM. Her essay also portrays the importance of connecting practical theology to field research, something Loder's work obviously lacked.

Part Four, "Loder and the Transformation of Christian Witness," includes just one essay by Dana Wright: "A Tactical Child-Like Way of Being Human Together: Implications from James Loder's Thought for Post-Colonial Christian Witness." Wright sets up a distinction between two ways of being human, the adult way of *strategics* and the child-like way of *tactics*, using Robert Penn Warren's masterpiece *All the King's Men* as the lead in. He then discusses how Loder's theological reconstruction of the crisis of infant ego formation explains how the "triumph of negation" takes hold of human development early on to engender "adult" ways of being human that distort the capacity for intimacy. This loss of intimacy ramifies throughout human experience as every level of human action takes on "strategic" or defensive postures that militate against the non-possessive delight in the particularity of the other that, according to Loder, the Spirit longs to bestow. Wright shows how Loder's understanding of the "negation of negation" in the action of Christ through the Holy Spirit transforms human nature and thought Christo-relationally, giving rise to a "perichoretic" or "tactical" pattern of life that is child-like in its on-going dependence on the Spirit.

We trust that all of these essays will be of help to academic discussions, to communities of faith, and to all persons and communities who long for a more just and humane world, encouraging all of us to live in the logic of the Spirit as the Spirit redemptively transforms all reality into the New Heaven and the New Earth that bears witness to Jesus Christ, who is our promised rest and our living hope.

Works Cited

Batson, C. Daniel. "Creativity and Religious Development: Toward a Structural/Functional Psychology of Religion." ThD diss., Princeton Theological Seminary, 1971.

Brooks, Cleanth. *The Hidden God: Hemingway, Faulkner, Yeats, Eliot, and Warren.* New Haven, CT: Yale University Press, 1963.

Coles, Robert. *The Spiritual Life of Children.* Boston: Houghton-Mifflin, 1990.

Fowler, James, *Stages of Faith: The Psychology of Human Development and the Quest for Meaning.* San Francisco: Harper & Row, 1981.

Gerrish, Brian. *Continuing the Reformation: Essay on Modern Religious Thought.* Chicago: University of Chicago Press, 1993.

Haitch, Russell. "A Summary of James E. Loder's Theory of Christian Education." In *Redemptive Transformation in Practical Theology: Essays in Honor of James E. Loder Jr.*, edited by Dana R. Wright and John D. Kuentzel, 298–324. Grand Rapids: Eerdmans, 1994.

Hamilton, Peter. *Talcott Parsons.* Key Sociologists. London: Routledge, 1983.

Hendry, George. "The Holy Spirit and the Human Spirit." In *The Holy Spirit in Christian Theology*, 96–117. Philadelphia: Westminster, 1961.

Homrighausen, Elmer. "A Study of Religion in American Life." *Princeton Seminary Bulletin* 14/4 (old series) (January 1958) 544–45.

Kovacs, Ken, E. "The Relational Phenomenological Pneumatology of James E. Loder: Providing New Frameworks for the Christian Life." PhD diss., University of St. Andrews, 2002.

———. *The Relational Theology of James E. Loder: Encounter and Conviction.* New York: Peter Lang, 2011.

Loder, James E., Jr. *Educational Ministry in the Logic of the Spirit.* Unpublished manuscript.

———. "The Great Sex Charade and the Loss of Intimacy." *Word and World*, 11/1 (2001) 81–87.

———. Interview by Dana Wright. Privately held tape recordings from April 13–20, 2001.

———. *The Logic of the Spirit: Human Development in Theological Perspective.* San Francisco: Jossey-Bass, 1998.

———. "Normativity and Context in Practical Theology: The Interdisciplinary Issue." In *Practical Theology: International Perspectives*, edited by Fredrich Schweitzer and J. Van der Ven, 359–81. Frankfurt am Main: Peter Lang, 1999.

———. "The Place of Science in Practical Theology: The Human Factor." *International Journal of Practical Theology* 4 (2000) 22–44.

———. *Religious Pathology and Christian Faith.* Philadelphia: Westminster, 1966.

———. *The Transforming Moment.* 2nd ed. Colorado Springs: Helmers & Howard, 1989.

Loder, James E. Jr., and Jim Neidhardt. *The Knight's Move: Relational Logic of the Spirit in Theology and Science.* Colorado Springs: Helmers & Howard, 1992.

Miller, Arthur I. *Picasso, Einstein: The Space, Time, and the Beauty That Causes Havoc.* New York: Basic, 2002.

Moorhead, James H. "Princeton and Deepening Pluralism, 1959-2004." In *Princeton Seminary in Religion and Culture*, edited by James H. Moorhead, 458-502. Grand Rapids: Eerdmans, 2012.

Nelson, C. E. *Where Faith Begins*. Philadelphia: John Knox, 1967.

Prenter, Regin. *Spiritus Creator: Luther's Doctrine of the Holy Spirit*. Philadelphia: Muhlenberg, 1953.

Root, Andrew, with Blair Bertrand. "Postscript: Reflections on Method—Youth Ministry as Practical Theology." In *The Theological Turn in Youth Ministry*, edited by Andrew Root and Kenda C. Dean, 218-37. Downers Grove, IL: InterVarsity, 2011.

Shults, LeRon. "The Philosophical Turn to Relationality and the Responsibility of Practical Theology." In *Redemptive Transformation in Practical Theology*, edited by Dana R. Wright and John D. Kuentzel, 325-46. Grand Rapids: Eerdmans, 2004.

Tiss, Tamara. "James Loder: Our Christlike Father and Gracious Friend." *Princeton Seminary Bulletin* 23 (new series) (2002) 71-73. First delivered at James Loder's memorial service, Miller Chapel, Princeton Theological Seminary, Nov. 14, 2001.

Torrance, Thomas F. "Forward." In *The Knight's Move: The Relational Logic of the Spirit in Theology and Science*, edited by James E. Loder Jr. and Jim Neidhardt, xi-xii. Colorado Springs: Helmers & Howard, 1992.

Wright, Dana R. "Afterword: The Potential Contribution of James E. Loder, Jr. to Practical Theological Science." In *Redemptive Transformation in Practical Theology*, edited by Dana R. Wright and John D. Kuentzel, 401-31. Grand Rapids: Eerdmans, 2004.

———. "Are You There? Comedic Interrogation in the Life and Witness of James E. Loder, Jr." In *Redemptive Transformation in Practical Theology*, edited by Dana R. Wright and John D. Kuentzel, 1-42. Grand Rapids: Eerdmans, 2004.

———. "The Contemporary Renaissance in Practical Theology in the United States: The Past, Present, and Future of a Discipline in Creative Ferment." *International Journal of Practical Theology* 6/3 (2002) 289-320.

———. "James E. Loder, Jr." *Christian Educators of the Twentieth Century*, 2002. Online: www.talbot.edu/ce20/.

———. "Paradigmatic Madness and Redemptive Creativity in Practical Theology: A Biblical Interpretation of the Theological and Methodological Significance of James E. Loder's Neo-Chalcedonian Science for the Postmodern Context." In *Redemptive Transformation in Practical Theology*, edited by Dana R. Wright and John D. Kuentzel, 216-51. Grand Rapids: Eerdmans, 2004.

———. "Prophetic Practical Theology As Testimony: A Loder Legacy?" *Inspire* 63 (Spring 2002) 20-21.

———. "Ruination unto Redemption: A Short Biography of a Reformed 'Wise Guy.'" *The Princeton Seminary Bulletin* 23 (new series) (2002) 75-85.

Wright, Dana R., and John D. Kuentzel. *Redemptive Transformation in Practical Theology*. Grand Rapids: Eerdmans, 2004

Wright, Dana R., and Kenda C. Dean. "Youth, Passion, and Intimacy in the Context of *Koinonia*: James E. Loder's Contribution to a Practical Theology of *Imitatio Christi* for Youth Ministry." In *Redemptive Transformation in Practical Theology*, edited by Dana R. Wright and John D. Kuentzel, 153-88. Grand Rapids: Eerdmans, 2004.

PART ONE

The Child Theology Movement and James E. Loder in Dialogue

1

Child Theology, Loder, and Holistic Child Development (HCD)

Keith J. White

Introduction

The original title of this paper was "Loder and Child Theology." You will see that I have taken the liberty not only of changing the title, but reversing it. "Figure and ground transformed," I imagine I hear James Loder saying! What's more, there is an acronym tacked on the end that you may not recognize. I plead guilty, and do so willingly because I found I could neither write the first part the other way round, nor finish without the second. Perhaps you will judge that the ensuing silence would have been a better option. We shall see!

The paper is in two parts. In the first I reflect on some of the emerging themes in Child Theology that connect with the work of James Loder. In the second part I make a plea to you to imagine and suggest with me some possible practical implications for the interface between theology and what has been called "Holistic Child Development."[1] HCD is closely related to Christian Education, the subject on which Loder was engaged directly and indirectly throughout much of his academic career. One of

---

1. For information on Holistic Child Development (HCD) see www.hcd-alliance.org.

the latent functions of the paper is to tell of my own debt of gratitude to Loder. Of course I am not a true apostle like some of those present at this colloquium, for I never met him in the flesh! I have arrived at Princeton for the first time too late. Like Paul I was "untimely born" in this respect. But the work of Loder has been of crucial significance to me in my daily life among children and young people, and in my writing about Christian education (in its broadest sense). I had resisted till the last a personal aspect to my paper, but on sharing a rough draft with a trusted friend, I realized that this would be as untrue to the facts as it would be to the work and example of James Loder.

All I knew of humanity through children, all I knew of theology, and all I knew of child development (and I freely admit that it all adds up to very little) came together in my book *The Growth of Love* (hereafter *Growth*).[2] And the fact is that I am not sure I could have written this book without the work of Loder. Now it is vital to emphasize that *Growth* is not Child Theology: indeed the book specifically points this out.[3] It is an exploration on the theme of love that is always open to human experience, secular theory, and biblical theology. It was Loder's diagram on page 75 of *The Logic of the Spirit* (hereafter *Logic*) that was of pivotal importance to me: that, and the observation of Thomas Torrance on the comparison between Barth's theology and Einstein's physics.[4] In my opinion, what Barth had done in theology and Einstein had done in physics, so Loder attempted in his work—notably *Logic* and *The Transforming Moment* (hereafter *Transforming*)—a revolutionary new configuration of understanding the relationships between previously disparate or unconnected aspects of reality and theory. In Barth's case we might say that the constant is God in Christ; in Einstein's it is the constancy of the speed of light; and in Loder's it is the constancy of the generative power and dynamics of the Holy Spirit.

As soon as I began to grasp this connection I saw at once that in much of my theoretical reflection I had been constrained by a rather Euclidean, two-dimensional world[5] of the social sciences, where ego

---

2. White, *Growth*.

3. It so happened that I wrote it speedily while working with Haddon Willmer on our essay in Child Theology, and it was therefore necessary to keep the two processes apart, for the sake of clarity.

4. Loder *Logic*, 32–33.

5. For Loder's exposition of the two-dimensional and four-dimensional worlds, see *Transforming*, chapter 3, 67–91.

development was one of the primary constants, implicitly or not. I had assumed that progress was the goal at every level, from the individual to the global, and that this progress was synonymous with human development, despite the scientific fact that we all die, that the planet on which we live is destined for destruction, and that we live between little and big infinities. That is, I had repressed or blocked out the Void (including death) and the Holy in myriad ways. By making the growth of love the central theme of my book, I was open to reality, because love does not run away from truth, or death, or the Void. Rather, it takes account of, and even embraces reality.[6] But enough of that for now!

What follows are five of the themes emerging thus far in an enterprise called Child Theology that resonate with the work of James Loder. You will see from the outset that my thoughts are by nature tentative and exploratory. At most they seek to identify possible resemblances, connections and analogies. There is little or no sense of arrival or completion. And this is, I suggest, as it should be. The fact is that we are at the earliest possible stage in a conversation. We are trying to establish terms and frames of reference to see if we are talking about the same things by other names. We have arrived at a place of meeting by different routes, and we are inquiring as to whether our respective experiences and knowledge thus far can be communicated one to the other. My hunch, or intuition, is that we will in time, even if not at this stage in the process, find new light thrown on our paths, and even that we have been walking similar paths without knowing it. We shall see.

Five Emerging Themes in Child Theology and Connections with Loder's Work

I will start from the work that Haddon Willmer and I have been doing,[7] rather than seek to encompass all that is going on under the banner of Child Theology worldwide. For example, Beth Barnett's paper in this volume (chapter 3) shows how she is working as a biblical theologian, exploring child and theology in the Pauline corpus. And in his paper (see chapter 2) Haddon Willmer connects his lifelong interest in forgiveness to Child Theology and Loder. Others are beavering away at differ-

---

6. I have in mind here particularly Rom 8:35–39.

7. We have been exploring Matt 18:1–14 together for over a decade. See our book *Entry Point*.

ent aspects of Child Theology. We ask: what are five emerging themes in Child Theology that connect to the work of James Loder?

The Child as Sign

This theme might sound so unexceptional as not to detain us, but it doesn't take long before its importance dawns on any who pause to reflect on child and theology. If, as we have done, you take the classic passage in Matthew 18:1–14 you will quickly see that theologians have treated the little child in very different ways.[8] Some have focused on the child to the detriment of nearly all else. The little child in her vulnerability, connectedness, spirituality, humility, virtue and whatever else, is presumed to hold the very keys to the kingdom! The child in this way of doing things has become the focus of the story, and possibly even of theology. Child spirituality is a natural outcome, or companion, of the approach. Others have gone in exactly the opposite direction and seen the child as representing the disciples (present and future), the "little ones" who are like lambs sent into a world of wolves. The child has been brought in like a Power Point slide to illustrate a point, and can be dispensed with as soon as we have seen that she represents others (You might prefer the image of the husk and the kernel of a grain of wheat).

Child Theology has paused to reflect on the meaning of this child placed in the midst by Jesus as a sign.[9] Please note, we are not trying to be dogmatic or doctrinaire. We are trying to do justice to Jesus, the text and the context, as well as to the child![10] And we have found that pausing yields dividends. There is, arguably, nothing quite like this action and teaching in the Gospels. There is a real little child, about whom we know nothing, including gender. There are disciples. And Jesus places the child among them, as well as in the midst of their argument about greatness in the kingdom of heaven. The child is there beside Jesus as some sort of sign, clue, key, or perhaps even catalyst. And it is Jesus, the teacher or leader of his disciples, who tells us what the child means or signifies. He interprets the sign, because like any sign the little child

---

8. I have tried to cover some of this ground in White, "He Placed," 353–74.

9. An example of such reflection is White, "Children as Signs," 41–59.

10. When using the word "child" it is necessary to bear in mind that what we understand and mean by child in the contemporary world is not identical to what it meant in the time of Jesus. Given that we are trying to see "child" as sign, this is a vital point. It is all too easy for modern readers to interpret the sign wrongly.

requires interpretation, by definition. Signs can by themselves mean many different things. A sign is not a carrier or communicator of a plain meaning. Jesus helps us to see what the child is signing. As his disciples we must tread carefully lest we read it wrongly and go off track.

Some of you will already have seen the creative connections with this theme and the argument of *The Transforming Moment*. There is little doubt that Jesus intended his action and accompanying teaching to be just such a moment: a disclosure, a convicting experience, and therefore a potentially "transforming event" (to use Loder's term). But, if you have seen this link, you will be equally quick to point out that in no way did the disciples experience the incident as a transforming event. And this is where another term that Loder uses in *Transforming*, "eikonic eclipse,"[11] may be of relevance. He uses it to mean something typically precise: the erroneous way in which rationalist discourse cuts off reason from its generative sources. But the term may be of wider use when considering the child as sign (*ikon*) in this episode. For some reason the disciples neither have eyes to see what the sign revealed, nor ears to hear what Jesus was saying in relation to the sign. And this, sadly, can be taken to represent much, if not most, theological inquiry and church practice down through the centuries. We might therefore say that there has been an eikonic eclipse both in the case of the disciples present with Jesus as he placed the little child among them, and also in church history from Pentecost to the present day. Using Dewey and Piaget, Loder explains how they bring a frame of reference to the object of their study which rules out as much discontinuity as possible.[12] And that is a distillation, he argues, that lies at the heart of eikonic eclipse. So when Jesus introduces a radically new dimension of reality, the kingdom of God, and does so in this instance with a radically new sign, it would be understandable if the disciples were thrown back on to their traditional, existing frames of reference in order to cope with the threatening discontinuity. And perhaps theologians have done the same down through the centuries. Be that as it may, for whatever reason the sign of the child has generally suffered eikonic eclipse.

Loder offers further reflections on signs that are of general significance to Child Theology, as well as of specific relevance to an understanding of this passage. In *Transforming* he focuses on convictional

11. Loder, *Transforming*, 26f, 223.
12. Ibid., 47.

experiences, like his own accident, and like the conversion of St Paul. Such experiences risk being discredited (marginalized) theologically on the one hand, or given canonical significance on the other.[13] And this is where he shows an acute awareness of what is at stake with a sign. Bear in mind as you read this that Child Theology starts, as it were, in the middle of an argument about the kingdom of God.

> ... [t]here are important theological observations to be made. These experiences may be understood under a category of biblical theology such as "signs of the presence of the Kingdom of God." This is a helpful category because it prevents the experiences themselves from being worshipped, and points to God of whose Kingdom they are signs. Moreover, relegated to the status of "signs," they are prevented from being strictly private experiences, granting personal powers and divine privileges to the convicted person. This strips away the narcissism that accumulates around these events and confirms the experience as belonging not pre-eminently [sic] to an individual but to all who have eyes to see..."[14]

This statement puts very well one of the extremes that we have been seeking to avoid in CTM: the canonization of the child. I think we are all aware of the attraction and strength of what is often called the "Child Spirituality Movement." It represents much careful observation and exploration, but it is always open to the temptation of placing the child on some sort of pedestal from which adults are deemed, *pace* Wordsworth, to have fallen. Loder points out towards the end of *Transforming* that "a child's innocence provokes ... religious longing,"[15] and a "nostalgia for the more deeply repressed longing for the enduring face."[16] It seems to me that we must be careful to keep this nostalgic longing within proper bounds. Child as sign may be a helpful contribution to this process. We will explore it a little further in section 3 below.

Before leaving this matter, let me say that I wonder whether the work of Loder, at Princeton or in the wider Christian academy, has not itself suffered eikonic eclipse. Is he so impossible to locate in our existing theological and developmental categories that we tend to rule him out

---

13. Ibid., 18, 19.
14. Ibid., 19.
15. Ibid., 177.
16. Ibid., 166.

(generally that is, not among those here) by retreating into our preconceived frameworks? Is the discontinuity he brings far too threatening, I wonder? And am I alone in finding it hard very often to know whether he is writing about a sign or about substance?

Entry to the Kingdom of Heaven

The sign of the child is accompanied by the words of Jesus: "unless you change and become humble like the little children you will not enter the kingdom of heaven."[17] There is something inherently scandalous about this teaching that may well help to explain why it has not been given due attention. It is not long before the disciples ask Jesus, "Who then can be saved?"[18] (This is a good theological question, if ever there was one!). The disciples take it for granted that they are already in the kingdom: the only thing to be settled is the pecking order! Jesus deconstructs (Loder talks of "rupture in the knowing context"[19] and "conflict") their whole understanding (if they could but take it in). They see things in terms of linear progress and development, or perhaps investment of time and energy in the hope of a return. Jesus challenges fundamentally their frame of reference, replete with the idea of high status as a reward for loyalty for the insiders, as distinct from the "others."

Now let's be clear, the whole idea of the Kingdom of God (to use the term more frequently used outside the Gospel of Matthew), and what it means to enter it, is far from easy theologically. People and denominations still seem to fall into errors very similar to that of the disciples. But given the action and teaching of Jesus, here and in his parables, and the centrality of the Cross to his mission, he brings a sweeping and comprehensive challenge to human systems and assumptions. Jesus has spoken the unthinkable to his disciples. He says, in effect, "You are outsiders, who make the very mistake that you see in the Pharisees, by thinking that you are the true, the only insiders." But Jesus does not just challenge their rather parochial and personal thinking. He places their culture, tradition and hope under question.

---

17. Matt 18:4.
18. Matt 19:25.
19. Loder, *Transforming*, 37.

And this is where Loder, like Barth[20] and Kierkegaard (to name but two), is willing to be open to the scandal of the teaching of Jesus, and to the rupture of knowing that this scandal demands, if it is to be allowed to become active in the process of change. Loder is willing to be guided by the leading and logic of the Spirit, as the Spirit illuminates his understanding of the teaching, life, death and resurrection of Jesus. He is, if you like, willing to walk by faith where this illumination leads. The transcendent God is God, and we are His creatures. Nothing we can do can contribute as much as a single brick to build a bridge across this infinite gulf. The kingdom of God is not, *pace* Harvey Cox *et al*, another way of understanding human progress, but almost exactly the opposite. Jesus specifically points this out very soon after this incident in Matthew's Gospel.[21]

Even allowing for the subtlety and mystery of the whole notion of the kingdom of heaven, it might be said that Fowler's *Stages of Faith* has more than a little to do with entry into it. And I think that we all know what Loder thought of that![22] But we must also take account of the full range of developmental theory, human longings, ambitions, schemes and not forget religion. Jesus is not making general points here, whether about the kingdom of God, or about the Gospel, although we may well find some universal truths or principles. He is talking specifically about entry. And the disciples need to unlearn most if not all of what they have assumed or learned about that. *Transforming* and *Logic* both have much to contribute to this particular theme.[23] The section in *Transforming* where Loder refers to H. R. Niebuhr's treatment of *metanoia* may be especially relevant here.[24] And *Logic* as a whole is a deconstruction of

---

20. It is one of the main themes of Barth's commentary on Romans that no human being has a possible place or position above any other when it comes to the matter of God's grace.

21. Matt 19:26, "With man this is impossible, but with God all things are possible"; Matthew 20:25 "You know that the rulers of the Gentiles lord it over them . . . not so with you."

22. Wright, "Loder," 13.

23. Loder, *Transforming*, argues that convicting experiences or moments, which can be taken as points of entry, are automatically resisted by well tried and tested processes. In *Logic* he argues that the Spirit is ceaselessly at work trying to deconstruct the false enterprise of the ego in order that God's grace might be received.

24. Loder, *Transforming*, 19–20.

every aspect of human endeavor that believes it can build its own way to God, and "gain entry to the kingdom" by its own means.

Like Loder, in taking Jesus at his word, CTM finds itself questioning much of the Christian establishment, with the challenge that those who see themselves not only as insiders, but as leading lights or exemplary organizations and churches, may need to consider seriously whether or not they are outsiders, in need of repentance. And this message does not guarantee a warm reception. "Don't rock the boat" is one phrase that has been used by the leader of a Christian organization. Indeed, the underlying and controversial message of *Logic* is that much human energy, effort and achievement is based on what Loder sees as the falsely and inadequately founded, and ultimately vain, enterprise of the human ego.[25]

The Child and Christ

There is in the story as told by Matthew a remarkable closeness between the child and Jesus that is more than mere physical proximity. At no point does Jesus attempt to draw any distinction between the little child and himself, and his words imply the opposite. By welcoming one such little child in Christ's name one welcomes Christ (and the one who sent him, if we draw from the accounts of Mark 9:33–37 and Luke 9:46–48). Yet, the child is not Christ, and Christ is not the child. That distinction is critical in the account of the story, and of our theological understanding of it. But we are still confronted with a connection between them that seems too close for comfort.

Here we find all sorts of theological approaches being taken and the arguments are varied. Some immediately think of the birth narratives: Jesus the little child. They invite us to see Jesus especially in every child. Thus the child represents childhood, which is the theological state of all humans before God as distinct from adult, which is a human construction. And so on. But what is the meaning of the sign of the child in relation to Christ in Matthew 18? Does the context help us at all? One thing is clear and very important: Jesus does not look back to his own childhood, but looks forward to the Cross. He confronts the Void. Can it

---

25. While thinking about and preparing for this paper I had been rereading Barth's second commentary on Romans, and the congruence of his message with that of CTM and Loder is uncanny.

be, therefore, that the little child is a reiteration of the call to his disciples to take up the Cross? Could it be that to embrace a child in an act of welcome or reception is to embrace the Cross?

We must, as always, be careful. It is not that the child is Christ or vice-versa, but that in welcoming the little child one welcomes Christ. The key is the action of welcoming or receiving the child. Earlier I referred to the way in which a sign can be worshiped, and quoted Loder on the risk of narcissism. The meaning of the child in the story is often taken to be that there are childlike qualities that the disciples should cultivate. Thus "change . . . and become humble like the little child" is seen to require spiritual commitment and discipline on their part. Without decrying the place of such discipline, it is vital to note that at no stage does Jesus hint at anything like this. Rather he gives the following statement: "when you receive a child in my name you welcome me."

Note that we have moved from "little children" (plural, verse 3) to "child in my name" (singular, verse 4) in the words of Jesus. This is not a general call to get involved with children. Remember that the parable of the single lost sheep is just around the corner in Matthew's account (verses 10–14)! What if the process of changing and becoming humble happens as an integral part of welcoming a child? We may need to pause to take this in. If such an interpretation is on the right lines, then the focus is no longer on spiritual development in myself, but on opening myself to receive a little child. Now surely the testimony of parenthood in general, and motherhood in particular, is that a full and healthy reception of a little child requires a considerable amount of change, all in the direction of stooping! So this may help us to understand the element of change that Jesus requires of his disciples.

But you reply, where is there any self-awareness of welcoming Christ in the process? The answer is that there isn't any. The kingdom is not entered as a result of a conscious spiritual act, but as an unconscious by-product of a welcoming action. It is just like the story Jesus will tell of the eschatological judgment recorded in Matthew 25. There it is precisely the absence of this awareness of welcoming Christ in both contrasted groups that is the key feature of the narrative. In welcoming others we have welcomed the Son of Man. Such a reading of Matthew 18 is therefore not only of practical relevance, but also of consistent exegesis. The alternative notion—that is, of receiving a child as a means of achieving spiritual virtue—though not uncommon in church history, and possibly current Christian education, is surely as repugnant as it is theologically unsound. The motive for welcoming a little child in the name of Jesus is not for any purpose other than love or compassion.

If we keep the concept of welcoming or receiving a little child firmly within the overarching concept of love and loving the child, then Loder has this to offer from his chapter in *Transforming*, "From Negation to Love": ". . . to continue to love as one has been loved is the only way to abide in the transformation effected by His Spirit . . . the only way to participate in it is to give love as it was given."[26] The disciples were still a long way from this practice, with the key word being "abide." As the child stands among them they are not living in, or embracing, the present reality and situation. Rather, they are looking back to what they have done. But relating to Jesus is never a case of stopping to count, as it were, the credits, as if the metaphor of a balance sheet is in any way relevant, let alone adequate. And he does not ask the disciples to list the number of children they have received in his name. In the here and now a child stands before them. The kingdom is as fresh as the morning dew, the *manna* in the wilderness, green as a leaf. Welcoming and love are lived in the present with no reckoning on anything remotely related to greatness or littleness in the kingdom.

Before we move on it is worth noting that the "*I yet not I but Christ*" unity[27] and dialectic that is central to Christian theology and to the work of Loder may be helpful in understanding the relationship between the little child and Christ as in so much doing of Child Theology. Is there a strange, Mobius-type loop here, I wonder? What if the way in which Christ becomes part of me is by means of welcoming a little child? Certainly the disciples strongly resist acceptance of the real Christ, the Suffering Servant, who must be rejected and die an ignominious death. Does welcoming the child at least indicate a way in which some of this resistance might be overcome? We must move on, because Loder does not, so far as I am aware, explore this particular passage in this context or way, but we have made a mental note to revisit it.

---

26. Loder, *Transforming*, 180.
27. Loder, *Logic*, 120, 145.

The Child, the Cross and Negation

The themes of Cross and Negation are arguably two of Loder's most widely-acknowledged, yet neglected and misunderstood, contributions to human development theory from a theological perspective.[28] These themes remain underdeveloped, both in terms of practical research as far as I know, and also in terms of theology's relationship with the human sciences. Much more time is still spent working with Augustine's *Confessions* and his concept of Original Sin, than with Loder's theory of Negation, for example. Child Theology, to be serious, has been trying to understand sin, Original Sin, and all sin with particular reference to the child.[29] And this is no easy matter. But Loder draws our attention to possible ways forward. If you put together pages 91–94 and pages 122–24 of *Logic*—his analysis of child or ego development and the doctrine of Original Sin—there is an obvious invitation to consider these themes together. It is a tantalizingly brief reference to so influential a subject, but one that deserves theological attention. Another connection is the way that the development of an individual human being mirrors, reflects, or is congruent with, the development of the universe. And still another connection is the way that human civilization represents an extension of the vain attempt of the individual's ego to build an identity, a name, or to seek security and safety for itself by denying or repressing the Void (do I hear Karl Barth say "Amen!" in the background here?)[30] Echoing Ivan Illich's notion of the "ritualization of progress,"[31] Loder refers to the way in which this "distortion of the human spirit is repeated as a widely exercised dynamic in socialization systems from the achievement-oriented family, to the public school classroom, and American business practices

---

28. Loder developed this theme in *Transforming*, 157–69 as well as in *Logic*, 91–94 and 122–24.

29. See Willmer, *Experimenting*.

30. "This world has . . . form and shape; and it possesses a law, a general pressure towards concreteness, to light-created light. This pressure towards enjoyment, possession, success, knowledge, power, rightness; this vigorous movement towards an attainable comprehensible perfection; this pressure . . . forms the mysterious pivot round which the whole world of human genius revolves . . . and . . . genius is . . . our beloved ego" (Barth, *Epistle*, 433–34).

31. Loder, *Transforming*, 166, referring to Ilich, *De-Schooling*, chapter 3.

. . ."[32] The key to understanding the source of much human and societal dynamics and structures is the little child in our midst.

Stooping to welcome one little child is, in a sense, a way of turning away from the lure and temptation of participating in the great human project, which is to build a reassuring and impressive home and a name for ourselves independent of God in Christ. And when we see this we can also recognize how easily the religious project can work in tandem with society, with scant recognition of the nature and dynamics of the kingdom of God and its transformational logic. It is also a reminder to anyone who would canonize this little child as a paragon of virtue, forgetting that the child who has passed the toddler stage has already begun, albeit unconsciously, to construct an ego against the Void. The disciples, of course, as human beings and as members of their oppressed nation, have done the same. The idea of the Kingdom of God that they have as their guiding framework is about a political restoration of power to Israel. And the sign and call of Jesus to the Cross works toward a negation of this negation of God's will and the logic of the Spirit of Christ.

In our study of this incident as told by Matthew we have been increasingly drawn to the conjunction of the little child and the Cross. But this conjunction is so counterintuitive that we need faith even to begin to venture into such new territory. We did not come across it via the idea or metaphor of the face (see below), but rather by beginning to understand the little child placed by Jesus as a reiteration of the call to the Cross. Both involve turning, and becoming humble. But the Cross, in and of itself, is a call to total denial, loss and emptiness, whereas receiving the little child is a call that involves a degree of new life. We need to explore the twin calls to take up the Cross, and to become humble like little children in relation to Loder's work. Intuitively it would seem to be exactly the sort of dynamic we might expect of the logic of the Spirit, with its paradoxes and negations that lead to life in Christ.

The scandalous reality of the Cross, with its horrendous void epitomized by the cry, "My God, my God, why hast thou forsaken me?," is often rejected in practice by Christians and the Church throughout history. And likewise the idea of child and negation has largely been rejected (whether consciously or not), in human development and theological studies. I sense a hidden link or congruence here, yet to be uncovered and explored. The Cross is about Negation in its starkest form.

32. Loder, *Transforming*, 166.

What happens, I wonder, if we connect the Cross with "the triumph of negation" in the little child?

The Face

This last concern leads us naturally to the matter of the Face, because the argument about negation in Loder takes place within the context of the search for the Face that is the inevitable consequence of cosmic loneliness. This theme is developed on pages 118–21 of *Logic,* and on pages 162–69 in *Transforming* with particular reference to Jesus as the Face of God. As we worked slowly through Matthew Chapter 18 we were, of course, brought to the very same word *prosopon*: "See that you do not despise the least of these little ones, for I tell you that their angels always behold the face of the Father in heaven."[33] This is not the place to attempt a biblical and theological exposition of such an important theme. But we do well to remind ourselves that the face described in the Servant Song in Isaiah 52 and 53[34] is the very stumbling block to greatness in the kingdom of God that Peter represents for Jesus and trips over himself.[35] Jesus will look at Peter face to face.[36] And we too are destined to meet that Face, face to face in the life beyond.[37] The reference in Matthew 18:11 bristles with questions for those who seek to understand it aright: Who or what are the angels, and what do they represent? What difference do they make to little children on earth? What about the orphans, many of them child soldiers or prostitutes, who cry into the Void and hear nothing but the hollow echo of their lonely weeping? Loder is one of many who have seen some of the profound implications of the child's search for a face, and the fact that theologically speaking, all human faces represent but a dim reflection of the Face of the Father. Fathers and mothers may forsake children but the Lord is always there to welcome

---

33. Matt 18: 11.

34. "His appearance was so disfigured beyond that of any man and his form marred beyond human likeness . . . He had no beauty or majesty to attract us to him, nothing in his appearance that we should desire him . . . Like one from whom men hide their faces he was despised, and we esteemed him not . . . " (Isa 52:14; 53:2–3).

35. Matt 16:21–23. This exchange concludes with the words of Jesus, "Get behind me, Satan! You are a stumbling block to me; you do not have in mind the things of God, but the things of men."

36. Luke 22:61.

37. 1 Cor 13:12.

and receive them.³⁸ This is the epitome, source and end of all acts of welcome and reception that lie at the heart of entry into, and the life of, the Kingdom of God. For no welcome is complete without the Face that greets you at the door, as C. S. Lewis, for example, portrays so vividly in *The Last Battle* at the end of time.³⁹

You will see from this short excursus that starting this way, with Child Theology, has led us to connect with some of the key themes in Loder's work. You might even imagine *his* face smiling and lighting up as we happen upon thoughts and insights that he had been mulling over for years. It is vital to be clear on one point: this reception is not about a simple affirmation of the status quo. The reception of the child in the name of Jesus brings change, even disturbance. There are avenues opening up in CTM that will necessitate new thinking through a sustained engagement with Loder's work. At the same time you will notice that there are themes in Loder that CTM has not yet actively explored. For example, little attention has been given to the Holy Spirit and the child, although there is every indication that this theme will prove rewarding when it commences.⁴⁰ And you may well have your own observations about what remains still to be connected. CTM would welcome any thoughtful contribution to the developing conversation that is beginning now.

Towards an Integrated Christian Education

Now let me turn to the second part of my paper, dealing with some other avenues that could open up as a result of the conversation between CTM and Loder. I guess that a few of these possibilities have become apparent already, but here are some suggestions. All the time we must bear in the mind that we risk talking only to the converted. Most theological study

---

38. Ps 29: "My heart says of you, 'Seek his face!' Your face, Lord I will seek. Do not hide your face from me . . . Though my father and mother forsake me, the Lord will receive me" (vv. 9–10).

39. Lewis, *Last Battle*, 144: "The others looked in the face of Aslan and loved him . . ."

40. There is, of course, the famous quotation by the prophet Joel: "Your sons and daughters will prophesy, your young men will see visions" (Acts 2:17). And in the 2011 CTM Nairobi conference there was some initial discussion of children. See the group discussion summary in White et al., *Now and Next*, 84–86 and the paper by Samuel, "Church," 87–100.

and Christian children's activity are being done in ignorance of Loder's potential contributions. It is the intention of CTM that we should give due weight, possibly most weight, to the matter of how we go about connecting with those thinkers like Loder whose work we sense is relevant to our mission. If a publication is a good way of doing this, let's consider it; but should we be thinking of research, lecture tours, consultations or what?

A key text here is Dana Wright's essay, "The Potential Contribution of Loder to Practical Theological Science."[41] In essence Wright addresses the same concern as that which I intimated at the outset of our conference, and as I think we all realize, that the work and potential insights of Loder have not percolated into mainstream Christian discourses, whether theology, counseling, or human development. Much though we enjoyed meeting together and sharing our testimonies (see below), the gathering out of which this book emerged resembled a salt cellar rather more than a shaking of salt that gives flavor to the body of Christ. It is light hidden under a bowl.

Perhaps we should ponder why this is so before trying to remedy the situation. There are some formidable challenges in such an enterprise.

Some Obstacles to Overcome

First, Loder's work, like Child Theology, is radical, if not revolutionary in some of its dimensions and implications, despite (or because of) the fact that it is at the same time very traditional in dogmatic terms. We should not underestimate the tenacity with which humans and human institutions cling on to everything that would seem to offer them the illusion of keeping afloat in an existential situation which could be said to be worse than the moment after the Titanic had hit the iceberg. Loder, like Barth and Kierkegaard, never tired in pointing out the *krisis* represented by the utter creatureliness of human beings and the transcendent holiness and otherness of God who is God. In seeking to help individuals and institutions in many and varied ways Christians can so easily collude with the endemic, original strategy and tactic of humanity in believing that we can make a name for ourselves. We find security by what is in effect shifting the deckchairs on a ship that is doomed and sinking. This is a far from comfortable message, and it is not to be wondered that, like

---

41. Wright, "Afterword," 401–31.

the message of the Cross (and it is an essential part of the message of the Cross), it proves to be as scandalous to the Christian community as it is to Jews and Greeks.[42]

Second, there is the whole question of language and the level of difficulty involved in learning Loder's work well. Put crisply, Loder's work requires translation and mediation before he can be understood. Some time ago I gave my first tutorial on the work of Loder. There were two students: both graduates with PhDs, and both senior academics in their respective fields. I recall it well, but for reasons that will become obvious, will not divulge any more details of place and people. Within a couple of minutes I was struggling with the most basic elements of Loder's thought. Some of us who gathered for the conference may have become so used to it that we fail to see how forbidding his work is to the uninitiated. He demonstrated, rather like Karl Barth, a quite remarkable knowledge of philosophical and scientific, as well as theological disciplines throughout his work. He went further and sought to connect and integrate them. But how on earth does this kind of interdisciplinary thinking get communicated, broken down, handed on? I needed to read *Logic* three times before I felt I had grasped most of it, and by the way, I was also writing a summary for my students! CTM is committed to open and inclusive gatherings of followers of Jesus. And so there must be the gift of interpretation. Perhaps we are being called to become Jim's interpreters while he still speaks in tongues!

Third, there is no apparent active community of scholars that is taking on Loder's work, putting it under the microscope, exploring it in relation to theological and contemporary developments.[43] There may be a rather loose network of interested scholars and practitioners, as this symposium testifies, but it is rather eclectic and linked by personal connections. There are no academic chairs related to Loder's work, and few courses being offered that feature his theory. This must, of course, include critiques of Loder's work, such as the possibility that he relies on a *tertium quid*, despite his aversion to such alien concepts.[44] Could this conference mark a beginning, I wonder, of a more sustained engagement

---

42. 1 Cor 1:22–23.

43. Wright, "Afterword," 408–9. Wright identifies human sciences, social theorists, theologians, and natural scientists, among others, who have not sufficiently analyzed Loder's work, connected the "dots" of his overall theory and joined them up.

44. Ibid., 412.

with Loder's thought? The Board of CTM is open to suggestions about how this kind of engagement might be nurtured including, of course, this publication of papers and any recommendations that might emerge from it. Could we agree on say five key topics,[45] that "cut the world at its [relational] joints,"[46] and hold conversations on them?

If genuinely new thinking is to take root, it must be tested in and through research. And if we are to take Loder's work seriously as intentionally scientific, it needs to be both theological and practical research, in that the topics we might sketch out must be amenable to research.[47] CTM has post-graduates working on PhDs right now, and we believe that more will come on stream. Would the five themes I have briefly sketched out above be worthy of some further consideration, I wonder?

Fourth, if Wright is correct that Loder is a practical theological scientist,[48] then there is the very difficult task of trying to decide where he fits on the academic bookshelf.[49] This might seem an arcane task, but it is in fact the very opposite—not least if someone suggests "A" for Alchemy![50] There may be other obstacles that I have not seen or mentioned, and if readers of this volume are aware of them, please let us know. Rather than try to cover a whole field of possible connections I have endeavored to narrow my remarks down to something reported to be developing fast around the world—namely, Holistic Child Development.

A Challenge to Holistic Child Development

Some of you may be aware of the attempt by HCD to stir seminaries around the world into action. The lead organization is Compassion International, and the relevant website is www.hcd-alliance.org. I think that the term has much in common with what is meant by Christian education, and whether you know of it or not, I would like you to imagine what might be meant by the term when used by Christians, and if there is

---

45. Ibid., 420–30 for his list of sixteen possible challenges Loder's work poses for practical theology. My hope is that we could distil them to something more manageable and perhaps categorize them in families.

46. Ibid., 417, Wright notes the origins of this phrase from Colin Gunton.

47. One effort to connect Loder to current research is the essay by Wendy Sanders in this present volume, chapter 10.

48. Ibid., 403–8.

49. Ibid., 410.

50. Ibid., 405, 408ff.

sufficient agreement, how we might go about advocating and practicing holistic child development in a theologically rooted and grounded way. The people engaged in the process to date genuinely aspire to do what its name indicates. But what a task for Christians it represents, given all that Loder and CTM have helped to draw to our attention! Among the immediate and significant questions come to mind are the following: How does Christian theology relate to theories of child development and the social sciences? How do we go about teaching interdisciplinary thinking? Who can teach it? Why does it matter? If HCD comes to find Loder's work unhelpful, for whatever reason, then where can it turn? At the very least, surely, we must include one of Loder's texts, *Logic*![51]

The movement is, I believe, still looking for some sort of synthesis, rather than accepting inherent contradictions between the different discourses that make up the components of an integrated approach. The implicit metaphor is I think, mosaic. This image suggests that individual pieces retain their particularity, and do interact with or affect any other piece. The unity, whether conceptual or in practice, is not organic.

Jesus confronts HCD in and through the sign of the little child with a dramatic challenge to change. He calls us to consider that we might be fundamentally mistaken, or on the wrong tack—i.e., not just that we have made one or two minor errors, or slipped up occasionally, but that we are heading in completely the wrong direction. Of course we find it unthinkable that we might be outside the kingdom of God and getting further away in our striving for greatness in it! But hopefully we can see that there is a real practical problem here about process: the way any form of conceptual integration might be achieved. Furthermore, one notices that there was no one here at the Loder event from Compassion, World Vision, or any such Christian-based organizations committed to child development. Why not? This is a pertinent question, because it is not for want of trying! There seems to be a disconnect between what Loder was trying to do, and what organizations like Compassion need to do better—that is, integrate theology and practice. A bridge needs to be built, and this conference and CTM may have roles to play in its construction. My belief is that Loder, and those who understand the significance of his work, could be crucial partners in this constructive possibility.

---

51. See White, "Model," 166–206.

The task of integrating theology and child development, though difficult, is crucial. Yet there is serious resistance, and we need to understand why the prevailing frameworks of so much that pass for Christian engagement with children remain overwhelmingly secular. One finds Christian education students trotting out the basic terms and frameworks of Maslow, Erikson, Piaget and the like without a moment's thought. At a very basic level there is limited interdisciplinary integrity between Christian theology and social science theories. Loder has critiqued, with due respect, this lack of theological integration and has shown us a way forward. In *Logic*, for example, we see his model of how this integrative task might be understood in term of human development theory. And Loder's collaboration with physicist Jim Neidhardt in *The Knight's Move* offers an expansive integration between theology and the natural sciences.[52] How might we take Loder's concern for interdisciplinary integrity further? How do we construct the outlines of a theologically informed and integrated curriculum that really makes a difference in practice?[53]

Child Theology, as developed in the essay that Haddon Willmer and I are writing, is too narrow to infuse and accompany HCD, though it may prove to have other critical and visionary functions. But by talking about human development, Loder is more fitted to give HCD the theological accompaniment it so obviously needs. He works with the same kinds of theory of human development as those at HCD. Building on the five themes and suggestions I have made thus far I suggest here two possible lines of rapprochement with Loder and HCD.

A Basis for a Curriculum Based on a Lifetime

First, Loder is concerned with human development up to, and in light of, death. This existential focus gives his work a perspective and a challenge that HCD ducks, for HCD confines itself to children, and to that segment of a life. Thus, HCD does not ponder what child development develops into. Its work is in theory and practice too closely aligned to modern education, preparation for independent living, employability, citizenship and parenthood. And like modern education of children

---

52. Loder and Neidhardt, *Knight's Move*, provides us with a very useful coordinate as we seek to understand the way Loder goes about the interdisciplinary task. For this connection to human development see *Logic*, 17–45, esp. 44 n. 16.

53. For more insight into Loder's interdisciplinary method in relation to Christian Education theory see chapter 7 of this book.

generally, HCD remains insulated from issues and visions which only appear later in life. What is offered to children does not have the human breadth and depth that people enter into by living a life to the end. Older education in humanities, by introducing children to drama, poetry and sacred texts, expands child education all the way between little and great infinities. But most education is shaped by what the child is deemed to be able to take in and understand within her assumed conceptual ability. So, years ago in the UK, the Bible was taken away from children on educational grounds that they were not cognitively "ready" for it. The secular social forms of this kind of education are extensive. Education becomes training in skills for employability, and little else.

HCD, of course, is in principle dedicated to the well-being of the whole child. But it cannot give a good answer to its own concerns, because dealing with the child in the terms set by childhood only (i.e., segregated from life as a whole), does not make for well-being. When HCD deals with children in this segregated way it runs two risks. One is that it will tend to over-privilege, or even idolize, children, as argued above. The other is that it tends to see children as needing care, protection, and training from within a social management concept of society. Because it does not take a serious view of children as human beings with a lifetime to live, it cannot do justice to them as persons. Loder offers help, starting with a reshaping of curricula. Instead of a curriculum packed with studies of children and child-care, with a bit of child-ideology tacked on, the base and breadth would be holistically human. It would be a syllabus that illuminated and asked questions of the young adult students and the old, nearly dead teachers, as well as for the little children.

Theology and Wholeness

The second connection to Loder is theological. In Christian contexts, holistic is a word that is used to express a double commitment. It indicates, as we have just noted, concern for the wholeness of the child, as that is seen in an everyday way of care for *mens sana in corpore sano*. But wholeness (we note the deep link with holiness) also makes a claim for the religious dimension of life that, it is hoped, must be respected by secular humanists, because this dimension is part of the whole. So HCD includes care for the spiritual development of children, and therefore for a distinctive and explicit Christian shape, texture and color in the whole training for and practice of child care. Though HCD is seen in this way in Christian contexts, it seems, as argued above, that the Christian element (religion, theology) is rarely integrated with the main studies of child development, where secular theories dominate. There is some desire for this situation to be changed, but for various reasons nothing seems to change. Theology (in the widest sense) may be put along side development studies, but it does not begin to transform them.

Loder offers an example for effecting theological change without compromising the integrity of the other sciences. He raises key questions about how it could be done. He uncovers some methodological and substantial choices that affect any Christian HCD course. His work is structured throughout by the distinctive relationality of human and divine Spirit. This relational dimension is not for him an item of doctrine, a single piece of theological information disconnected from the secular. It is a way of seeing a complex and transcending reality, which time and again in a lifetime comes into view (darkly), in one way or another. It is even more than an observer's scientific theory. In Loder's vision, divine and human spirits converse in the deep turmoil of life, so that the teacher and student cannot insulate themselves from the Spirit's presence. The teacher, the counsellor, and the father confessor come together in practical experience where the steady course of education may be fundamentally disrupted by spiritual transformation.[54]

We must take good note that Loder's theological understanding of human development can be grasped and shared only by those who are living in the relationality of divine and human spirit with the same sort of openness, courage and articulacy we sense in Loder himself. We must not make Loder the model and recruit imitative disciples. That would turn his work into nonsense. But he inspires us to be aware of, and persevere with, the holistic human requirements of doing genuinely holistic (holy?) child development, which most of us would find more than demanding: actually frightening and discouraging. Most education, like most of church and most of all human life, are so ordered that specified outcomes can be achieved without making people aware of their human limitations, or frightened by their own inability.

If Loder was deployed to shake up HCD et al, it might then produce a situation in which the participants and their organizations could and would notice the child in the midst as a sign of the Kingdom of God. At present, meanwhile, HCD seems not at all concerned with the kingdom

---

54. For example, see the case of "Helen" in *Logic*, chapter 3, 46–78.

of God, as God's great disturbance. On the one hand, they seem satisfied with the secular models and theories on offer and in fashion. On the other hand, they want to promote the future of the church in some way, but without any apparent need to embody a theological openness, curiosity, humility, or wonder Loder associates with life in the Spirit. Perhaps HCD is merely satisfied that the church gives them God's program and a place in it.

Conclusion

It has become clear to me, not least through the references to research at the end of Dana Wright's summary of Loder's life and work, that hundreds have been influenced by Loder in one way or another. Could we find a way of drawing together their testimonies?[55] In some ways that is what we have here at this event and in these essays. I am going to conclude with my own testimony. And, perhaps implicitly, each of those of us who attended this gathering and who contributed essays to this present volume is also testifying to what we know. Are we not all like the case studies Loder used to illustrate his thought? He always argued that these testimonies, along with his own stories of redemptive transformation, "belong to the church"! So why don't I give an example of how some of this has begun to come together for me?

As a sociologist and theologian, committed to living in a residential community of hurting children called Mill Grove, I have sought to integrate my faith, life, theory and practice. This lifelong vocation and practice has led me into two sorts of reflective activities: teaching and writing. In my teaching I have focused on children and childhood, and currently lecture on the HCD course in Penang. I started with the theological foundations, and am now working my way through how this foundational work relates to other aspects of child development. In my writing (probably best described as eclectic) I have been trying to draw together strands, and make sense of disparate elements of life and experience. One book is *Growth of Love* that I have already mentioned. It describes love that I have witnessed growing in and through many

---

55. As it happens, I did not mention this part of my paper at the Loder conference, although I sensed that testimonies were the very things called for. In the event Tom Hastings therefore demonstrated what could and had to be done without any prompting from me! See his highly personal essay in this present volume, chapter 5.

of those living at Mill Grove. And as I started with real human life and stories, and in this way, it was only when I discovered Loder that I was able to begin to make sense of the data of my lived experience. Accepted understandings of developmental stages were unhelpful to my work for all sorts of reasons. But in Loder I found someone so well versed in the theologians and theorists that I knew his work was likely to be relevant to much of my life and experience.

Putting together my experience, the corpus that makes up "child development theory," and theology, I came to the conclusion that for love to grow there are five key elements or dimensions to the process: Security, Boundaries, Significance, Community, and Creativity. They resisted a meta-framework, such as stages in a progression, levels in a hierarchy. I knew this, and Loder confirmed it. But now I see that the final theme in the list, creativity, is both the beginning and the end of the process, as well as running right through it. Properly understood it bears the hallmarks of *Spiritus Creator*. I have used this combination of insights in my teaching and will be producing a course-book next year. I would welcome the comments and peer review of this work by some of those who have gathered for this event. It would be a practical way of taking the process forward.

In all this we must never forget that the key that unlocks the door to the kingdom of God is welcoming or receiving a little one in the name of Jesus. And that is what I have been seeking to do throughout my life. Notice, this is not just a "secular" receiving, however gracious and loving that may be. This is receiving in the name of Jesus. And it is in this "moment" (if we allow ourselves a Loderian and Barthian-laden word with which to close) of reception, that the negation of the ego is negated, by the responsive face of a human being, as a sign and perhaps even more, of the welcome that God in Christ has had in store for us from before the dawn of time, has been breathing into creation by the Spirit, and which awaits us at the end of the age.

Works Cited

Barth, Karl. *The Epistle to the Romans*. Translated by E. Hoskyns. London: Oxford University Press, 1933.
Bunge, Marcia J. *The Child in Christian Thought*. Grand Rapids: Eerdmans, 2001.
Illich, Ivan. *De-Schooling Society*. New York: Harper & Row, 1971.
Lewis, C. S. *The Last Battle*. London: Harper Collins, 1990.
Loder, James E., Jr. *Educational Ministry in the Logic of the Spirit*. Unpublished manuscript.
———. *The Logic of the Spirit: Human Development in Theological Perspective*. San Francisco: Jossey-Bass, 1998.
———. *The Transforming Moment*. 2nd ed. Colorado Springs: Helmers & Howard, 1989.
Loder, James E., Jr., and Jim Neidhardt. *The Knight's Move: The Relational Logic of the Spirit in Theology and Science*. Colorado Springs: Helmers & Howard, 1992.
Samuel, Vinay. "The Church and the Child—A Challenge to the Churches." In *Now and Next: A Compendium of Papers Presented at the Theological Conference on Children, Nairobi, Kenya, 2011*, edited by Keith J. White et al., 87–100. Penang, Malaysia: Compassion, 2011.
White, Keith J. "Child Theology is Born." Unpublished address given at the annual meeting of the UK Christian Child Forum, February 5, 2002.
———. "Children as Signs of the Kingdom of God: A Challenge to Us All." In *Now and Next: A Compendium of Papers Presented at the Theological Conference on Children, Nairobi, Kenya, 2011*, edited by Keith White et al., 41–59. Pengang, Malaysia: Compassion, 2011.
———. *The Growth of Love*. Abingdon, UK: Barnabas, 2008.
———. "'He Placed a Little Child in the Midst': Jesus, Kingdom and Children." In *The Child in Christian Thought*, edited by Marcia Bunge, 353–74. Grand Rapids: Eerdmans, 2001.
———. "A Model of Applied Theology: James E. Loder, *The Logic of the Spirit*." In *Introducing Child Theology: Theological Foundations for HCD*, 166–206. Penang, Malaysia, Compassion, 2010.
White, Keith J., et al., eds. *Now and Next: A Compendium of Papers Presented at the Theological Conference on Children, Nairobi, Kenya, 2011*. Pengang, Malaysia: Compassion, 2011.
Willmer, Haddon. *Experimenting Together: One Way of Doing Child Theology*. London: CTM, 2007.
Willmer, Haddon, and Keith J. White. *Entry Point: Towards Child Theology with Matthew 18*. London: WTL, 2013.
Wright, Dana R. "Afterword: The Potential Contribution of James E. Loder, Jr. to Practical Theological Science." In *Redemptive Transformation in Practical Theology*, edited by Dana R. Wright and John D. Kuentzel, 401–31. Grand Rapids: Eerdmans, 2004.
———. "James E. Loder, Jr." *Christian Educators of the 20th Century*, edited by Kevin Lawson. California: Talbot Seminary. Online at www.talbot.edu/ce20/educators.

2

Forgiving Constitutes the Person

HADDON WILLMER

Introduction

This paper is a meandering comment on a part of James E. Loder's *The Logic of the Spirit*, which caught my fancy.[1] I have thought much about human development, having lived through a lot of it myself, seen and messed about with it in other people, but I have no competence in the science of human development. I found a meeting point with Loder when I saw some resonance between his description of the creative work that has to be done by the infant as a growing person and ideas I have cultivated for decades about the fundamental way in which forgiving is constitutive in the being of persons and societies, if they are to have a plausible claim to be humanly good.[2]

Composing a World

"The child must construct, compose and construe the world in a predominantly trustworthy or untrustworthy way" (88). The child cannot avoid doing this work, for the child is within a "chaos of forces unleashed

---

1. Loder, *Logic* (pagination noted in the text).
2. Willmer, "Forgiveness as Permission," 79–98; "With My Missing Hands," 141–48; "Forgiveness and Politics," 1–10; "Forgiveness," 245–47.

at birth." The child cannot read a blueprint, but he must find a way to live as a person. It is not as though the child is offered a variety of paths, all equally safe and rewarding. If that were so, it would not matter which way the child went forward. The child does not have leisure of that kind. Already the child is threatened by the negative. This is not a merely alien external negation, but takes form and comes close through the experienced unreliability and fragility of the child's own achievement in personhood.

Loder described this achievement in terms of the Face, which is in the first place a gift from the personal and person-evoking environment, which conveys the message, "You're wonderful." The mother's contribution to bringing a person out of the chaos is not merely quickly accepted by the child (who soon smiles readily) but is internalized by the child in her own work of self-creation (or is it evolution?). That reminds us of an important point: What the environment gives is not a determination; it is rather material to be worked on and with and made the child's own. So, "the face phenomenon is not strictly something that comes only from the environment; it is also a construct created by the child and developed out of the child's inherent resources and deep-seated longing" (91). It is also important that, in this process, the environment does not function simply as a quarry of inert material for the growing person to control and shape in sovereign freedom. That would reduce the environment to passivity as well as building *hubris* like Nebuchadnezzar's into the person's being.[3] Rather, the environment, which is mediated and personalized by persons like the mother, gives itself to the project of the little person. While the environment taken as a whole wears many different faces, some of them dark and hostile, the welcoming, encouraging, and affirming Face which calls persons into being is sufficiently shown by the environment for the infant to see it. That is so for many, even though what the infant sees is less a clear continuous path, and more like fingerholds in a rock face. Only if the environment (in this broad unspecific sense) gives itself so that a friendly Face can be descried in it will it be plausible to construe the world as trustworthy.

---

3. Daniel 4: 30: Nebuchadnezzar said, "Is this not great Babylon, which I have built by my mighty power..."

Meeting Negation

The Face goes away: that is an early and inescapable discovery of the infant. As a result, the world the child was finding as a habitation that makes life in hope possible is shattered and dissolved. The Wolf huffs and puffs and blows down what the Piglet built using all he could find—straw. The Negation, this "No!," is, says Loder, "traumatic." Thus, the anxiety of non-being becomes integral to the child (and remains with us). He has no power to counter it, unless he learns and borrows from what he has been given: the No. So he defends himself against this world that does not keep its promise by raiding its armory, seizing its No, so that he learns to turn the No upon the negating world. To protect himself, he closes himself against what is other.[4] "The much-lauded achievement in the first year and a half of life is ultimately ironic." The child takes the negative into and onto herself and is shaped and burdened by it for life.

The child encounters Negation, in the form of frustration and disappointment. This encounter is not only traumatic at the time, but carries great danger for the future. To understand this danger, there is no need to put a deterministic interpretation on the early development of the child. It is enough that negation influences the formation of character or spirit and builds a habitual style of limited living.

The Way of Hope in Life

Because of the Negation, there is real struggle, uncertainty about outcome and, even, defeat. But there is also a hope which persists through life because divine Spirit does not give up. So the human spirit at each stage of life may find sufficient grace to build on its capacity and creativity (95). The person develops through negotiating a path where Negation cannot be avoided. The pilgrim way, as Bunyan narrated it, is illuminating here. Pilgrim enters the way to life, from the City of Destruction, through a narrow gate. He must get past the Lions, through the Valley of

---

4. How does this compare with the tragic stupidity of some war? "*It became necessary to destroy the town to save it*" is a famous disputed quote from the Vietnam War. We might also remember the fearful Cold War slogan, "Better dead than red," which justified MAD (mutually assured destruction) defence policies. It is an ancient homely wisdom that tells us not to cut off our nose to spite our face. We should not act out of pique, or pursue revenge in a way that would damage oneself more than the object of one's anger.

Humiliation, through the fight with Apollyon who "straddled quite over the whole breadth of the way, and said, 'I am void of fear in this matter, prepare thy self to die, for I swear by my Infernal Den, that thou shalt go no further, here I will spill thy soul,'" through Vanity Fair and Doubting Castle, till he comes to the inescapable River of Death. Negation is given vivid and various dramatic expression in *The Pilgrim's Progress*. Bunyan speaks to the soul, Loder speaks about the soul, and both give hope for living through Negation. Are we who have Loder now, better or worse off than the many generations who had only the Bible and *Pilgrim's Progress*?[5]

It is possible to avoid being determined by the Negation, though it is not certain. Coming through positively seems to be given to people in different measures. There may be some to whom it is hardly given at all. Hope placed in mere humanity is fragile and erratic, tossed about by luck and accident. Sure or firm hope is the gift of divine Spirit engaging with the human. But the divine Spirit is not easily accessible, not on tap, it seems (does not the story of "Helen" suggest that?).[6] Loder describes moving forward hopefully on this threatened way as:

> a stage transition dynamic that begins in conflict and moves through scanning to the construction of an insight about one's place in the world, or the construction of a new way of construing personal world order out of chaos, followed by the release of tension bound up within the original conflict. Now new energy is available to be redistributed, and thus development proves out and moves ahead, building on this newly constructed sense of order. This pattern, built into the earliest period of a child's life, works to make the difference between life and death. Partly because of the sheer survival power of this pattern, but also *because of its uncanny capacity to construct the world, the child creates a future that is indebted to but not controlled by the past. Indeed, the past is totally reworked and reconstructed as new forms of relating self and environment emerge* [my italics]. For these and other

---

5. And do not let us say Loder includes children in his account of human development but Bunyan left them out—at least let us not say that till we have read the second part of *Pilgrim's Progress*.

6. See Loder, *Logic*, chapter 3. Loder tells the story of Helen who came to him for counselling. Helen's story serves as a case to illumine his thesis that "when ego-development is disturbed from the beginning . . . the transformational power of the human spirit must be seen as transcending the constraints of any stage–developments or any distortions that may occur therein" (55).

reasons, this pattern of transformation typifies the work of the human spirit in the creation of the human ego and all its adaptational functions . . . early development discloses the hidden potential of the lifetime that is to come (88–89).[7]

Integral Unnamed Constitutive Forgiving

Amid much that I only dimly understand, I see in this account of what goes on in the child's development something which I want to name as forgiving, a forgiving integral to the development. I only see this because of the way I have come, over many years, to understand forgiveness and its relation to being. Loder does not use the language of forgiveness here but I think he is describing something that has forgiveness family resemblance. It is that family resemblance I look for. Forgiveness occurs and works in human living, individual and social, in many different ways. If we presuppose a particular definition of forgiveness we may not see it. Sometimes people look for whatever they define as "real" or "true" forgiveness, and then they despise and miss imperfect or incipient or indirect forgiving. It could be that some forgivings we do not name are the most important in opening the way of life to us. It is possible to speak of forgiveness (and to speak and act forgivingly) without using the word or having a simple definition of it. The reality of forgiveness in practice can be described without using words such as forgive. The traces of forgiveness in living often go unnamed, and operate hiddenly. Life is humanized and divinized by sensitivity to and appreciation of the unlabelled and the uncelebrated. That is the gentleness and humility of being. That is why I do not work with an authoritative definition of forgiveness but see the word itself as representative of a big and fruitful family. One sees there is a family likeness among the members, within the repeated disconcerting surprise that all these different people are a family.

Loder's omission of the word, then, is not a ground for declining to see the real thing at work in what he is talking about. Given the dominant cultural understandings of forgiveness, it is not surprising that he did not use the word. We mostly do not have the antennae to see forgiving as essential to the construction and sustaining of being. There are many contexts in which we do not expect it, so we do not find it. If

---

7. Hutchinson, *Johanna*, 314. See Willmer, "Forgiveness as Permission," 79–98.

we think of forgiving at all, it is something that persons, who already have being, receive or do in response to what occurs within what already exists and can be taken as given. We thus follow the powerful pattern derived from Genesis, which dominates much of our religious and even secular culture: first creation, then Fall, then redemptive forgiveness. The goodness of creation implies that what *is* does not need forgiving, so we never think being and forgiving together. The beginning is simply good, and nature is innocent.

The alternative pattern set by God in Christ has a different order: first forgiveness, and so New Creation which defines the reality within which we are given to live. In this pattern, the Fall is not denied but is revealed as overcome and repaired in the primal creative act, by which the initial and sustained divine Yes takes the weight of the No into itself and disempowers it.[8] The Fall so overcome by God at the beginning is not, however, a dead past but shows itself powerfully in human life every day. Within this pattern, to fall, to sin, is not to lose innocence and break from original goodness. It is rather to refuse to believe and respond to the divine forgiving in which and by which we are created, constituted in being.

There are several ways in which forgiveness appears in Christian and secular discourse. We tend to look for forgiveness when a law is broken or not fulfilled so that we fall under some kind of penalty. And we look for forgiveness in quarrels and conflicts between persons and groups. We think forgiving might be relevant in peace-making, but not in infant or adult person-making. Recently, the world has learnt that forgiving is practical and prudent in dealing with unpayable debt.[9] It is now widely understood that forgiving is not an exclusively religious or interpersonal practice. Nor is it a Christian invention (despite Arendt's oft-quoted, complex and in some respects misleading remarks about Jesus).[10] Nevertheless, specifically Christian contexts like church, and extensions of church such as Desmond Tutu's activity in the Truth and Reconciliation commission, are major carriers of the advocacy and

---

8. I am indebted to Karl Barth, who was forever making this point, and taking it with his own peculiar kind of seriousness as the key to evangelical faith. As he is noted to have said, "Sin scorches us when it comes under the light of forgiveness, not before."

9. See "Jubilee, 2000." Online: http://en.wikipedia.org/wiki/Jubilee_2000.

10. Arendt, *Human Condition*, 238ff.

practice of forgiveness.[11] Not that Christianity can be presented as a forgiving religion in contrast to all others. It is, however, a religion under continual critical pressure from the revelation by which it is called to be forgiving in response to God's Forgiving. So in the Church, at least, we think we know what we are looking for in forgiveness and when we find it we celebrate it repetitively till it is reduced to a cliché. Or we narrate special instances of it as wonders, which surpass what is expected in ordinary life with ordinary people. But looking for it in this way means we do too little to explore forgiveness as it happens through time (process) and especially we do not look to see how forgiving is integral to ordinary everyday being. Overuse and over-definition of words like forgiveness (or "God" or "ransom"[12]) wears them out and even makes them unbearable. So it is a refreshing practice to try to talk about the reality of forgiveness without using the common or obvious word.

Because it is possible to forgive, and to talk about forgiveness, without using the word, many apparently barren fields in the world hold the treasure and the seed of it. I like to read all sorts of stories and texts as a prospector who in looking at mere rocks sees gold waiting for him. Of course he may be gullible and dig where there is nothing to be found. But sometimes he strikes lucky for, in some rocks, there is gold.

Past and Future

One feature which belongs to the family of forgiveness is a distinctive range of ways of dealing with past and future. There is an example of this in the italicised words in the passage quoted above: "*Because of its uncanny capacity to construct the world, the child creates a future that is indebted to but not controlled by the past. Indeed, the past is totally reworked and reconstructed as new forms of relating self and environment emerge.*" The past is not thrown away as useless; that is, it is not condemned. The refusal of condemnation and outright discarding of what is inadequate for the future is an essential element in forgiving. The admittedly inadequate, failed past is utilized in making way for a better, richer future. Approached in a forgiving way, the past gives itself as a resource for the future, even in the moment when it is being surpassed. The past is saved, redeemed and valued (not disvalued) by being transformed. Forgiving

---

11. Tutu, *No Future*.
12. Lewis, *Voyage*, chapter 9.

does not see the past as simply what has failed and therefore will fail to make its way in the demanding present. Forgiving does not write off as hopeless those who are responsible for making the mess. Somehow, forgiving sees that the one who made and thus now suffers the past, who is now therefore confronted with achieved inadequacy, is rightly to be valued, loved, and so hoped for, because love hopes all things. Forgiving not only sees this person more clearly, but acts to open the door of hope even for the one who has failed. This way of relating past and the present, opening out to the future, helps us to see what forgiveness is, what it has to work at and what it may achieve. Forgiveness values and hold on faithfully to what is good from the past, even if that good is now no more than a discredited promise of potential. It rescues and builds on the little that it finds, taking it into a future where its value can be realized and recognized openly.

We picture persons as having continuity through change, including rise and fall, growth and decay. If growth is by incremental enlargement, where new goods are added to and built on an existing good, a seamless continuity of goodness is realized. And then forgiveness has no place or function. Often this is how we see traditions we favor or believe in, as for example, the apostolic succession of bishops. In reality, all continuities are broken by interruptions, contradictions and blocks, so that to perceive continuity is itself a determined act of repair. Continuity is achieved by going back to pick up the lost stitch, to find the lost sheep or the wandering son, or by building bridges over chasms. This work of knitting up the discontinuous belongs to the family of forgiveness. Growth by forgiveness is necessary because the negation means there are no steady unbroken progressions in life. We are always beginners—forever beginning again.[13]

Forgiveness is not so much a way of settling an account from the past, writing it off and getting free from it, as opening a new and different future of surprising rescue. In the Gospel of God in Christ, forgiving comes in the present anticipatory actualization of the New Future of God. Desmond Tutu entitled his book, *No Future without Forgiveness*. But the converse is equally true and important: there is no forgiveness without the future. It is the promise and venture of a specific future which gives the power and the vision to escape what the past seems to

---

13. Barth repeatedly made this point, see his *Christian Life*, 78–82. See Willmer, "Karl Barth and Thurneysen."

be prescribing, namely, revenge, grudge, caution, building negation on negation. "Your Kingdom *come*" is the ground that gives validity to the prayer, "Forgive us our sin . . ."

Seeing Forgiveness through Active Forgiving

Forgiveness is central, though not exclusive, to Christian faith. Christian experience and presentation of forgiveness have been shaped, predominantly, by the human need to be forgiven and by the joy of being forgiven. God forgives: human beings are forgiven. We receive forgiveness or let ourselves be forgiven. Thus, active forgiving is left to God—either because it is his sole right to judge[14] or because it is his *métier*.[15]

We can see this passive forgiveness played out in the history of baptism. From early times, baptism was a washing for forgiveness of sin. Because baptism was seen in that way, Tertullian had argued that children should "become Christians when they have become able to know Christ. Why does the innocent period of life hasten to the remission of sins?" Little ones had done nothing wrong yet: he could not see that they had any need to be forgiven. Augustine turned the argument the other way: because infants are baptized, they must have some kind of sin to be washed away. Protestant Evangelical Christianity often makes more of conversion than of baptism. But there too, the priority of God's grace in forgiveness is emphasized. Being forgiven is at the heart of the human experience of desiring salvation and being given the dynamic of new life. So human beings relate to forgiveness as God offers it, sheds it abroad and actualizes it in saving ways, centrally in Jesus Christ. Some liturgies, like the communion service in the Anglican 1662 *Book of Common Prayer* are shaped throughout as a plea and a search for forgiveness now and at the Last Judgment. Recent liturgical revisions have relieved congregations of a sustained level of mournful penitence that the "easy conscience of modern man" does not want to bear.[16] In all these various

---

14. Cf. many of the contributions in Wiesenthal, *The Sunflower*.

15. Attributed to Heinrich Heine and others, this saying seems to affirm forgiveness, because it is God's doing, but then cheapens it by treating it as God's expertise and habitual practice. In both ways, forgiving is made unimportant for the daily earthly living of human life. Neither God nor forgiving are taken seriously. He also said, "One should forgive one's enemies, but not before they are hanged," which is another way of quoting the Gospel and making it of no effect.

16. See Niebuhr, *Nature and Destiny*, 99–131.

ways, it is in the passive reception of being forgiven that we discover and trust the grace of God.

We do of course know that we are to forgive as we are forgiven, but in spiritual experience and in most theology, our active forgiving does not weigh as much as being forgiven. For a variety of reasons, (is it fair to say?) when Christians are actively forgiving, they do not find themselves so powerfully in and with God as when they receive forgiveness. Can we forgive without assuming superiority? If we cannot, it is spiritually and socially dangerous to forgive others. In any case, our forgiving is so feeble and spasmodic and really nothing to crow about, whereas God's forgiving is sufficient, unstinting, creative, renewing. We are bowled over by the generosity of God to "miserable sinners." So it would seem obvious that we should persist in rejoicing in the glory of God's forgiving, and being very modest about ours.

It can be argued, however, that while this is true as far as it goes, it is not fully faithful to the challenge and the gift of God's forgiving in Christ. We are not rising to the height of our calling to *forgive as we are forgiven*. We are not to minimize the wonder of God's gracious forgiving, in relation to which we are simply beggars. But it is a mistake to fear that our forgiving could somehow compete with and thereby lessen God's forgiving. Our forgiving is a tribute to and a fruit of God's forgiving. It is an active form of gratitude, trust and acceptance of what God offers in decisive action. The measure of our appreciation of God's forgiving us is not that we sing songs of thanks for what we have received but that we give ourselves in the practice of life in the world to sharing with God in what God does. We are invited, indeed commanded, to let ourselves be taken in to the fullness of God's forgiving grace, by giving ourselves to active forgiving. This is our due response, the living sacrifice of our whole life in the body (Romans 12:1–2). God's grace is full, not because it is what God does from his side quite without us, and in distinctly divine action, but because it is what God does with and in and through his human partner, elect in Jesus Christ, in the reality of the world as his creation, where God is imaged actively and visibly by those created after his image and likeness.[17] God's forgiving is a central key to God's reconciling us to Godself and adopting us as his children. It is an inseparable aspect of the greater whole of our fellowship with the Father and the Son in the Spirit.

17. Hall, *Imaging God*, 88–112, especially 108.

This partnership of God and humanity is expressed plainly in the Gospel teaching about forgiveness. We are forgiven as we forgive. This is not to make our forgiving a condition of our being forgiven, though it can be read that way, and too often it needs to be read so.[18] It is rather to invite us to be forgivers like God and with God. So we must work with conceptions of forgiveness that do not set God and human being over against each other, but rather (like Loder) find appropriate ways of relating the divine and human spirit intimately. It is in pardoning that we are pardoned. It is in trying to go God's forgiving way and to share God's forgiving work that we come to know we need to be forgiven and receive it. We are taught to pray, "Forgive us our sin." And we can be more specific, "Forgive us our unforgiving," a core sin in the light of the Gospel. But we also thank God that we are able to forgive within his forgiving, thus sharing what we are given. We know our forgiving often falls short, and we are not very good at it. So within the active life-creating fellowship with God, we take our prayer further: "Forgive us our forgivings. Come and perfect what we do." When we pray this way, we confess that God's forgiving is the beginning and the end, and thus our hope. But we do not make that confession as supine recipients, mere dependents rather than partners.

What Has All This to Do with Loder . . . ?

As I understand it—and I understand very little in this area—the person forms the ego through dealing with an immediate practical make-or-break issue. The child encounters the No when the Face which sparks its world into being disappears, thus destroying nascent trust. Working amid this traumatic threat to being, the child makes a covenant with death (to borrow from Isaiah 28:14–22) or, in Loder's account, co-opts the No in order to hold on to and define itself against the No (94). This tactic gains success in ego-building, but "under the surface, existentially speaking, negation has triumphed." "The human spirit has been forced by the sense of dread, 'the anxiety of non-being,' to contradict itself

---

18. It is needed because we are prone to take advantage of forgiving grace, Rom 6:1, 15; 3:8; Matt 18:23–35. The leverage of fairness is a useful instrument to form and stir the careless conscience. Why expect anyone to be generous to you, if you are not generous to them? (2 Sam 12:1–15). But we lose the generosity of God if this lever ceases to be like a schoolmaster leading us to Christ, and becomes the law of forgiving as a mere *quid pro quo*.

and lose touch with its original creation, the face phenomenon, and its power to shape human destiny in the direction of the divine." The "powerful hidden longing" for the remembered and lost Face "continues to influence the ego from under the surface as the human spirit continues to scan for ways to overcome this deep fault in the bedrock of human development" (94). This scanning is the will to forgive, exploring how to make something of a compromised position by forgiving. Loder says the achievement of the child in this early period is "ironic." The child has achieved no more than "a defensive functional solution to an existential and theological crisis" (95). It is not difficult to hear some resonance with traditional notions of Original Sin. That would be a measure of the grievousness of the situation. But it would leave the child with a one-sided need to be forgiven. Loder does not refer us to anything like original sin here. If this ironic solution is a step in a life of hope, then hope has its source elsewhere, transcendently, beyond the holding position achieved by the child.

Human existence throughout the rest of the life span, especially through the great eruptions of adolescence, the middle years, and later life, urges persons toward a more adequate solution that will nullify the existentially formative power of negation, transform the ego and its defences, and put the totality of human existence into a relationship with the One who is the cosmic ordering, self-confirming Presence—the Face of God who does not go away (95). This indicates the positive, hopeful way Loder leads us through the whole book. Because he does not name the initial stage as a forgiving, the later stages are not presented as ventures in forgiving either. Yet I think the family likeness can be seen in all these stages of life. It is wise to face the existential challenges flung at us in a lifetime with a spirit ready to forgive and to read the challenges as invitations to forgive. Even when the challenges arise within ourselves because we make covenants with death and because our achievements are merely ironic solutions, forgiving shows us how to go forward. Forgiving symbolizes a style of practical living, in which the persistent pilgrim–experimenter in forgiving looks for and enters God's coming new creation where forgiveness is beyond irony, generous and effective.

...and with Child Theology?

Jesus placed a child in the midst of the disciples who were so anxious about greatness in the Kingdom of God that they put their bare entry into it in doubt (Matthew 18:1ff.). Jesus gave them the child, signaling humility as the way into the Kingdom of God. When they received the child, they received Jesus—and the One who sent him—and thus were already brought to the heart of the Kingdom—the King. The child placed by Jesus is thus full of profound, demanding and saving meaning, but is also, significantly, without any trace of parental, or modern, or psychological interpretation.

Loder puts the child before us, with meanings that are modern products. True or not so true, these meanings suggest some of the ways in which we might see the child so that the child illumines what it is to be human. Theory of this kind is not only useful for looking after children in appropriate ways, but it helps us to understand what kind of beings we are in the whole of a lifetime. Yet we should not glibly assume that we can put Loder's child, or any other modernly-perceived child (certainly not the fancifully idolized or the affluent child) into the center of the argument about the Kingdom of God. We have to be clear that Jesus served the Kingdom of the Father by centering a child who was not any one of our modern preferred much loved, abused or studied children. We are not called to receive an idealized child, who exists in our dreams and not in her own bodily presence. And to ignore children, as they are now, in order to work in theological purity with the child as formed in a first-century Palestinian culture, would be an idealization. So, while we must be humbly cautious, we should not be frightened off by the dangers of putting ourselves in the story where the disciples were and where the child from next door was being placed by Jesus. It is not consistent with faith and obedience to God in Christ to refuse to work with this story because we fear to contaminate it by putting a modern child there. That kind of refusal is the exegetical sin of hiding one's talent in the ground. Rather, we must have courage to follow the story along all the tracks it opens up, including recognizing that the child here is real, not a product of idealization, and that the real child placed by Jesus bears saving meaning for those who would like to enter the Kingdom of God.

There is encouragement for us to take this risk with the story and even, if it comes to it, to "sin boldly" as Luther said. If we see forgiving is naturally necessary to the child's inescapable person-making process, we can build a bridge between the child as we know her today and the child who was placed by Jesus. Loder's child, if I may use that shorthand, is not totally alien to the child by whom Jesus signed the Kingdom of God. Forgiveness, passive and active in unity, is the typical core of the Kingdom of God, as Jesus presented it (i.e., as he made it present in his action and words). Matthew 18 begins with the child in the midst and leads into a major discourse on forgiving. The child is placed in the midst to be received. Shockingly, the child is often not received but is despised and rejected (Matthew 18:10). This rejection is actively resisted and overcome by God who typically goes in search of the lost straying sheep (18:12–14). Bringing back the lost is a concrete image of forgiving. It highlights the costly venture that forgiving involves. Forgiving is not a mere "letting it pass" with a casual "no problem." Remember the pathos of the hymn, "The Ninety and Nine"? Having prepared the way, Matthew 18 then speaks about dealing with faults in the church and forgiving brothers up to seventy times seven. Its climax is the story of the unforgiving servant. He missed entry into the Kingdom of God altogether, because, though he was blessed by the king's merciful forgiveness of his debts, he did not forgive a fellow servant whose debt was small by comparison.

The inner life and being of the person grows and is sustained by a process which is set out in these stories about interpersonal forgiving, coupled with directions for social living which befits the Kingdom of God. Person-constituting forgiving, which we see in Loder's child, harmonizes with God's forgiving in Christ, which constitutes New Creation. Matthew 18 is a discourse about forgiving in which the child has a crucial function, not as a teacher or a priestly minister of forgiveness, but as an eye-opening sign in the argument Jesus is having with his disciples. The disciples are missing the way into the Kingdom of God and they need help. They are not primarily called to get into the Kingdom of God for themselves, but to open it for others. They are partners with Jesus in his mission, called to be servants rather than mere beneficiaries. They need to be forgiven by being released from the sin that is driving them into darkness.

Jesus does not give up on the disciples. Nor does he uncritically stand by them, because they are his own people, right or wrong. Instead of covering up for them, he sharpens the issue. He makes clear how they are going seriously wrong. And then he acts to give them a vision of the way, and to open it up for them. That is the fundamental content of any forgiveness, opening up a new and better possibility. It is quite new for the disciples because it was never going to come out of what they were or were making of themselves. What is, and what has been done, blocks this new better possibility. Forgiving engages with persons who are locked into the habits of the past, and finds ways—which may be costly and inventive—to liberate them for the new and better. Hence forgiving takes the form of holistic persuasion to conversion. It aims at more than a change of a particular behavior. It seeks a transformation of the whole person, so that that person may live fully and freely in the identity that belongs in the new and better possibility (the Kingdom of God).

This transformation is not and cannot be achieved in a moment or by magic. It is concerned with the whole person, who has a lifetime to live, and indeed a calling to the Kingdom of God which transcends what can be seen in a lifetime. The concept of a person with a life to live goes beyond our capacity to grasp. We do not understand ourselves in our own self-awareness, whether we approach it with ordinary amateur autobiographical narrating, or with the help of a theory of human development like Loder's. Whatever way we take, we are brought to Bonhoeffer's end, which is also the beginning, as it is expressed in his poem, *Who Am I?*:

> Who am I? They mock me, these lonely questions of mine—
> Whoever I am, Thou knowest, O God, I am Thine.[19]

Not merely, then, is this transformation not to be achieved in a moment. Transformation is not in our hands or in our time. We can see hints of what it might be like, but we cannot comprehend it fully. We are waiting till we know as we are known. We may know that we shall be like him, for we shall see him as he is.[20] But it does not yet appear what we shall be—and what does not yet appear cannot be put into our account or our planning. And yet, this should not push us back into passive reception of forgiveness. It rather clarifies what it is to live a life as an active forgiving partner and follower of God in Christ, forever seeking to open the way where it is blocked.

---

19. Bonhoeffer, *Letters*, 347.
20. 1 John 3:1–3.

Social Forgiving

This leads me to a final comment on Loder. I get the impression from his account that lifetimes are lived by individuals. He does not deny that we are social beings, but our relations with other human beings seem to be underplayed or allowed to stand at the margins, as unproblematic reality. The Face is structurally vital for the infant. But, after that, the structure of the adult seems to be that of a self-possessing individual. There is no exploration of the ways in which, at every step of life, *I am because we are*. Paul asked, "What have you that you have not received?" (1 Cor 4:7). What am I if all the persons who have somehow given themselves to me and entered into my being, are ignored? What the Face tells us about being a person reveals a pattern of being which is not left behind by the adult, but becomes more complex, enriching or bedevilling as life goes on. The middle years, for example, bring to many of us all the blessings Job enjoyed—wife, children, property, social responsibility and respect—so that if they all are taken away, unnaturally and against the promise of the gracious creator, we are plunged into Job's unbearable questions about our meaning and hope. Reduced to bare existence, an individual depressed by the loss of sociality, Job demanded to see the Face (Job 13:3; 23:1–7).

It might be argued that in Loder's account, individuality is opened up to sociality because of the relationality of divine and human spirit which runs through the whole book. Certainly a fully social account of living should be the result of thinking about humanity in relation to divine Spirit. In Christian sources, it would seem that Holy Spirit, the Paraclete, is sociable and socially creative (e.g., Acts 2). But does this social Spirit shape Loder's overall picture? Or does the divine Spirit tend to be individualized through being related mostly to the human person who has an individual lifetime to live? Is this individualization of Spirit a consequence of Loder's working with modern Western people and with modern Western concepts, culture and religion?

The Spirit can be individualized because, to some extent, we live life individualistically. Each stage of life presents the individual with the challenge to make some sense of this individual life and to "be the best that I can be." This individuality has power and significance. Many people (how can we know whether it is every body?) have an incessant inner life, a dialogue with and in the self, and they are happy if this dialogue gives them a sense of control and hope and self-esteem. But few manage a lifetime as nothing more than an interior process. Even if we seek seclusion, the world of others interrupts us in happy and unhappy ways. For example, we become parents and a once individual life is siphoned off into the children—unless of course we choose to walk away from them. We become citizens, and may complain about the intrusion of government. But most of us, the canny rich even more than the poor, expect the state to be there to help us. We may want individuality without encumbrance. But when we discover, through hard experience, Aristotle's insight that to live outside the *polis*, we must be either god or beast, most people turn back to have another go at being human even if it means living with other human beings. A human life is a mix of private and social. So the divine Spirit is to be understood and sought not only in relation to the private life, but also the social.

What is the place of other people (either as individuals or in various sorts of groups) along the individual's way to the transformation the Spirit brings? Are persons transformed solely by a direct solitary engagement with Spirit? Forgiveness, as we see it for example in Matthew 18, is essentially social. I have already quoted part of Loder's account of the infant's development: "There is real struggle, defeat, uncertainty about outcome. But there is hope which persists through life because divine Spirit does not give up and the human spirit at each stage of life may find sufficient grace, capacity and creativity" (95). I recall this quote now to make the point that, often—indeed mostly—hope persists throughout a lifetime because the divine Spirit works through other people around the individual. The Spirit hopes in those who hope for those who do not hope for themselves. We need brother or sister to be "as Christ" to us, holding "the Christ-light for us in the night-time of our fear." Some people do not have faith for themselves. Some people need others with a faith that carries the weight of a stretcher and even breaks through the sanctity of property to bring a friend to Jesus.

> For those who have no prayers to say,
> Who in despair are dumb,
> Teach us to live as well as pray
> "O Lord, your kingdom come!"[21]

---

21. Cf. Mark 2:1–12; Smith, "Remember," 274.

The infant does not manufacture the Face out of nothing. Nor does the Face come directly from the divine Spirit in her solitary invisibility. The infant needs the earthly, personal mother, to show and give something that is at least a plausible sign that living is viable, because there can be a world as a habitat for life. God comes and works through mediation. That is one implication of the doctrines of the trinity and Christology. In Loder's case study of "Helen," she would not have prayed without Loder praying with her. The divine Spirit did not transform her without the "father confessor" sharing in the process. In the Christian understanding of God, there is a complex of reciprocating and mutually helpful mediations and representations. So God in Christ holds the place open for human beings, and human being in Christ holds the place open for God.[22]

Of course there is the danger that, in the intricate, sometimes dense webs of mediation, the divine Spirit is denied because lost to sight. Created actors, human and other, fill the stage, presenting their story so convincingly that there seems to be nothing outside what we see in their action. Again and again, in Christian history, the living God, the divine Spirit, has been lost. The Church can be overwhelmed by the busyness that quenches the Spirit. Often the loss comes about not with an atheist intention—i.e., by denying that there is any Other Agent apart from human beings and all the other evolved and visible creatures in the universe. It comes because those who trust and honor the divine Spirit live with joy in the plenitude of God's created gifts. They live to the full the life given them now on earth, giving and taking, losing and finding, sharing and growing. All this humanism, they say, is the life they have from and in God—and so it is. But God gets hidden in the plenitude of the humanity that flourishes by the divine generosity, where the Spirit, with self-endangering humility, gives the stage to creatures.

Some carelessly, some cautiously, some with finesse accept that the dissolving of God in the human world and in religion is unavoidable. We have to work with it and can be hopeful within it. Theologians like Schleiermacher lead us here. But being Christian with God in human solution is not restricted to followers of particular theologians. Loder's Barthianism, if that is what it is, has a point. Without it the relationality of divine and human spirit, which is essential to his whole enterprise, melts down into an undifferentiated religiosity, where there is no persuasive or

22. Soelle, *Christ*, 104, 116, 130.

transforming transcendence. The integrity of God and creatures, each truly themselves, is essential to this relationality. To lose the difference of divine and human identity in the blending intimacy of oneness would be fundamentally inconsistent with Loder's theology, anthropology and soteriology.

Works Cited

Arendt, Hannah. *The Human Condition*. Chicago: University of Chicago Press, 1958.
Barth, Karl. *The Christian Life*. Edinburgh: T. & T. Clark, 1981.
———. *Dogmatics in Outline*. London: Hodder and Stoughton, 1936.
Bonhoeffer, Dietrich. *Letters and Papers from Prison*. Edited by Eberhard Bethge. New York: Collier, 1972.
Hall, Douglas John. *Imaging God: Dominion as Stewardship*. Grand Rapids: Eerdmans, 1986.
Hutchinson, R. C. *Johanna at Daybreak*. London: Michael Joseph, 1983.
Lewis, C. S. *Voyage to Venus*. London: Bodley Head, 1943.
Loder, James E., Jr. *The Logic of the Spirit: Human Development in Theological Perspective*. San Francisco: Jossey-Bass, 1998.
Niebuhr, Reinhold. *The Nature and Destiny of Man, Vol. 1*. London: Nisbet, 1941.
Soelle, Dorothee. *Christ the Representative*. Philadelphia: Fortress, 1967.
Smith, Timothy Dudley. "Remember, Lord, the World You Made." In *A House of Praise*, 274 Carol Stream, IL: Hope, 1981.
Tutu, Desmond. *No Future without Forgiveness*. London: Rider, 1999.
Wiesenthal, Simon. *The Sunflower*. Paris: Opera Mundi, 1970.
Willmer, Haddon. "Forgiveness." In *The Oxford Companion to Christian Thought*, edited by Adrian Hastings, 245–47. Oxford: Oxford University Press, 2000.
———. "Forgiveness and Politics." In *Embodying Forgiveness Project 13*, edited by Stephen Graham, 1–10. Belfast: Centre for Contemporary Christianity in Ireland, 2004.
———. "Forgiveness as Permission to Live." In *Wounds That Heal*, edited by Jonathan Baxter, 79–98. London: SPCK, 2007.
———. "Karl Barth and Thurneysen." Online: http://www.childtheology.org/new/docuploads/Karl_Barth_and_Eduard_Thurneysen.pdf.
———. "With My Missing Hands." In *Remembering to Forgive: A Tribute to Una O'Higgins O'Malley*, edited by Enda McDonagh, 141–48. Dublin: Veritas, 2007.

3

James E. Loder and Paul in Conversation

Discourses of Development and Disruption

Elizabeth Waldron Barnett,

Introduction: Paul, Loder, and Child Theology

I find myself as one who has been strangely but warmly gathered here among brothers and sisters, many of whom have journeyed long with the writings of Loder, some of whom knew him personally. He is emerging in my imagination from your anecdotes, quotes from conversations, and archival material as a character who spilled the boundaries of Princeton, the academic discipline in which he worked, the ecclesial traditions and the professional teacher/student divisions of status. It seems that one of the characteristics that you celebrate is that he was personally disruptive.

I come to this space by the challenging invitation of Keith White, my colleague in the Child Theology Movement, who knows me as a biblical scholar and one who, in exegetical method, presses against the tide of scholarship to hear readings of our texts that do not privilege age—particularly the age of adulthood—as normative. Following the same manner as feminist theologians, and a polychromatic, and poly-vocal ensemble of theological voices from the global south, and joined by theologians who have recognized that the inherent ambiguity of being human means that we are all both abled and disabled—I am challenged as a female, ambiguously abled, from the so-called global south, to appropriate this challenge afresh to the normativity of "adult" spirituality, "adult" readings of our precious texts, "adult" functionalities in relation to life in God.

Unlike many at this symposium, I did not know James Loder personally. This puts him on an even footing with the author of texts which are the focus of my study—that wild character, a first century author on the fly, whom you might think of as Paul of Tarsus, the Apostle Paul, Paul the Persecutor, Paul, missionary to the Gentiles, or perhaps just Paul. Both Paul and Loder can be identified simultaneously as products of their culture, but also as those who resisted the dominant discourses of their time. They resisted in their own thinking—and furthermore catalyzed more extensive resistance thinking beyond their own work. Part of the value of what we are doing here, at Princeton, in a symposium on the fecundity of Loder's writings for nourishing the infant field of child theology, highlights this very aspect of their work—that there was a *kenotic* dynamic to the writings of both Paul and Loder. This *kenosis*, given in a regenerative "Logic of the Spirit" and the pregnancy of their thought, means that we still have things to consider, things over which to wrestle. Or, if you like a Pauline metaphor—and I for one love Pauline metaphors—we still have ideas to birth, nurse and suckle, and whose faces and bottoms will need wiping and nappies will need changing. Allow me to briefly offer a cameo of this dynamic for each character in relation to the dynamics that I think are important in creating a methodology for reading each of them.

Paul

Paul lived in the midst of an overtly imperial and colonial age. The logic of power was unchallengeable without facing violent restraint, isolation and humiliation possibly ending in the conclusive *quod erat demonstrandum* via death. The dominant discourse of Paul's world was epitomized in the rhetorical socio-political philosophical monologue—the art of oratory: a form of speech which was engineered entirely for the purpose of enlarging the honor and status of the speaker—and to have that concretized in accolades of various types.[1] Is it ironic, then, incon-

---

1. We think of the fantastical Mark Antony's speech at the funeral of Julius Caesar,

gruously or intentionally so, that Paul himself was an inheritor of status via this discourse. He appealed within the system for privilege—though it was for the sake of the gospel—as a Roman citizen, appearing before emperors and pressing for an audience in Rome. For a radical, Paul inhabited the center of the discourse of power with uncanny confidence and skill.[2] Paul also occupied a privileged place within a second social system, Jewish covenant and law. Reading the writings of Paul keeps us ducking and weaving as we try to follow the way he both exploits, commandeers devices and reappropriates from the dominant Hebrew cultural and scriptural authority, while at other points, he critiques, inverts or disposes of these discourses of power and honor.[3] Thus, he both accommodates and authenticates using Hebrew scripture and tradition. Paul rejects the authority of Jewish practice for Gentile believers at many points, but daringly and dangerously—from both sides of the religio-political fence—he reinscribes the status of Israel into the Gentile community (Philippians 3:3) and he doesn't always get away unscathed.

As we enter the narrative within and around the text, we will need to pay attention to follow which of these maneuvers he is doing. And moreover, we must be aware of our own superimpositions of superstructures on to the text. The hegemonic discourses of our time are mostly of "super-ness": (a) the presumption of a "natural" imperative to progress, in both the microcosmic and macrocosmic fields; (b) the instrumental means to achieve this, and (c) the attendant values systems that reinscribe meaning and authentication via the loop of the discourse itself.[4] We have been serving up our texts with lashings of double domi-

---

which Shakespeare renders for us so artfully. He moves the crowd to tears in self-deprecation—and rises in honour and power. He speaks, perhaps Paul would say, with the tongues at least of men and maybe of angels. It dismays me that so much of our communication and so called kerygma in twenty-first-century church and mission still apes this style of communication.

2. Castelli, "Interpretations," 199. Castelli notes: "The Kingdom of God exists as a discourse of power."

3. Heil, *Rhetorical*, 261. "In some cases Paul has skillfully adapted or reshaped his scriptural quotes and references to enhance their rhetorical effectiveness for the particular purposes of his argumentative strategy. Paul thus relies not only upon the divine authority but upon the rhetorical effectiveness of each of his scriptural quotes or references to engage or powerfully persuade his Corinthian audience."

4. Pieterse, "Dilemmas," 6. "The central thesis of developmentalism is that social change occurs according to a pre-established pattern, the logic and direction of which are known. Privileged knowledge of the direction of change is claimed by those who

nance discourse cream for some centuries now. We have grown fat upon it—and a good deal of it has dribbled right down into the cracks, where it is barely noticed. In my exegetical offering to our conversation we will seek to track the discourse and to sound some resonances with the work of Loder that we might further explore, leading to a critique via the conversation between Paul and Loder of both the first century Imperial power discourse and the nineteenth and twentieth century Progress discourse.

Loder

Here I try to tread softly on the cloths of heaven, as I speak of one who some of you knew with a great tenderness and respect. Nevertheless, what I offer here are observations not of him personally, in the same way as I could not speak of Paul of Tarsus personally—I am articulating how the writings of Loder sound to at least one auditor, who stands admittedly in the hermeneutic of suspicion for the modernist triumphs of rationalism, individualism, capitalism and the terrible Trinitarian expression of all three, Developmentalism. Loder wrote explicitly engaging the broadest of scopes—"holistic" I think he would be termed now.[5] But he also chose a particular, and in that, limited circle of conversation partners and disciplines: from Psychology—Freud and Jung; from Sociology—the stage theorists, Piaget, Erikson, Kohlberg, and Fowler; and from Philosophy and Theology—Heidegger, Kierkegaard, Pannenberg, Brunner and Barth. He was broadly educated by all means, but these were his particular wrestling angels to whom he returned as reference points. They formed "the court of reputation" which in some senses he needed to satisfy. Beyond this cluster was the larger panoply of the scientific academy. Working at the end of the twentieth century, this establishment was arguably the (mythical) epitome of authenticating reality and *veritas*. Loder was a man of stunningly original thought. Or, using his own terms, he was one open to the transforming moments

---

declare themselves furthest advanced along its course. Developmentalism is the truth from the point of view of the centre of power; it is the theorization (or rather, ideologization) of its own path of development, and the comparative method elaborates this perspective."

5. Loder's friendship and collaborative thinking and writing with physicist Jim Neidhardt attests to the gamut of his intellectual vision.

of convictional knowing.⁶ And yet he allowed these conversation partners and courts of reputation to set the terms, the vocabulary, and the rules of engagement. So in strange ways Loder's radical reworking of an essentially Developmentalist agenda used the constructs, and in many ways the constraints of scientific modernity, with its powerful discourses of domination, colonization, and instrumentalization. Nevertheless, this very methodology caused creative disruptions and saw him:

- expanding dimensionally (and I'd like to suggest this not be seen as additional but an exponential) from two to four dimensional epistemologies in his work on convictional knowing
- extending the liminalities of stage theory beyond linearity and temporality
- rewriting the internal grammar of psychosocial identity formation in Christological or Chalcedonian terms, whilst negotiating scientific rationalist empiricism
- engaging the content and encounter of evil (a radically non-scientific category) in the appropriation of negation and the void in psychosocial human development

There are numerous other contributions of course, but these four stand out for this author as those that hold the tension of Loder's creativity and conformity most stringently. These also correlate to disruptions of the logic of power and progress that Paul detonates with his unrelenting reiteration of the center of his own convictional knowing—Christ crucified.

Moving from those preliminary and summary sketches of the general dynamics of Paul and Loder's methodological relationships, we turn now to examine in detail Paul at work in the Corinthian community. In yoking Loder and Paul in dialogue, we must address the overt framework of Developmentalism in Loder's methodological starting point, and assess the misappropriation of this discourse in an exegesis of Paul, in this case specifically 1 Corinthians 13.

---

6. "Convictional experience" as a term is first introduced in Loder, *Transforming*, 6.

The Dominance of Developmentalism in Pauline Commentary

Central to our concern is the place and understanding of the child in Paul's discussions and our exegesis. The classic assumption that the ways of the child are to be eschewed in the name of progress and growth towards a higher maturity will come under revision. I suggest that Paul places a child in the midst of his argument, providing a radically positive model of the ethics and qualities he desires in the Corinthian community. The child provides Paul, the Corinthians, and us with a touchstone for the vision of humble, other-oriented love. Paul's central concern throughout 1 Corinthians is corporate and personal disunity. The Corinthian community is rent with competing claims of status. Knowledge, wisdom, prophecy, tongues, allegiance to leaders, cultic license and ascetic purity, present themselves as a mass of relational dysfunctions—pride, alienation, judgment, partisanship—accompanied by serious inferences of immorality, injustice and abuse. The community is afflicted by a disconnection between thinking and being. This schism of whole personhood might be seen as an unfortunate side effect, or as an intentional pursuit of the Corinthians, in an aspiration towards a spiritualized liberation of mind, body and soul. Either as programmatic purpose or coincidental consequence, Paul rejects such divisions. We will see that it is "dis-integration" of person and/or community that exercises Paul theologically and pastorally. The presence of child language within Paul's response represents a model for re-integration, offered through the highest ethic of Love.

However, plenty of divisions, antitheses and distinctions populate the text. Most exegetes have assumed that νήπιος and τέλειος invoke a direct antithesis of child against adult, in which child is understood as a deprecating term, used to chastise the hearers to "move on" or "grow up" and become that which is deemed desirable: that is "adult" or "mature." Little attention is paid to the underlying slur that this casts on the category of child. A quick survey of some standard commentaries on 1 Corinthians discloses the extent to which this negative assumption accompanies childhood terminology and the unilateral application of a direct antithesis of νήπιος ("child"/"infant") against τέλειος ("complete," "whole," "perfect"; though curiously, and I argue, incorrectly, in some places, "mature").

Jeremy Corley divides Paul's vocabulary into neat binary pairs and he documents the proximity of νήπιος and τέλειος and their derivatives in thorough detail.[7] However, while he identifies their association (they do turn up together frequently), he has assumed an antithetical relationship. His presentation of νήπιος and τέλειος applies this dichotomization consistently. The formal contrast between the word pair as a set predetermines the meaning of the individual appearance of the word.[8]

Anthony Thiselton looks more broadly than many others at the different types of thinking (calculating, reasoning, considering etc.) that are attributed to the child in 1 Corinthians 13:11. However, this broader appeal doesn't lead him to a positive valuation of the child.[9] For Thiselton, νήπιος had a clearly more pejorative meaning [in 1 Corinthians 3:1] where we translated it as *infantile*. Here [1 Corinthians 13:11] it serves also in contrast to *maturity*, but in the more value neutral sense of the child.[10] While Thiselton supposes that his reading of the child in 1 Corinthians 13 is more positive than in chapter 3, we are struck by the assignation of any human as "value neutral." It sounds rational and even-handed, but is in fact a gloss: value neutral equals worth nothing.

> For just as in 2:6 the wisdom for *the mature* is not for those who exhibit childish self-centeredness and immediacy, even so here Paul is about to draw the same contrast with being *infantile* or *childish* or *childlike* in v. 11a and the *goal* of mature adulthood. Hence it combines the two related notions of *fulfillment* or *goal* and the *completed whole*.[11]

---

7. Corley, "Pauline Authorship," 260. According to Corley, the noun νήπιος ("babe, child"), used in 13:11, occurs ten times in the undisputed Pauline letters, and elsewhere in the NT only five times. Akin to the contrast of νήπιος ("child") with το τέλειον ("what is mature/perfect") in 1 Cor 13:10–11 is the contrast of νηπιαζετε (be babes) with το τέλειοι ("mature [persons]") in 1 Cor 14:20. A similar contrast occurs between εν τοισ τελειοισ (among the mature") in 1 Cor 2:6 and ωσ νηπιοισ ("as to babes") in 1 Cor 3:1. A comparable antithesis also occurs in Eph 4:13–14.

8. The focus of Corley's article is in presenting evidence against Walker, that 1 Cor 13 belongs in the category of Pauline material, not a particular evaluation of childhood terms. However, he almost works against himself, and a less mechanistic approach to these terms would have helped his argument when he comes to thematic evaluations.

9. Thistleton, *First Epistle*.

10. Ibid., 1066.

11. Ibid., 1065 (emphasis in the text).

However, Thiselton does not maintain even a "value neutral" explication of the child. Explicitly following Augustine, he attributes negative values to the (perceived) "self-centred interest" of children but reckons positively the sustained pursuits of the ambitious adult.

> A child, as Augustine reflects, inevitably views life with a self-centred set of interest which steadily develops into *concern for the other*; chaotic drives address, for the child, the gratification of the *immediate present*, whereas the adult *coherently orders strategies* which serve *long-term goals* with *self-discipline*.[12]

Here, without reference to any criteria, Thiselton values one kind of "selfwardness" (an adult goal-oriented self-discipline) against another (the child exploring and discovering the world in relation to itself). In some codes of value, the adult who "coherently orders strategies . . ." may be regarded very poorly. We think of the "successful" but relentless manipulator who systematizes their existence, encroaching on the lives of others in order to achieve a high-status self, a self to be secured and maintained at the expense of other agendas—sometimes the agenda of justice or love, freedom or diversity.[13] The point at this stage is not to determine which of these visions is preferential, but to acknowledge that a set of values has been assumed on this text, which will need to be set aside for a fresh reading.

Hans Conzelmann is unremarkable is his unchallenged acceptance that "the antithesis between child and man is a standard rhetorical theme."[14] His significant contribution to biblical scholarship lies with his large schemata of Salvation History chronology, and its implication for Jesus' self-understanding. This orientation of linear time progression providing theological order is expressed through eras or (referencing the language of Fowler[15]) stages. It leads Conzelmann to accept "stages" in the Corinthian's faith, which require training—a program of improvement. Even while subscribing to this reading, Conzelmann concedes that the "pedagogical verdict"[16] is only "suggested" and is not developed. But he nevertheless reiterates: "they are beginners in the field of Christian

---

12. Ibid., 1067 (emphasis in the text).

13. Sometimes this "self" is not a human individual, but a system, corporation, or policy

14. Conzelmann, *1 Corinthians*, 226.

15. Fowler, *Stages*.

16. Conzelmann, *1 Corinthians*, 70.

knowledge. They can make progress but they must show it."[17] I am suspicious that this comment belongs in a theological college course outline handbook under "learning outcomes" rather than within Paul's sphere of concern—the human followers of Jesus becoming and living as the body of Christ in unity. I am not sure what the "field of Christian [sic] knowledge" would mean for Paul.

N. T. Wright[18] skillfully expresses his serious scholarship intentionally in accessible terms for a non-academic readership. He demonstrates what this interpretive assumption might look like in the parlance of the lay-led home group.

> The first image is of a child growing into maturity. "When I grew up, I stopped behaving like a child. Tongues prophecy, clever sounding words of knowledge: child's play, says Paul. Give me the grown up stuff, the real spiritual, emotional and personal maturity. Give me the humanness that will last, enhanced and unimpeded, through to God's new world. Give me, in other words, love: the love described here, the love which is the highest form of knowing and being humans can attain in this world or the world to come.[19]

None of the superiority of adults is lost in this common-speak paraphrase. And yet some of the inconsistency of this polarity is exposed in the vernacular phrases. "Give me the grown up stuff," sounds selfish and petulant. "Give me, Give me, Give me . . ." is offered as the pattern of the "spiritual maturity" of adults, presented in contrast to the undefined "behaviour of a child." We can't be sure what Wright imagines childhood behavior is, but his "adult" Christian is throwing a self-centred tantrum. The individualism and acquisitive flavor of this passage is not at all typical of Wright's theological vision. So this example only serves to highlight the incoherence of assumed images of child and otherwise comprehensive and integrated theology.

Raymond F. Collins has been "doing his sums" and counted the five occurrences of child in 1 Corinthians 13:11. But this is not statistically compelling for him, and the singular adult male is preferred as

---

17. Ibid., 72.
18. Wright, *Paul for Everyone*.
19. Ibid., 178.

the dominant and desirable typology.[20] Collins' focus is on adult male behavior, and moreover it is personally linked to Paul's adult behavior.

> Paul is an adult. His adult behaviour contrasts with his behaviour as a child, whether in speaking, thinking or doing his sums. The fivefold use of "child" (νήπιος) provides a vivid contrast with his state as an adult male (ἀνήρ). The gender specific "man" denotes a mature human male; the child is only an infant.[21]

Collins avoids the negative connotations of "foolish and silly," which he understood as implicit in Greek constructs of the child. Instead it is the "partially developed" limitation that he takes as the central purpose of the metaphor. Collins goes so far as to acknowledge that Paul himself identifies *rhetorically* with the incompleteness of a child. Nevertheless, Collins exaggerates the frequency and importance of Paul's "father" identity. And when it comes to the troublesome Corinthians, he slips back into a negatively slanted valuation in which they are "really just infants" (with the subtext that they shouldn't be).

> In classic and Hellenistic Greek "child" was often used metaphorically to describe someone who is childish, silly or foolish. This is not Paul's meaning; he simply wants to capture the partial human development of someone (himself in his *ethos* appeal) who is only beginning to speak, think and enumerate. Paul describes himself as a child in 1 Thessalonians 2:7 (with a textual problem); more commonly he describes himself as a father (cf. 4:14–16). The Corinthians on the other hand, who think of themselves as fully mature (2:6) are really just infants when it comes to the things of Christ.[22]

Many other commentators present similar tropes, however there are some exceptions that provoke further consideration.

Gordon D. Fee[23] rejects the idea that Paul is using a child/mature metaphor to approve some behaviors and chastise others, by calling the Corinthians "childish" as a shaming tactic. A larger vision is at stake.

---

20. As it is, somewhat more surprisingly, for Reidar Aasgaard, who counts these repetitions as a device which "underscores the deplorable state of the child, the immature human being." See Aasgaard, "Like a Child," 262.
21. Collins, *First Corinthians*, 486.
22. Ibid.
23. Fee, *First Epistle*.

> Paul's point in context does not have to do with "childishness" and "growing up," but with the difference between the present and the future. He is illustrating that there will come a time when the gifts will pass away. The analogy, therefore, says that behavior from one period in one's life is not appropriate to the other; the one is "done away with" when the other comes. So shall it be at the Eschaton. The behavior of the child is in fact appropriate to childhood.[24]

Fee recognizes the eschatological theme at work, as Paul's response both encompasses a broad ethic, and addresses individual behaviors. Fee also affirms the integrity of childhood. The things of children are important for children.

C. K. Barrett,[25] like Conzelmann and others, emphasizes the eschatological content of Paul's message, and the reading of *totality* in preference to *maturity* for τέλειος. The implications for the processes into τέλειος accompanying each of these two readings would be vastly different. Barrett also accepts the imperfection of even the grownups, our experience and expression of love, and the revelations of God grownups (and possibly children?) might receive now.

> This reference to childhood is an illustration, suggested by the use of the word *totality*, which in other contexts denotes *maturity*. Paul does not mean that he himself is now mature in the sense that he is able to dispense with prophecy and knowledge and practice perfect love (Philippians 3:12). For him (unlike Stoics and other Greek thinkers) *totality* remains an eschatological notion to be realised only at a future point of time determined by God. In this age when men love imperfectly, there is room for other instruments of revelation, imperfect though they too may be.[26]

He connects with Paul's desire to redefine the parameters of apostleship in the eyes of the Corinthians as he concludes:

> Before God, we are all, including apostles, little children.[27]

Therefore, from Corley's textual atomization, to Barrett's universal affirmation, the prevailing responsiveness to the place of the child in the

24. Ibid., 646–47.
25. Barrett, *Commentary*.
26. Ibid., 307.
27. Ibid.

text is at best warm but perfunctory, and more commonly dismissive and at least slightly deprecating. Personally, I consider the deprecation of children in scholarship to be warrant enough to sound a call for further examination of the text. But failing that compassionate motivation, we might at least redress the oversight of our premature dismissal of a significant motif in Paul's thought.[28]

I could go on and on, citing the ways in which the childhood metaphor is pejoratively predetermined—but there is no need. No doubt we are well accustomed to such a hermeneutical slant. What is important to note here is the resulting dissonance between the general theological vision and the way this particular aspect of the text is handled. Commentators assert that boasting in achievements and works, attainments and success are antithetical to the kerygma of Paul. My suspicion is that in these cases the dissonance is caused by an overlay of developmentalist assumptions upon the theological content of the model of child. I am asserting that to read Paul with the grain of Developmentalism is inappropriate.

- It is historically inappropriate—Paul was not an inheritor of the enlightenment.
- It is also literarily inappropriate—We miss the explicit subversions of Paul's rhetoric and literary devices, if we try to force particular antitheses or suppress allusions suggested in the structure.
- It is theologically inappropriate—There are theological inconsistencies in Paul's writings for sure, but this is not one of them.[29]

What follows is my attempt to resist the inertia created by several centuries of cultural and intellectual Developmentalist superscription. We are evaluating a fresh reading of child as a positive paradigm that contributes—or "incarnates"—Paul's obsessive vision of Christ crucified as the primary structural determinant for the new community of the Way. While fully cognizant and articulate in the discourses of power,

---

28. It is hard to assess what statistical evidence would qualify child language as a "significant motif," but given that some key theological terms such as "sin," "salvation" and "forgiveness" are more scarce than "child" in 1 Corinthians, there is merit in investigating the terms Paul does use.

29. Horrell, *Introduction*, 57.

status and purity, Paul privileges no court of reputation, but simply the ethic of Love.

1 Corinthians 13

> If I speak in the tongues of mortals and of angels, but do not have love, I am a noisy gong or a clanging cymbal. 2And if I have prophetic powers, and understand all mysteries and all knowledge, and if I have all faith, so as to remove mountains, but do not have love, I am nothing. 3If I give away all my possessions, and if I hand over my body so that I may boast, but do not have love, I gain nothing.
>
> 4 Love is patient; love is kind; love is not envious or boastful or arrogant 5 or rude. It does not insist on its own way; it is not irritable or resentful; 6 it does not rejoice in wrongdoing, but rejoices in the truth. 7 It bears all things, believes all things, hopes all things, endures all things. 8 Love never ends.
>
> But as for prophecies, they will come to an end; as for tongues, they will cease; as for knowledge, it will come to an end. 9 For we know only in part, and we prophesy only in part; 10 but when the complete comes, the partial will come to an end. 11 When I was a child, I spoke like a child, I thought like a child, I reasoned like a child; when I became an adult, I put an end to childish ways. 12 For now we see in a mirror, dimly, but then we will see face to face. Now I know only in part; then I will know fully, even as I have been fully known. 13 And now faith, hope, and love abide, these three; and the greatest of these is love. (New Revised Standard Version, 1989)

The center of our thinking here rests on the image of the child in verse 11. Western biblical scholarship has persistently read the childhood metaphors in Pauline literature and in particular, verse 11 and 12 of 1 Corinthians 13, "through a glass darkly"—i.e., with a distorting lens. The King James Version mis-imagines the Greek εσοπτρου for us as a glass lens which, though cloudy may reward closer introspection with a "window" into perception. But Paul knew of no such device. His mirror was in the impenetrable polished metallic reflection that offers nothing beyond itself, the individual. And in that reflection he speaks of being only "in part." Which part is envisaged in the mirror? Only the head,[30] (and this becomes symbolic of the manipulative prioritization of rationalism, and that which is "higher" and "above"), a part that sees nothing beyond its own visage. This is the self-absorbed view.[31] And this individualist—and I will come to argue, rationalist and developmentalist—metal mirror jarres with as much optical distortion against the primary vision of Paul—Christ Crucified—as the clanging cymbal of eloquent and divine but loveless speech (13:1) clashes against the central kerygma of Paul. The task here is to outline the discords heard in the literature on this passage. Following this, I suggest the simple, yet probably subversive ways in which we might restore Paul's childhood imagery. Paul's child-self is both positive and programmatic. Paul's intention is not to elevate that status of the child. Status seeking and elevation are the very postures he critiques. Rather, Paul calls the new community of Christ to remodel their life together around a new ethic, given in other-facing love, and for which a child offers a radically challenging prototype.[32]

DISCORD 1. The metaphor of the child is presumptively presented as a negative metaphor, and the following metaphor of man is construed more positively. We need to revisit the value assignments, which pre-empt meaning and the structural compulsion of binary dichotomizations.

DISCORD 2. A three-stage sequence: child . . . man . . . perfect, is uncritically adopted and assumed to idealize progress or maturity in linear, progressive and developmental positivist terms. The modeled trajectory towards "the perfect" obligates leaving behind childhood thinking, speaking and accounting, and via the thinking of manhood the trajectory then continues towards "the perfect." Gendered language (here highlighted specifically in "man" [Gr. anhr] not the more general ανθρωōποσ) is an

---

30. In chapter 12, Paul has already challenged the fragmented self-focus in the community, with his question; "If all were a single member, where would the body be?" (1 Cor 9:12). In this mirror metaphor, we might add "Are we all a cerebellum? Is everyone a frontal lobe?"

31. Stendahl, "Apostle Paul," 199–215. Stendahl exposes the Western application of individual conscience on the writings of Paul, obscuring a collective agenda within the text. This is partly the result of a developmentalist agenda within the history of theology and biblical scholarship.

32. In other places Paul uses the equally disturbing prototypes of slave (1 Cor 9:19); fool (1 Cor 1:20; 4:10); weak (1 Cor 4:10).

important aspect of the way the language functions. The association of childhood with female modeling suffers the implications of reinscribing distinctions of value along gender and age lines. Hopefully the alarm is clanging loud now. What? Do we arrive at the perfect through being an adult? But so many millions never become adults. It is only a Western privileged worldview that could subscribe to such an exclusive reading. Nevertheless, the outworking of this adult, rational, consent-mediated faith has also colonized many global ecclesiologies.

Discord 3. Typically cast in essentially individualist terms, it is the individual who is exhorted to become mature. The individualism of "a man" "thinking" is here interpreted in rationalist terms, and moreover privileges the rationalist imperative rather than in the broader terms which such a diverse palette of skills and processes such as "thinking" can encompass. Imagining, reckoning, accounting, evaluating, discerning, wisdom-ing, logic-ing, reasoning, wondering, remembering, considering . . . many of which are uncomfortably constrained if required to conform only to rationalist forms. As we revisit Paul's model of child, expressed in the triad "When I was a child I spoke as a child, I thought as a child, I calculated as a child"—it is worth asking what kinds of thinking do children do? And what is lost when one sheds such thinking? Here is an invitation for us to return to our lexicons and sound out some other terms and listen for the clanging cymbal or the voice of the child.

Discord 4. Finally, and most significantly, a progressive staged-development reading of the child metaphor loses its function, which is to reorientate the destructive claims and posturing of the Corinthians in discourses of power and status and honor. I hope to offer a reading of the child metaphor in which the value of the child metaphor is reclaimed. I suggest that Paul places the child in the midst of the discipleship community—a community rent with competing claims of status and honor and power according to various but all false paradigms—eloquence, knowledge, capital, agency and ability.[33] The Corinthians were a discipleship community preoccupied with the question of "who is the greatest?" Paul responds in a way that parallels the action of Jesus in Matthew 18.[34] He places a child (in Corinthians, metaphorically) in

---

33. Paul and his colleagues likewise placed themselves as children in the midst of the Thessalonians (1 Thess 2:7 ἀλλὰ ἐγενήθημεν νήπιοι ἐν μέσῳ ὑμῶν).

34. See Mark 9:36 and Matt 18:2 (ἐν μέσῳ αὐτῶν, but not in Luke 9:47 [παρ' ἑαυτῷ]).

the midst of the arguing grown up disciples, consumed with forms and claims of greatness. Child Theology as an emerging methodology follows this same pattern and intentionally places "the child in the midst as a sign of the kingdom," not to be superseded in moving to further stages of growth, but to be ever present. As we attend to the conversation of Paul and Loder, this child must be in our midst as well, that we might be ready for the disruptions of the kingdom.

Three Negative Examples: Speech, Knowledge, and Gifts.

Chapter 13 of 1 Corinthians is often read in sentimental, quasi-romantic tones. The presence of the word "Love" has been abstracted from the context of the chapter, and the surrounding rhetorical material. Chapter 13 read aloud is an exercise that begins in dramatic irony and parody (vs. 1–3). It shifts to pragmatic action mode (vs. 4–7) and concludes with poignant lament, reality bites and, finally, hope. Most important is resisting the glorification of the figure(s) in vs. 1–3. These are not inspirational personalities but parodies of ego, drawn from each of the categories of status that the Corinthians themselves have variously claimed.

1 Corinthians 13:1–3 sketches a grotesque caricature of an eloquent orator, a prophet initiated into the deepest of mysteries and knowledge, a miracle working giant of faith, cashed up with resources for generosity and prepared for dramatic martyrdom, but who is tragically loveless. Paul exaggerates this extreme character in two directions—hyper-endowed with spiritual and human competencies and honor, but love/ἀγάπη impoverished. This is not a *persona* that simply requires the embellishment of love, or an "upgrade" to another level in order to fulfill the notion of τέλειος. The call of this passage is not to improve or develop the quality of one's spiritual gifts by adding love, in order to become mature. Our character in all his incarnations doesn't need to grow up. He is already too big for his boots. Transformation of a different kind is required. Loder points us to the reality of the "Void" as the negation of being, and also what must be recognized prior to the encounter of the "Holy." Here Paul uses the parallel language of "nothing" (ουδεν is repeated three times). The character is in Paul's estimation, nothing.

This opening triad of (disrupted) claims is hypothetical. "If I . . ." speculates Paul. The subjunctive pronoun creates a tenuous identity, which Paul casts off in verse 11, using the stronger personalizing model

"When I was a child . . ." A contrast is thus drawn between the Void adult in verses 1–3 and the unpretentious child in verse 11. We do well to attend to both the construction of this inversion of status, as well as the content. The child is not over-endowed with qualities to eclipse the model in verses 1–3, but is presented plainly—speaking, thinking and reckoning. A comparison is obvious looking back, but moving through the image of child, Paul avoids a simplistic antithesis. The three parts of the metaphor—the child . . . the man . . . and the perfect—help us avoid a black and white *child*/adult, immature/mature, remedial/advanced, good/bad, dichotomized interpretation. A moment of great grace occurs in the turn of the story from *child* to man. Paul does not claim to have moved from *child*-ways in to "τελιoσ" but he has become a man (ανηρ). The bald honesty of this statement allows for all of the development, as well as all of the flaws. "Men" (and women) do not all think maturely and rationally. Mental health is precarious for many. Age, rather than ensuring an ever-evolving sophistication of thought, frequently brings dementia, confusion, memory loss, atrophied assumptive patterns, mixed with breadth and depth of wisdom, and a gathering of thoughts and memories.

And so we hear the humble admission of Paul "as a man I see puzzles and riddles." Reimaging the model of child is also a powerful and grace-filled myth-buster for our models of adulthood, in which ages outside certain windows are suppressed and disempowered. I confess I come to reading the text with a thirst for justice—but a true justice that will be justice for everyone. If there is a direct contrast to be made, it may just as easily be made between the clarity in which the speech and thought and reckoning of a child is done, and the puzzlement of the adult man. Nevertheless, we have three images in succession, not simply two. And the story arc from the child to the man does not proceed with affirmations of progress, but with laments of puzzlement, lack of clarity, and confessions of self-absorption. We also observe an elegant literary balance between verses 1–3 and verse 11. The *persona* of verse 1–3 is qualified by speaking, knowing, and accounting. In each of these verses our super saint is in fact disqualified, despite, excellence in all areas.

The child *persona* of Paul in verse 11 is remembered in terms of speech, thought and reckoning. Some of our translations "flatten" this out to read: "I spoke like a child, thought like a child and reasoned like a child." But such a translation unnecessarily draws thinking and reasoning together, and obscures the diversities of thinking, reckoning, accounting, wisdom-ing, and many other modes of thinking that are possible. Nevertheless, the image of the child is a foil for the obscenities of the super spiritual but loveless adult. This is a familiar Pauline device, in which Paul inhabits the text autobiographically, but radically presents himself as weak, broken, impoverished, powerless, foolish, inarticulate, disempowered. We ought not be surprised that Paul identifies himself as a child, or that this identification operates as a positive and programmatic model, inviting imitation. Where Paul does this, it is in solidarity with the inarticulate, weak, broken, foolishness of the crucified Christ.

A critical review of readings of 1 Corinthians 13 must address the individualization of maturity. If we read "man"—third person singular—as the prototype of maturity, we read against the trajectory of the text, which is towards τέλειος, a vision of completion and perfection. Paul's cosmological scope, and eschatological paradigm locate τέλειος Christologically, that is, in Christ in God. The location of the child or the man here in completion and perfection is in reconciliation with the whole of creation in Christ. In humility we recognize that anything that might appeal to us as "mature" is relativized in such a radically reordered panorama.

"Now we see in part" confesses the partial identity that we each are when viewed through the mirror of self. Not only do we not see ourselves wholly, but we are in fact, imaged as an isolated individual, not complete. We need "other"—not just one other, but one another—as Paul has expounded in chapter 12. "But then when the perfect comes"—not a matter of parts being perfected, but of a different way of knowing—knowing as we are known "face before face." Here there is no developmental continuity, but a relational transformation. Paul's eschatological yearning is not for attaining perfection or completion, and far less maturity, but for intimately knowing God as the infant fully knows the mother.

A More Excellent Way: Paul's Model of Child and Relational Discourse

It is important not to romanticize, idolize or idealize childhood. But we also do well to remember that it is adults who cheat on their taxes, cheat on their spouse, who drive under the influence, who gamble their livelihood. Grownups are not so enviable. Both Paul and the Corinthians know this. A man has been sleeping with his father's wife. The rich have been greedy eaters. Their sexuality is expressed abusively. They have been unable to settle their squabbles. They are adults who don't know how to eat, sleep, dress, love, talk or shut up.[35] Paul places the image of the child in the midst (ἐν μέσῳ) of this divided and competing community. Perhaps his action reminds us a bit of Jesus, placing the child amongst the disciples arguing over who is the greatest. The gift of the child in 1 Corinthians 13 is that it provides a positive model for us. There is likely no argument against the destructive power of individual ego-flexing and social orders based on any criteria of competence, functionality, or individual condition. But what are we to do instead? As Paul places the child in our midst, alternate paradigms of status—rationalist, capitalist, individualist or developmentalist—are disrupted. In choosing the child, the question of status is replaced by the question of relationship. From Paul's childhood terminology we receive not an alternative imperative[36] to reorientate around a confined idolization of a childhood state, but an inclusive relational ethic of love. Broad dimensions and a multiplicity of modes are affirmed by the universality, vulnerability and non-utilitarianism of childhood. Not all of us will become useful, not all of us will become clever, not all of us will become adults. Development itself is disrupted.

Paul offers himself in reflection as a vulnerable, but thinking, perceiving, communicating, relating child—a positive model, and an anticipation of completion in the future of God and a demonstration of faith (I am not self reliant), hope (I am not yet perfect), and love (but my reality is other-oriented and defined within God). The vision of the inarticulate, vulnerable, naked, weak, powerless, dependent one is visible both in the crucified Christ and in the image of the child. What then shall we say is the consequence of accepting a positive and programmatic "child metaphor"? We do not ask: "Am I strong, wise, advanced

---

35. Eat: 1 Cor 8; 1 Cor 11:20ff.; sleep: 1 Cor 5:1; dress: 1 Cor 11:4ff.; talk: 1 Cor 13:1; love: 1 Cor 13:4–8; shut up: 1 Cor 14:28.

36. Castelli, "Interpretations," 197–222. Castelli critiques the conditions of power operating in the Corinthian discourse which assert Paul's voice as a "powerful and authoritative agent in the text." This sensitivity is important, and while Castelli works in exclusively adult (mostly sexualised) terms in her reading, her purpose is to "create space" for "the more muted subjugated discourses" (204). I would submit that the positive valuation of the child as relational qualitative model is one such voice.

enough to survive, to see in the Eschaton?" Our question is relativized collectively and in relation to the dynamics of the Cross: "As a body of followers of Jesus, are we young, weak, vulnerable enough to be reborn, reformed, made New Creation?"

We have taken a long time with Paul, whose company I am most enthralled by. Is Loder still with us? Those who know the work and person of Loder more thoroughly than I (it is a very deep and dense forest in which to walk) will no doubt identify other resonances and wrestlings which I would welcome heartily. I can suggest a few opening and obvious launching places for conversation between Paul and Loder around the metaphor of the child.

Liberation from the Imperative Taxonomic Ranking Inherent in Developmental Structures

Loder demonstrates a "flexibility" of life ordered, not by some mechanistic, automated process, but open to and reoriented by the action and initiative of God.

> "Reversibility" has two closely related meanings. The first is that the meaning of past experiences and of the inevitable future experiences such as death may be automatically or subliminally altered. The second is that one's self consciousness is liberated to resist the past or to anticipate the future with increasing flexibility or freedom. Thus the linear unfolding of life through a prescribed sequence becomes, in effect reversible for further development and self-understanding. God's action in effecting both forms of reversibility is decisive.[37]

Furthermore, this flexibility in regards to "development" carries a transposable logic or grammar from the personal to the social to the relational to the transcendent. Thus Paul's insistence that social orders are reordered by gospel logic—that is, by the cruciform life—is mirrored in Loder's transformational description.

> First note that there are several strata of the developing personality within which transformation unfolds. At the biological level the transformational pattern is most clearly expressed in orthogenesis. As stage transition process, it is expressed both at the level of part processes (such as language and intelligence) and

---

37. Loder, *Transforming*, 209–10.

in ego development. Then, transposed to the level of intentional conscious behavior, it is expressed in the act of creation and in narrative forms. Transposed again, it is the internal pattern of the healing process in the context of redevelopment. As indicated earlier, it also transposes into development in interpersonal, social and cultural contexts. Most significant for our concern here is its transposition into the pattern of God's action as Spiritus Creator. However the Spiritus Creator transforms all transformation in the course of affecting his purposes at all level so of human development.[38]

Thus, just as Paul disrupts the dominant discourse of his first century Greco Roman culture with a relativization of all their categories, finding them in the face of the glory of the crucified Christ, trivial reductionist distortions of humanity and human community, similarly Loder disrupts his own methodologies of psychoanalytic theory and Developmentalism. He avers: "To follow the psychoanalytically oriented approach alone and by itself, is to truncate the human spirit and trim its contributions to the size and shape of the human ego. The human spirit cannot be so constrained."[39]

Christology

The primary structural determinant for Paul is cited by Loder as affirming the Christological, explicitly, the cruciform Christological center of identity. Many scriptural passages support and highlight the parts of this event but, for Loder, the most comprehensive and succinct account of the whole logic of transformation as it structures the Christ event is probably Phil 2:5–11. The "Chalcedonian" vision of Loder correlates to the pre-Chalcedon integrative thought of Paul, in whom the relational ontology of Love is fundamental. We have heard Paul in 1 Corinthians 13, so let's now hear Loder: "The Chalcedonian relationality between God and humanity play out into the relationality of eternity and time, and so ontological priority is given to the eternal without denying, separating or confusing the two views."[40]

---

38. Ibid., 157.
39. Loder, *Logic*, 63.
40. Ibid., 76.

The Void

A simple but profound correlation occurs between Loder's explication of the Void and the Holy as systematic categories where Paul offers a narrative of ontological, actional, and acquisitional "nothing." Paul makes this assessment of all that is loveless, not that it lacks something to be added, but is Void, void of God. Loder begins here, and affirms: "Because the abyss between the human and divine is humanly unfathomable, it must be crossed by the act of God; but the argument from above is that this has already been done in the paradox of God's becoming fully human while remaining fully God in Jesus Christ."[41] The legacy of "development" may be seen as implicit in Loder's response to this: "What remains for us is the awakening to this reality and to all this implies for the conviction, illumination and sanctification of the development of persons."[42]

Paul clearly seeks to understand these processes in the light of the "already done" of God's action. Yet Paul reminds us that this action of God is Love, expressed completely in Christ Crucified and fulfilled not in the enigmatic image of man, but in the "perfect" face before face. Together Loder and Paul disallow any continuity of human effort, growth or development between our starting point (the Void) and our teleios (the End). It is, in both cases, God in Christ who has disrupted what might be claimed as such a trajectory (false claims of human advancement) and simultaneously disrupted the inevitability of the void.

Face to Face Relationality

The locus of relational knowing and "face to face" intimacy and ultimacy is in the logic of the Spirit—the human spirit but initially the Holy Spirit—as Loder expresses it.

> I suggest that what is established in the original face-to-face interaction is the child's sense of personhood and a universal prototype of the Divine Presence. In the face- to-face, (whether actualized or remaining as innate potential) the child seeks *a cosmic-ordering, self-confirming, impact from the presence of a loving other*. Some Jungians may want to say the archetype is an independent and impersonal structure, beyond any facial or personal presence, and Freudians may want to say that the di-

---

41. Ibid., 12.
42. Ibid.

> vine presence is nothing other than the screened memory of the mother. However, in Christian context, the self-understanding of the convicted person combines the sense of personal presence and transcendent order. Thus the primal experience of the face as actual presence and its significance as symbolic expression provides a prototype for the convicting presence of God.[43]

Reflecting on this last quote, I would hold a differing view perhaps to Loder in regards to the meaning and capacity of this logic in the life of a child. While Loder affirms the origin of the Face in God, and correlation with the face of the parent, he still anticipates a fulfillment in the redeemed adult or at least in parts of the redeemed, therapeutized adult. I would stretch this further on the strength of Paul's positive model of the child. The face to face which we anticipate, not in adulthood, but in the Eschaton, the New Creation, is a return to our early face to face in which God's gracious presence is rarely (though perhaps sometimes tragically) more immediate than as a new born. Here the launch of life is strong, and we are, unmediated by rationalized, constructed or instrumentalized means, simply προσοπον προσ προσοπον, "face before face." I think Loder comes closer to Paul here: "To mature in Christ is to behold who we are in Jesus Christ as the Face of God, and so be held there while his Spirit transforms our spirits in conformity to his person. This is the one and only situation in which perfect conformity amounts to perfect liberty."[44] And he comes closest here, though we note that this quote appears in the midst of a discussion of young adulthood.

> The most powerful intimacy comes from the presence of the Spirit of God. It may be mediated, as in these cases. The spiritual presence of Christ is not dependent on the development of the ego, but it is a sanity-producing intimacy, that does call forth interpersonal affirmation and openness in a psychological and spiritual sense. This is, of course the satisfaction of the deepest longing of a person for presence implied in the significance of the primal longing for the Face, the Face that will not go away. This satisfaction occurs at a deeper level than the psychological *intimus*, the innermost being of the person.[45]

---

43. Loder, *Transforming*, 167 (emphasis in the text).
44. Loder, *Logic*, 122.
45. Ibid., 265.

Conclusion

In seeking and constructing conversation with Loder and Paul, I hope that whatever other mis-readings or long bows I may have drawn, that I have not done what Loder himself wryly lamented had been done—as predicted to Kierkegaard, one of his most stimulating conversation partners—to "hide from the existential claims of the incarnation behind cultural constructions of our own making."

> Kierkegaard's thought has been cropped and co-opted by the philosophers, reduced and abused by psychologists, poeticized by the literati, fictionalized by the fanciful, and misunderstood or held at arms length by theologians—all of whom do what Kierkegaard predicted. He knew ahead of time that his thought would be made, in multiple modalities, an object of study that would permit the professional thinker to hide from the existential claims of the incarnation behind the cultural constructions of his or her own making, yet all the while calling those constructs "Kierkegaardian."[46]

We have had to risk the dangers of "Pauline" and "Loderian" constructions. But I trust that the "child in the midst" of this conversation has been disruptive enough to two-dimensional knowing and has yielded some transforming moments of perpendicularity, as the vulnerable, inarticulate, foolish, non-status of the child reveals the incarnate presence of Christ crucified, the eschatological vision of face to face knowing of God and the call to Love.

---

46. Loder, Review of *Kierkegaard's Vision*, 640.

Works Cited

Aasgaard, Reidar. "Like a Child: Paul's Rhetorical Uses of Childhood." In *The Child in the Bible*, edited by Marcia J. Bunge et al., 249–77. Grand Rapids: Eerdmans, 2008.

Barrett, C. K. *A Commentary on the First Epistle to the Corinthians*. London: Adam & Charles Black, 1968.

Castelli, Elisabeth. "Interpretations of Power in 1 Corinthians." *Semeia* 54 (1991) 197–222.

Collins, Raymond F. *First Corinthians*. Collegeville, MN: Liturgical, 1999.

Conzelmann, Hans. *1 Corinthians: A Commentary on the First Epistle to the Corinthians*. Philadelphia: Fortress, 1975.

Corley, Jeremy. "The Pauline Authorship of 1 Corinthians 13." *Catholic Biblical Quarterly* 66 (2004) 256–74.

Fee, Gordon D. *The First Epistle to the Corinthians*. Grand Rapids: Eerdmans, 1987.

Fowler, James. *Stages of Faith*. San Francisco: Harper, 1995.

Heil, John Paul. *The Rhetorical Role of Scripture in 1 Corinthians*. Atlanta: Society of Biblical Literature, 2005.

Horrell, David G. *An Introduction to the Study of Paul*. London: T. & T. Clark, 2006.

Loder, James E., Jr. *The Logic of the Spirit*. San Francisco: Jossey-Bass, 1998.

———. Review of *Kierkegaard's Vision of the Incarnation: By Faith Transformed* by Murray A. Rae. *Theology Today* 56/4 (2000) 638.

———. *The Transforming Moment: Understanding Convictional Experiences*. San Francisco: Harper & Row, 1981.

Pieterse, J. N. "Dilemmas of Development Discourse: The Crisis of Developmentalism and the Comparative Method." *Development and Change* 22/1 (1991) 5–29.

Stendahl, Krister. "The Apostle Paul and the Introspective Conscience of the West." *Harvard Theological Review* 56 (1963) 199–215.

Thistleton, Anthony. *The First Epistle to the Corinthians: A Commentary on the Greek Text*. NIGTC. Carlisle, UK: Paternoster, 2000.

Wright, N. T. *Paul for Everyone: Corinthians*. 2 vols. London: SPCK, 2003–2004.

PART TWO

James E. Loder and Christian
Education Theory and Practice

4

The Transforming Moment and Godly Play

JEROME W. BERRYMAN

Introduction

Jim Loder's challenge still rings true: "Christian education is structuring the creative act for the purpose of expanding the boundaries of freedom. Without this central emphasis, it becomes fantastic, and in Kierkegaard's words: 'Christian education is a lie.'"[1] This chapter is about how to put the creative process at the center of Christian education for children and why this is important.

Loder was a theorist interested in Christian education, while I am a Christian educator with a taste for theory. My life work has been an approach to Christian education with a well-developed theory, method, curriculum, and understanding of its place in the history of theology.[2] The approach Thea Berryman and I developed is called "Godly Play" and has "the creative act" as its "central emphasis." Research classes for Godly Play began at Pines Presbyterian Church in Houston in 1974. They followed the Montessori method and reframed Christian education as

---

1. Loder, *Religious*, 228.

2. See Berryman, *Godly Play; Children and the Theologians;* and especially *Complete Guide*, 8:156–69.

spiritual guidance.³ Loder's publication of *The Transforming Moment* in 1981 was an important influence on its development.

Godly Play teaches children the art of using classical Christian language to make existential meaning, so they can take an active part in their community of worship and their own spiritual guidance as they mature. The absorbing and activating of this language domain uses Montessori-like teaching objects and Maria Montessori's method to show how to use the sacred stories, parables, liturgical action, and contemplative silence of the Christian language system to make existential meaning while it is being learned. This process, which follows the same deep structure as the Word and Sacrament of the Holy Eucharist, helps children know themselves as creators and the Creator in whose image they were created.

Children Coming Close To God in Godly Play

The first major influence on Godly Play's creative center was Dorothy L. Sayers, who published *The Mind of the Maker* in 1941. I first read this book about 1960, as a student at Princeton Theological Seminary, and was struck by the bridge she built from literary creativity to knowing the Creator. Her book was neither an argument for Christianity nor an expression of her personal religious belief. It was "a commentary" on the Christian creeds and their claim to be factual. She argued that all language is metaphorical, so we always know something in terms of something else. "If the word 'Maker' does not mean something related to our human experience of making, then it has no meaning at all."⁴ The logical analogy is obvious, but Sayers was not talking about logic. She was talking about a Reality that can be interpreted by the way we use language. Making meaning with Christian language while it is being learned is good pedagogy. Participating in the Creator's being while creating meaning is good theology. When classical Christian language is absorbed and activated through the creative process, children come close to God and God comes close to children. They are intertwined like a magnificent, invisible braid, so the language they are learning can function appropriately.

---

3. Berryman, *Spiritual Guidance*.
4. Sayers, *Mind*, 21.

Sayers was "inclined to believe" that the pattern of the creative process "corresponds to the actual structure of the living universe" so if people feel at odds with the universe or feel powerless in its immensity they are merely stating that they, for whatever reason, are not conforming to the pattern of their true nature. What is this pattern?

> I can only suggest that it is the pattern of the creative mind—an eternal Idea, manifested in material form by an unresting Energy, with an outpouring of Power that at once inspires, judges, and communicates the work; all these three being one and the same in the mind and one and the same in the work. And this, I observe, is the pattern laid down by the theologians as the pattern of the being of God."[5]

This is why Godly Play is Trinity-centered and God is invited, verbally and nonverbally, to come join in the play with the children as they make meaning together with the language that flows out of the life, death, and resurrection of Jesus to give us a way to find our way back to that reality and to move forward to spiritual maturity.

God Coming Close To Children in Godly Play

While Sayers bridged literature and theology, Loder bridged theology and science.[6] Loder's aspiration resonated with me, because I had been working on interdisciplinary teams since 1974, especially at Texas Children's Hospital, M. D. Anderson Hospital, and later at Houston Child Guidance Center. The creative process was our common currency. Loder related the natural creative process to ultimate matters by talking about a "fourfold knowing event." We compose a reality "out there," which in turn composes us.[7] We also create relationships, which imply "being-itself." The "self cannot be itself unless it is grounded in the

---

5. Ibid., 172–73.

6. This agenda was set in part by D. Campbell Wyckoff, who was Loder's professor and mentor at Princeton, as well as my own. Wyckoff was working on his *Theory and Design* when they first met. Wyckoff's book stressed the need for one clear objective "intended as a guide for the whole education process" (62). Wyckoff argued that theology provides both the content for Christian education and is "a source of insight and direction in determining the context, scope, purpose, process, and design of curriculum" (94). He also cautioned that the behavioral sciences should not be neglected. Loder embraced the behavioral sciences and physics in his bridge building. His key organizing thought was the "transformational moment."

7. Loder, *Transforming*, 72.

Source," as he said, which "lets it be."[8] The third part of the "knowing event" takes place when our two-dimensional world, where we usually live and relate to others, is "violated" by the Void.

To speak of "nothing," Loder cautioned us, is "a semantic anomaly" because it allows us to speak of nothing as if it were something.[9] Still, he pressed on to talk about the Void, as the negation of the first two kinds of knowing. The fourth dimension of this knowing event is when the Holy moves from the background behind the Void into the foreground and replaces it, as one's primary existential reference. This is the "transforming moment." Loder stressed the immediacy of this event and wrote that the graciousness of being-itself "comes out of nowhere and mediates between God and humanity."[10] He called such events "convictional experiences," because they are decisive and self-authenticating, although it seems to me that it is difficult if not impossible for any event to be "self-authenticating." There is always a context and a history to consider, as in all of Loder's illustrations.

Loder's great contribution was to apply the ordinary use of the creative process to the existential setting. As he said, "in ordinary experience transformation begins and ends with the development of the personality's creative and adaptational capacities." In "the theological context" the pattern begins with "Christ's initiative" which brings one through the experience of the Void into faith to guide one's daily life and worship.[11]

Godly Play talks more about "limits" and "boundaries" than the experience of the Void. Either way, as Gabriel Marcel has reminded us, there is no "tower" one can climb up to look over the existential boundary to see what is on "the other side." There is only the boundary. What is at stake is to discover a way to cope with the always present, ultimate and nonspecific threat, which stimulates our existential anxiety, caused by the limits to our being and knowing. Creating meaning about our limits to being and knowing cannot be solved without remainder like a problem in simple mathematics or in a detective story. This is because the totality of our being is involved. We can talk in general about our limits, as we are doing now, but to know them personally we need to

---

8. Ibid., 80.
9. Ibid., 80–81.
10. Ibid., 87.
11. Ibid, 115–16.

participate in their mystery and that leaves us speechless. To engage the ultimate environment the self must become permeable to allow the mystery to seep into us to be known.[12]

What is *beyond* the limits to being and knowing makes us existentially anxious, because we don't know exactly what to fear. Godly Play helps children cope with this non-specific danger by inviting them to enter classical Christian language, such as the Parable of the Good Shepherd, with their senses, reason, and contemplation. Since the non-specific danger is to the whole being, the whole person needs a way to respond with awareness without being overwhelmed.

Loder's four-fold act of knowing influenced Godly Play in general, but the more specific influence comes from Irving Yalom's *Existential Psychotherapy*. Yolam, now Emeritus Professor of Psychiatry at Stanford University School of Medicine, encountered four primary existential limits in his clinical practice. They were death, the need for meaning, the threat of freedom, and aloneness.[13] Such issues do not yield to therapy. They are realities one must cope with and they define us, so they need to be brought within our awareness as part of our authentic being. If this is not done, the energy that could be used for living and healing is drained away to keep the walls of repression in place.

The repression of our existential limits is a major reason why adults maintain the fiction that children are always happy. Adults hope this is so, but that is cheap hope. It masks adult limits, shared with children, and hides from the responsibility to listen respectfully when children try to tell us about their ultimate concerns. This neglect traps children in a double bind. They must either please the adults and repress their anxiety or express their anxiety and risk having adults ignore, dismiss or shame them. This is why children usually remain silent about their ultimate concerns, which ironically seems to confirm that they are always happy.

The play therapists at Texas Children's Hospital, especially Jackie Vogel, in the mid-1970s were the first to understand Godly Play and what "the chaplain's strange language" had to do with children's ultimate concerns, which are hard to ignore in a hospital setting. The play therapists knew quite well how to help children cope with the fear of the un-

---

12. Marcel, *Creative*, 172. Marcel preferred the term "permeability," arguing that "participation" was too ambiguous. When "permeable," the boundary of the self becomes open to experiencing both what is beyond, beside, and within as with the Holy Trinity, which is also a mystery.

13. Yalom, *Existential Psychotherapy*, 8–9.

known. For example, they could help children play this out with a model of the hospital's surgical suite to make going there more familiar and to help the children talk about their fears. However, when children asked, "Am I going to die" something changed in the communication. This was not a question about the unknown. This was about the unknowable, so a whole different kind of language was needed. The Parable of the Good Shepherd needed to replace the model of the surgical suite.

Children know that talking about death is different, so they don't ask about death so much as dying. Will it hurt? Will you stay by me? Will you help me? Life at the edge is leveling. It is hard to tell who is a child and who is an adult. Children know that death is personal and that they are a case of one. They are not distracted by statistics. This is why it is good to meet children as a storyteller rather than an expert about religion. "The Parable of the Good Shepherd"[14] is told, not explained. It is placed between the storyteller and the child so the two of them can enter the middle realm in between to engage the story where meaning with God is created.

The sheep are brought out from the safety of the sheepfold and are moved through the grass, by the water, and through places of danger back to the sheepfold. The wolf approaches and an ordinary person runs away, but in the parable the wolf can also be touched. Should it be buried? Pushed away? Should it come into the sheepfold? Will it change? How can the Good Shepherd stand between you and the wolf? Does he really give his life for the sheep? *Telling* the story and *moving* the pieces of the parable provides a way for the child to make meaning with the parable and with his or her whole body. The mentor shows how to do this by being involved in the story with the child and with the Parable Maker.

Making meaning and being close to God are experiences that the creative process helps happen. This makes the pattern of the creative process important, because it maps how to move through the whole process from opening to closing to draw both meaning and God's presence with it.

---

14. Berryman, "Parable," 3:77–86.

The Pattern of the Creative Process

The literature has changed enormously since Loder first described the structure of the transformational process as "the Hypnagogic Paradigm" in 1966.[15] This was 40 years after Graham Wallas published *The Art of Thought* with its four steps for the creative process—preparation, incubation, illumination, and verification—and 46 years before R. Keith Sawyer's second edition of *Explaining Creativity: The Science of Innovation*. Sawyer included a comprehensive history of the concept's interpretation as well as an up to date analysis of its many dimensions.[16] Still, within this almost 90 year span there is still much to learn from Sayers and Loder about how the process feels and its relationship to knowing God. Their two descriptions of the pattern of the creative process may be compared as follows:

Sayers	Loder/Godly Play
1.—	1. Opening the Process
2.—	2. Scanning
3. The Idea (Insight)	3. Insight
4. Incarnation (Appropriate Form)	4. Development
5. Communication	5. Closure/Communication

Sayers did not speculate on where "The Idea" comes from for the human maker, but the two views agree on most details about the steps in the process for making meaning and the analogy between the human and divine creators.

Descriptions of the creative process in Godly Play have likewise evolved. In *Godly Play* and *Teaching Godly Play* the description turns around the circle of how the process feels, but in *Children and the Theologians*,[17] the four dimensions of the creative process are pictured

---

15. As a student of Freud, Loder began his study of the creative process with the work of Herbert Silberer (1882–1923), a Viennese psychoanalyst, whose work strayed from Freudian orthodoxy toward Jungian themes, such as the occult and alchemy, to the extent that he was rejected by the inner circle and hanged himself. However, he wrote an important article in 1909 about the hypnogogic state, the state of consciousness between waking and sleeping. Loder does not mention Silberer in *Moment*, but he relied on him almost exclusively in *Pathology* to develop his view of the creative process. See Loder, *Religious*, 179–91, 200–202, 207f.

16. Sawyer, *Explaining Creativity*, 15–34.

17. Berryman, *Complete Guide*, 93–135, especially 102, 150; *Teaching*, 116–28 and

in parallel to show how flow, play, love and contemplation are similar in structure so they are likely to have come from the same source. We turn now to a five-step overview of the process.

Opening

The process begins with a conflict, as Loder suggested, but there are hard openings and soft ones. A hard opening usually involves a dramatic loss such as the death of a loved one, or a doctor's diagnosis of cancer, which shatters one's assumed world. Soft openings result from encountering some richness in life that dissolves one's ordinary worldview. Examples are a beautiful sunset, tiny tundra flowers above timberline, and the ocean's placid calm or wild fury. Such events, or the art that evokes them, cause one to wonder. Positive wonder stimulates scanning as much as a negative crisis does.

Loder's examples from his life and from counseling sessions were usually hard openings, but he included a few examples of soft openings such as when Bulgakov, the great Russian Orthodox theologian, was "driving across the southern steppes of Russia" or when he encountered Raphael's Sistine Madonna in a Dresden art gallery.[18] Most regular spiritual guidance with children involves soft openings, which is why Godly Play emphasizes wonder, beauty, and play in its method. But mentors are alert to hard openings such as in the hospital when a child's assumed world is shattered by treatment or in the parish when a divorce threatens to fragment a child's sense of world coherence.

Scanning

The second step for both Loder and Godly Play is scanning. Loder counseled that the search can be brief, only a few minutes, or much longer, such as my ten-year search for a method (1960–70) to enlarge the capacity of Christian education. The scanning process moves relentlessly toward a new and more adequate meaning once it begins, as Dorothy Sayers also recognized. When a more adequate vision is intuited, it forces its way into consciousness as an insight, like when I was watching our girls in a Montessori school and discovered the key to my rethinking

---

136–37; and *Theologians*, 230–44.

18. Loder, *Transforming*, 204.

of Christian education. Insight, however, is not inevitable. Frustrations such as rigidity and repression can block the process and it can be used in destructive ways. We will return to this in a moment.

Insight

Insight can be correlated to a burst of brain activity. There is "a spike of gamma-wave rhythm," which is the highest electrical frequency generated by the brain.[19] The moment of insight can also be predicted by a steady rhythm of alpha waves emanating from the right hemisphere about eight seconds before the insight takes place.[20] What this confirms is that we are not "imagining" things when we sense that the creative process is at work or that an insight is about to happen. This scientific description, however, only provides a correlation between the biological phenomenon described and one's awareness of the process's movement. Shifting to the domain of scientific language and custom does not necessarily demonstrate a cause.

Loder divided the insight into two parts, the insight itself and another step, which is a sense of moving forward. Godly Play combines these two aspects within the insight, because they usually occur simultaneously and to give more emphasis to the next two steps, which are development and closure.

Development

The development of an insight is optimally channeled through one's special interests and capacities. In Godly Play these alternative pathways are recognized, and Howard Gardner's description is used to give this awareness specificity. Gardner's multiple intelligences (MI) contradicts the idea that human beings have a single, general intelligence. Gardner looked back over almost thirty years of the development of his idea in his 2011 book *Frames of Mind: The Theory of Multiple Intelligences*. He wrote, "I am sticking to my 8 ½ intelligences, but I can readily foresee a time when the list could grow, or when the boundaries among the intelligences might be reconfigured."[21] The frames of knowing he presently

---

19. Lehrer, *Imagine*, 17.
20. Ibid., 30.
21. Gardner, *Frames*, xxi.

recognizes are: linguistic, musical, logical-mathematical, spatial, bodily-kinesthetic, interpersonal, intrapersonal, and naturalistic. The one-half frame is an existential one, which is when people are drawn toward ultimate things. For the most part he has included spirituality and moral sensitivity within each of the other frames, but the "one-half frame" at least acknowledges that there are children with a special interest and sensitivity to matters of ultimate concern. People who spend much time in Godly Play rooms with children have known this for many decades.

Gardner specifically related his theory of multiple intelligences to creativity in his *Creating Minds: An Anatomy of Creativity*,[22] citing examples from both the arts and the sciences. A creative insight might be developed in intra-psychic terms like Freud, in mathematical terms like Einstein, in visual art like Picasso, in music like Stravinsky, in words like T. S. Eliot, in dance like Martha Graham, or in social terms like Gandhi. Godly Play mentors are attuned to the many ways that children prefer for make meaning so they can support the development of their existential insights in an optimum way.

Questions have been raised about whether Gardner's criteria for defining his frames are adequate. A second query is whether all of his "intelligences" are really needed to adapt to life's demands. For example, couldn't dance and music be "talents"? Third, is there sufficient empirical evidence to support his conceptualization? Despite these important queries, the use of this theory in education for about thiry years has established its credibility and Godly Play makes use of it.

Closure

Loder's last step is verification, but that is part of Godly Play's development step. Godly Play gives more emphasis to closure than in Loder's scheme. Perhaps this is because he was describing the overwhelming presence of Christ, which was considered "convictional" or self-authenticating, and he may have assumed that the process virtually closes on its own in such a case. On the other hand, closure might even be *forced against* one's will by internal or social pressures or both. Closure also involves the creator's decision-making style and will-to-close, as well as the need to balance the lure of perfection against what is good enough to carry one's new idea forward to completion and communication. All

---

22. Gardner, *Creating*, xiii–xiv.

of these considerations are relevant, whether one is creating a new idea or becoming recreated by an encounter with God.

The closure of this process after the development of an insight can be hard and soft, as with the opening. A hard closure is rigid and is focused on the idea alone. A soft closure is firm but not rigid. It is focused on the creative process as a whole, as integrated with the person, rather than on the idea alone. The creative process is not isolated as something we do. It is connected with who we are.

The Use and Misuse of the Creative Process

When the creative process becomes detached from the *Imago Dei* as our deep identity it can be used for destructive purposes. Winnicott (1896-1971), the English pediatrician, child psychiatrist and psychoanalyst, recognized this. The transitional space he discovered in infants is the place where creativity, play, art, and religion come from, but it can also be corrupted to be the source for stealing, lying, fetishism, obsessive rituals and other destructive practices.[23] There is nothing in the pattern of the creative process that guarantees constructive outcomes unless it is integrated with the flow, play, love, and contemplation that is at our core as creative beings.

The misuse of the creative process for theft is a familiar one and a cornerstone for white-collar crime. A more action-based kind of theft was studied by Ikuya Sato. He reported in "Bosozoku: Flow in Japanese Motorcycle Gangs" that the thieves he studied exhibited all the personal satisfaction of creative flow, but the outcome was still anti-social and destructive.[24]

The misuse of the creative process for lying has also been studied. Dan Ariely at Duke University examined this in *The (Honest) Truth About Dishonesty*.[25] It takes creativity to lie to others, but the more destructive use of the creative process takes place when we deceive ourselves into having the confidence to deceive others well. This deception uses the creative process to attack the fundamental core of who we are meant to be. The lie most used for self-deception is that we are more intelligent and popular than we are. We create the illusion that we are

---

23. Winnicott, *Playing*, 5.
24. Csikszentmihalyi and Csikszentmihalyi, *Optimal*, 92–117.
25. Ariely, *(Honest) Truth*, 163–89.

too clever, too well liked, or too important to get caught. Another misuse is related to the rigidity of the closure. Loder noted that sometimes "people who have undergone remarkable experiences of transformation become authoritarian about scripture and spiritual laws." He wondered what caused the incongruity between "the freeing transformation and the rigid aftermath" and proposed three causes.[26]

The first cause of rigidity is fear. The "awesomeness of the Holy" results in "the suspicion that one is not quite oneself afterward." People begin to worry about "losing the good thing that has happened." The fear of losing control and of losing "the good thing" can combine with the "fear of aspersions cast on the experience by other people" to produce "an aggressive, authoritarian posture to defend the authenticity of the Holy and to drive away all detractors."

The second cause of rigidity comes from confusing God's power with personal power. When the dramatic experience of "the Spirit begins to wane, one tries to keep it or retrieve it, resulting in the temptation to substitute personal power for the Power of God." The resulting arrogance, *even if unconscious and not intended*, is blasphemy, a lack of reverence for God and contempt for the Holy.

The third cause of rigidity is a "general lack of thoughtful language about God's Spirit." People who experience God's presence desire to speak about it, but they are not always well equipped. As Loder put it, "One wants to say more but, not knowing how, says the same cliché three times, with ever-increasing volume." The "general lack of thoughtful language" does not necessarily indicate a lack of biblical language, which may be parroted, but because it is not integrated with one's constructive core, it can even be used to attack others and one's own well-being. This problem of rigidity continued to be considered by Kim V. Engelmann, a Presbyterian minister and one of the two Loder daughters. She addressed the need to be courageous, realistic, and prayerful to break out from a cycle of "false spirituality."[27]

Since scripture and liturgical practice is not declaimed, proclaimed, or announced in an overly solemn and authoritarian way in a Godly Play room, and since rigid and authoritarian behavior is not modeled there, it is unlikely that children will become rigid or get trapped in a spinning, self-defeating cycle of false spirituality. Instead, children are invited into

---

26. Loder, *Transforming*, 209–10.
27. Engelmann, *Running*, 45–61.

the experience of knowing God and the language of God through their own creative core. Godly Play fosters the art of playful orthodoxy to be deeply grounded and at the same time open to the potential of becoming graceful people.

Christian Language and the Wholeness of the Creative Process

The creative process has two phases, opening and closing. There is a danger of getting stuck in either. The "liberal" part of the process is related to opening and the "conservative" tendency is related to closing. Supporting the use of the whole process while learning Christian language helps prevent irrationally separating these two tendencies into two ways of life or political positions within or outside the church. Each of the five steps in the creative process also has a type of person who is especially drawn to it. There are openers, scanners, discoverers, developers, and closers. You may have served on adult committees where all five types were represented and in a Godly Play room you will also see all five types of children moving about. One of the many benefits of an open classroom is that mentors, who are sensitive to the steps in the creative process, can guide children who are stuck in a particular step toward enjoying the whole circle of the creative process to help reintegrate their fundamental core.

When hard or soft openings are experienced some people are eager to proceed. These are the openers. Their opposite, the nay-sayers, however, will not budge. They sit by the doorway to the creative process with their arms folded, challenging anyone to arouse wonder or openness in *them*! Both openers and nay-sayers can get stuck in the first step of the process. Scanners, however, love to open and continue on to scan, but they are not very interested in discovering any particular insight, which might require taking responsibility for it. Discovers are open to and tolerate the anxiety caused by the chaos of scanning, because they enjoy the thrill of the insight. Once the insight is discovered, however, this kind of person often loses interest and does not always follow through to develop the idea. Developers do not like the chaos of opening, scanning, or the thrill of the insight, so they are likely to take over another's insight and develop it. Finally, the closer can't stand any of the preceding four steps. She or he likes to stand back and decide which ideas, developed by other people, to keep and which to throw away. We need all five kinds of people. They all play a role, especially on teams for joint projects, but people who can move all the way through the whole process from opening to closure find a satisfaction that comes from exercising their fundamental wholeness, which contributes to their spiritual maturity.

Children in a Godly Play room, who say things like "Oh, we had that already," are encouraged to move towards openness. Parables are especially useful for this. The scanners, who may wander aimlessly about in the open space, are supported to get out some specific material to make their own discoveries and to develop them. Children who love insights are especially encouraged to develop their discoveries and bring them to fruition. Children who copy other children's work to develop it are guided to use their own creative process to make personal meaning. Children who stand off to the side and make comments about other children's work are encouraged to move through the whole process from beginning to end so they can experience evaluating *their own work*. When mentors guide and support children through the whole process, children tend to find more satisfaction in completing the whole circle than living with the fractured grace of being stuck in one of the steps. This wholeness liberates them from cultural constraints and their inner limitations to be truly free to develop into graceful people.

The Creative Process and Graceful People

We are creatures with biological, psychological, social, and spiritual dimensions, so our origin can be expected to be as complex as it is powerful. Complexity is not the opposite of simplicity, because it is more than intricacy, which only suggests something involved or perplexing. Complexity is the property of being closely connected and yet distinct. The creative process at our core begins in unity and then develops into four dimensions as the child grows and develops language, which is the major tool for making such distinctions.

The unity of our original grace falls apart into four dimensions of the creative process, each with its own language and use. This fracturing of our original wholeness is part of original sin and is part of our maturing, which cannot be avoided. As we grow, however, the potential to rejoin the four dimensions always remains and the return to original grace in a non-naïve way, despite original sin, can result in graceful moments and even graceful lives. It is this kind of spiritual maturity that

Jesus pointed to when he spoke about "becoming like a child" to enter his realm.

To say more about our core complexity, let's borrow a strategy from comparative biology called "homology." This is the study of similar traits in different animals. The similarity in the differentness suggests a common ancestor. For example if a particular bone is noticed in the forearm of a human, the leg of a dog, and the flipper of a whale, then, a single source is suggested. In the same way the psychological, social, biological, and spiritual dimensions of the creative process share the same structure, so, a common origin is suggested. Let's examine each one of these four dimensions to explore this structural affinity.

The Psychological Dimension of the Creative Process: "Flow"

The psychological study of the creative process took a leap forward in 1975 when one of the modern pioneers, Mihaly Csikszentmihalyi, published *Beyond Boredom and Anxiety*.[28] He argued that creativity appears in a middle range of activity between the extremes of tedious rigidity and anxiety-producing chaos. He found that this was true of many, seemingly diverse, activities, such as painting and mountain climbing, which he investigated. When one is over-whelmed by chaos or under-whelmed by boredom, creativity is frustrated. The middle way between chaos and rigidity is when creativity works best. Csikszentmihalyi used the term "flow" to describe how the creative process feels when it is working smoothly. In 1990 he published a book that focused on flow's structure as the optimal experience.[29]

Flow involves deep concentration. The sense of self disappears. Time is altered and the experience is enjoyed for itself rather than for any product that might arise out of it. When feedback is relatively immediate and the goals are clear, then flow is sustained. One's skills need to be stretched but not overwhelmed by real challenges. The placing of creativity in a middle realm between being over-whelmed and under-whelmed is different from but does not exclude Loder's overwhelming "transforming moment" in an encounter with the void. Such a conflict stimulates the creative process to create existential meaning.[30] But in

---

28. Csikszentmihalyi, *Beyond Boredom*, 35–54.
29. Csikszentmihalyi, *Flow*, 43–70.
30. Loder, *Transforming*, 18–26. Loder *appears* to stress justification and regenera-

theological terms Loder leaned more toward the dramatic experience of justification and regeneration where God's grace prevails while Csikszentmihalyi's theory leaned more toward the theological concept of sanctification, as an optimum experience, where God and the individual cooperate not for a transforming moment but for a lifetime.

There appears to be a natural rhythm between these two kinds of experience that finds its way into many religions in many centuries. Harvey Whitehouse, who works in the overlapping fields of archaeology, history and psychology proposed such a theory.[31] He called the two tendencies toward drama and continuity, "imagistic" and "doctrinal." Each is related to a specific kind of cognition, the "episodic memory system" for drama and the "semantic memory system" for continuity. Both are needed because the punctuation of the drama keeps the consistency alive and the consistency is needed to provide context for the drama.

Csikszentmihalyi's focus on optimum experience led him to argue that flow is the key to the good life and intrinsic motivation.[32] His scientific description of optimal experience, therefore, is a good companion for the theological study of the graceful person. Godly Play helps children dwell in the middle realm as they absorb and activate classical Christian language through the flow of the creative process, which links this language system to the dynamic source for becoming a graceful person.

The benefit of flow can also be seen by studying what happens when it is missing. Csikszentmihalyi did this in *The Evolving Self* and concluded that people will always seek the happiness associated with flow, even when they lack the discipline and knowledge to achieve it. They will settle for its *simulation*. He wrote that, "in such cases, the result of seeking enjoyment is entropy, rather than harmony."[33] In other words, flow cannot be maintained by artificial means, such as by drugs, because the

---

tion, which are acts of God alone, to the detriment of sanctification, which involves the person's involvement as well as God's grace. In my view Loder has a better balance between these two theological doctrines than is sometimes seen. The "Holy Spirit converges with the Eucharist" (114) and there is a "sanctifying unity" with Christ (115). He also talked about "doing something about one's convictional experience" (194) and the "sacramental community" (196). In addition he emphasized at times "continuity," "process," and "human agents" as being instrumental for the Christian life (208–9).

31. Whitehouse and Martin, *Theorizing*, 11, 205.
32. Csikszentmihalyi and Csikszentmihalyi, *Optimal*, 10–11.
33. Csikszentmihalyi, *Evolving*, 197–99.

real and constructive challenges for true creativity are missing. Godly Play seeks to stimulate and support the reality of flow and to support its close relationship to play, love, and contemplation to help keep alive the potential for all four dimensions of the person to be unified.

The Social Dimension of the Creative Process: Play

There is a great deal of overlap between flow and play. In fact, Csikszentmihalyi thought at first he was studying play before he carefully distinguished it from the creative process. As his project became clearer, he energized other students of creativity. Howard Gardner noted in his *Creating Minds* that when Csikszentmihalyi asked him, "Where is creativity?" instead of the usual, "What is creativity?," the scope of his study changed and took on new life.[34] Three years later Csikszentmihalyi published the next step in his life long study of creativity, which affirmed that creating is about two-thirds social.[35] In 2012 Jonah Lehrer's *Imagine: How Creativity Works*, a popular review of the field, was divided into two major sections: "Alone" (139 pages) and "Together" (114 pages). His presentation balanced the importance of the social and the solitary aspects of creativity, but he added that it takes the right mixture of people for the social aspect of creativity to work well.[36]

Creativity may be both individual and social, but play is always social, even when it appears to be solitary. Take a climber alone on a moun-

---

34. Gardner, *Creating*, 37.

35. Csikszentmihalyi, *Creativity*. Creativity's social dimension has three centers of influence. The first for Csikszentmihalyi is "the domain," where "a set of symbolic rules and procedures" reside. In Gardner's terminology this is "the work." It includes the relevant symbol system of the domain in which the creative individual is working. A second center is "the field," which for Csikszentmihalyi includes "all the individuals who act as gatekeepers to the domain." For Gardner this part of the creative process is called "other persons." They are family and peers in the early years. This group later expands to rivals, judges, and supporters (Gardner, *Creating*, 9). An idea, which is personally novel, becomes socially significant through the interaction among individuals, domains and fields (Gardner, *Creating*, 36). The third center of activity is "the person," who works in a particular domain (or sets up a new domain) and moves beyond personal creativity into being creative socially when the field accepts the new idea (Csikszentmihalyi, *Creativity*, 27–28). Gardner notes that a creative person "solves problems, fashions products, or defines new questions in a domain in a way that is initially considered novel but that ultimately becomes accepted in a particular cultural setting" (Gardner, *Creating*, 35).

36. Lehrer, *Imagine*, 139.

tain wall. The creative moves are made *with* the mountain and changing weather. The mountain's challenge is personal and existential, a matter of life and death. A less dramatic example is watching people play solitaire. They look alone, but the cards represent an imagined playmate they are interacting with. Perhaps, the most radical view of play's social dimension, however, was that of Johan Huizinga, the Dutch historian. In 1938 Huizinga played with the Latin title of his book *Homo Ludens*, to claim that human beings are fundamentally players. This characteristic defines them more fundamentally than the ability to create and work with tools (*Homo Faber*) or the ability to use reason (*Homo Sapiens*). Huizinga's view of play has often been misunderstood. He was not talking about amusing ourselves, silliness, or leisure activities. For him play was not an element *within* culture or an *alternative* to culture, both of which are interesting. He went much farther. Huizinga argued that play *is* culture, which is challenging.

We will use Catherine Garvey's study of play to show how it is related to the creative process. Her study was first published in 1977 and claimed "play" to be indefinable, so she carefully listed five characteristics, instead of proposing a definition. The characteristics are that "play is pleasurable," "has no extrinsic goals," "is spontaneous and voluntary," and "involves some active engagement on the part of the player." The fifth quality was that "play has been linked with creativity, problem solving, language learning, the development of social roles, and a number of other cognitive and social phenomena."[37] In the enlarged edition of 1990 she added two new chapters both of which amplify the social dimensions of play. Garvey's five characteristics of play are similar to Csikszentmihaliy's description of flow's characteristics.

The focus of Godly Play is on what is *personally* new for children in order to affirm the flow of the creative process for each child. When children create something new, it is renewing. Encouraging such self-directed learning was part of the Montessori tradition from the beginning. To create meaning, rather than being told answers, personally integrates the meaning made. Since ultimate meaning is about one's personal life and death, it needs to be personally discovered.

We have surveyed the similarities between flow and play. We turn now to the biological dimension of the creative process to examine its affinity with the creative process as well as its structural similarity to

---

37. Garvey, *Play*, 5.

flow, play, and contemplation. The biological dimension of the creative process is love.

The Biological Dimension of the Creative Process: Love

Love is usually thought of as a strong emotion, one that involves affection and attachment. The descriptions of love emphasize different elements, from a mother's love to loving one's enemies. Still, the many kinds of love have a strong biological base. For example "making love" results in the *creation* of new biological life and the attraction that draws people together is also very physical. A "limbic resonance" makes the match while the neocortex makes up reasons why the match is right.[38] The limbic system is where our "emotional intelligence" resides. It is "a capacity that profoundly affects all other abilities either facilitating or interfering with them." Since it developed before the neocortex, it can at times override our rationality.[39]

Thus, the biological dimension of love is so deep in our origins that it has links to all our seven basic affect systems. The more cerebral nuances of feeling and thinking are blends, derived from these primary systems located in the old brain. Jaak Panksepp and Lucy Biven identified the seven systems as: seeking, rage, fear, lust, care, panic/grief, and play.[40] Love is seeking. It moves toward newness, satisfaction, and creativity but is complicated by the rage associated with competing for scarce resources. Fundamental fear is not learned. It is a primal warning about danger during seeking. Lust is what pushes us toward creating offspring but is at times balanced with nonsexual caring for offspring and each other. Panic and grief come from the potential or actual loss of care. And play is how we learn how to manage the conflicts in the other affect systems, which provide the basis for the bio-psycho-social-spiritual blend we call love.

The kind of language most appropriate for connecting our thinking and emotions about love is poetry. It links the neocortex and the limbic system. In *A General Theory of Love*, the authors used an abridgement of

38. Lewis et al., *General*, 63.
39. Coleman, *Emotional*, 80–83.
40. The biological grounding of love incorporates the whole chorus of our affective systems. The study of the ancient parts of our brain is an expanding field, as demonstrated by such books as Jaak Panksepp's *Affective Neuroscience* and his book with Lucy Biven referred to in the text, *Archaeology of the Mind*.

Robert Frost's famous saying, at least among poets, to make their point. The saying was taken from a letter to Louis Untermeyer (January 1, 1916) and is: "A poem begins as a lump in the throat, a sense of wrong, a homesickness, a love sickness. It is never a thought to begin with."[41] This explains why the poetry of the Christian language system needs to be respected and celebrated. It can help connect the verbal and non-verbal aspects of love, so St. Paul's poem of love (1 Corinthians 13) will be our classical text used to describe love.

Choosing Paul to describe love may sound odd when stressing the biological dimension of the creative process. Wasn't Paul against the body? This view of Paul may come from reading him through the lens of the third to the fifth centuries. Theologians such Origen, Evagrius, The Cappadocians, and Augustine contrasted the spiritual to the physical and used metaphors for the maturation of spirituality like climbing a ladder or a mountain toward God and away from the physical. This view was heavily influenced by the Greek philosophy of Neo-Platonism. Paul's own view of the body was different.

Philip Sheldrake argued in *A Brief History of Spirituality* that what Paul meant by "the spiritual" was "life in the Spirit."[42] The Pauline letters contrasted "spirit" (*pneuma*) with "flesh" (*sarx*) as "two attitudes to life." If Paul had intended to contrast the "spiritual" and the "physical" he would have likely used the word "body" (*soma*). Sheldrake concluded that for Paul, "A "spiritual person" (see 1 Cor 2:14–15) was simply someone within whom the Spirit of God dwelt or who lived under the influence of the Spirit of God."[43] There is nothing in his poem of love that negates the body.

Paul claimed that love is freely given and received. It is patient, kind, not jealous, not boastful, not arrogant, and not rude. Love is also deeply engaging. He wrote that it bears, believes, hopes and endures all things. Love is so engaging that it lasts forever. Loving is done for itself. There is no extrinsic goal. That is why jealousy, arrogance, and boasting are not part of its reality. Language without love is empty. It is like "a noisy gong or a clanging symbol." Love, also, has links to other kinds of activities, such as ethics and creating meaning, much like play does. In Paul's terminology love is connected to the spiritual gifts, which are

41. Quoted without a source in Lewis et al., *General*, 34.
42. Sheldrake, *Brief*, 3.
43. Ibid., 2–3.

nothing without love (1 Cor 12:27—13:2) and to ethics and physical action, where loving one's neighbor fulfills the law (Rom 13:10).

In addition love is pleasurable, but this pleasure is profound. It incorporates both the pain of the crucifixion and the longed-for but perplexing wonder of the resurrection, which Paul personally experienced on the road to Damascus when Jesus turned his life around. Love, therefore, includes the depth of pain and the height of happiness for the whole person. The mixture of pain and happiness produces joy, which is the realistic and quintessential Christian emotion. When Paul contrasted God's Kingdom to the Roman Empire, he drew attention to a different kind of "place." It was a domain of righteousness, peace, and joy in the Holy Spirit (Rom 14:17). By contrast the Roman Empire was comprised of geography and *Pax Romana* was kept by force of arms and taxes.

Paul's poem in the context of the collection of the letters ascribed to him provides a richly nuanced and expansive view of love with a structure that is similar to and connected with the other three dimensions of the creative process. This brings us to the fourth dimension of the creative process, contemplation.

The Spiritual Dimension of the Creative Process: Contemplation

John Cassian (c. 360–435) learned about contemplation from the variety of contemplatives in the desert of Egypt in the fourth century. He then traveled to Constantinople, where he was ordained deacon, and then to Rome. Finally, he settled in Gaul, near Marseilles, and in 415 built the Abbey of St. Victor, which shaped Christian monastic life for centuries to come. His work influenced Benedict's Rule in the sixth century and, thus, the later reforms of the Benedictine order by the Cistercians and Trappists.

Richard of St. Victor's classic definition of contemplation is the one we shall use. Richard, who was probably born in Scotland, traveled to Paris to study with the Augustinian canons, especially Hugo, at the Abby of St. Victor. He was Abbot from 1162 until he died in 1173, and was the primary spiritual writer in the West during the twelfth century. In the next century his work influenced Bonaventure (1221–74), who was Minister General of the Franciscan Order and taught at the University of Paris, overlapping briefly the time that Thomas Aquinas taught there. Bonaventure's *Itinerarium Mentis in Deum (Journey of the Soul into*

God) is the main work that continued Richard's influence during the thirteenth century. In the next century Dante (1265–1321) wrote in his *Paradiso* that Richard of St. Victor was a person "who in contemplation was more than man."[44]

Richard was at home in the disputations of the University of Paris and in the quiet of the cloister, so from personal experience he could distinguish the knowing of the body by the senses, from the knowing of the mind by reason, and the knowing of the spirit by contemplation. He also lived in a century when the traditions of romantic and divine love influenced each other and "fed into the development of affective mysticism which in turn encouraged greater interest in the development of spiritual guidance."[45]

Richard's definition of contemplation was that: "Contemplation is the free more penetrating gaze of a mind suspended with wonder concerning the manifestations of wisdom."[46] Contemplation sets all distractions aside by the openness of wonder to be with God without words. This definition of contemplation shares the same basic structure as the other three dimensions of the creative process.

Opening is connected to the giftedness and voluntary aspect of the four dimensions. You cannot force someone to love, enjoy flow, play, or contemplate. *Scanning* is linked to the deep engagement and searching quality in all four dimensions. *Insight* is associated with engaging this process for itself without much thought of any product that might result. Insights appear, seemingly of their own volition, rather than being forced. *Development* connects flow, play, love, and contemplation to other parts of life. *Closure* brings satisfaction and enables the discovery to be communicated.

There are some differences among the four dimensions, but these are matters of detail. They do not contradict but enrich each other. For example the details from Csikszentmihalyi's description of flow fill in, rather than conflict with, the ways that love, play and contemplation are discussed. Csikszentmihalyi and Garvey have both added helpful nuances to Richard's "more penetrating gaze of a mind" and "suspension with wonder." They also help extend the meaning of his "manifestations of wisdom." The shared structures, therefore, help interpret and enrich

---

44. Dante, *Divine Comedy*, 115.
45. Sheldrake, *Brief*, 77.
46. Richard of St. Victor, *Twelve*, 157.

each other as well as give definition to the creative process from which they come.

Conclusion

Making the "creative act" the "central emphasis" of Christian education (the spiritual guidance of children) not only involves the learning of classical Christian language while creating existential meaning as the means for spiritual guidance and community. It also involves knowing God. This approach follows both the path of Sayers (coming close to God) and Loder (God coming close to us) to integrate the dramatic and ordinary experience of God, to keep in creative tension the traditions of Jonathan Edwards and Horace Bushnell in touch with each other, and to hold together the theological doctrines of justification and regeneration with sanctification and natural theology with grace.

Karl Barth wrote at the beginning of *Church Dogmatics*: "I regard the *analogia entis* as the invention of Antichrist, and I believe that because of it it is impossible ever to become a Roman Catholic, all other reasons for not doing so being to my mind short-sighted and trivial."[47] This startling statement stimulated a decade long discussion between Barth and Roman Catholic theologians such as Przywara, who wrote the book about the *analogia entis* in 1932 that Barth was reacting to, and von Balthazar, who wrote a study of Barth which Barth himself said was the best ever written about him. In 2012 this discussion was reopened in a less absolutist way than Barth left it by a collection of articles, including both Roman Catholic and Protestant theologians, entitled *The Analogy of Being: Invention of the Antichrist or the Wisdom of God?*[48] The resulting discussion, embodying both agreement and disagreement, affirms the approach taken in Godly Play.

The distinction made by Barth very early in the *Church Dogmatics* softened as his theology continued to develop, although he never admitted that he had misunderstood Przywara's view of the *analogia entis*, which is the consensus of scholars today. Nor did he withdraw his early statement. It is probably true that "Barth had found in the notion of the *analogia entis* a foil with which to reiterate the Reformation negation of Catholic natural theology—a task made all the more urgent by what he

---

47. Barth, *CD*, 1/1, xiii.
48. White, *Analogy*.

took to be liberal theology's retrieval of all that was wrong with traditional natural theology."[49] Barth was, perhaps, reacting to Schleiermacher even more than he was to Przywara's book. An analogy keeps its terms separate or it cannot function beneficially and does not blur them in mathematics or theology, as Barth feared. In addition in both Catholic and Protestant theology the analogy is made within the context of Christ's revelation in scripture and worship.

At the heart of Godly Play the influence of Barth's Christocentrism and the classical metaphysics of being stemming from St. Augustine and St. Thomas are correlated, rather than blurred, in a unified approach to the spiritual guidance of children, as coming close to God and God coming close to us. If one really considers God to be transcendent, then, as David Bently Hart says, "True divine transcendence, it turns out, transcends even the traditional metaphysical divisions between the transcendent and the immanent." There is a kind of "transcendent immediacy." God is not "the supreme being set atop the summit of beings, but the one who is transcendently present in all beings, the ever more inward act within each finite act."[50]

In Godly Play both the *analogia entis* (analogy of being) and Barth's similar *analogia fidei* (analogy of Christ) are available to children verbally in the lessons by speaking of people coming close to God and God coming close to people. These words are coupled with the nonverbal openness of the children's mentors to this mystery. One's relationship with God is, after all, a relationship that involves knowing God from beyond in creation (*analogia entis*), knowing God beside us as a redemptive companion (*analogia fidei*), and within us as the Holy Spirit (God's presence without words "within each finite act")—all at once, all of the time, and in every place within the experience of creating and being like the Creator, who recreates us by grace.

---

49. Di Noia, "Forward," xii.
50. Hart, "Destiny," 408.

Works Cited

Ariely, Dan. *The (Honest) Truth about Dishonesty: How We Lie to Everyone—Especially Ourselves*. New York: Harper, 2012.

Barth, Karl. *Church Dogmatics, 1/1*. Translated by G. W. Bromiley and T. F. Torrance. London: T. & T. Clark, 2004.

Berryman, Jerome, W. *Children and the Theologians: Clearing the Way for Grace*. New York: Morehouse, 2009.

———. *The Complete Guide to Godly Play*. Vols. 1-8. Denver: Morehouse Education Resources, 2002–2012.

———. *Godly Play: An Imaginative Approach to Religious Education*. Minneapolis: Augsburg, 1995.

———. "The Parable of the Good Shepherd." In *The Complete Guide to Godly Play*, 3:77–86. Denver: Morehouse Education Resources, 2002–2012.

———. *The Spiritual Guidance of Children: The Montessori Tradition and Godly Play*. New York: Church Publishing, 2013.

———. *Teaching Godly Play: How To Mentor the Spiritual Development of Children*. 2nd ed. Denver: Morehouse Education Resources, 2009.

Coleman, Daniel. *Emotional Intelligence*. New York: Bantam, 2005.

Csikszentmihalyi, Mihalyi. *Beyond Boredom and Anxiety: The Experience of Play in Work and Games*. San Francisco: Jossey-Bass, 1975.

———. *Creativity: Flow and the Psychology of Discovery and Invention*. New York: HarperCollins, 1996.

———. *The Evolving Self: A Psychology for the Third Millenium*. New York: Harper Perennial, 1993.

———. *Flow: The Psychology of Optimal Experience*. New York: Harper Perennial, 1990.

Csikszentmihalyi, Mihalyi, and Isabella Selega Csikszentmihalyi. *Optimal Experience: Psychological Studies of Flow in Consciousness*. Cambridge: Cambridge University Press, 1995.

Dante Alighieri. *The Divine Comedy: Paradiso, Volume III, Part I*. Translated by Charles S. Singleton. Princeton: Princeton University Press, 1991.

Di Noia, J. Augustine. "Forward." In *The Analogy of Being: Invention of the Antichrist or the Wisdom of God*, edited by Thomas Joseph White, i–xii. Grand Rapids: Eerdmans 2011.

Englemann, Kim V. *Running in Circles: How False Spirituality Traps Us in Unhealthy Relationships*. Downers Grove, IL: InterVarsity, 2007.

Gardner, Howard. *Creating Minds: An Anatomy of Creativity Seen Through the Lives of Freud, Einstein, Picasso, Stravinsky, Eliot, Graham, and Gandhi*. New York: Basic Books, 1993.

———. *Frames of Mind: The Theory of Multiple Intelligences*. 3rd ed. New York: Basic Books, 2011.

Garvey, Catherine. *Play: The Developing Child*. 2nd ed. Cambridge, MA: Harvard University Press, 1990.

Hart, David Bentley. "The Destiny of Christian Metaphysics." In *Analogy of Being: Invention of the Antichrist or the Wisdom of God*, edited by Thomas Joseph White, 395–410. Grand Rapids: Eerdmans 2011.

Lehrer, Jonah. *Imagine: How Creativity Works*. New York: Houghton Mifflin Harcourt, 2012.

Lewis, Thomas, et al. *A General Theory of Love*. New York: Random House, 2000.

Loder, James E., Jr. *Religious Pathology and Christian Faith*. Philadelphia: Westminster, 1966.

———. *The Transforming Moment*. 2nd ed. Colorado Springs: Helmers & Howard, 1989.

Marcel, Gabriel. *Creative Fidelity*. Translated by Robert Rosenthal. New York: Fordham University Press, 2001.

Panksepp, Jaak. *Affective Neuroscience: The Foundation of Human and Animal Emotions*. Oxford: Oxford University Press, 2004.

Panksepp, Jaak, and Lucy Biven. *The Archaeology of the Mind: Neuroevolutionary Origins of Human Emotions*. New York: Norton, 2012.

Richard of St. Victor. *The Twelve Patriarchs: The Mystical Ark; Book Three of the Trinity*. Translated by Grover A. Zinn. New York: Paulist, 1979.

Sawyer, R. Keith. *Explaining Creativity: The Science of Human Innovation*. Oxford: Oxford University Press, 2012

Sayers, Dorothy L. *The Mind of the Maker*. London: Mowbray, 1994.

Sheldrake, Philip. *A Brief History of Spirituality*. Oxford: Blackwell, 2011.

White, Thomas Joseph, ed. *The Analogy of Being: Invention of the Antichrist or the Wisdom of God*. Grand Rapids: Eerdmans, 2011.

Whitehouse, Harvey, and Luther H. Martin. *Theorizing Religions Past: Archaeology, History, and Cognition*. Walnut Creek, CA: AltaMira, 2004.

Winnicott, D. W. *Playing and Reality*. London: Tavistock, 1982.

Wyckoff, D. Campbell. *Theory and Design of Christian Education Curriculum*. Philadelphia: Westminster, 1962.

Yalom, Irvin D. *Existential Psychotherapy*. New York: Basic Books, 1980.

5

Baptizing John Dewey

James Loder's Pedagogy of Presence in Theory and Practice

THOMAS JOHN HASTINGS

> *. . . transformational logic may be called the grammar of the knowing event, and the knowing event may occur in contexts as seemingly alien as puzzle solving, scientific discovery, poetry writing, and religious conversion*
>
> —JAMES E. LODER, *TRANSFORMING MOMENT*

Loder's Debt to, and Transformation of, Dewey

After teaching a seminary course for many years in the philosophy of education that included an intensive segment on John Dewey, it dawned on me one day that the transformational epistemology of James Loder is a philosophically-nuanced Reformed theological expansion of Dewey's scientific method. One of Loder's lifelong conversation partners, Dewey saw the scientific method as the best way to equip an educated citizenry to become competent to make the kinds of rational judgments that contribute to a robust democratic society. That Loder's theory takes a page directly from Dewey's book is obvious when you place the steps of the scientific method next to the steps of transformational logic:[1]

Dewey: Scientific Method	Loder: Transformational Logic
1. Problem	1. Conflict
2. Rational Formulation	2. Interlude for Scanning
3. Exploration/Hypothesis	3. Constructive act/Imagination
4. Best Hypothesis Selected	4. Release and Opening
5. Hypothesis Tested	5. Interpretation

Loder's educational philosophy, which I want to call a "pedagogy of presence," focuses on our participation in the life of God as both the source of the human spirit and the goal of "its genuine but blind longing" across a lifetime.[2] While Loder was highly appreciative of Dewey's experience-centered pedagogy that sought to nurture well-informed Americans for participation in democratic social institutions, he was equally critical of his instrumentalist ideology that repudiated the humanistic educational tradition and left no time or space in the curriculum for metaphysics or the life of the spirit. If Dewey's pedagogy of experience has a proximate or pragmatic end, Loder's pedagogy of presence has a theological or transformational end. Yet it would be a serious error to conclude from this that Loder was a teary-eyed, other-worldly mystic when compared with Dewey, the hard-nosed, this-worldly pragmatist.

As just one example of how Loder defies such a caricature, he offers in chapter 4 of *The Transforming Moment* a Christian alternative, on the one hand, to Eastern spiritual transformations that appear to take people "out of historical reality,"[3] and on the other hand, to "an erroneous Western Christian view of transformation" that accentuates "the historical, almost to the exclusion of the spiritual." He calls instead for "authentic Christian conviction" that retains both "continuity and the power of transformation." While he was not yet using the formulation of Chalcedon to depict asymmetrical bi-polar relational unities, the

---

1. This presentation of Dewey's scientific method is taken from Loder's own presentation of Dewey's *How We Think*. See Loder, *Transforming*, 44.

2. Loder, *Logic*, 12.

3. It must be said that Loder's understanding of Eastern thought was very limited, and the fact that he mentions Japanese Zen Buddhism probably should be read more as an apologetic gesture at a contemporary Western trend rather than a result of a serious study of Zen in its Japanese context.

Christocentric logic is already present here in tacit form.[4] "Christianity, true to the complete logic of transformation, returns every insight, vision, or image to its historical context as the locus of God's redemptive action."[5] Because Jesus Christ is in Kierkegaard's Chalcedonian shorthand the God-man, his followers resist spiritualties that either denigrate or idolize history. It is Loder's willingness to hold on to this core paradox that gives his theory its dynamic biblical, theological, and scientific character.

To return to Dewey, in chapter 2 of *The Transforming Moment* Loder is critical of Dewey's paradigm, and by extension Piaget, for two faults: (1) Failing to take the imaginative and intuitive dimensions of the knowing event seriously; and (2) For being overly concerned with "consistency in performance and conformity to known frames of reference." Loder had a conviction of a deep or hidden order toward which transformational epistemic events move and was therefore sensitive to the need for the broadest possible range of perceptual modalities to disclose this order. For knowing to more faithfully plumb and reveal the inexhaustible richness and depth of this four-dimensional order,[6] he thought it must embrace imaginative and intuitive forms of knowing, as well as more rationalistic formulations. Hence, it would be a huge misunderstanding to conclude that Loder rejects rationalist formulations *per se*. Rather he insists on the need for reason to be complemented by other registers of knowing.

---

4. Of Chalcedon, George Hunsinger writes, "The minimalism of Chalcedon, in other words, is not only constitutive but also regulative. It is constitutive with respect to salvation, and regulative with respect to interpretation. More precisely, it is constitutive regarding Christ's person in the work of salvation, and regulative for the church in its interpretation of Scripture. As a hermeneutical construct in particular, Chalcedon offers no more and no less than a set of spectacles for bringing the central witness of the New Testament into focus. It suggests that just because Jesus was fully God, that does not mean he was not also fully human; and that just because he was fully human, that does not mean he was not also fully God. When the New Testament depicts Jesus in his divine power, status, and authority, it presupposes his humanity; and when it depicts him in his human finitude, weakness and mortality, it presupposes his deity. No interpretation will be adequate which asserts the one at the expense of the other" (Hunsinger, "Karl Barth's Christology," 128).

5. Loder, *Transforming*, 96.

6. Loder described four dimensions of human existence, as they are related to the logic of transformation, in terms of knowing events within "the lived world," "the self," "the void," and "the Holy." See Loder, *Transforming*, 67–91.

Charging that the imaginative theoretical breakthroughs of both Dewey and Piaget actually subvert their epistemically restrictive paradigms, Loder writes, "Had Dewey followed this procedure (= the scientific method), he would have remained a philosophical idealist; Piaget would have stayed with Simon in Paris constructing standardized tests, and neither would have made the contributions for which they are so widely noted." Loder claims Dewey and Piaget fall prey to the eikonic eclipse, "a theory of error in which rationalistic assumptions about truth cut off reason from its generative sources in personal knowledge and the imagination."[7] Loder is challenging what he sees as an excessive rationalism and reductionism in the scientific method and, while highly valuing its contribution as far as it goes, seeks to open it up to the personal and imaginative dimensions of knowing. Into this critical discussion of Dewey and Piaget, Loder introduces Einstein as a scientist who positively exemplifies the transformational pattern and whose "intuition and insight bypassed experimental findings to generate new facts."[8]

To reiterate, in terms of pedagogical theory, while Dewey believed the scientific method is the most practical way for building a healthy democratic society, Loder believed that the living God is bringing about the reordering of persons, history, and the cosmos through divinely-initiated transformations that conform to the cruciform pattern of the Risen Lord Jesus Christ. Hence, the relation of Loder to Dewey is not as an other-worldly mystic to a this-worldly pragmatist. Rather, it is as a nuanced confessional Reformed theologian who maintained strong doctrines of incarnation (as source) and redemption (as destiny) to a pragmatic philosopher or ethicist who had abandoned metaphysics in the interest of building a good modern society. Loder never lost his sense of deep respect for Dewey. He acknowledges his debt to the final step of his scientific method, saying, ". . . once the results of transformational thinking are given and one enters the last step of 'correspondence,' Dewey's paradigm becomes useful."[9] In this way, the structural overlay of Dewey's scientific method and Loder's transformational logic remain, even as they are clearly distinct on presuppositions, ultimate ends, and epistemic boundary conditions.

---

7. Loder, *Transforming*, 223 (text slightly altered).
8. Ibid., 47.
9. Ibid., 48.

Having briefly touched on how transformational logic both builds on and breaks open the framework of the scientific method to imaginative and intuitive forms of perception, I will now switch to an autobiographical narrative style in order to unpack how I personally experienced Loder's pedagogical practice at a key turning point in my life and vocation. The point here is not to draw attention to my own story *per se*, but to offer a personal example of what I call a "pedagogy of presence." Taking his cue from Kierkegaard and Polanyi, Loder saw subjectivity or personal knowledge as integral to genuinely scientific work. Thank you for bearing with me as I briefly recount my personal story in the interest of demonstrating Loder's theory in practice.

Embodying the Theory in Practice[10]

Briefly, transformational logic includes the five moments: (1) *Conflict*, when we sense and become concerned that our current understanding no longer provides an adequate account for new experience; (2) *Interlude for Scanning*, when we actively seek out possible approaches and solutions to the conflict; (3) *Constructive Act of the Imagination*, when a convincing solution suddenly appears; (4) *Release and Opening*, when energy is released and we are opened up in a new way to our original context; and (5) *Interpretation*, when we make sense of how the solution relates back to the original conflict (congruence) and what it may offer to a broader public (correspondence).[11]

I had already spent six and one-half years teaching in Japan when I arrived at Princeton Theological Seminary as a special student in fall of 1991. I came there to study with the person who wrote *The Transforming Moment*, a book that had given me an adequate if not exhaustive language for understanding my own adult conversion experience or reaffirmation of faith. Dr. Loder was assigned to be my advisor, and on that first day we met in the seminary cafeteria, I shared with him some version of the following story.

Born into a somewhat devout pre-Vatican II, working-class Irish Roman Catholic family in Massachusetts, my mother had hoped I would someday take up a vocation in the priesthood. Up until my early

---

10. In his recently published dissertation, Kenneth Kovacs comments on Loder's educational and counseling methodologies. See Kovacs, *Relational*.

11. Loder, *Transforming*, 35–44.

teens, I attended confession every Saturday, mass every Sunday, and Confraternity of Christian Doctrine classes every week. Mom prayed for us every morning before we set off for school. I regularly prayed the rosary before sleeping, attended daily mass and Stations of the Cross during Lent, and sometimes, special late night Easter vigils with my dad in the darkened sanctuary of Saint Joseph's, our parish church. I always looked forward to the visits from my mother's first cousins, Father Hugh, a Franciscan priest who lived in a monastery in the Midwest, and Brother Bill, a Xavierian Brother who taught at an all boys' high school in Brooklyn. As a child, I knew myself as one called to a life of worship, wonder, and witness, and my yet-to-be-realized vocation was nurtured within a supportive religious community.

I attended local public schools in Massachusetts, which were then under the strong influence of Dewey's educational theory and a Puritan or post-Puritan ethos that was not overly hospitable to newly arrived Catholic immigrant families like mine. Entering adolescence in the middle of the turbulent 1960s, I began to mourn not only the loss of my own childhood, but also my belief in the inherent goodness and trustworthiness of human beings, most especially, of course, adults over the age of thirty. The churches I knew seemed hopelessly out of synch with the turbulent times. (Let's call this my "conflict in context" that launched an "interlude for scanning" lasting several years). Feasting on dangerous books such as *On Walden Pond, The Naked Ape,* and *Soul on Ice*, I started skipping Sunday Mass at 13 and came out publicly as an agnostic at age 16. At Boston College, I studied literature and philosophy, critically absorbing the Christian humanism if not the piety of the Jesuit tradition. After graduation, I took a job teaching at a private, residential school for serious juvenile offenders. But it soon dawned on me that I was unable to help those deeply troubled young people with literature and philosophy alone.

Just then I met Carol, the daughter of Revs. Bill and Marilyn Jo Tolley, the first Presbyterian clergy couple in the history of New York Presbytery. On the surface, our backgrounds could not have been more different—she purportedly a descendant of William Bradford, the first governor of the Massachusetts Bay Colony—and me a third generation Irish American. But with our lives in close conjunction, we gratefully acknowledged that we both had been nurtured by caring Protestant and Catholic families and faith communities. We were married in August,

1977 in Carol's parents' church in Brooklyn. Yet at this point neither of us expressed any interest in returning to church.

In November that year we were sent to Western Samoa by the Peace Corps to teach in a government high school. Christianity had been seamlessly woven into the fabric of traditional Samoan culture, and because of the efforts of a vibrant Youth for Christ movement, the faith of many of our students had been strangely rekindled. Carol and I were both puzzled and moved by our students' exuberant and sincere expressions of love for Jesus Christ. However, I still insisted on calling myself an agnostic. I was still scanning for possible solutions to my original conflict. In Samoa, we also made friends with Japanese volunteers and decided that Japan would be the next stop on our journey. We both got jobs teaching English in Japan where we met a bright, evangelical missionary who knew I was seriously engaged in the practice of Zen Buddhist meditation. He prodded me to read the Gospels with him. I took up his challenge with the secret intention of hoping to undermine what I then viewed as his hopelessly naïve and narrow faith. However, the more I read and reflected on what we were reading, the more I felt drawn to Jesus as he comes to us in the narratives and sayings of the Gospels, and the more I felt a rekindling of the earlier sense of God's calling on my life. One night soon after Rose, our first child, was born, I suddenly felt a strong impulse to pray in the name of Jesus Christ (This was my "constructive act of the imagination" that burst upon me unexpectedly). It was the first time I had prayed in many years. As I prayed, I felt a sensation of being bathed in a warm embrace.

Carol and I started attending a local Japanese Protestant church. We spent much time praying, studying the Bible, discussing theology, and trying to discern the will of God for our lives, which had now taken a very unanticipated turn (My "release and opening" and "interpretation"). We publicly reaffirmed our faith in Jesus Christ and began to discern a call to serve in Japan. When we returned to the States, I taught in a private, interdenominational Christian school. Our second and third children, Paul and Sarah, were born. After receiving a full scholarship to attend Wheaton College Graduate School, we headed to the Midwest. There we spent two very happy years studying and living in student housing with Christians of all backgrounds from Argentina, China, Germany, Ghana, Hong Kong, Japan, Korea, Nigeria, and the U.S. After graduating from Wheaton, we returned to Japan and in 1988 we were officially appointed as Presbyterian mission co-workers with our first assignment at a junior college for women. After completing a four and a half year term, we were given a home assignment and I enrolled at Princeton Theological Seminary as a special student taking doctoral seminars and courses for ordination.

This finally brings me back to my first personal encounter with Dr. Loder and what I want to call his "pedagogy of presence." Frankly, as a cradle Irish Catholic and graduate of Boston College, as one who had studied Zen and experienced a reawakening to Christian faith in Japan, as a Wheaton grad and now as a foreign missionary, I felt like something of an outsider at Princeton Theological Seminary in 1991. Some faculty and students seemed to have some need to communicate to me that they thought PTS was intellectually, theologically, and indeed culturally superior to my cradle Irish Roman Catholicism and adopted liberal evangelicalism. However, Dr. Loder embraced my Irish Catholic upbringing, my Jesuit and evangelical education, and the many twists and turns in my journey that had led to my adult reaffirmation of faith and my missionary calling to Japan. Most of all, he affirmed and celebrated my sincere hunger for a more adequate language to comprehend what had happened to me and what happens to others who perceived themselves as having been touched by grace. While he had what is considered to be an elite education in this country, at Carlton, PTS, and Harvard, he was not an elitist. In short, he did not judge me according to his own native sociocultural or economic background. Nor did he try to reduce me or my story to some pre-determined framework. He warmly accepted and welcomed me in my full subjectivity and limitations. It was soon obvious that he had a radically egalitarian view of the human person, not because of a political ideology but because of his conviction of the Spirit's free and sovereign operation. Indeed, since his real interest was in how the Holy Spirit opens up the human spirit to hitherto hidden ranges of complexity and possibility, he was not in the least bit uncomfortable with, or threatened, by my background. I think he took great joy in witnessing the countless, unique ways that his students experienced the logic of transformation. Like a midwife assisting in the delivery of a child, he always seemed to be expecting the approaching arrival of new insight or discovery. From the time we prayed at that first meeting in the seminary cafeteria and subsequently up to the time of his death in 2001, when I was finally able to return from Japan to PTS to complete my doctoral work, I always felt the sensation of God's embrace through him. This is perhaps the greatest gift a teacher can give.

Conclusion

I know that many graduates of PTS could similarly testify to the embrace of the Spirit through the ministry of this unusually gifted and passionate mentor. In conclusion, I would like to suggest some tentative characteristics of Loder's "pedagogy of presence" (transformational logic in action) that might help inform our own interactions with learners of all ages.

Attention to Presence

Paying attention to the presence of God and to the presence of the other person in the presence of God. Jim made time for me and always listened very carefully before responding to me. This attentiveness was more than a counseling technique he had picked up at the Menninger Clinic. It was a spiritual or prayerful attentiveness that shaped his own spirit over a lifetime of discipleship, a discipleship characterized by much personal suffering or passion. Both in one-on-one situations and in the classroom, he always embodied this prayerful and passionate disposition. Whether I unexpectedly ran into him on campus or had a scheduled meeting, he acted as if our encounters were sacred, and I felt like I was participating with him in an unfolding sacred story. I never once got the sense I was keeping him from more important things. He never looked at his watch. He listened carefully to try to discern the Spirit's work in me.

Active Faith in the Holy Spirit's Transforming Work

Trusting the Spirit will eventually give language that adequately expresses insights into the hidden order that arise from our perceptual and cognitive experience. Neuroscientists also say that perception, in conjunction with cognition, drives the motors of our language and decisions. Through the window of this evolutionary pattern of perception-cognition-language-action, Jim was moved with wonder and seemed to glimpse the agency of the Holy Spirit. He was very widely read and densely articulate. Able to converse intelligently on a broad range of subjects, some say he was the smartest member of the PTS faculty. However,

I should also mention that some of his colleagues have reported that he had a competitive or argumentative streak. Thankfully, it seems he was more merciful with his students than with some of his colleagues. Unlike some pedagogical relationships where there is always a tacit or even explicit power dynamic at work, I never felt oppressed by Jim even though he had the highest academic standards. There was a sense that there was much more at stake in this pedagogical relation that transcended the institutional restrictions and requirements of PTS. I felt inspired by him and worked very hard. He communicated his personal support in the unflinching conviction that God was always at work, even in the mundane environs of the classroom or library. While I often felt tongue-tied when speaking with him, he never put me down for my inadequate knowledge. He never overtly or even subtly compared my ability with that of other brighter or more articulate students. He actively encouraged me to keep thinking and keeping seeking adequate words even when I felt like I was stammering. He loved to quote Polanyi who said "we know much more than we can tell." His confidence in the Spirit's work in me gave me the confidence that my perception and cognition had intrinsic value and that they would eventually find adequate expression in language and action. This was a huge gift and one I have sought to emulate in my own life and work.

Imminent Expectation

Expecting new light to burst upon every pedagogical encounter, Dr. Loder seemed to expect that God the Holy Spirit, the Real Teacher, would show up at any minute. While he was brilliant, he was open to the Spirit and teachable. He loved, for example, to hear me share my experiences and insights into Japanese Christianity or theology and would say, "I did not know that." Just before he died, we met to discuss my work in progress. He said, "Tom, I have so much more to learn, I feel like I am just beginning to understand, so I think the Lord really wants me to keep teaching." I hear in Jim's eschatological urgency an echo of the conclusion of T. S. Eliot's *Four Quartets*.

> With the drawing of this Love and the voice of this Calling
> We shall not cease from exploration
> And the end of all our exploring
> Will be to arrive where we started

And know the place for the first time.
Through the unknown, unremembered gate
When the last of earth left to discover
Is that which was the beginning;
At the source of the longest river
The voice of the hidden waterfall
And the children in the apple-tree
Not known, because not looked for
But heard, half-heard, in the stillness
Between two waves of the sea.
Quick now, here, now, always—
A condition of complete simplicity
(Costing not less than everything)
And all shall be well and
All manner of thing shall be well
When the tongues of flames are in-folded
Into the crowned knot of fire
And the fire and the rose are one.[12]

Jim Loder never stopped his explorations, but he was grateful for, and contented with, the proleptic glimpses of the hidden order that points toward the ultimate transformation of all things when we will know fully even as we have been fully known. May we also convey a robust attention, faith, and expectation in our own pedagogical theory and practice.

12. Eliot, *Four Quartets*, 145.

Works Cited

Eliot, T. S. *The Four Quartets.* In *The Complete Poems and Plays, 1909–1950.* 19th ed. New York: Harcourt, Brace and World, 1971.

Hunsinger, Geroge. "Karl Barth's Christology: Its Basic Chalcedonian Character." In *The Cambridge Companion to Karl Barth*, edited by John Webster, 127–42. Cambridge: Cambridge University Press, 2000.

Kovacs, Ken E. *The Relational Theology of James E. Loder: Encounter and Conviction.* New York: Peter Lang, 2011.

Loder, Jame E., Jr. *The Logic of the Spirit: Human Development in Theological Perspective.* San Francisco: Jossey-Bass, 1998.

———. *The Transforming Moment.* 2nd ed. Colorado Springs: Helmers & Howard, 1989.

6

Pedagogical Implications of Loder's Theory of Transformation

LAUREN SEMPSROTT FOSTER

Introduction

James E. Loder, in his 1979 inaugural address for an endowed chair at Princeton Theological Seminary, offered a theory of transformation as well as pedagogical implications of that theory. He gave this address prior to the published work entitled *The Transforming Moment*. Loder addresses the important pedagogical implications of this transformational process and the kinds of perversions in education that might lead to stunting and arresting transformation. He specifies five types of learning in their positive and negative forms that may encourage or retard transformation. These five types of learning go hand-in-hand with his work on the five steps of the transforming moment. That is, he presents the steps here not as a part of a moment of transformation but as types of Christian learning tasks, "intentionally fostered forms of learning by which one comes to participate in the ongoing transformational Spirit of Christ."[1] Thus we find that in this inaugural address, Loder presents five types of learning that relate deeply to transformation in Christian education and give concrete form to the grammar of transformation in learn-

---

1. Loder, "Transformation," 21.

ing. For Loder, transformation is intrinsic to human meaning making. Therefore it is logical for one to use transformational logic in designing learning experiences. In light of this belief, there are ways to practically apply Loder's five types of learning to designing learning experiences towards opening up opportunities for redemptive transformation.

Transformational Grammar and Learning

For Loder, transformation is more than a simple discovery that changes a person's thinking or actions. He writes, "The convicted person believes that the very nature of one's being is changed by the Convictor through the transforming event."[2] This type of redemptive transformation is quite different from the idea of transformation as seen by the rest of the world and is an important idea to consider when beginning to think about transformational grammar and learning in Loder's terms.

Loder specifies in his presentation of the five steps of transformation that one may enter into the pattern at any point and work either backward or forward through the process. It is important to keep in mind that no matter where one enters into the pattern there must be some sense of fluidity and relationship among the steps. Likewise, there must be relationship among these types of learning in order to create space for transformation. Transformational logic seeks completion because it bears a sense of an ending. Therefore, to isolate the steps is to cut off this drive of the human spirit for completion. The five steps, then, are: (1) A conflict borne with persistence; (2) Interlude and scanning; (3) Insight felt with intuitive force; (4) Release and redirection of the psychic energy bound up with the original conflict; and (5) Interpretation, which tests the insight for coherence with the terms of the conflict and for correspondence with the public context of the original conflict.[3] All of these steps relate directly to the five learning tasks that Loder addresses. Interestingly enough, Loder acknowledges that each of these learning tasks can be arrested or perverted in an educational context. It is vital, therefore, to begin Christian education with the belief in the guiding principle of transformation.[4] Even the soundest types of learning may be perverted if the educators and/or learners are not guided into

---

2. Loder, *Transforming*, 67.
3. Loder, "Transformation," 14.
4. Ibid., 21.

transformation by the Spirit of God. Assuredly, the work of the Spirit of God is not finally contingent on educators or learners. It is not contingent on state of the art materials, the perfect learning space, or the most effective curriculum. God can move in and through all that we do or don't do pedagogically, like it or not. But the real pedagogical question remains: Is there a way to create space for the Spirit of God to be ushered into the educational process of transformation? This creation of space in Christian education transforms the learning environment into a place for holistic and healthy educational practices that lead to receptivity in the transformational process. The transformational process is not entered into necessarily consciously, but there are learning tasks, guided by transformation and set up to create a space for it, that allow learners to more fully enter in to the spiritual process of transformation that is involved in learning.

As practitioners of Christian education, though, the pedagogy behind these learning tasks may matter more than the tasks themselves. Do we believe in the guiding principle of transformation by the Spirit of God? Do we believe in the sacred moments of cognition that occur in the transformational process and that lead to transformed living and thinking? This is the first task of the educator: to submit to God's mighty work of transformation and to create space for transformation to occur in the lives of both educator and student alike. Transformation in education is a vulnerable work to undergo. It requires submission, honesty, critical reflection, praxis and evaluation. Transformational learning, therefore, requires the whole person and relationships among whole persons. Without this pedagogical framework, the learning tasks are easily perverted and lead to retardation of learning.

The first step, although not always entered into first in the transformational grammar, is *a conflict borne with persistence*. The belief behind conflict is that once the conflict is entered into the *psyche* seeks to resolve it and is resistant to giving up the work of conflict resolution. One may understand, then, that in conflict the educational process becomes in some way "soul work." As we enter into conflict there is a desire from the soul to resolve it. Theologically, this could relate to the knowledge within humanity for the redemption of all things. The hope placed within us for final resolution urges us forward and onwards into truth-seeking. Loder writes:

> Theologically, all views of time come under the perspective of eternity, as is manifest to us proximately, in transforming moments of life-embracing significance. Such moments encompass the . . . fullness of the present and so redefine all of life for us . . . To grasp the whole, while still in the midst of relentless and unforgiving clock time . . . is a gift of God's Spirit.[5]

The human soul seeks resolution in the present in relation to the ultimate resolution in the eternal.

With regards to the learning task, this initial step involves *learning to face and embrace appropriate conflict with perseverance*.[6] Loder addresses head on an important issue within this theme: "One cannot create what he/she does not care about and persist in."[7] Caring relates the learning task to the felt needs of a person, which will be defined as the practical concerns and struggles of an individual. Appropriate conflict as a learning task, therefore, is conflict that originates with the felt needs of the person. The key in this stage is that upon entering into the conflict one does not stay there but is urged onward to a heightened consciousness of God's action in the world. Jim Plueddemann clarifies this concern as he presents a new paradigm of education that views the learner as a pilgrim. Although pilgrimage is certainly not a new concept, the idea of pilgrimage in the educational process is a different way of viewing learning which is not often addressed. "Jesus never taught subject matter which was divorced from life, nor did he teach solutions to practical problems without teaching the Word."[8] The task of educators, then, is to create space for conflict that begins with the felt needs of the learner and leads to a heightened awareness of God's action in the world. One of the two parts of embracing appropriate conflict is insufficient; both must be present in order for learning to be healthy. Transformation is not to be separated from the Holy, as true transformation is convictional and redemptive. Loder writes: "A vision of the Holy is a vision of a reality so magnificent that the human self longs for the Holy to be all in all, totally transforming existence in the fullness of its light and being."[9]

---

5. Loder, *Logic*, 339–40.
6. Loder, "Transformation," 22.
7. Ibid.
8. Plueddemann, "Do We Teach," 3.
9. Loder, *Transforming*, 90–91.

Paulo Freire speaks of the perversity of this learning type as well. He writes: "Our traditional curriculum, disconnected from life, centered on words emptied of the reality they are meant to represent, lacking in concrete activity, could never develop a critical consciousness."[10] In order to heighten awareness and understanding so as to face conflict with persistence, first there must be a connectedness to the life of the person involved. Thomas Groome states this conflict borne with persistence as a "certain wrestling" which must occur in education in the journey to maturity in faith.[11] The perverse form of this lack of connection to real life might be seen in the banking method of education, which assumes that education is simply a matter of depositing information in passive receptacles.[12] Piaget goes so far as to claim that cognition must be grounded in a present/active reflective process. How then do we create space for this conflict borne with persistence?

Practically there are several ways for Christian educators to go forward in this learning type. Dialogue is key to "reinventing" what is already known[13] and bearing it with conflict. Beginning to enter into bearing with conflict should lead to ways of opening up learners to critical reflection, which is borne through dialogue. Dialogue will in some way be a part of each educational learning type, because it creates in education what Parker Palmer refers to as "a space where obedience to truth is practiced."[14] In regards to dialogue, this learning type is also one in which the educator is able to ask questions and give information and insights that open up new doors in the minds of the students and allows them to possibly address and engage conflicts that they have not considered before.[15] The role of the educator in this sense is one of opening up learning space with a designed activity, a theory, a piece of information, a text, or a question, and then trusting learners to wrestle with the theme at hand. This role is one that involves trust and humility as learner and educator work together to embrace conflict. Another aspect of creating a space for conflict to be embraced is that both abstract or imaginative means may be used to enter in. Forms of this space creation

10. Freire, *Education*, 37f.
11. Groome, *Christian*, xv.
12. Ibid., 7.
13. Ibid., 8.
14. Palmer, *To Know*, 88.
15. Ibid., 69–71.

include instructional simulations in which reality is represented in ways in which events can be controlled, synectic problem-solving activities that increase creativity and critical reflection, and role-playing situations that enhance empathy and foster new perspective. Designing intentional activities help learners to answer some of the following questions: "What are you/we currently doing related to the topic? What situations are you/we in? What is your impression or reaction to this situation? How do you/we feel about this problem? What does this conflict mean to you? What does it mean in your life? What is your understanding about this event? What message do you hear from this situation? What do you/we believe about this conclusion? Answering these questions can open up space to bring learners to a place of embracing and bearing the conflict with persistence.

Furthermore, these activities that educators design to create an experience of embracing conflict in a healthy way should include the senses. Imaginative forms of educational tasks might help to connect ideas that relate to the lives of the learner. This task involves the educator as well. The focus of the educator is in designing activities, questions, and methods that will lead to discovery-based education. The task of the educator is not to direct all conversations or to give answers to learners. It becomes the work of the learner to embrace and work through conflict with the educator as guide.

The next step is *interlude and scanning* which relates to the learning task of contemplative wondering. Loder speaks of a strong inner hunch that leads the learner in this learning task to an "expectant searching" that takes place.[16] Here the educator creates space for transformation by guiding and redirecting this search instead of supplying answers that require no depth of learning. The information or activity has already been presented in the first step. Now it is the role of the educator to step back and allow the sometimes-uncomfortable stage of contemplation and wresting to occur. Contemplative wondering and mindfulness are a practical part of this task. They lead to "satisfying deeper longings"[17] which could not be satisfied by simple transmission of information. Learning is a sacred experience as we learners seek to know God and to be known by Him in the process. Thomas Groome puts it this way: "[I]t must always be remembered that only by the help of the Holy

16. Loder, "Transformation," 3.
17. Ibid., 23.

Spirit can the truth be known."[18] This learning task is centered round this remembrance as we contemplate with the Holy Spirit as guide in the sacred process of learning. Interestingly enough, Groome, in his second movement of shared praxis, follows the same flow of learning as Loder by beginning critical reflection after the first step of naming present action.[19] This time the learning process becomes an invitation to reflect. The primary task of this learning is to "enable participants (the educator included) to reflect critically on their present action, their reasons for it, and the consequences of it."[20] Dialogue is still useful if it is dialogue that leads to rumination. Parker Palmer speaks of this rumination period in this way: "In silence more than in argument our mind-made world falls away and we are opened to the truth that seeks us. If our speech is to become more truthful it must emerge from and be corrected by the silence that is its source."[21]

Contemplative wondering takes several practical forms in a learning space. One is to allow for times of silence in learning, as well as a slowed pace in dialogue and discovery, not only for the learners but also for the educator. *Lectio Divina* is another practical form of this type of learning because it revolves around the rumination and internalization of Scripture. This method allows for sacred reading at a contemplative pace that allows reading to open, not fill, our learning space.[22]

The third learning task is *insight felt with intuitive force* or "learning from convictional experiences or from insights that reach the proportions of convictional significance."[23] These are the moments of cognition that were spoken of earlier, in which one becomes conscious of a deeper truth that heightens his or her awareness of God and his work in the world. One may wonder how an educator goes about creating space for moments like these that cannot be forced or fabricated. Loder speaks about the repeated awakening to the transformation of all things into the glory of God that is an essential part of the Christian faith. Being awakened to the transformation of all things leads to worship. These spiritual awakenings have a "prophetic role" in education and in the lives

18. Groome, *Christian*, 201.
19. Ibid., 211ff.
20. Ibid., 213.
21. Palmer, *To Know*, 80.
22. Ibid., 76.
23. Loder, "Transformation," 24.

of learners that "expose, however momentarily and partially, the nature of the reality into which all of life is being integrated."[24]

Worship in the context of education may seem difficult to place but may be seen as a natural outflow of the convictional experiences that come from learning in the transformational process. This worship is such a natural outflow of conviction that it seems absurd to try to design ways for it to come about. Here we are not speaking of worship in the celebrational sense of the word, but instead in the worship that comes of "holy wondering" that leads us into the presence of the Spirit. Here we find that once again dialogue is key, not in forcing a convictional experience, but in creating the space for it to be possible. Paulo Freire gives guidelines to dialogue that are especially useful in this learning task. Groome refers to the fourth of these five guidelines in this way: "Dialogue requires hope, a hope that is aware of our incompleteness but is determined not to settle for silence or escape from reality. It is an active hope, but not an impatient one that gives up or continues only if there are results."[25]

As learners continue to wrestle with conflict in a dialogical relationship that is healthy, these moments of conviction are a natural outflow of listening and loving others in the learning context. This is also the time of illumination by the word of God, in which we bring back our findings and wrestlings to rest in and find space in the transformative power of Scripture. In the synectic problem-solving activity or simulation, this is the debriefing process in which learners are encouraged to make connections between classroom learning and outward truth. In this way, the classroom is a place "in which obedience to truth is practiced."[26] The learner of Christian education finds and glories in the fact that what happens in the classroom is happening in the world.[27] This obedience to truth will be seen once again in the fifth phase, but is appropriate here since insight felt with intuitive force leads back into the desire to connect discovery with broader learning.

The fourth phase addressed by Loder is *release and redirection of psychic energy*, which may also be seen as *learning to celebrate*.[28] The first

24. Ibid.
25. Groome, *Christian*, 190.
26. Palmer, *To Know*, 88.
27. Ibid.
28. Loder, "Transformation," 23.

question to consider in this learning task is, "What is being celebrated?" Loder would respond that we are celebrating the discovery of the hidden order of things, the fundamental but hidden order of all things undergoing transformation into the glory of God.[29] And what a reason to celebrate that is! This celebration should lead learners back into the celebration of God and should develop more of a sense of awe and wonder at the nature of the Creator. In other words, celebration of discovery of created order should lead back to the Creator of that hidden order and should thus be a part of a continued awakening to transformation.

Practically speaking, this is the time for learners to present findings and share with others what they are learning about the hidden order of all things. This presenting creates a space for learners to celebrate in community the truth that they are embracing. This learning is also seen in the desire to continue learning and dialoguing after class or after "formal" learning has finished. The discovery-based learning has so incited energy and passion that comes from critical consciousness that it drives learners to continue dialoguing, brainstorming, and for reconsidering practical ways of implementing learning. There is a kind of dreaming that comes into play during this release and redirection of psychic energy; not a dreaming that is detrimental to learning or that leads to wasted ideas, but a dreaming that leads to the desire to learn more and to "live out" new discoveries and beliefs.

Finally, Loder presents the fifth phase of the grammar of transformation which is *interpretation* that tests the insight for coherence with the terms of the conflict and for correspondence with the public context of the original conflict and that in relation to its learning task may be seen as *learning interpretation and responsible action*.[30] This task is related deeply to Christian praxis which promotes a lived Christian faith, and believes that authentic reflection cannot exist apart from action.[31] The transformational process of education is not fully entered into if it does not lead to transformed living. This is the work of the Spirit within the learner and the learning space—to take discovery that reveals the hidden order of created things and thus the Creator himself and that transforms the life of the learner by this revelation. Transformational learning leads to critical consciousness, or "depth in the interpretation of

---

29. Ibid.
30. Ibid, 22.
31. Freire, *Education*, 20.

problems . . . by the testing of one's 'findings' and by openness to revision . . . ."[32] Truly, transformational learning should lead to a greater desire for learning, as well as a greater desire for knowing and understanding the Creator.

This learning task is that which involves testing by trial and error. We have discovered something, and we must find the direction through which learning about that subject continues. We must find out where and how that subject may be appropriately applied in life. This stage of learning involves interpretation of discovery as well as evaluation of learning as learners begin to appropriate discoveries into a deeper context of reality. Thus, in some ways the discoveries are broadened while in other ways they are narrowed down. There is a broadening as reflective interpretation and appropriation of learning will lead to further learning and the sharing of learning with others in community. But there is also a narrowing down as evaluation and the "testing out" of discovery leads to concrete forms of application within a certain context and the focused study of specific elements of learning. By bringing back findings and presenting them in a community of learners that provide feedback and dialogue learners are able to reflect together and test out discoveries. Also, by thoughtfully and intentionally applying learning to practical situations learners are able to test and evaluate what they have come up with in the phase of *release and redirection of psychic energies*. This is where evaluational models come into play. Evaluation is a key part of the learning process. Evaluation allows learners to flush out what works and what does not in all practicality, and then to move forward from that place of evaluation into a redirection of energies and efforts. Elliott Eisner gives an overview of important pieces to the connoisseurship and critical process involved in education, which includes description, interpretation, and evaluation. Throughout the process of education there must be consistent description, interpretation, and evaluation so as to create space for critical reflection and ultimately lived-out learning that continues forward in growth. This fifth stage of learning is one that must continually be revisited, as redirection of energies will need to be re-evaluated and honed upon all persons throughout the learning process. This process is led by the Holy Spirit to serve as a time of setting learning

32. Ibid., 18.

expectations, which should be set in partnership with the Holy Spirit as educators partnering with God to fashion the people of God.[33]

Conclusion

The grammar of transformation is present throughout the educational process, as learners come to discover knowledge, critically reflect on it and internalize it, and then move towards living it out in community. If education may be seen as a "leading out" towards truth, the learning space should be one in which educators and learners alike depend on the transforming power of the Holy Spirit of God to take learning and to embed it—i.e. to use it as a catalyst in the lives of the learner, and to then impact others in community. Loder gives key insights into transformational pedagogy that may be applied in practical ways for all those involved in the educational process in which learning is centered on the subject of Truth and involves those seeking it in community.

33. Harris, *Fashion*.

Works Cited

Freire, Paulo. *Education for Critical Consciousness*. London: Continuum, 2005.

Groome, Thomas. *Christian Religious Education*. San Francisco: Harper & Row, 1980.

Harris, Maria. *Fashion Me a People: Curriculum in the Church*. Louisville: Westminster/John Knox, 1989.

Loder, James E., Jr. *The Logic of the Spirit: Human Development in Theological Perspective*. San Francisco: Jossey-Bass, 1998.

———. "Transformation in Christian Education." *The Princeton Seminary Bulletin* 3/1 new series (1980) 11–25.

———. *The Transforming Moment*. 2nd ed. Colorado Springs: Helmers & Howard, 1989.

Palmer, Parker J. *To Know As We Are Known*. San Francisco: Harper & Row, 1983.

Plueddemann, Jim. "Do We Teach the Bible Or Do We Teach Students?" *Evangelical Theological Society* 29 (2004) 4.

7

Educational Ministry in the Logic of the Spirit

A Loder Legacy?

Dana R. Wright

Introduction: "This is to be my Legacy!"

Late in our CTM consultation, Ajit Prasadam recalled his conversation with Dr. James Loder just before he died in 2001. Ajit had read Loder's unpublished manuscript *Educational Ministry in the Logic of the Spirit* and was troubled. "Why after 40 years of teaching the philosophy of Christian education at Princeton Seminary," he asked, "have you never written a book on that subject until now? Why have you written all of these other books?" Loder replied, "I had planned to write a book on Christian education all along but I wanted to get it right. I wanted to write something that I could say would impact the discipline and help get it more firmly established." Tom Hastings remembered Loder saying something similar about his yet-unpublished manuscript: "This is to be my legacy!"

After anecdotes like these were shared, we decided to add to this present book a contextual and critical assessment of *EMLOS*.[1] Our con-

1. See my introductory chapter in this volume. Also Haitch, "Summary," 298–324,

versation had revealed a difference of opinion among Loder's former students as to its scholarly quality. Some did not think it exhibited the same rigorous depth of his other books (*The Transforming Moment, The Logic of the Spirit, The Knight's Move*), implying that Loder had fallen considerably short with his "legacy" goal. But others held the book was worthy of Loder's overall project. One especially important value of this book concerned Loder's creative, theological reconstruction of Talcott Parsons' action theory that formed something of its substrate.[2] The incredible breath and depth of Loder's understanding of the full range of human action under the "logic of the Spirit" needed to be appreciated, especially if his theory as a whole was to fulfill its promise.[3] *EMLOS*, in this judgment, promises to make the kind of contribution to practical theology that Loder sought to make, at least in part.

Complicating matters is the fact that there are several different renditions of the manuscript itself in the Loder archive at Princeton Seminary.[4] Some of Loder's former students did not think that the 2001 version Loder sought to get published was the best edition. Yet Loder himself had given, or was about to give, the manuscript to a publisher, and he gave copies of it to several of his students, implying perhaps that he had some urgency about getting the book out in this form.[5] How he

---

and Wright, "Are You There?," 23f. I will abbreviate references to Loder's unpublished work as *EMLOS* in this essay.

2. *EMLOS* is organized in a chiasm based on the four domains of action theory in Parson's work. For an introduction to Parsons and his theory, see Hamilton, *Talcott Parsons*.

3. Loder's effort to show the action of the Holy Spirit transforming the human spirit in all four dimensions of human action (organic, psychological, social, and cultural) is absolutely essential for understanding the full breadth and power of his overall vision of what Christian education could be. Apart from his development of a theological transformation of Parson's action theory Loder's attention to individual convictional experience and transformational dynamics and the work of the Holy Spirit in human development, generally fails to connect redemptive transformation fully to corporate life in ecclesial or cultural experience.

4. During my time at Princeton (1991–2003) I saw about four different versions of this manuscript. Loder lectured from the manuscript in his ED 105 class and refined it through the years. The last manuscript, a copy of which Loder gave several of us in the weeks before he died, was noticeably different from the ED 105 notes I was used to. I suspected that an editor may have requested some of the changes.

5. Furthermore, there is the question of Loder's health in the latter years of his life. His closest associates noticed that he appeared to be struggling physically in those last few months. How his heath affected his judgment is not known.

himself thought about this manuscript is not fully known. He certainly changed some of it from the previous iterations based directly on his ED105 lectures.[6] After his death the manuscript was sent back from the publisher and, as far as we know, it remains locked away in a Princeton Theological Seminary vault. In lieu of the possibility that this book will never be published, the CTM gathering decided to make another analysis of the book available in order to give it a vicarious hearing. Charged with that task, I will seek to help the reader gain a fuller understanding of the book's context, content and purpose as I understand it. I will also render my own judgment about whether Loder achieved any worthwhile legacy with this *oeuvre*.[7]

To make such a judgment we must first take some care to look "behind" the book itself to the history of Christian education as an academic discipline charged with the task of equipping leaders to work for the renewal of Christian faithfulness in the modern (and now postmodern) world. We need to ask some preliminary questions: What might Loder have meant by the word "legacy," especially in light of the 110 year history of academic Christian education theorizing to which Loder was heir? What kind of legacy did the book represent for him in light of this history? How did he hope this book might make a major contribution to theories of practical theology and Christian education in the 21st century? What legacy might be appropriate for one who taught at Princeton Seminary for 40 years during a time in which a genuine renaissance in practical theology emerged, at least in the West?[8]

---

6. The most obvious change is the elimination of a chapter on curriculum that had been written by Beth Frykberg. He admitted that "curriculum" wasn't his thing. He also added a preface and changed some of the chapter headings. These alterations reduced the book from twelve to ten chapters.

7. Several of his former students have copies of the manuscript in various forms. I am quite sure that some of us could come together and collaborate on a posthumous publication of his work if we could be granted permission.

8. See the noteworthy summary of Loder's work at Princeton by Mikowski and Osmer in their bicentennial contribution, "Flowering," 133–176, esp. 148–163. Loder, along with Seward Hiltner and Charles Bartow, are presented in this chapter as exemplars of practical theology.

Shedding Some Light on the Meaning of "Legacy" for Practical Theology

We gain some insight into what Loder himself meant by "legacy" if we risk a tentative *theological* interpretation of this 110 year history of the academic field of Christian [religious] education, focusing especially on some of its key concerns: theological and interdisciplinary method, scientific cultural context, and the work of the Holy Spirit within human experience.[9] I have argued elsewhere, borrowing from theologian Ralph Wood, that academic practical theology has taken essentially two different meta-theoretical forms in the United States: the "Tragic-Apologetic-Synthetic" form that has dominated the discussion, and the "Comic-Kerygmatic-Analytic" form that has been influential but not dominant.[10] "Tragic-Apologetic-Synthetic" practical theology assumes continuity between human reason, the scientific disciplines, the symbolic meaning of Christian revelation in human experience, and a tendency to identify the work of the Holy Spirit with the creativity of the human spirit. Thus, human reason or experience, or the sciences of human development etc., can be synthesized with Christian meanings as they confront what Reinhold Niebuhr called the "permanent myths" that reveal the mystery of experience.[11] Niebuhr's kind of moral theology does not envision God acting in history through the risen Lord to establish his eschatological kingdom. Everything hinges, instead, upon the human quest for a proximate earthly justice as it is *symbolized* in the life and death of Jesus.[12] In shorthand, theology synthesizes nature and grace such that nature (or culture) sets the context for the meaning of grace and grace is expressed in immanent human categories.

---

9. Historians locate the origins of the modern discipline practical theology with Horace Bushnell's *Christian Nurture* (1846). But the modern search for scientific method arose with the Religious Education Movement (1903).

10. Wright, "Contemporary," 289–320. My development of the two strands of practical theology was suggested in Ralph Wood's study, *Comedy of Redemption*.

11. According to Wood, myth is especially useful to Niebuhr's non-dogmatic, American style of theology. He makes no radical distinction between divine revelation and human self-understanding, nor therefore between biblical and non-biblical myth. In his view, the human penchant for myth making is a universal phenomenon. Biblical myths are thus a particular species of an all–inclusive genus. For Tragic-Apologetic-Synthetic theologians like Niebuhr, to speak of "human existence as ultimate meaning" is (to quote Wood), to "go but barely beyond tragedy."

12. Wood, *Comedy*, 8.

In contrast, Comic-Kerygmatic-Analytic thinking, exemplified in Karl Barth, recognizes an ontological divide between the divine and the human that only God, not human beings, can (and has!) overcome in Jesus Christ. This kind of theology does not seek a synthesis between permanent myths and human knowledge based on human categories but privileges radical grace, a radical offense to human perspicacity in the modern world. Barth highlighted the scandal of this form of theologizing, both in and outside the church. Wood wrote:

> So to insist on the finality of God's self-disclosure in Jesus is, inevitably, to give offense. Barth insists, however, that the Gospel scandalizes Christians no less than secularists. The uncompromising precedence of divine revelation over all human potentiality sets both believer and pagan on the same footing—namely, in radical dependence on this "one truth which is superior to both of them." . . . What offends Christian and secularist alike is the refusal of this unique Word to be synthesized with other human words. The Gospel resists all attempts to join God's transcendent revelation with our own immanent creations and discoveries . . . philosophy . . . psychology . . . the arts . . . world religions . . . not even politics or the church. "There is no legitimate place," Barth asserts, "for projects in the planning and devising of which Jesus Christ can be given a particular niche in co-ordinating with those of other events, powers, forms and truths. Such projects are irrelevant and unfruitful because as the one Word of God He wholly escapes every conceivable synthesis envisaged in them."[13]

Most practical theologians in the United States (and Europe) generally regard assertions like Barth's with considerable skepticism, if not downright disdain.[14] No doubt what generated this skepticism against this so-called "positivism of revelation" was the Enlightenment heritage

---

13. Wood, *Comedy*, quoted in Wright, "Contemporary," 294.

14. Recall Gerrish's words, quoted in my introduction to this book: "Anyone who believes that theology is possible and meaningful in the church alone, that it begins with God in his revelation in Jesus Christ, and that it is scientific just insofar as it corresponds to the word of God through obedience of faith, will need to come up with a quite different account of theology's credentials as a university discipline, or may prefer to pursue it somewhere else." What is true of the "secular" academy is also true for practical theology in the guild. Note, for example, the general dismissal of the work of Karl Barth in Browning's *Fundamental Practical Theology*, 5. While Browning suggests that Barth is "partially right" in his theological approach, it is difficult to detect how Browning has appreciated Barth at all. Also see McCormack's, "Unheard Message," 59–66.

in the West, which one could argue reached the apex of its power at the end of the 19th and beginning of the 20th century when the notion of religious education as a science was gaining credence.[15] Optimism that a scientifically constructed "democracy of God"[16] could be virtually engineered through the modern tools of rational thought, empirical scientific insight, entrepreneurial spirit, and the goodness of human nature (properly educated and cultivated) shaped religious education theory in the first half of the twentieth century (and continues today). Christianity's function in the modern world was essentially ethical and democratic.[17] Modernization would flourish using a "demythologized" gospel to legitimize the scientific and technological promise of social salvation—ushering in "the Christian century!" But before the first half of this *Christian* century played out, this ethical, scientific and technological optimism shattered. The *inevitable* progress of Christianity's fusion with modernity instead set humanity "slouching toward Bethlehem," a "Second Coming" of grotesque and monstrous and unimagined proportion devastatingly know in the cruel nomenclatures of Auschwitz, Hiroshima, and Silent Spring.[18]

In response to the horror, something of a *kerygmatic* revolution in theology emerged to expose the hubris underlying synthesis. Kierkegaard's "attacks" on Christian culture found a new hearing, and the "Barthian bombshell," *Der Romerbrief,* called theologians to "reckon" with Christian revelation and to recover the biblical categories of eschatology and apocalyptic, revelation and Word, evil and grace, in

---

15. For an analysis this history see Osmer and Schweitzer, *Religious Education.* See also Osmer's dissertation, "Practical Theology."

16. "Democracy of God" was George Albert Coe's phrase for the "kingdom of God." Coe, a major player in the rise of the Religious Education Association, self-consciously abandoned an early hope for religious conversion and determined to develop a scientific and immanent approach to religious education.

17. For example, William Hutchison summarized the optimism that attended the organizers and participants of the first Religious Education Association meeting in Chicago in 1903: "[T]he liberals of the nineties . . . articulated a program . . . that was prophetic of twentieth-century changes in mission theology . . . [that] entailed the search for a quintessential Christianity suitable for export; the conversion of the idea of Christian finality into an almost purely ethical conception . . . [a] 'Gospel for Humanity'" (Hutchison, *Modern,* quoted in Wright, "Contemporary," 302).

18. William Butler Yeats gave us this image in his poem "The Second Coming" (1919).

order to make sense of things.[19] For a time, religious educators working from a Barthian sensibility chastened the apologetic dominance of the human sciences in religious education.[20] But the kerygmatic theologians generally failed in their efforts to effectively integrate needed insights from the sciences with theology in compelling ways, fueling criticisms by apologists that revelation too must be chastened in a scientific world.

During the late 1950s and early 1960s renewed efforts by religious/Christian educators to integrate the apologetic and kerymatic concerns emerged with new intensity. By the 1970s, taxonomies describing different methods of integration appeared as practical theology truly sought to endow itself with a fully constructive and interdisciplinary academic pedigree.[21] During this period the methodological question—the relation of apologetic and kerygmatic concerns in a scientific context—continued to dominate the discussion.[22] By the 1980s into the 1990s, the constructive and interdisciplinary trend clearly again favored apologetic-synthetic theorizing, though the concern to take revelation seriously as well continued.[23]

19. See Smith, "Let Religious," 45–51, reprinted in Westerhoff, *Who Are We?*, 97–109. Brooks Holifield noted how the realist theologians like Tillich and H. R. Niebuhr resisted the apologetic assertions of liberalism. Tillich, for example, asserted that Liberalism's "language of adjustment was merely a reflection of a capitalist culture that sought only control over mind, nature, and God . . . [but] . . . the divine was precisely the reality that resisted control" (Holifield, *History*, 250).

20. Canadian James Smart is generally regarded the early exemplar of kerygma-dominant Christian education theory during this time. See his *Teaching Ministry*.

21. Lewis Mudge and James Poling, for example, outlined three general types of practical theology: (1) A critical naturalist method in which secular disciplines provide the basic framework and Christian tradition plays secondary role; (2) A critical correlation method which imagines a collaborative yet critical dialogue between secular and theological disciplines; (3) A critical confessional method in which the Christian tradition provides the normative framework within which the human sciences find their proper value for hermeneutical decisions. See Poling and Mudge, *Formation*.

22. See Don Browning's paper "Struggle," delivered at the first planning meeting of the International Academy of Practical Theology, Princeton Seminary, summer 1991 (unpublished copy). Concerning the interdisciplinary task of practical theology Browning wrote: ". . . the Academy is interested in practical theology as a distinct discipline . . . [which] as a scholarly organization . . . is dedicated primarily to the theory of practice . . . It is . . . concerned with the development of models (of practical theology) accounting for their theoretical coherence and unity. This means that the Academy is interested in developing and investigating comprehensive frameworks for ordering practical theology itself and its relation to the other theological disciplines."

23. Browning outlined seven emerging trends in practical theology. (a) Theological

Right here is where James E. Loder's neo-Chalcedonian science of practical theology sought to make a startling contribution. Demonstrating an expansive theological and interdisciplinary imagination, Loder articulated a truly scientific theory of Christian education grounded in the deep coherence he intuited lay at the heart of all reality when the human spirit awakened to, and was empowered by, *Spiritus Creator*. His audacious claim was that the true ground for both *kerygma* and *apologia* was the same—the Reality of Jesus Christ known in the depths of a transformed human spirit through the power of the Holy Spirit. To substantiate the radical significance of this claim, we need to understand how Loder addressed his own colleagues on the methodological question. Then we will look at *EMLOS* in detail.

Alleluia and Eureka: Integrating Kerygmatic and Apologetic Concerns through Redemptive Transformation by the Spirit

For Loder, the key to recovering the integrity between divine and human action for a scientific world was nothing less than the action of the Holy Spirit bearing witness deep within the human spirit to the Christological relationality that holds all reality together. Loder explicitly "came clean" with this claim in two papers he wrote around the turn of the century, papers through which his passion for neo-Chalcedonian yet scientific practical theology finds powerful articulation. In the first paper, "The Place of Science in Practical Theology: The Human Factor," Loder argued that discovering the ultimate meaning of all scientific knowing depends upon the self-involvement of the knower—the human factor.[24] Furthermore, self-involved knowing is given to us definitively in Jesus Christ, discerned as the dynamic relationality between Christ's divine and human nature in the Chalcedonian formulation. When the human

---

thinking begins with an analysis of practice in context; (b) Practical theology implies public theology as well as ecclesial theology; (c) All practical theology is intrinsically interdisciplinary when properly conceived; (d) Practical theology has an integrative role to play both within its own purview and within theological education as a whole; (e) Practical theology is scientific and critical; (f) Practical theology attends both to "critical norms of practice" and "the dynamics and the rhetorics of transformation"; (g) Practical theology may be the fulfillment of all theological reflection practically.

24. Loder, "Place of Science," 22–44 (pre-published copy). Loder's indebtedness to Michael Polanyi concerning the "personal" nature of scientific knowledge is seen throughout his *oeuvres*.

spirit is awakened through convictional experience to this Chalcedonian Reality, the true ground of both theological and scientific knowing is revealed in human experience as the mind of Christ.

In this analysis Loder exposed as false the reigning "orthodoxy" that deems so-called "detached and objective" scientific knowing superior to self-involved or "subjective" knowing central to postmodern science and theology. Loder refuted this "heresy" from the Enlightenment that he believed had (1) distorted our understanding of how new knowledge is acquired and also (2) rendered the classical integrity of science-theology relationality impossible. That is, Loder argued that a powerful and pervasive confusion of science and technology had sponsored an "eikonic eclipse" in epistemology that occludes the "human factor" in all truly scientific understanding, the factor that makes true science a compelling dialogue partner with theology.[25]

> . . . in the theology-science dialogue, science [not] technology, is the primary dialogue partner with theology. However, no view of science is adequate that fails to recognize that all knowledge of the universe is incomplete and probably misleading until it includes the person, the knower himself or herself. Indeed, it is precisely through persons that the universe becomes conscious of itself . . . Thus, the dialogue between theology and science, which is so central to practical theology, must take place at the level of personal knowledge if its outcomes are to be truly comprehensive.[26]

Drawing upon the work of Michael Polanyi, Loder articulated the dynamic nature of all knowing as self-involved discovery. The deep knowing of the human spirit is dependent upon a gestalt-like figure-ground structure and the power of insight, generated through the knower's passionate indwelling of the nature of the reality she/he seeks to know. The

---

25. On the notion of "eikonic eclipse," see Loder, *Transforming*, 27–33, 223. For Loder it was a "pressing" concern that practical theology recover "the mutually enriching and deepening interplay between theology understood as the studied participation in God's action in various forms of culture" and "human action embedded in the created world which science seemingly interprets so much more effectively than theology." See Loder, "Place of Science," 22–44.

26. Loder, "Place of Science," 6. Loder summarized three great scientific revolutions in the 20th century associated with Einstein (relativity), Heisenberg/Bohr (complementarity), and Prigogine (chaos theory) in light of the programmatic work of Michael Polanyi, to assert why the "human factor" is crucial to understanding the relation of theology to science.

depths of personal knowing is revealed in the testimonies of geniuses like Einstein, Werner Heisenberg, Niels Bohr, and Ilya Prigogine, all of whom "reach[ed] intuitively into the phenomenon and grasp[ed] at a tacit level the deep inner structure of the phenomenon."[27]

What generally is the nature of the relational coherence that emerges in discovery through personal knowing? Loder argued that postmodern science had discerned something like infinite patterns of complexity in the universe that participate in a dynamic movement from order, through disorder, to emergent new order while retaining relational purpose and meaning in the process. From the greatest reaches of the macro-universe to the infinitely small dominion of quantum worlds, and including all natural and cultural reality in between, these complex, self-organizing patterns can be discerned because they are already present dynamically in the knower herself. Like reality itself, these hidden, dynamic patterns constitute the knower herself as a meaning-maker.[28] Reality is revealed to be relational and transformational at its core when the spirit of the mind engages it dynamically according to the spirit's own power. Therefore, reality can only be known relationally and transformationally—that is, dynamically or kinetically—which means scientifically. Loder averred: "As the anthropic principle taken in its strong sense makes very clear, the moment of the big bang initiated immensely powerful relationships which had to remain in an infinitely

---

27. Ibid., 8f. Loder cites T. F. Torrance's discussion of Polanyi in *Transformation and Convergence*, chapter 3, 107–74. Loder drew on Polanyi's description of what the Greeks called "prolepsis," which is "an implicit apprehension that is imprinted upon the informed mind because the internal structure of the phenomenon bears a kinship to our knowing and what we can know as we allow ourselves to indwell the phenomenon. At a tacit level where we know more than we can tell, we come upon hitherto unknown patterns, a novel or unexpected order of things . . . [that] is generated out of indwelling and allowing the gap that stretches from experience to idea to be bridged by an intuitive surmise evoked by deepening coherences [sic] that gradually emerge from the interaction between the knower and the known and eventually lay bare the internal structure of the reality being investigated" (Loder, "Place of Science," 9).

28. Loder is perhaps most well known for his investigation of the transformational pattern of human knowing at the heart of convictional experiences and through human development. He is less known for what this transformational pattern implies about the nature of reality itself and our knowing of that reality. His works *Transforming* (convictional experience), *Logic* (transformation in human development), and *Knight's Move* (the transformational nature of reality revealed to science and theology) need to be read as a whole.

delicate balance for the physical universe to give rise to human intelligence by which the universe could become conscious of itself."[29]

Loder connected this profound understanding of the nature and power of the human spirit in knowing to the theological claim that Jesus Christ, in His Chalcedonian identity as fully God and fully human, is the *definitive* relational Reality toward which all human and natural relationalities point and out of which they originate. When the human spirit is awakened to the Presence of this Christomorphic relational Reality, the Reality that created all things to bear the transformational pattern becomes the experiential Ground for life and thought. The human factor so awakened by the Spirit of Christ manifests what the Church calls *faith*, a truly scientific posture for knowing all things. Our awakening in faith to the God-Human structure of Reality as the Ground of all we are and think is the work of the Holy Spirit. Loder believed that the Reformed tradition, with its "Christ the Transformer of Culture" perspicacity, could help enable not only a revitalized Church but also a truly coherent scientific relationality upon which the renewed promise of Western civilization could be built.[30]

Thus for Loder, the integrity of *both* apologetic and kerygmatic concerns was precisely found *beyond* both in the action of the Holy Spirit, action which human beings can recognize and in which they

29. Loder wrote: "It is not exaggeration to say that it has taken the entire history of the universe, with its dying stars, its infinitely intricate relationalities, and the act of God to bring forth a child. The development of the child replicates *en nuce* the [patterns of order, disorder, new order, and relationality]. The rationality by which we learn to think scientifically is an emergent resultant of transformational dynamics operative in the context of human relationships. Delicately balanced relationalities are prior to the creation of conscious rationality by a series of transformations which bring new orders out of disequilibrated states exemplified by birth, adolescence, middlescence and senescence [sic]. Rational consciousness presupposes relationality and transformation by which it can become intelligent to itself" ("Factor," 19).

30. Theology's impact on culture had been lost by the dehumanizing dualisms underlying the faith–science split nurtured in modernity. See *Knight's Move*, 27–33. Of the promise of a renewed Reformed theology Loder wrote: "If Calvin was correct, we are missing the presence and power of the Holy Spirit testifying to and with our human spirits, in an expanding universe which is also a groaning creation, that the coherence of what now seems fragile and fragmented has been revealed in the nature of Jesus Christ by the power of his Spirit. We are in profound spiritual need of knowing what the nature of that coherence is. Our immediate task, then, is to reclaim some of the logic of coherent relationality revealed to us in Jesus Christ . . . Scripture and tradition must be set forth in terms that directly and critically address the dualistic forces pervading modern culture" (*Knight's Move*, 32).

can participate and hope, but over which they have no final control, methodological or otherwise. Loder sought more than interdisciplinary sophistication and integration for the sake of academics. He sought to bring theological and interdisciplinary coherence to human participation, thought and action, in the very life of God, and to articulate this relational Reality with scientific and theological integrity to the world.[31] For Loder, discoveries in nature by science and discoveries of the divine nature through convictional experiences reveal the deep connection between "Alleluia!" and "Eureka" built into the universe—the Mind of Christ powerfully present in all human experience.[32]

Loder regarded the Spirit's restoration of the quality of human knowing as essentially dynamic and existential, a relationality he called "imageless" to communicate the self-relational or spiritual nature of our being created in the *imago Dei*. In *The Knight's Move* he had written:

> ... inherent in any description of the Holy Spirit there is a perennial difficulty in bringing the self-relational quality of the divine Spirit to bear on the self-relational quality of human experience. Nevertheless, precisely this difficulty is the decisive aspect of the concept of "spirit" to be addressed in our recovery of coherence in Christ. In opposition to distorting dualistic assumptions and the consequent fragmentation of our current world views, we need to reengage and reinstate self-involvement in objective

---

31. Loder, "Place of Science," 9. Loder discerned another analogy between the "leap of faith" in Christian experience (Kierkegaard) and the "uncertainty principle" in quantum physics (Heisenberg). Both of these experiences point to a paradoxical and asymmetrical relationality underlying all human knowing in depth, which governs the interdisciplinary and asymmetrical relationality at the heart of the theology–science dialogue. When this relationality becomes the framework for an epistemology that "indwells" reality and allows reality to remain "subject" (i.e., disclosing how it is to be known rather than an "object" to be mastered), the "uncertainty principle" in sciences is transformed into the "passion of faith." And the human spirit's power to discover the nature of God and God's relation to creation becomes a function of the Holy Spirit in us, the "inner teacher" promised in the New Covenant who teaches us to know as we are known—relationally and transformationally. Indwelling the Kerygma reveals that we are "being known" such that our knowing is derivative, "a human mirror of the indwelling presence of God's Spirit in the investigator."

32. Loder's own testimony of redemptive transformation by the Spirit bore the marks of intellectual depth and breadth commensurate with the deep things of the Spirit acting to transform the self–relational quality of his own spirit. His work was testimony to the presence and power of the Spirit in his life inspiring theological reflection originating beyond himself, not reducible to his own intellectual or imaginative powers but fully involving them.

knowledge and objectivity in self-knowledge within the work of the human spirit; correlatively, we need to reclaim God's self-involvement within the created order and at the same time the contingent interdependence of that order within and upon God's grace by the power of God's Spirit.[33]

Loder argued that the restoration of the *imago Dei* becomes, in the new creation, the *imago Christi*, the fulfillment of the promise of the New Covenant, which could be communicated through neo-Chalcedonian practical theological science. The coherence and integrity of "imageless" Christ-to-believer relationality revealed in the Gospel is Chalcedonian in structure, which overcomes the objective-subjective split inherited from the Enlightenment and reveals a kinetic or dynamic relationality grounded in the Living Christ, the Mediator. "Thus, spiritual coherence in Christ may be envisioned as a Chalcedonian-like union of the Divine Spirit with the human spirit, giving evidence that the human is heir of the renewal by God of all creation (Rom. 8:16ff.)."[34] Such coherence revealed in Christ places relationality at the heart of knowing as well as being. As Loder averred:

> [C]onscious human existence is inevitably and irrepressibly self-relational. Moreover, the *relationship*, not either polarity alone, is the vital center of human existence . . . It has now become obvious that, even in the hardest of sciences, the observer is a necessary part of the natural order to be investigated . . . the intelligible order of reality is not in the mind, as Kant thought, or in nature, as Newton thought, but it resides in the relationship between the mind and nature, the observer and the observed.[35]

Loder believed that the God-Human structure of reality was communicated Spirit to spirit with human beings and communities, empowering them to discern and experience reality itself as continually transformational. Human agency in Christ is "coordinated" and "integrated" existentially as human beings participate in the kinetic power of the Spirit. Only in the Spirit of Christ can the human spirit, the creative power of all human constructions scientific and otherwise, find and retain its own relational integrity as spirit.

---

33. Loder and Neidhardt, *Knight's Move*, 32f.
34. Ibid., 33.
35. Ibid., 42f.

> The human spirit then finds its true home only when it is in one accord with the Spirit of Christ. There its integrity is preserved and it becomes a human analogy for how the Holy Spirit, who never loses relational integrity, searches the depths of God so as to disclose to us the wisdom hidden for us in the mind of Christ. Thus, left to itself, the dynamic relationality of the human spirit will eventually actualize its inclination toward death by collapsing into . . . idolatry or dissipating into . . . anarchy, but transformed by the Holy Spirit of Christ it becomes a human figure for the Divine reality.[36]

Though Presbyterian, Loder believed the Lutheran Kierkegaard had grasped the dynamic structure of the "logic coherent . . . in Jesus Christ" for the modern world. That is, he believed that Kierkegaard uncovered the "kinetic connection between Christology and culture," the "dialogical logic of the incarnation" revealed in the crucifixion and resurrection of Christ and relevant to a postmodern culture.[37] The vital reality of Spirit-to-spirit relations revealed in the Gospel—the kinetic spiritual coherence of human and divine in Christ—may be envisioned and experienced as "a Chalcedon-like union of the Divine Spirit with the human spirit." The methodological corollary is that one cannot recognize the

---

36. Ibid., 48. Loder wrote: "Paul speaks of the secret and hidden wisdom that is able to be imparted to 'the mature' . . . This hidden wisdom must be grasped by the spirit of the person in communion with the Spirit of God; thus wisdom is acquired Spirit to spirit . . . [In Paul's analogy between the Holy Spirit and the human spirit] the self-relational essence of the human spirit and its capacity to draw upon the tacit dimensions of human existence are set forth in eloquent simplicity. However, this is not yet sufficient because the human spirit left to itself will begin and end in a human frame of knowledge . . . Left to itself, the human spirit is blind and fails to recognize when it has lost its relational integrity and collapsed into some form of objectivism or submitted to demagoguery. To stay transcendent, it must remain in that which transcends it" (47f.).

37. Loder wrote: ". . . what is that essential core [of Kierkegaard's work]? In a single phrase, it is the kinetic connection between *Christology* and *culture*. It is the dialectical logic of the incarnation, carried out in the crucifixion and resurrection, criticizing and reshaping the several diverse disciplines of modern culture for the sake of humanizing existence according to the nature of Jesus Christ. If one begins with the logic of the incarnation in its biblical context, one understands the irreducible starting point for the entire complex corpus of Kierkegaard's thought, and to correlate its logic with the diversities of modern culture is to understand why his thought continues to be so compelling and yet so unclassifiable. It is as deeply grounded as the biblical literature, as coherent as the incarnation, and as pluralistic as the modern mentality . . . Kierkegaard has . . . demonstrated that the inner intelligibility of human existence in faith as revealed through the logic of the incarnation is of a single piece with some of the most formative constructs in modern scientific culture" (*Knight's Move*, 65f).

integrity of practical theology as a theological *and* scientific discipline until and unless one's own spirit is *transformed theologically and relationally* through the power of the Spirit. The nature of the knowing self, as spirit, must itself be transformed by the Spirit in order to know reality accordingly to its own nature as new creation.[38]

The Core Generative Problematic: Redemptive Creativity in Practical Theological Method

In the second essay, "Normativity and Context in Practical Theology: The 'Interdisciplinary' Issue," Loder outlined the crucial priority of the second dimension of practical theology as a discipline, the *methodological* or *systematic* dimension.[39] He argued that for any discipline to have interdisciplinary integrity, the method that interrelates the different dimensions and the content of the discipline as a whole must be grounded in what does not change and therefore what governs the ongoing relations—what he called "the core generative problematic."

> The key to understanding the core of a discipline is to grasp what does not change or what maintains the continuity of the discipline as it unfolds historically. The core of a discipline . . . resides in the generative problematic which, functioning almost like a "strange attractor" in chaos theory, brings the object and ways of knowing it together in a concern that unites but transcends them both . . . [T]he point is that grasping the generative problematic of a discipline is what enables one to transcend the enculturated structure of a discipline and invent new paradigms which depart from, but nevertheless are legitimate heirs of, what has gone before. In practical theology, the core of the discipline is not its operations, procedures, practices, roles, congregations, and the like. Rather, its core problematic resides in why these must be studied; why these are a problem . . . what drives this discipline forward and generates its issues, is that such phenomena or events com-

---

38. We cannot think theologically or act with theological integrity unless and until we are convicted to see ourselves as fully implicated in the Reality Christ continues to make known to us through the Spirit. One's spirit and imagination must continue to be awakened to this theological coherence revealed in the power and presence of Jesus Christ making Himself known to us in our knowing of reality.

39. Loder, "Normativity," 359–381. Loder understood there to be five dimensions to practical theology as a discipline: (1) historical, (2) systematic, (3) ecclesial, (4) operational, and (5) contextual.

bining two incongruent, qualitatively distinct realities, the divine and the human, in apparently congruent forms of action.[40]

For Loder, the core problematic that generates insights for a *theological* and interdisciplinary discipline like practical theology must itself be (1) *theological* and (2) yet be able to retain the integrity of the scientific disciplines themselves for practical theology. But one cannot integrate the agencies of the human and the divine from the side of the human and retain relational integrity, for the only agency competent to render such integrations is the Holy Spirit, who transcends the constructive capacities of human beings and communities in order to connect them back to mundane reality as it was created. The Holy Spirit alone aligns human knowing with integrity to the way things are, theologically discerned.

As we might expect, Loder regarded the "core problematic" that generates insights deep enough for practical theology to be revealed in the God-Human, Jesus Christ, the Reality that holds all divine and human relationality in their proper integrity through time.[41] He wrote: ". . . theology may have a way within itself for relating itself to our postmodern mentality and specifically to experience and the sciences in human action, thereby unfolding its inherent richness and simultaneously extending the implications of experience and of those sciences into a more comprehensive view of what it means to be human."[42] As we have noted,

---

40. Loder, "Normativity," 2 n. 2 (pre-publication copy). Loder's formal statement of the core problematic for interdisciplinary practical theology was: "The core generative problematic [for practical theology] . . . is that such issues [like practices, programs, organizations, spiritual life, etc.] . . . require that two ontologically distinct realities, the divine and the human, be brought together in a unified form of action that preserves the integrity of both and yet gives rise to coherent behavior. This paradoxical problematic implies that God's action and human action, although ontologically distinct, are not ultimately dichotomous" (Loder, "Place of Science," 2).

41. For Loder, the problem of methodology in practical theology turns on the tendency of theorists to seek a non-theological mediation between human action and theology, what he calls a *tertium quid*. Such a move is problematic because, "under the surface of the interdisciplinary discussion, [a non-theological mediation] . . . introduces an alternative reality that is not explicitly accountable to the terms of the theology-human science dialogue itself." Predictably, "these approaches subvert the central problematic of practical theology as a discipline." For Loder, the tacit reality referenced by the mediating baseline controls the insights that fund the practical theological imagination in conformity with whatever ethos that baseline represents—therapy, adaptation, science, experience, etc. See "Normativity," 5–8 (pre-publication copy)

42. Ibid., 8.

this "way within itself" is "the person of Jesus Christ as described by the Chalcedonian formulation . . . the decisive form of relationality" through which "the world has been reconciled to God."[43] As the definitive form of relationality the pattern of Christ is "inexhaustibly" and "infinitely rich" and provides the inner coherence for interdisciplinary methodology as well as all dimensions of interpersonal relations. On analogy to the constant of light in an Einsteinian universe, Jesus is himself the Relational Constant toward which all reality bears witness and through which all integrated witness is born, even (and especially) a scientific witness.[44]

This Christomorphic relationality underlying all reality calls forth, in our fallen world, "a transformational dynamic which is repeatedly awakening us to contradictions between theology and the human sciences, intensifying oppositions until there is a new insight, finally bringing about a reappropriation of the original situation as parabolic of the relationality in Christ."[45] The transformational order-through-disorder-to-new order structure of reality created by *Spiritus Creator* is, in Loder's neo-Chalcedonian science, discerned in the transforming of the knower and in the interdisciplinary theory that encourages order-through-disorder-to-new order participation in Christian practice governed by the Spirit. Furthermore, the deep coherence revealed in the God-Human and actualized in the ministry of the Holy Spirit generates

---

43. Ibid.

44. Loder drew on T. F. Torrance for this understanding. In his reading of John's gospel on Jesus Christ as literally the Light of reality—that is, the relational constant through which all relations constituting reality are discerned and aligned Torrance argued: "Jesus as light can be seen as the constant of the universe. As that constant, all individual perspectives in and of space-time would be relative and contingent to the movement of that light. Jesus, as light, is not 'derivative,' as one might approach him through historical study, but 'ultimate principle.' Jesus is the light through which all history is seen, and cannot be 'defined by reference to any contingent reality beyond [him] self.'" Ken Kovacs comments: "Furthermore, Jesus as light is not bound by space-time, for space-time is defined and constituted through the relational encounter with the constancy of Jesus' presence throughout all space-time. Just as light is part of the created order and lights up the universe, yet is not defined by the universe, so too is Jesus the light of the world who illumines our reality in such a way that he cannot be defined or limited by the created order. Jesus participates in space-time even as he reveals and opens up, that is, allows us 'to see,' our lives within space-time. As constant, the light of the universe is the grace of God revealed in Jesus Christ, whose inexorable faithfulness remains in place for all time-space, but is not controlled by its contingencies" (Kovacs, *Relational*, 145).

45. Loder, "Normativity," 11 (pre-publication copy).

insights not only for Christian education thought and practice, but also for discerning what God is doing in the world to make and keep human life human (Paul Lehmann). Thus, Loder sought a *theological* resolution to the kerygmatic-apologetic tensions in practical theology grounded in the Christological Reality that alone holds all things together in creation itself. The radical nature of Loder's methodological claims for practical theology should now be apparent.

Loder's neo-Chalcedonian science "scandalizes" Kerygmatic-Analytic methods no less than Apologetic-Synthetic methods in practical theology. He showed how relational integrity cannot be derived from either polarity—kerygmatic or apologetic—but only from the Christological relationality that transcends and transforms human perspicacity, creativity, and practice even as it transcends and transforms creation itself. Deep coherence can only be found in the dynamic relationality that holds all polarities together—the God-Human structure of Reality, Jesus Christ—made known in human experience through the Holy Spirit. The work of the Spirit places theology and the human sciences, human thought and practice, on the same contingent footing—namely, in radical dependence on this Living Spirit of Truth that transcends and transforms all created reality. In short, Loder discerned that the work of the Holy Spirit and only the work of the Spirit made practical theology *theological* and gave it *interdisciplinary* integrity.[46] Theological reason and theological action are integrated only as they participate in the actuality of the Spirit's work in, with, among, under, and in spite of, human beings and communities and their best reflective-performative efforts. Loder's hoped-for legacy was to shift the center and

---

46. In this regard, Loder felt that the Church's understanding of the person and work of the Holy Spirit was scandalously underdeveloped in general and in practical theology in particular. The lacuna had been noticed in religious education but had not been fully addressed. In 1965, Edward Farley wrote two articles for *Religious Education*, both entitled: "Does Christian Education Need the Holy Spirit?" After surveying a field in confusion, Farley answered "No!" and proceeded to argue that the Holy Spirit had been reduced in Christian education to the status of an "X-factor" that was simply asserted. Farley concluded: "the Holy Spirit is simply superfluous in the program of Church education." The articles generated more heat than light. But as Russell Hatch contended, Loder's work can be considered a very careful response to Farley's indictment of Christian education's lack of Spirit. Loder wanted to re–describe the entire discipline of Christian education in terms of the work of the Holy Spirit. See Haitch, "Summary," 299–300 for the particulars of the debate. Loder sought to address this concern at every level, including especially the methodological level.

dynamism of practical theology to the work of the Holy Spirit redemptively transforming all human action and thought, so that both practical action and thought participated "kinetically" in the life of God.[47] Interdisciplinary method, for Loder, was crucial but was nevertheless *in itself* nothing more than "a truth producing error" apart from the Spirit. Methodological sophistication, whether kerygmatic or apologetic in formal structure, could in itself actually occlude the practitioner's dependence upon the work of the Spirit. Interdisciplinary method had to serve the Reality to which it was called to bear witness, or it wasn't practical theology in any Christian sense![48]

In my judgment, *EMLOS* was Loder's effort to articulate what might be characterized as a "self-liquidating" or "iconic" *conception* of divine-human action that encouraged dependence of all thought and action (method and practice) upon the tacit power and priority of the Spirit's creative work, even as it encouraged full human participation in that work. The explicit theory itself was designed to bear a "transparent" relationship to the tacit Reality to which it bore witness and upon which it depended.[49] All of his fundamental work prior to *EMLOS* was Loder's effort to describe, in fallible human language, the dynamic nature of created reality as it is revealed in Christ and experienced by human beings. In *EMLOS*, he sought to construct an "iconic" interdisciplinary theory that empowered communities of faith to reflect and embody the redemptively transformative medium of *Spiritus Creator*.

In light of this extended analysis of these two essays, therefore, *EMLOS*'s status as a "legacy" book may depend upon our acceptance of the "scandal" that all our theories and practices are insufficient in themselves to facilitate transformation in the Spirit. Loder believed the Spirit

---

47. The shift from anthropology to theology in Barth's corpus needed to be radicalized in terms of theological anthropology and the work of the Holy Spirit. I understand Loder efforts in some regard as a "revision" of Barth's magisterial effort to recover the theological side of *theo*-anthropology. Loder's pneumatology of Spirit-to-spirit relations provides a way to transform the Barthian project and make it more suitable for theology-science dialogue.

48. While Loder's methodology may seem to conform *formally* with the Comic-Kerygmatic-Analytic side of the discussion in my earlier analysis, the dynamism sought for by the method (its power to enable new life) was dependent on *both* theory or action becoming transparent bearers of the action of the Holy Spirit.

49. I understand the homiletical theory of John McClure, another Loder student, to seek this same kind of "self-liquidating" force in the service of the Spirit. See his essay "Way," 95–115.

continually placed human agents in theological conflicts of immense Christological proportion which alone generated the kinds of insights that "made way" for the Spirit's power. Christian educators are called to be provocateurs of the Holy Spirit who alone creates and maintains the New Being in Christ—the *imago Christi*—in human contexts.[50] From this perspective, the supposed lack of scholarly erudition of *EMLOS* as unworthy of his previous work may need to be reconsidered. In order for Loder to be faithful to his own understanding of the efficacy of the Holy Spirit, his "legacy" book *must* rely more on the tacit reality of the Spirit that his previous works render more explicitly. For his interdisciplinary theory of Christian education, less is more, lest theoretical sophistication or obsession about right practice occludes and replaces the work of the Spirit. The somewhat "impressionistic" discussions in *EMLOS* actually serve to enhance and vindicate the very point of Loder's theological science! He must not say too much (nor too little) in his specific theory of education (*EMLOS*) in order to be faithful to his neo-Chalcedonian science which claims that the Living Spirit alone brings a kinetic or living coherence to human thought and practice. The "legacy" Loder sought to leave with us was the courage to anticipate, discern, and actually participate in the Spirit's redemptive transformation of creation. In other words, if anything *EMLOS* is generally less "scholarly" in form, less comprehensive and more impressionistic than his other writings—*by design!*[51]

---

50. Loder, "Normativity," 16 (pre-publication copy).

51. My judgments in this extended discussion are supported, I believe, by the "Preface" to *EMLOS* that Loder sent to the publisher. Loder described his work in terms of "radical orthodoxy," but as distinct from the "radical orthodoxy" of so-called Milbank school. He wrote: "Radical orthodoxy, as it is understood in this volume . . . does not negate science, hard science or human science, but it seeks to use and transform its methods and claims. This book takes seriously the human sciences and the control they try to exert over human life from the organic and personal to the cultural and philosophical, but it argues that these forms of human understanding are too weak to make any difference unless they are empowered and directed by the Spirit of God as revealed in Jesus Christ." Loder's concern here includes empowering the next generation of the Church to live in the Spirit. "Thus this book wants to place self-revealed divine reality in Jesus Christ at the center of our thinking, especially as we think about educating the upcoming generation in the redemptive power of God's transforming work as redeemer of all creation." Loder's overall argument attempted "to establish the logic of the Spirit, both human and divine, as the speed of light equivalent for human affairs and so the norm for our educational perspectives and practices in the life of the church." See the "Preface" to *EMLOS*, 3–4.

Let us now turn to the "legacy" book itself to see if Loder successfully maintained the kind of delicate balance of thought he claimed was necessary to open thought and practice to the Spirit's empowerment of Christian education in a scientific world.

Educational Ministry in the Logic of the Spirit: An Extended Analysis.

Chapter 1

Loder began *EMLOS* with a programmatic chapter entitled "The Crux of Christian Education: Introductory Dilemmas and a Critical Perspective." His opening section was called "Theory and Practice in Christian Education." He argued (in a way consistent with his conviction about the Chalcedonian relationality that governs knowing noted above) that theory always exercises priority over practice in scientific knowing. Scientific thinking always privileges theory because theory determines what is (and can be) observed. Theory, like good theater,[52] penetrates beneath the socially constructed world of practice to disclose what is really happening relationally. Theories disclose "hidden orders of intelligibility" (i.e., what the gods are doing) lying tacitly below the surface of experience, so to speak. He noted: "Good theory in Christian education, then, like good theory in science or good theatre [sic] . . . is an ongoing disclosure and articulation of a hidden higher order of things in relation to and in light of the Truth of God's self-revelation. It thereby invites our faithful holistic [sic] participation in God's on-going redemptive transformation of all creation."[53] In other words, a scientific practical theology of Christian education requires extraordinary imagination about what God is doing in the world. Everyday practice must be re-imagined from the standpoint of the God-Human structure, an imaginative construct from the Chalcedonian theologians that remains extraordinarily compelling for discerning the inner relational structures undergirding reality from the standpoint of Christian faithfulness. That

---

52. Loder notes that "Theory," from the Gr. *thea*, means "the action of viewing, beholding or contemplating." We get our word "theater" from this word, which signifies in its true sense the kind of deep penetrating viewing of reality that is normally occluded by our social constructions of reality.

53. *EMLOS*, chapter 1, 7f. I am interacting with the 2001 copy of *EMLOS* Loder gave me, and will cite chapter and pagination from that manuscript in this review.

is, theological-scientific approach to Christian education requires what Loder, following Michael Polanyi, called "indwelling" the phenomenon under investigation.

When Loder "indwelled" Christian education—i.e. when he entered imaginatively into the inner structure of Christian education to discern the internal relations that constitute that reality, allowing Christian education to reveal how it is to be known—he discerned a version of the order-disorder-transformed order of creation-redemption discussed earlier—*socialization* and *transformation* in a fundamentally tensile or contradictory (or paradoxical) relationality in search of its true continuity.[54] Thus, two contradictory dynamic forces in tension, socialization and transformation, underlie the deeper intelligible structure and dynamics not just of the Christian education in particular but also of all socio-cultural domains of human action (and of all creation!). Loder discerned a latent and deeply contradictory disjunction at the center of human action that we must take seriously (a version of the core problematic that generates insight). We might schematize it as follows:

Christian←Contradictory Disjunction→education

Loder developed a model of these disjunctive dynamics in dialogue with the sociological insights of Talcott Parsons, whose work Loder encountered at Harvard and later reinterpreted theologically. I take his neo-Parsonian model as a theological description in scientific language of what Scripture calls the powers of "conformity" at work in the world and the church, the penultimate context of Christian education ultimately at odds with the Spirit's redemptive intention (cf. Rom 12:1).[55] From this theological model Loder argued that, apart from the Spirit, we are continually and inevitably resolving the contradictory disjunction underlying experience on the side of socialization dynamics that are finally entropic and resistant to the life-giving Spirit. Loder described socialization-dominant-transformation as "*a tension-reduction, pattern-maintenance process* designed to serve [in every register of human experience] the purposes of adaptation and incorporation into larger and more complex social milieu."[56] This adaptational power works in every

---

54. Ibid., chapter 1, 8 n. 5.

55. Loder took courses from Parsons at Harvard and imbibed or indwelled his thought, and later re-interpreted it theologically for Christian education.

56.. *EMLOS*, chapter 1, 12.

register of human agency and relationship in interpenetrating isomorphic patterns that inevitably conform all persons and institutions to societal goals based on survival and preservation. Rendered in Loder's theological imagination, socialization participates in the entropic dynamism that Scripture calls "death" in the biblical account of the Fall.[57] Socialization is, theologically, the potential progenitor of idolatry and death, understood perhaps as the power of disrelations woven throughout the social construction of reality. Socialization itself moves in the direction of death, always finally, apart from its transformation by the Spirit, contrary to the Spirit of Life revealed in Christ. From a theological viewpoint, socialization proves over and over again to be a false solution to the contradictory disjunction at the heart of all human action, a false continuity of the highest order.

On the other hand, human transformation-in-relation-to-socialization is understood by Loder as pointing toward the true resolution for human action in the God-Human, Jesus Christ, though its potential for distortion continues as well. He defined transformation as "a patterned process whereby in any given frame of knowledge or experience, a hidden order of meaning emerges with the power to redefine and/or reconstruct the original frame of reference."[58] Transformation as "a force of universal magnitude" provides the counterpoint to death and disrelation, seeking the renewal of life and power throughout reality—the true continuity.[59] In particular, human transformation-in-relation-to-socialization dynamics are also at work in four dimensions of human action—bodily, psychic, social and cultural—that make up the relational matrices of the social construction of reality, from human development in context, to family dynamics, to international relations, etc. But the power of unredeemed socialization is entropic and, therefore, under the conditions of the Fall, dominant over transformation, always tending toward pattern maintenance, tension-reduction, spirit-constricting adaptation to socialized interests for the purpose of survival and/or control. The power of transformation is pattern expanding, reality-opening, and

---

57. Ibid., chapter 1, 13.

58. Ibid., chapter 1, 14.

59. Loder's forays into physics substantiated that transformation is more powerful than entropy. Following Prigogine he argued that out of entropic disorder in the universe are self–organizing capacities at every level, from the universe to the human mind that studies the universe (Ibid., 1, 4f, n. 8).

spirit-enabling. "When transformation is dominant, then it is clear that all socialization is unto transformation, preparatory to the emergence of a higher but hidden order in keeping with God's action in the world."[60]

But naturalistic transformation, like socialization, cannot bear the Spirit's redemptive transformational initiatives until and unless these dynamics themselves are transformed according to the nature of Jesus Christ. Human powers of socialization-transformation, until redeemed in Christ, have no final power to withstand or overcome either the conforming powers of socialization unto death or the "loose cannons of creativity" that mark unredeemed human transformations. For Loder, under the conditions of sin and the power of death, socialization ultimately dominates the socialization-transformation relational matrix, placing even scientific creativity under the power of ego and in service to forms of disrelation endemic in the unredeemed world.[61] Socialization domesticates transformation and distorts relations that transformation seeks to regenerate and enliven. Human transformations cannot sustain their transformational potential for reversing the dominance of socialization. "All natural forces, including transformation itself, must be transformed," according to Loder, through the power of the Spirit.[62] The Spirit negates the negation of the entropic power of unredeemed socialization-transformation dynamics and reverses this distorted relationality so that transformation gains ontological priority in alignment with the redemptive transforming power of the Reign of God. "[I]t is through the eyes of faith in Jesus Christ that we can recognize the ontological priority of transformation over any other force in the universe . . . because the creative pattern of this force operative throughout creation is analogous . . . to the pattern by which all creation is renewed and will be redeemed by the Creator Spirit."[63]

---

60. Ibid., chapter 1, 15.

61. Miller, *Picasso*. Miller, not to be confused with the playwright Arthur Miller, was Professor of the History and Philosophy of Science and University College London from 1991–2005. He is now a writer, commentator, and consultant on cognitive theory and creativity.

62. *EMLOS*, chapter 1, 16.

63. Ibid., chapter 1, 16f. What Loder has done in this chapter is to discern what the Scripture in its polemics calls "the world" or "the principalities and powers." This theme has become crucial in theological constructs through the wide-ranging works of such thinkers as Paul Lehmann, William Stringfellow, Walter Wink, Richard Horsley, John Dominic Crossan, Jeorg Rieger, Timothy Gorringe, Johan Baptist Metz, Jürgen

In the remainder of chapter 1 Loder described the "challenges" socialization ("education") and transformation ("Christian") bring to each other. He argued that the tension between the two forces must be heightened and indwelled in order for the discipline of Christian education to retain its theological and interdisciplinary integrity as a provocateur of the Holy Spirit's power. To help conceptualize the tension, Loder re-imagines Talcott Parsons' isomorphic-structured theory of action that interrelates biological, psychological, social, and cultural registers toward the goal of adaptation.

In this construct, "transformation is tacitly present in each subsystem and in the transitions among them," even as the "decisive dominant force is socialization and the drive toward adaptation."[64] Socialization is latent and pervasive in all experience and works to master transformational disruptions and bring them into conformity to the goals of the social construction of reality—including especially Christian faith itself. This domesticating power of death is the challenge of "education" to "Christian" in Christian education. Loder argued that socialization dynamics cannot be "Christianized" to serve the Gospel's transformational initiative, contrary to the methodological efforts of theorists to do precisely that.[65] The false continuity of socialization is too strong.

Moltmann and others. The Church is in the world but the world is in the Church, and practical theology needs a way to discern how the distortions of the world impact the Church. Loder's particular contribution to this concern is the impotence of human transformations in the face of socialization. Human transformation-socialization dynamics must themselves be transformed if they are to fully participate in the redemption of the Holy Spirit and be liberated from the "powers."

64. *EMLOS*, chapter 1, 22.

65. Loder's critique of socialization, developmentalism, and the more recent iteration of practice–based models of Christian education remains consistent on this score. See below.

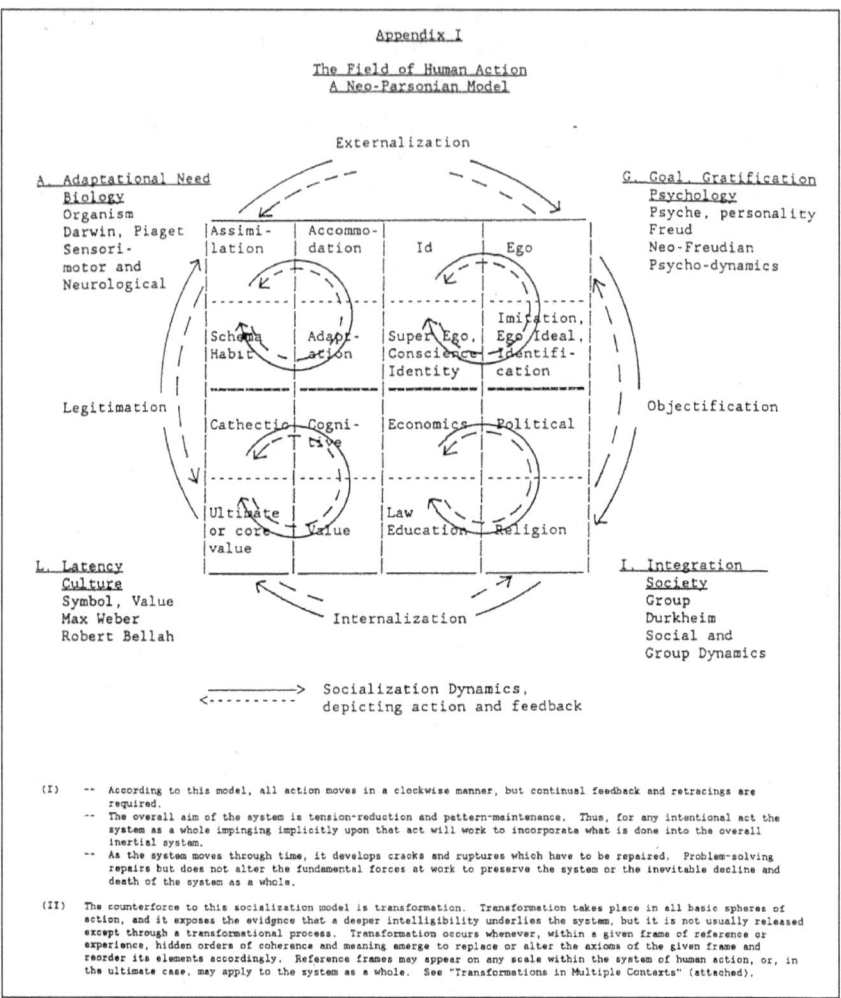

Loder's Theological Interpretation of Talcott Parsons' Action Theory

The challenge of "Christian" to "education" is even more powerful. Loder wrote, "When the nature of Jesus Christ is the transcendent reality toward which emergent coherent orders of meaning point, transformation as a power characterizes life in the Spirit of Christ. As such the predominance of transformation over socialization focuses in dynamic terms the Christian challenge to education."[66] Loder drew on Kierkegaard to make his case that "Christianity will not yield to habit"

66. *EMLOS*, chapter 1, 26.

since "the dynamics of habitation and socialization are not sufficient . . . in their efforts to be bearers of Christian truth."[67] There must be "a coherent relationship between the content of the faith and the dynamics by which it is conveyed." And since Christianity reveals a dynamic transcendent relationality, Christian faithfulness cannot be taught apart from the Spirit's transformational power at work to redeem every register of human action and thought dominated by socialization. In the unity of Christ's person as fully divine and fully human, the true coherence of the relation of "Christian" to "education" is discerned and appropriated in the Spirit. The remainder of the book comprises Loder's effort to articulate the "how" of the Spirit's work of redemptive transformation through the practice of Christian education.

Part I, Chapters 2, 3, and 4

After this programmatic introduction, Loder began Part I of his study, "Socialization Dominance: The Malleability of Culture" with a lengthy chapter entitled "Socialization and Transformation: A Brief History." First of all, Loder used his neo-Chalcedonian lens to assert the "irreducible relationality of God and humanity"[68] as this relationality is portrayed in Scripture (the Tower of Babel and Pentecost), in Christian interpretations of world history (van Leewen's *Christianity in World History*[69]), and in the power of civil religion and the history of Christian education in American culture. Loder's scientific reconstruction of Chalcedon's Christology revealing a "bipolar relational dynamic" (spelled out in *The Knight's Move*) "has interpretative power" for re-envisioning the history

---

67. Ibid., chapter 1, 28.

68. Loder quoted Karl Barth in the epilogue to the chapter: "Starting with Jesus Christ and with Him alone, we must see and understand what in the Christian sense is involved in the mighty relationship, to which we can only point again and again in sheer amazement, about which we cannot help being in danger of great error, when we say God and man." See Barth, *Dogmatics*, 66.

69. In this same chapter Loder used A. van Leewen's controversial study *Christianity in World History* to argue that the socialization-transformation relationality can be used cross–culturally to discern "ontocratic" and "theocratic" world views operative in cultures throughout history. Loder noted: "The main point here is that the seductive power of socialization makes it evident that the typology van Leewen described is not fundamentally an ancient–modern or an east–west dichotomy, but . . . better interpreted dynamically as a socialization/transformation struggle played out differently in different epochs in both east and west" (*EMLOS*, chapter 2, 17f).

of socialization-transformation dynamics even as it appears in narrative form in Scripture or in so-called "secular" historical contexts. So, the metaphors of "Jerusalem" and "Babylon" can show forth socialization-dominant disrelational culture (Babylon) and transformation-dominant relational culture (Jerusalem or the Church) as these realities are portrayed in the biblical narrative. Amazingly, the portrayal of Babylon as a "closed system" of domesticated culture in Genesis 11 (the tower of Babel story) "is not altogether different from contemporary systems of socialization which attempt an all-inclusive integration of psychological, social, and cultural organization."[70] Similarly, the birth of the Church narrative (Acts 2) functions as the anti-type of Babylon to reveal an "open system" in the power of the eschatological Spirit redemptively transforming socialization-transformation dynamics at Pentecost according to the nature of Jesus Christ. Loder approved of Barth's "elegant" Chalcedonian description of human reality redemptively transformed in the Spirit:

> The work of the Holy Spirit . . . is to bring and to hold together that which is different and therefore, as it would seem, necessarily and irresistible [sic] disruptive in the relationship of Jesus Christ to His community, namely, the divine working, being, and action on the one side and the human on the other, the creative freedom and act on one side and the human on the other, the eternal reality and possibility on one side and the temporal on the other. His work is to bring and hold them together, not to identify, intermingle or confound them, not to change the one into the other nor to merge the one into the other, but to coordinate them, to make them parallel, to bring them into harmony and therefore to bind them into a true unity.[71]

The same lens is useful for interpreting human history as the interplay of these same dynamic forces. Loder engaged A. van Leewen's dialectic of "ontocratic" (socialization dominant) and "theocratic" (transformation dominant) forces outlined in his controversial 1964 book *Christianity in World History* to show the interpretative power of Chalcedonian relationality in history. According to Loder, the "desacralization" intrinsic to "theocratic" patterns that took root in the West (deeding a relative autonomy to human creativity largely closed off to the

---

70. *EMLOS*, chapter 2, 7.
71. Ibid., chapter 2, 13, quoting from Barth, *CD IV*: 3, second half, 761.

East's ontocratic imagination), gave the West its relatively "open-ended and contingent" sensibility essential to the development of science and to fostering a climate for ongoing social revolutions. Even so, however, the power of socialization in the West domesticates the more dynamic theocratic pattern in ways that replicate "Babylonian Captivity." Thus, the "theocratic" pattern must itself be continually transformed by the Spirit of Christ if culture is to experience the truly generative, life-giving power of Christ in the world.[72]

Loder's third illustration of the power of his Chalcedonian model relates to the history of civil religion and its impact the history of Christian education in America. He outlined the "Great Awakenings" in American history as events of transformation pointing to the transformation of all reality in Christ. While these awakenings have inevitably been socialized, they nonetheless point to our culture's "permanent need" to be grounded in the Spirit of Christ. Transformation-socialization dynamics come to "critical mass" in times when "what is publicly recognized as the ultimate court of appeal is brought directly into conflict with the particulars . . . of a well-socialized sphere of human action." In such cases "transformation . . . is calling those ultimate claims into engagement with specific aspects of the interlocking arenas of a society turned

---

72. Ken Kovacs' recently published dissertation *Relational Theology of James E. Loder* explores precisely this concern in chapter 4, "A Radicalized Spatio-Temporal World." Through the lens of Chalcedon and the work of the Spirit, human history itself, and our reading of human history are exposed as idolatrous human constructs that bear ultimate negation until and unless transformed by the Spirit of Christ. When Loder conceived of the nature and task of Christian education, the reach of his theory goes beyond culture and incorporates human history itself in its powerful effort to constrict the human spirit within its own "fear of absence." Negation is not woven only into human development or the social construction of reality but into human history itself as a construction of meaning. The "triumph of negation" is found especially in efforts by theology to mediate the continuity of Christ through historical processes like tradition or dogmatic development or practices. This effort is ironically unhistorical in the sense that it composes historical process in abstractions in an effort to "repress" the "sense of absence" perceived in the early church's experience of the "delay of the Parousia." Historical constructions betray the human fear that incoherence and a sense of absence or void is all there is. History is used "functionally" as the effort to restore order and meaning amid the corruptibility of historical experience. In essence human history rehearses over and over again the "Babylonian" effort to "make a name for ourselves" and to "built a tower to heaven" to cover our existential sense of abandonment and aloneness (Gen 11). History must be read "Christologically" if the full four-dimensionality of human experience is affirmed, including the dimension of human death that pervades and largely determines human agency. See Kovacs, *Relational*, 113–52.

in upon itself by socialization dynamics." In such events "the socialized sphere of action yields to the transforming vision, or . . . [to] the power of socialization . . . suppressing emergence of a new axiomatic order."[73] Loder showed how the power of socialization has exercised dominance in Christian education theory and practice in American history, and thus how the Church has distorted the nature of Christ even as it has pretended to honor him.

In the last half of this extended chapter, Loder discussed the socialization theory of Christian education offered by C. E Nelson, one of the most sophisticated theorists in the field. His in-depth analysis focused on Nelson's influential book *Where Faith Begins*.[74] While he affirmed aspects of Nelson's book, he strongly criticized Nelson's efforts to "Christianize" the powers of socialization. He argued that relational reality communicated Spirit-to-spirit in Christ contradicts the disrelations intrinsic to socialization-transformation dynamics until and unless those dynamics are themselves transformed by the power that negates the negation riven into unredeemed socialization-transformation reciprocity.[75] "My basic objection to Nelson's approach is that it seeks to socialize the transforming work of God's Spirit. It needs to be the other way around. God's Spirit is much larger than society and socialization."[76]

> To take the action of God's Spirit and the action of God in the community, and bring them under the canons of social science is in these very fundamental ways a violation of what we would want to say theologically about God's action. God stands over and against the socialization process. When God uses socialization, it is to transform it, which means that socialization is in the service of transformation. But if we take Nelson's premise, experiences and events which bring us into relationship to God socialize transformation at best. The theological premise regarding the priority of transformation over socialization makes all the difference.[77]

Therefore, socialization is at best "a truth producing error" in both theory and practice. What Christian educators must emphasize and

---

73. *EMLOS*, chapter 2, 24.
74. Nelson, *Where Faith Begins*.
75. *EMLOS*, chapter 2, 39–53.
76. Ibid., chapter 2, 53.
77. Loder, "Socialization Approach," undated version of chapter 2.

discern is "the translation of the substantive nature of Jesus Christ into this bipolar relational dynamic [i.e., the Chalcedonian model]" which has "the interpretative power for re-envisioning [*sic*] the history of this field and for moving it into the future under the guidance of a dynamic interpretation of the *hypostatic* union, as the unified bipolarity of the person of Christ has been classically designated."[78]

In chapter 3, "Lifestyles: Taking Social Reality Seriously," Loder developed Nelson's proper emphasis on "life style" as the "fashioning of power" in every register of human action.[79] But he showed how such power operating through socialization on a massive scale actually permeates and shapes life styles that reflect "Babylonian" ways of being human incongruous to life in the Spirit. Indeed, congregational relations tend to be held in thrall to distortions of spirit promoted through various cultural lifestyles prevalent in American society, all of which have been studied by the social sciences. But from a theological point of view the self-alienating, communion-corrupting impact of socialization dynamics on Christian faith needs to be appreciated and resisted if the Church is to live in the Spirit of Christ. Loder takes up four lifestyles that can be summarized as follows:

1. THE ACHIEVEMENT LIFESTYLE. Perhaps the most pervasive and influential life style shaping mainline denominations, achievement obsession distorts love relations or intimacy. Closely associated with Parsons' goal-setting register (the psycho-social box), this lifestyle is grounded in the organism's ends-means instincts which, in Western culture, tends to overshadow "ascriptive worth potential," the person's true context for receiving rewards. Loder noted, "Originally children are balanced [in means-ends instincts and ascriptive worth potential]. But what happens to this balance in our achievement-oriented society is that we gradually inform the child in subtle ways that she is really

---

78. *EMLOS*, chapter 2, 2.

79. Loder is speaking of "life style" in the strongest sense of "how one fashions the energy of a lifetime" (Whitehead), a fashioning that is pervasive and persistent in a person or community's existence. Unredeemed, these powerful lifestyles tend to create Christian "faithfulness" in their own image, thus actually destroying the possibility of Christian faithfulness. "A lifestyle is a relatively stable, patterned process whose core characteristics govern life in all four major areas of human action" (*EMLOS*, chapter 3, 3). This understanding is consistent with Cornell West's idea of "normative gaze." See West, *Prophesy*, 53ff. See also Loder, *Knight's Move*, 7.

worth a lot more for what she can do, than she is for just being there. Thus, the dominance of goal getting gets established in the psychic life."[80] This is the basic ego posture underlying the achievement personality and it is reinforced continually and relentlessly through socialization and "schooling's" commitment to the "ritualization of progress."[81] Loder argued that socialization brings this achievement distortion into the heart of congregational life and shapes life styles that erode the inner life and suppresses ascriptive worth. Christianity itself becomes dominated by the wrong spirit, a spirit that ever seeks to deserve the love one gets.

2. THE AUTHORITARIAN LIFESTYLE. This lifestyle, the distortion of power governing social relations, also pervades Western cultures, especially in military, education, business, or religious settings. The origins of this lifestyle take place early on in the Oedipal/Elektra struggle between primitive urges and social constrains on those urges. In normal development children learn to identify with the parents of the same sex in order to learn the basic social role. But in homes where fear and violence prevail, identification dynamics change as the child identifies with whatever adult has the most power out of fear of punishment. One learns to always side with power over others in order to be in control. Unable to identify with ambiguities or complex inner feelings, the child learns to live in a black-and-white world of weak and strong, in-group and out-group stereotyping, of superstitious and fatalistic sense of history, and a concern to punish the other.

3. THE PROTEAN LIFESTYLE. This lifestyle distorts the longing for freedom in all of us and is particularly generated in our media-saturated society, which connects to the culture box in Parsons' schema. The pervasive anxiety over nuclear war (now also environmental or terrorist catastrophe), social dislocation caused by "de-territorializating" power of globalization, and media saturation explains the emergence of this lifestyle in which the self is always "in process." In such contexts "virtual" realities tend to prevail and the child is left to continually "create" herself amid an illusive and ephemeral cultural context. A protean lifestyle is marked by cynicism and self-evasion, a longing for community but a fear of commitment, a vague moral confusion and indifference to society,

---

80. *EMLOS*, chapter 3, 8.

81. Ivan Illich discerned the power of these elements in his book *De-Schooling Society*.

and the absence of superego. This lifestyle is particularly influential on young persons.

4. THE OPPRESSIVE LIFESTYLE. This lifestyle distorts justice and connects to subsistence living in the organic box in Parsons' structure. This lifestyle engenders a pervasive sense that one cannot achieve, is perpetually an outsider, and is powerless to overcome these circumstances. This sense oppression is passed on through parents chronically oppressed. The lifestyle is characterized by pervasive sense of low self-esteem, repressed anger covered over by jocularity, distrust and hostility and agitation due to fear of loss of control, and passivity or resignation, and a vague sense of oppression by "the system," which remains unnamed.

Thus, chapter three provides the reader with an extraordinarily rich neo-Chalcedonian scientific analysis of how the human spirit becomes distorted within a variety of depraved lifestyles inevitably woven into the disrelational fabric of our social constructions of reality.

Chapter 4, "Human Development and Personality Formation," shows how the same relational distortions Loder described in society and culture are generated in so-called "normal" human development. He defined key terms in the literature—development, interaction, adaptation, intelligence, structuralism—and reviewed the central features of those whose contributions have shaped the field—Freud, Erikson, Piaget, Kohlberg, Fowler, and Gilligan. Essentially this chapter reviewed his argument in *The Logic of the Spirit*, focusing especially on the work of James Fowler's faith development paradigm.[82] Loder valued Fowler's work in terms of his research method and the reliability of aspects of his developmental theory. But he asked, "What developmental phenomenon is [Fowler] studying?" He argued that Fowler's biblical and theological understandings are deficient in the way he attempts to portray what he calls faith development.

> What we have here is one of the most pointed examples of the triumph of socialization over transformation. "Faith" is here the structure of one's own capacity to adapt to the largest sociocultural environmental range possible. My own predisposition would be to say that the main title and subtitle of Fowler's

---

82. For the core of Loder's critique of Fowler, see *Logic*, 256–59. See also the responses Loder and Fowler made to one another's work in Loder and Fowler, "Conversations," 133–48.

book should be reversed to read, "The Psychology of Human Development and the Quest for Meaning: Stages of an Aspect of Faith." It seems to me that Fowler's work is a sensitive, insightful study of the ego's competence in structuring meaning, but it is only potentially, not necessarily related to faith in a biblical or theological sense.[83]

In contrast to "faith development" as a function of the executive ego creating and composing reality toward cultural adaptation, faith is actually a relational reality governed by the Spirit. Following Gerhard Ebeling, Loder argued that biblical faith

1. gives certainty to existence from beyond the ego's capacity,
2. opens up the future beyond developmental stages,
3. participates in the power of God through the exercise of "power made perfect in weakness,"
4. is witnessed to from outside the structural potential of the developing ego,
5. is particular and exceptional rather than inevitable and automatic, and
6. is decisively salvific in relation to God rather than an expression of human potential.[84]

Biblical faith connects persons to the theological question "Why do I exist?" in a way that goes beyond the capacity of the human ego.

Thus, according to Loder, Fowler's whole project "seems to reflect rather than correct the 'ritualization of progress' in an achievement obsessed society."[85] Thus, it celebrates, against Fowler's own intention, the dehumanizing distortion of the human spirit woven into the warp and woof of American society. Fowler's theory cannot penetrate to the core generative problematic discerned through Christ, because the Living Christ is not understood in his paradigm to be the center of the personality. So called "normal development, as described by Fowler, is theologically abnormal."[86] Thus, Loder argued that "normal" human

---

83. *EMLOS*, chapter 4, 33.

84. Loder is dependent on Ebeling's study of the synoptic Gospels, *Word and Faith*, 201ff.

85. *EMLOS*, chapter 4, 37.

86. Ibid., chapter 4, 40.

development under the unredeemed ego tends to deepen the "captivity" of the human spirit to the Babylonian power of death.

Part 2, Chapters 5, 6, 7, and 8

How the Holy Spirit works the transformation of the socialization-transformation "captivity" in all dimensions of human agency is the subject of the middle section of *EMLOS*, "The Holy Spirit and Human Transformation." Chapter 5, "Transformation in Theology: Analogy of the Spirit," rehearsed the argument of *The Transforming Moment* for its generative insights into the transformation of the human spirit by the Holy Spirit. Loder argued that the power of socialization dominating the social constructions of reality actually determines the subjectivity of human beings and communities in sub-Christian ways unless and until the Spirit works an ontological transformation in the knower. He called his disclosure analogy the "*analogia spiritus*" (analogy of the spirit), which describes the dynamic relationality that exists between the creativity of the human spirit and the creativity of God's Spirit (*Spiritus Creator*). The similarity of the analogy is that both the human spirit and the Holy Spirit create reality out of conflicts through a patterned transformational logic that combines continuity and discontinuity toward a telos.[87] But the dissimilarity of the analogy is crucial in that the Holy Spirit transforms the transformational pattern of the human spirit according to its larger, theological frame of reference. "What we want to do is shift to a frame of reference that includes [the] first two dimensions [of human existence, the self and the "worlds" we inhabit], but then go [sic] beyond them to include the whole scope of human existence . . . we will have to learn to think in terms of four dimensions: the self, the world, the Void, and the Holy . . . human existence in a redeemed creation."[88] We might summarize Loder's understanding of these dimensions as follow:

1. THE SELF. The "I" creates and composes the world and is shaped by the world, which is embodied in, and yet transcends, the body.

2. THE WORLD. The creative "I" creates and recreates livable environments ("worlds") that in turn create and shape the creative "I" according to

---

87. The patterned "logic of the spirit" is (1) conflict in context, (2) scanning for solutions, (3) insight, (4) release of energy bound up with the conflict, and (5) interpretation.

88. *EMLOS*, chapter 5, 25f (Slightly emended)..

the power of socialization. The "self" and the "world" comprise the two dimensions governed by socialization.

3. THE VOID. Hidden "under" the social construction of reality is a third dimension of our existence, the presence of an absence or "nothingness" that "haunts being." The proximate forms of the Void (loneliness, alienation, disease, conflicts, etc.) all point to the possibility that Nothing is all there is, and our true destiny.

4. THE HOLY. The Living Presence that comes to us from beyond the Void and the social construction of reality but enters into the three-dimensions to transform them according to the nature of Jesus Christ. While the human sciences can take seriously the first two dimensions, they cannot in fact take seriously the nothingness underlying the social construction of reality (the third dimension) or the Presence of the reality-transforming power of the Spirit (fourth dimension).

Only the Spirit of Christ working in a Chalcedonian calculation reveals these deeper dimensions underlying the social construction of reality and calls us to embrace reality fully with the courage of our convictions. Loder described this reality-discerning transformation as follows:

> These are the four dimensions within which the Holy Spirit of God lives and moves, bestowing grace and engendering faith. Faith, then, is abiding in the fourth dimension while the power of faith transforms the other three. The effect of abiding in the fourth dimension is not to become so transcendently spiritual or spiritualistic that out of every pore there oozes some sort of heavenly glow. Abiding in the fourth dimension means that you are put back into the ordinary world . . . the ordinary world then becomes the bearer of the extraordinary. The "I" becomes "I, not I, but Christ" . . . dialectical identity . . . The world also gets transformed because the world that you are working and building, extending yourself into is now not a world you composed, [but] . . . rather . . . the world you see Christ composing . . . the kingdom of God. Even the void gets transformed because the void is no longer this deep silence behind silence . . . [but] a shadow, the foreshadowing of grace . . . the optimal occasion within which you can recognize grace as thoroughly gracious . . . Holy gets its sharpest, clearest definition in the context of void . . . The Holy Presence of God becomes the ultimate milieu within which all

other dimensions are embraced and seen as such [i.e., in their proper fullness].[89]

In chapters 6 through 8, Loder described the impact of the Holy Spirit in more detail in terms of three of the four dimensions of human action: human development, social relations, and culture. In relation to psycho-social development (chapter 6), the Spirit's intimacy with the human spirit transforms the defensiveness and control sought by unredeemed ego by placing ego in the service of the relational integrity of Christ. The ego's power is affirmed, but discerned to be the sponsor of profound disrelational (defensive) propensities that must be "crucified" by the Spirit in order that truly non-coercive, non-possessive relations with God and with others might be liberated and released. Loder used Scripture, parables, and case studies from his own counseling to illuminate the Spirit's work in ego transformation.

In relation to social reality (chapter 7), Loder showed how the search of ego for a non-coercive and intimate relational context is found in the *koinonia*, the communion-creating reality of Jesus Christ. In this domain the Spirit works the transformation of non-intimate, role-based relations by "crucifying" the dehumanization implicit in role structures in order to engender the more intimate relationality revealed in the Trinity as the living foundation of communion on earth. Loder asserted that

> . . . the "communion-creating reality of Jesus Christ," the koinonia, frees us from the double-binding conditions that role structures place upon us. This is because the koinonia relationship is grounded in and secured by the spiritual Presence of Christ. So, as Lehmann understands it, koinonia is a four-dimensional phenomenon. It exists only because the power of Christ as the fourth dimension creates and sustains a set of relationships among us. By love, the Holy Spirit is transforming us into each other, while building up in us a corporate awareness of Christ's Presence; the fourth dimension is here at work transforming the other three. It is making us aware of the inherent negation in role structured and role determined institutional life. It is putting us into a two-dimensional world with a four-dimensional perspective so we can mutually create each other. As one student suggested, this is

---

89. Ibid., chapter 5, 42f. Loder spells out the *analogia spiritus* and the transformational grammar working in four dimensions in his trope on "the Emmaus Event" in Luke 24. See Loder, *Transforming*, 97–120.

a corporate version of our dialectical identity in Christ . . . "we, not we, but koinonia."[90]

Finally, in relation to cultural dynamics (chapter 8), the power of the Spirit works to render language, images, and symbols transparent to the Reality to which they tacitly or explicitly refer, negating the negation of their tendency to lie (i.e., offer two dimensional resolutions to four dimensional reality).[91] In particular Loder focused on the power of master images to distort and "lie" until they are transformed through the Spirit of Christ and rendered transparent signs of the Reign of God. Culture in all its particulars is affirmed as a potentially meaningful context that nevertheless serves the interests of dehumanization by being bonded to master images that "capture" and "control" the relational dynamism that inspired those images in the first place. But when the Spirit works, the negation implicit in these captured images is negated to empower the human knower to look "through" the master image to behold its relation to the "imageless" Presence of Jesus Christ—i.e., the Living Presence beyond the cultural construction of reality through which all cultural images find their ultimate meaning. "The transformation of culture . . . does not eliminate culture but makes it iconic, a visible and tangible occasion for entering into the invisible and intangible presence of God."[92]

All in all these chapters demonstrate the redemptive transformation of the Holy Spirit transforming developmental, social and cultural reality by negating the negation riven into that reality in order to rightly relate all dimensions of human action to the coherent Presence of Christ. Loder offered valuable clues for the Church to discern the Presence of the Spirit at work both within the community of faith and in the world. This outline of the soteriological transformation of the Spirit in every realm of human action suggests the enormous promise of Loder's Chalcedonian science for the current concern for "public" practical theology. Loder addressed the underlying dynamic structures of all experience private and public, individual and social, personal and cultural in a way that reveals the "logic of the Spirit" at work in all of human experience individual and collective. I regard this theological transformation

90. Locer, "Society: Koinonia and Social Transformation," chapter 7, 21f.
91. "From the Cynics to the Epicureans, from Nietzsche [sic] to Freud, from existentialism to deconstructionism, the point is made again and again: it is extremely difficult, if not impossible, for language to tell the truth" (Loder, *EMLOS*, chapter 8, 1).
92. *EMLOS*, chapter 8, 40.

of Parsons' action theory as perhaps the single most important aspect of Loder's practical theology still largely unheard and ignored by practical theology today.

Part 3, Chapters 9 and 10

In the final section of this book, "Human Participation in Divine Action: The Claims of the Theory," Loder outlined (in purposely impressionistic ways) the practical or explicit operational dimensions of his theory of Christian education practice. In chapter 9, "Structuring the Vision," Loder reminded us again that the purpose of theory is to continually indwell the reality being disclosed so that "its tacit implications may become generative for focal or explicit forms of practice." He argued, "to indwell the theory is just the opposite of what trivializers of theory think . . . [Theory] is designed to create the most profound reciprocity possible between cognition and experience, between understanding and action, between the life of the mind of the theorist and the life and mind of God. Theory calls for indwelling, so that both the 'Christian' and the 'education' of Christian education may disclose their underlying meaning."[93] More than that, Christian education theory is designed to disclose and draw upon the deeper intelligibility of the Trinitarian enfolding of human history in particular ways and contexts. "The ultimate intelligible order on which Christian education theory is based is the inner logic of Christ's nature given in Scripture and formulated for the Church especially as it was articulated by the Chalcedonian theologians. This is not to set up a monotheism of the second person of the Trinity because the whole Trinitarian life is present in each of its persons, but it is in the incarnation that the inner life of God is disclosed to us in terms most like our own."[94] Here in this opening part of chapter 9, Loder summarized the claim he made for the power of his theory to foster participation in the Chalcedonian interplay of human and divine relations revealed in Christ.

> Looking through the lenses of [Christ's] nature, we have seen that the crux of Christian education is an interplay between socialization and transformation. Christologically, socialization is as essential to the enterprise of Christian education as

93. Ibid., chapter 9, 2.
94. Ibid., chapter 9, 3.

> the humanity of Jesus Christ is essential to his nature . . . By the same Christological analogy, transformation is as essential to Christian education as is divinity to the nature of Jesus Christ. Thus, as we plan and enact educational activities in the life of the church as the body of Christ, we must always deal with both sides of this interplay, both sides of his nature . . . The Chalcedonian interplay is the crux of Christian education and it embodies the ultimate intelligibility in which the theory of Christian education is grounded.[95]

When Christ's nature governs this interplay, Christian education becomes redemptively transformational and four dimensional, accord to Loder. Only in the Spirit are congregations empowered in explicit practice to live in and through the four-dimensional reality revealed in Jesus Christ. The theoretical principles Loder developed in this chapter to guide educational practice cannot guarantee the Spirit. But they do suggest "a systematic integration of perspectives that permit appropriate responses to whatever educational situation occurs so that the work of the Spirit may prosper."[96]

Loder used a version of the reporter's "interrogative hermeneutic" to demonstrate how his neo-Chalcedonian theoretical lens illuminates the explicit purpose (why?), scope (what?), context (where?), process (how?) personnel (who?), and timing (when?) of educational praxis that participates in the Spirit. We can summarize Loder's insights here as follows, beginning with the process (How?):

1. PROCESS (HOW?). When the eschatological *Spiritus Creator* is present in any situation the potential for redemptive transformation in four dimensions consistent with the God-human structure of reality may be realized. Educators who undergo transformation by the Spirit learn to discern the Spirit's work in four dimensions transforming two-dimensional reality to participate in the life of Christ. Loder sought to make "Christ's redeeming activity in the world" articulate to a scientific culture.

2. PURPOSE (WHY?). Transformation of the corrupt being-unto-death into the image of the New Creation in Christ, toward the fashioning of Christ's power in every arena of human action, is the purpose of

---

95. Ibid., chapter 9, 3f.
96. Ibid., chapter 9, 15.

Christian education in the Spirit.

3. SCOPE (WHAT?). The whole of human experience and history becomes intelligible as a four-dimensional, transformational, and Christocentric reality so that whatever is taught or learned bears the marks of *Spiritus Creator*. All reality is rendered "parabolic" or "iconic" through the spiritual transformation of human beings and communities in Christ.

4. CONTEXT (WHERE?). "The context of Christian education is the present and coming reign of God, the proleptic form of which is the dialectic between koinonia and ecclesia."[97] Such a context must foster creativity through empathetic practice characterized by open authority, imagination, positive value on conflict, complexity, appreciation of difference, and periodic restructuring, and movement toward worship as ultimate value.

5. PERSONNEL (WHO?). The Holy Spirit is the teacher working in all contexts for redemptive transformation. The human teacher/learner is "the provocateur of the human spirit." The pattern of transformation may be learned from within and appropriated as the grammar of the Holy Spirit. It is in this way that the human teacher in the power of Spiritual Creator "prepares (in two dimensions) the way of the Lord (in four dimensions)."[98] Such people must be filled with the Spirit in that they practice wonder, play with language and symbol, suffer with others in learning, celebrate the presence of Christ, learn themselves in the act of teaching, and trust the mediation of Christ. "The point [of teaching] is to awaken [the human spirit], to name it, to affirm it, to celebrate it, and lead it in the context of worship."[99]

6. TIMING (WHEN?). When *kairos* (God's time) transforms *chronos* (human time) the Spirit is discerned to be working. "The matrix of socialization is sustained for the sake of 'the moment' because the

---

97. Ibid., chapter 9, 27.
98. Ibid., chapter 9, 38.
99. Ibid., chapter 9, 45.

'moment' is that which gives the sequence its meaning."[100]

All of these dimensions of practice outlined here find their redemptive power only when their interrelations are re-constituted in the pattern of Christ through the Spirit's redemptive initiative.

In chapter 10, "Climax in Worship," Loder summarized how the relational reality celebrated in worship becomes the paradigm of redemptive transformation for the whole of the believing community, and for the world at large. "The aim of Christian education is for every human life to become an act of worship . . . [such that] all our creativity is offered to God, and thus worship becomes a way of life."[101] Loder summarized four types of learning—

1. Classical conditioning;
2. Operant conditioning;
3. Symbolic learning; and
4. Paradigm shift.

He argued that worship is best understood educationally as the latter. "It is as if a whole new constellation of meaning emerges within a field of study, usually from the mind of the key investigator. As a consequence, the data that had been organized under some previous structure of meaning (paradigm) within the field is not falsified, but given new significance and meaning."[102] When the reality in view is the Presence of Christ redemptively transforming the personality or the community through the Spirit, "this paradigmatic form of learning transforms all previous, as well as all subsequent, learning."[103] Loder continued: "This fourth type . . . is inherent in the worship of God as understood in the Reformed tradition, particularly the liturgy of the Word."[104]

---

100. Ibid., chapter 9, 33.

101. Ibid., chapter 10, 1–2.

102. Ibid., chapter 10, 12. Loder relates this learning to Kuhn's *Structure of Scientific Revolutions*, to Piaget's understanding of the cognitive growth, and to Jungian experience of ego transformation. All of these paradigm shifts must undergo redemptive transformation if the significance of worship is to be understood as the paradigm shift for learning in the Spirit.

103. *EMLOS*, chapter 10, 13.

104. Ibid., chapter 10, 14.

> An act of worship, like any other transformational pattern will include all [four] . . . forms of learning but it is or should be designed to let the hidden order of meaning—ultimate meaning—emerge to challenge all previous frames of knowledge or contexts of explanation or conditioning. In order to help this to happen—to prepare the way of the Lord—worship must be structured so as to allow God to speak God's Word to us for our redemption and for the redemption of the world. This is exactly what the liturgy of the Word is designed to do.[105]

Loder focused on worship (the liturgy of the Word) as a paradigm case for the use of theological language and symbol. The latent four-dimensional significance of the symbolic world of worship (language that negates conventional meaning in order to refer beyond the social constructions of reality to the Presence of Christ) corresponds to the four-dimensional transformation of the one who comes to worship in faith, embodying the "*I yet not I but Christ*" dialectical identity. Loder used John McClure's unpublished dissertation to discern how the liturgy embodies four-dimensional transformations in all dimensions of human action in four phases.[106]

1. PHASE 1. The minister mediates the move from marketplace language to "divine" language (Call to worship, prayer of confession, assurance of pardon).

2. PHASE 2. The Bible mediates the Word of God spoken directly to the people (*Lectio*).

3. PHASE 3. The sermon mediates the Word in marketplace language, such that "the marketplace is reclaimed as the arena of God's action, but now by God's own Word."

4. PHASE 4. The Word of God is now born by ordinary people into the world, the koinonia that becomes "the corporate version of the four dimensions inherent in the language of theology used in worship."

The four-dimensional work of the people (liturgy) gathered for worship becomes the four-dimensional work of the people (liturgy) dispersed in the world, such that the koinonia participates in the me-

---

105. Ibid., chapter 10,15f.
106. Ibid., chapter 10, 19f. See the dissertation of John McClure, "Preaching."

diation of Christ's presence in the world. Worship is nothing less than the kenotic pattern of Christ revealing the hidden order of intelligibility underlying all creation amid the world (on analogy with E=MC² in physics). We are baptized into this pattern and are called to live it out in the world. The same pattern lived out in the world exposes and crucifies the patterns of Adam that we create through socialization dynamics and encourages us to flourish according to the new being in Christ. Christ reverses history and provides the means by which human beings are liberated from the socialization-dominant "worlds" they create, without removing them from these "worlds."[107] Four times in the liturgy the pattern of Christ is enacted.

> Moving through the extremities of the four dimensions, from Void to Holy, thrusts us into a liminal state, the threshold of the ego boundaries, where we may be informed and transformed by the Word of God to us. To worship as these theological symbols provoke us to do is to be pressed in every act of worship to the limits of existence in order to rediscover our identity in Christ. This works to create a Christian style of life because, given this pattern, each act of worship is a reenactment of the life of Christ, whose life, as traditions have it, was an act of worship.[108]

From this standpoint, worship is the most fully reality-affirming, reality-reforming, reality-transforming practice there is. We discern in worship that the so-called "real" world defined and defended by the social construction of reality (*schema*) is not fully real at all until and unless we see and experience the world through the Presence of Christ (*morphe*). Worship is the rehearsal of judgment and redemption of the world through Christ crucified and raised, the "world without end" to which we are called to witness. In worship in the Spirit, the koinonia experiences proleptically the New Being in Christ amid the present world characterized and governed by death.

---

107. Loder discussed the implications of Phil 2:5–11 using Paul's suggestive differentiation of "*schema*" and "*morphe*." Jesus took on the "form" (*schema*) of humanity (i.e., socialized humanity) in order to redeem humanity in terms of its true form ("*morphe*") in the image of Christ. Christ overcame the death woven into *schema* and grounded human life in his own nature as the "true humanity" (morphe). See *EMLOS*, chapter 10, 20–28.

108. *EMLOS*, chapter 10, 28.

Conclusion

In my judgment, *Educational Ministry in the Logic of the Spirit* does indeed provide Christian education specifically, and practical theology generally, with a compelling legacy of immense import in the 21st century. In it James Loder demonstrates how profound academic reflection and methodological insight (the *schema* of the task of practical theology) can be placed in the service of Christ's nature to reveal its true, generative source (the *morphe* of practical theology). The more "impressionistic" treatment of the subject matter of *EMLOS* is by design, because Loder was concerned that the *schema-morphe* relationality of human practice served the "logic of the Spirit" in order to participate in the God-Human structure of reality revealed in Jesus Christ. All of his works must be taken together as a complex theory of how Christian communities (and all human social constructions of reality large and small) participate in the generative power of the Spirit in witness to the world. *EMLOS* was designed as an "iconic" theory of Christian education that directly addresses the apologetic-kerymatic methodological concerns of the field of Christian/religious education and calls it to bear witness to Jesus Christ crucified and raised and actively transforming the world in his image through the Spirit.

Works Cited

Barth, Karl. *Dogmatics in Outline*. New York: Harper & Row, 1966.
Browning, Don. *Fundamental Practical Theology: Descriptive and Strategic Proposals*. Minneapolis: Fortress, 1991.
———. "The Struggle Over the Future of the Church: The Contribution of Practical Theology." Paper given at the inaugural planning meeting of the International Academy of Practical Theology, Princeton Theological Seminary, Summer 1991.
Bushnell, Horace. *Christian Nurture*. Grand Rapids: Baker, 1979. Reprint of the 1861 edition published by Scribner.
Ebeling, Gerhard. *Word and Faith*. Philadelphia: Fortress, 1963.
Farley, Edward. "Does Christian Education Need the Holy Spirit?" *Religious Education* 60/6 (1965) 427–36, 479.
Gerrish, Brian. *Continuing the Reformation: Essay on Modern Religious Thought*. Chicago: University of Chicago Press, 1993.
Haitch, Russell. "A Summary of James Loder's Theory of Christian Education." In *Redemptive Transformation in Practical Theology*, edited by Dana R. Wright and John D. Kuentzel, 298–324. Grand Rapids: Eerdmans, 1994.
Hamilton, Peter. *Talcott Parsons* (Key Sociologists Series). London: Routledge, 1983.
Holifield, E. Brooks. *History of Pastoral Care in America: From Salvation to Self-Realization*. Nashville: Abingdon, 1983.
Hutchinson, William. *The Modern Impulse in American Protestantism*. Durham: University of North Carolina Press, 1992.
Illich, Ivan. *De-Schooling Society*. New York: Harper & Row, 1971.
Kovacs, Ken E. *The Relational Theology of James E. Loder: Encounter and Conviction*. New York: Peter Lang, 2012.
Kuhn, Thomas. *The Structure of Scientific Revolutions*. Chicago: University of Chicago, 1996.
Loder, James E., Jr. *Educational Ministry in the Logic of the Spirit*. Unpublished manuscript.
———. *The Logic of the Spirit: Human Development in Theological Perspective*. San Francisco: Jossey-Bass, 1998.
———. "Normativity and Context in Practical Theology: The 'Interdisciplinary' Issue." In *Practical Theology-International Perspectives*, edited by Fredrich Schweitzer and J. A. van der Ven, 359–81. Frankfurt am Main: Peter Lang, 1999.
———. "The Place of Science in Practical Theology: The Human Factor." *International Journal of Practical Theology* 4/1 (2000) 22–44 (pre-published copy).
———. "Socialization Approach: Emphasis in Culture, Nelson as Paradigm Case." Unpublished, undated, essay.
———. *The Transforming Moment*. 2nd ed. Colorado Springs: Helmers & Howard, 1989.
Loder, James E., Jr., and James W. Fowler. "Conversations on Fowler's *Stages of Faith* and Loder's *The Transforming Moment*." *Religious Education* 77/2 (1982) 133–48.
Loder, James E., Jr., and Jim Neidhardt. *The Knight's Move: The Relational Logic of the Spirit in Theology and Science*. Colorado Springs: Helmers & Howard, 1992.
McClure, John. "Preaching and the Pragmatics of Human/Divine Communication in the Liturgy of the Word in the Western Church: A Semiotic and Practical Theological Study." PhD diss., Princeton Theological Seminary, 1984.

———. "The Way of Love: Loder, Levinas, and Ethical Transformation through Preaching." In *Redemptive Transformation in Practical Theology*, edited by Dana R. Wright and John D. Kuentzel, 95–115. Grand Rapids: Eerdmans, 2004.

McCormack, Bruce. "The Unheard Message of Karl Barth." *Word and World* 14/1 (1994) 59–66.

Mikowski, Gordon, and Richard R. Osmer. "The Flowering of Practical Theology During the McCord and Gillespie Years." In *With Piety and Learning: The History of Practical Theology at Princeton Seminary, 1812-2012*, 133–76. International Practical Theology 11. Berlin: LIT 2011.

Miller, Arthur I. *Picasso, Einstein: Space, Time, and the Beauty That Causes Havoc*. New York: Basic Books, 2002.

Nelson, C. E. *Where Faith Begins*. Philadelphia: John Knox, 1967.

Osmer, Richard R. "Practical Theology and Contemporary Christian Education: An Historical and Constructrive Analysis, Vol. 2." PhD diss., Emory University, 1985.

Osmer, Richard R., and Fredrich Schweitzer. *Religious Education between Modernization and Globalization: New Perspectives on United States and Germany*. Grand Rapids: Eerdmans, 2003.

Poling, James, and Lewis Mudge. *Formation and Reflection: The Promise of Practical Theology*. Philadelphia: Fortress, 1987.

Smart, James. *The Teaching Ministry of the Church: An Examination of the Basic Principles of Christian Education*. Philadelphia: Westminster, 1964.

Smith, Shelton H. "Let Religious Educators Reckon with the Barthians." *Religious Education* 24 (1934) 54–51.

Torrance, Thomas F. *Transformation and Convergence in the Frame of Knowledge*. Grand Rapids: Eerdmans, 1984.

Van Leewen, Arend Th. *Christianity in World History: The Meeting of Faiths of East and West*. Translated by H. H. Hoskins. London: Edinburgh House, 1964.

West, Cornell. *Prophesy Deliverance: An Afro-American Revolutionary Christianity*. Philadelphia: Westminster, 1982.

Westerhoff, John. *Who Are We? The Question for Religious Education*. Birmingham, AL: Religious Education, 1978.

Wood, Ralph. *The Comedy of Redemption: Christian Faith and Comic Vision in Four American Novelists*. Notre Dame: University of Notre Dame Press, 1988.

Wright, Dana R. "Are You There? Comedic Interrogation in the Life and Witness of James E. Loder, Jr." In *Redemptive Transformation in Practical Theology*, edited by Dana R. Wright and John D. Kuentzel, 1–42. Grand Rapids: Eerdmans, 2004.

———. "The Contemporary Renaissance in Practical Theology in the United States: Past, Present, and Future of a Discipline in Creative Ferment." *The International Journal of Practical Theology* 6/3 (2002) 289–320.

Wright, Dana R., and John Kuentzel. *Redemptive Transformation in Practical Theology*. Grand Rapids: Eerdmans, 2004.

Yeats, William Butler. "The Second Coming." In *The Norton Anthology of English Literature*, edited by M. H. Abrams et al., 2:1880f. 6th ed. New York: Norton, 1994.

PART THREE

James E. Loder's Relevance to Psychology, Counseling, and Sociology

8

The Healing of Memory as a Pathway to Transformation

A Case Study Presenting James Loder's Counsel

MARK KOONZ

Introduction

For nearly four decades Professor James E. Loder's public lectures at Princeton Theological Seminary attracted a high degree of student interest, but in addition to his teaching career he also gave a lot of his time to spiritual and therapeutic counseling. He had a reputation as a gifted psychologist who sometimes achieved remarkable results, although he would say he did not "achieve" anything but was privileged to witness the transformational power of the Holy Spirit. Colleague Richard Osmer wrote:

> One of the many losses that resulted from his untimely death was that Jim did not have the opportunity to write up in book form his approach to spiritual counseling. My sense is that his counseling was something quite unique among contemporary approaches to spiritual formation and direction, for it took seriously the insights of depth psychology without being reduced to another form of psychotherapy . . . [H]e learned from psychotherapy while placing its insights in a fundamentally different

pattern of spiritual practice . . . [This is one of the] many areas that must be brought forward by his students and colleagues because of his sudden death.[1]

The purpose of this paper is to focus on one aspect of Loder's spiritual counseling, namely, his practice of praying with people for the healing of hurtful memories. Recordings of conversations in which we discussed prayer and pastoral counseling provide the primary source material underlying this paper. These private sessions were recorded with his permission.

When Memory Requires Healing

The work of Robert Kegan focuses on the process of meaning-making moving from infancy to adulthood, and to the end of life. The way in which a person interprets the world and his or her relationship to it, as well as his or her own interpretation of self and identity, is a significant part of the meaning that results in this on-going process.[2] Loder's interest in Kegan's work stems from the importance of the meaning-making process in all human development, and in particular the dynamics of the human spirit in the search for meaning and order in life. The human spirit impacts the meaning-making process, not according to a timeline required by a particular stage of development, but according to the strength or weakness of the human spirit itself. This means that a strong human spirit can make advances and discoveries that open up new vistas, but a wounded human spirit adversely affects not only the meaning-making process, but also the actual meaning that is made. A wounded human spirit can distort a person's perceptions of reality, including perceptions of self and identity, and can truncate a person's true range of freedom. One way in which Loder discussed mental illness was as regression to an earlier stage of meaning-making involving confusions and constrictions, rather than appropriate distinctions and liberations that enhance personal wholeness and communal relations.

The role of memory is not unimportant, because memory impacts our sense of identity and relationships, as well as our emotions.

---

1. Osmer, "Forward," xi.
2. Kegan, "There the Dance," 403–40; See also idem, *Evolving Self* and *In over Our Heads*.

Emotions also impact the meaning-making process.[3] When a past trauma is etched in memory, that memory may work in harness with a wounded spirit to feed anger or fear, as well as distort crucial aspects of meaning-making. Memories are not just detached mental pictures of a past event. As Os Guinness says, "Sometimes even the memory of previous pain at a particular point is enough to summon up the pain again."[4] David Seamands pointed out that poignant memories may have an on-going impact, with almost the power to become *present experiences* of the total person. "Memories are the experience of whole persons as they remember something, and not simply brain-stored pictures of the past. Memories include feelings, concepts, patterns, attitudes, and tendencies toward actions that accompany the pictures on the screen of the mind."[5] Some memories are laden with emotional pain, which hinders our relating to people or coping with life, distorting both personality and behavior patterns. Repressed painful memories have power to damage health, but even when memories are accessible or in a person's focal awareness, they may operate just as powerfully and negatively. Depending on the event or circumstances remembered, the meaning that is made from a memory may then add to or detract from its power to wound, even wound repeatedly over the span of a person's life.[6] In

---

3. Carlsen, *Meaning-Making*, 22. "In any discussion of meaning and its referents emotional factors must be taken into consideration. Meaning–making is not just a detached, analytical, intellectual enterprise; it involves our excitements, our griefs, our passions as well." There are significant connections between emotions and cognitive ability. See Immordino-Yang and Damasio, "We Feel," 3–10. I owe this reference to Wendy Sanders.

4. Guinness, "Scars," 135. Guinness's chapter discusses a type of doubt that is not based on intellectual problems but on emotional problems. This type of doubt seems protective against disappointment, and cannot be resolved by reason but only by the healing of damaged emotions. Cf. Seamands, *Redeeming*, 111–14.

5. Seamands, *Redeeming*, 113.

6. Early in my ministry, a woman in her seventies spoke with strong emotional bitterness about her mother, who abandoned her and her sister when they were school girls during the Great Depression. The bitterness had not subsided in over sixty years. Yet there are examples of valiant human attempts to deny soul sorrow and bitter memories the power to distort life. Sir Martin Gilbert tells the difficult story of a group of Jewish men who survived the Holocaust. They survived the horrors of brutal mistreatment and malnutrition in Nazi concentration camps primarily because they were young and had strong physical constitutions. As they were in their mid to late teens when they were rescued at the end of the war, they had many decades to rebuild their lives. Yet as adults they had to live with incredibly painful memories and a pervasive sense of grief—in many cases no other member of their family survived—so that struggles with

this regard, memory is powerful. This says nothing about the accuracy of the memory details, nor of the human ability to distort an aspect of interpretation. Our concern here is the way in which on-going memory impacts the human spirit in an adverse way.

Seamands observes that prayer for the healing of memory is not designed to erase the memory. "But the power of the emotions which surround those memories—the sting, the pain, the fear, the hate, the hurt, the lust—will be broken."[7] This is because the meaning of the memory may be radically changed by the healing presence of Jesus Christ, the transcendent Lord of space and time.[8] The affirmation here is that Jesus Christ can work with both our past and our future. Therefore "the so-called normal sequence of human development may become reversible." Loder explained, "Convicting experiences may encourage reliving periods of early childhood and/or the anticipation of death," because Christ is in "a unique transcendent relationship to the ordinary course of human development." This means that the past can "undergo a healing change, directly or indirectly as a result of a convictional experience. The future also may be anticipated and profoundly affected through convictional experience."[9] An important implication is that the meaning of the past as well as the (anticipated) future may be altered.

---

depression were often constant problems. After the war, these young male survivors were rehabilitated together in Great Britain, and formed associations that lasted for the remainder of their lives. Their organized charitable work was quietly implemented after several of them became successful in business. Many of the men were guided by the insight that they could not allow their lives to be dominated by anger: if they gave in to hatred it would mean a victory for Hitler! They intended to deny Hitler any victory that would define the meaning of their lives. See Gilbert, *The Boys: Triumph over Adversity*, published in the United States as *The Boys: The Untold Story of 732 Young Concentration Camp Survivors*.

7. Seamands, *Putting Away*, 21ff.

8. Loder used biblical examples to illustrate the way Christ radicalizes space and time. Distance and space could not prevent Jesus from seeing Nathanael under the fig tree. In fact, he could look right into Nathanael's mind and heart and see his true character, declaring that Nathanael was free of deceit. On the Mount of Transfiguration Jesus could radicalize time and connect with two men who lived hundreds of years ago in the past—Moses and Elijah. Of course there are other ways to view these stories, but Loder used them to emphasize that Christ is the Lord over our space–time universe. This means Christ can interact with human thoughts and emotions, as well as physical bodies, bringing gifts of love and healing. Thus there is no barrier to the presence of Christ entering a memory. The gift of healing Christ brings is never separated from his presence. The gift and Giver belong together.

9. Loder, *Transforming*, 201–2. This reference is to the 1989 second edition, which

Convicting experiences have a place within a pattern or logic of transformation, which was the central focus of Loder's *The Transforming Moment*. Whether in artistic or scientific discovery, or in personal therapeutic discovery, the pattern containing five key parts is often at work:

1. the threatening problem or conflict;
2. an interlude for scanning in search for a resolution;
3. a convictional insight that comes as an "Aha!" moment or "Eureka!" shout of discovery;
4. a release of energy is made available to test the insight; and
5. interpretation: the insight is interpreted in a search for confirmation that the resolution fits the conflict and resolves it.[10]

The sequence does not have to be in this order, as sometimes the answer comes before the question, and one can enter the logic at any of the five major turning points and then work backward and/or forward.[11] Therefore when the convicting insight or revelation comes, the convicted person is able to work through all five parts of the transforming pattern. In the end, the initial question or problem has been resolved and set in a new frame of reference.

Insofar as many of these discoveries are only two-dimensional, involving the self and the composed understanding of the world, the transformations based on these discoveries are themselves in need of transformation. They are not ultimately strong enough to endure in the face of death, the real threat of annihilation, which Loder called the "Void." The void negates all that we cherish and find meaningful, for ultimately death negates life itself. But the presence of the Holy (shorthand for God's Presence) is stronger than death, and so the Holy is able to negate the negation of the void (which has so many faces) and remove even the fear of death. This is the ultimate four-dimensional transformation that brings the deepest spiritual and psychological healing.

Loder affirmed that convictional experiences involving the encounter of the Holy Spirit and human spirit, removing the threat of the Void, transforming human life and making all things new, are always events

---

is preferable because it contains important revisions and a glossary.

10. Ibid., 35–40.
11. Ibid., 131.

and movements which are initiated by Jesus Christ. Christ is the Initiator and the Finisher—the Author and Sustainer (even the Repeater)—of all four-dimensional transformations. This is why in prayer we call on the presence of Christ, or the Holy Spirit, who always works to connect us to Christ, to initiate the transforming process and bring it to completion. Prayer for the healing of wounded memories is part of praying for four-dimensional transformation. We pray this way because Jesus is the transcendent Lord over space and time, over past, present and future, and over death itself. For this reason human development, memories, and meaning-making may be included in prayer seeking Christ's healing work. Loder summarized:

> A common version of the healing move backward in developmental time is emerging in a contemporary Christian emphasis on the "healing of memories." Popular Christian literature abounds with accounts of people revisiting previous traumatic experiences through an imaginative reconstruction of the past (similar to Carl Jung's view of "active imagination"). In the healing of memories, Christ, preferably as the one who has initiated conviction in the rememberer, is invited to enter the trauma, to remold the memory, or to do whatever else may be necessary for wholeness. This often brings quite unexpected results.[12]

By way of illustrating this type of prayer and an unexpected result, Loder discussed the case of "Georgia" in *The Transforming Moment*. Georgia was a woman who "had in childhood often been abused by a domineering older brother." As an adult she dreamed repeatedly of an approaching monster, which the counselor connected to her childhood fear. In the course of prayer that centered on the loving presence of

---

12. Ibid., 202. Loder does not reduce healing prayer to Jung's concept of "active imagination," which was a mediation technique thought to enhance the process of communication between the subconscious and the conscious mind. One element in common, however, between the Jungian technique involving awareness of images in dreams and Loder's "visit-in-prayer" concerning the mental images of a hurtful memory is that both approaches refrain from manipulating the dream images on the one hand, or the images in the memory on the other hand. Loder invited the presence of Jesus Christ into the memory, but he does not declare or suggest what the counselee should experience or see *happen* as a result. See Jung, *Jung on Active Imagination*. Loder was very critical of other aspects of Jung's theory, yet he did not discard all of Jung's insights. See esp. Loder, *Logic*, 306–9, Cf. two Christian responses to Jung which have been recommended by psychologist Paul Vitz: William A. Johnson, *Search for Transcendence* and Leanne Payne, *Healing Presence*.

Christ, the counselor felt prompted to encourage her to "*love* the monster." When she prayed for God to help her love the monster, she saw the image of the monster crack open "like a hollow shell. Inside, quite apart from her conscious intention, and even to her surprise, she saw a little boy curled up in a fetal position, crying." Many truths began to unlock and become clear about her own life and her brother's life, and she made progress in forgiving him. The end result was that the dreams did not recur, and "her fear of her brother was healed to the extent that she could at last enjoy being in his presence."[13]

In numerous cases Loder prayed with people who were haunted by memories that continued to wound their spirits and distort their personal meaning-making processes, often long after the tragedy or brutality had occurred. In the course of discussing one case in particular, a teenage boy I was then working with, he offered guidance about praying with people for the healing of their memories. A few years later he published his most extensive discussion on this aspect of his spiritual therapy: "Human Development Reenvisioned: The Case of Helen," chapter 3 in *The Logic of the Spirit*.[14] It is not my purpose to review everything Loder wrote there, but rather to recall some of the verbatim guidance he gave me while counseling this teenage boy. Before moving into the details of this case, however, it may prove helpful to review some of Loder's key convictions about prayer.

Loder's Three Rs of Prayer[15]

Dr. Loder practiced intercessory prayer in both his private prayer life and in his counseling sessions. Intercessory prayer is prayer on behalf of another person, family, or group of people, and is a sub-category of petitionary prayer. He was not in the camp of Friedrich Schleiermacher, the early Nineteenth Century theologian who negatively influenced significant numbers of European Christians, over several generations, to think that prayers of petition or intercession were not appropriate. Some Christian circles and institutions in North America were impacted by

---

13. Loder, *Transforming* 202–3.
14. Loder, *Logic*, 46–78.
15. All quotes from Loder in this section come from a recording of an undated conversation that took place a few months after my graduation in 1990, henceforth referenced as *Essentials*. See also Koonz, "Prayer." See also Angella Pak Sun's interviews with Loder televised in 2001 for additional information on Loder's view of prayer.

this attitude, as well as by the deistic mindset that maintained God's remoteness from human activities and concerns. Schleiermacher thought only prayers of resignation to God's will or prayers of gratitude were appropriate.[16] Loder did not accept the validity of Schleiermacher's position. His prayer practice was influenced by his own experience of God's presence, as well as his biblical studies. The heart of the "Lord's Prayer" is petitionary, containing several important petitions, and in numerous places Paul requested prayer for his own work or admonished congregations to "pray one for another." When Loder prayed for others in their presence he did so in order to give them explicit encouragement, and to connect them with the One who can truly help.

The first "R" of prayer is *Recognition*. "Recognize Who you are talking to when you pray; it's important to behold the face of God in Jesus Christ. To behold Christ, to behold the One through whom all things were made—it's *big*!"[17] The size of God's creative activity is a revelation of God's enormous love, because the universe has to be as large as it is just to support life on earth![18] Therefore Loder believed in the enormity of God's love as well as the enormity of God's power, and said, "Don't ever pray small." Part of God's majestic greatness is God's power to do the particular. God tends not only to the infinite reaches of space, but also to what seems infinitely smaller to us, even an electron or a human life. The

---

16. Mackintosh, *Types*, 92–93.

17. Loder, "Essentials."

18. Block, *Universe*. The universe expands in direct relationship to its age. Its long time-span is required to produce stars that develop, age, and send carbon into the universe as they expand and break apart. Carbon is necessary for all biological life. Without a universe this old and this large, none of us would be here. T. F. Torrance saw many scientists open themselves up to theistic and Christian belief with this insight in mind. "More than one distinguished scientist has recently become a Christian, for the advance of scientific knowledge has undermined their atheism or their agnosticism . . . . They have in mind not least the discovery known as 'the anthropic principle,' that the expansion of the universe has taken place governed by a very fine tuning of both its strong and weak forces, which against all the laws of probability has adapted it as the home of humankind. But they also have in mind the fact that, as far as they are able to see, the whole universe in its quite incredible immensity is needed for human existence on Planet Earth" (Torrance, *Preaching*, 24–25). Loder and Torrance were mutual friends who both saw the size of the universe as an indication of the great size of God's love for us as human creatures dwelling on Earth. God's providential love has been in place throughout the lifespan of the universe, preceding and anticipating our existence, and is meant to be a presupposition for Christian prayer in every context, especially when coupled with the revelation of God's love in Christ.

magnificence presented to us in the face of Jesus Christ makes possible "more than you can even imagine, conceptualize, or even participate in, except by the Spirit."[19] Recognition helps us focus in prayer. Recognition also empowers us to approach God with an attitude of reverence.

Loder added, "Once you recognize Who this is, then you realize that you're in a relationship." The second "R" of prayer is *Relationship*. "And all the things you know about a relationship on a human level pertain here. This is not esoteric; this is respect, and this is sensitivity, and this is attention. This is person-to-person: the reality in which you are moving in prayer is relational."[20] Because it is relational, it is vital and living. There's no way to grasp relationality in order to control it, like an object that can be put on a shelf or used at one's pleasure. Relationality requires attentive participation.

Relationality with God, however, means that in this relationship "you are known through and through, in the biblical sense . . . you are *known*." In this relationship God's Spirit gives us the possibility of knowing God, an act of grace without which we cannot know God, but in a context in which God already knows us. We cannot hide the truth of our lives. In fact, we can go to God to learn the truth, for God knows us better than we know ourselves. This means that God must define the relationship when we pray. Loder said, "This puts you into a relationship in which you really want Him to do most of the talking." This divine priority applies to petitionary prayer for other people.[21] God may speak or communicate to the one praying and direct the prayer based on God's knowledge of the other person's situation. As Loder put it, "There are so many more ways for the Spirit to communicate to you than there is for you and me to communicate with each other. There's just infinite ways . . . so let Him talk to you. Let Him show you something."[22] God may also direct the prayer based on God's knowledge of the person praying. For example, when in prayer for another person, the person praying may have a word from Scripture come to mind; such as "I will never leave you nor forsake you."

---

19. Loder, "Essentials."

20. Ibid.

21. A good example of this point is the case of "Mike" in Seamands, *Putting Away*, 22–24.

22. Loder, "Essentials."

The person struggling in prayer on behalf of a sick or dying person may respond, "But that isn't what I'm asking. I'm praying for this other person's needs." To which God's Spirit may impress on the intercessor's mind, "You cannot pray for this person until you know that I will never leave you nor forsake you." God knows when our prayers for others include our own fears, as when it seems to us that the person in a hospital or a nursing home bed has been abandoned by God, and we fear being abandoned by God (as we interpret it) and suffering in the same way. That fear may have to be addressed before we can continue in prayer. This is an illustration of why God must direct our intercessory prayers. God knows our own condition as well as the life history of the one for whom we are praying. Loder believed that the Spirit often does not tell us how to pray until assuring us of who *we* are in relationship with God. In this context, receiving assurance or guidance requires attentive listening on our part. God's Spirit may also guide based on knowledge of the recipient's life, as in the case of "Georgia" when the counselor was led to suggest, "Now love the monster."[23]

Another corollary of knowing that God knows us through and through is that we can and should pray honestly and without sophistication or pretense. God does not want us to dress up our prayers to make them "acceptable" or proper. Private prayers are not public prayers guiding a congregation in worship. Loder believed that God responds to humans who cry from their heart in total honesty. A graduate student, who received prayer when counseling with Loder described his surprise at the way Loder prayed. He said Loder prayed almost like a child and held his hand while they prayed together. At that time he found it to be disconcerting, but at the same time he found it to be strangely comforting.[24]

Loder also believed that many of the people we may pray for are "deeply resistant to any kind of truth, they do not want the truth." This is a serious problem in the context of prayer and counseling. "Under the surface, so many people we pray for really want to die. Their hearts are set on dying."[25] Of course they will not say anything so depressing. They will say that they want to live, but they are resistant to their own healing. Loder made these comments based on his own observations and insights as a therapeutic counselor, but his conclusions are affirmed from

---

23. Loder, *Transforming*, 202–3.
24. Private communication with the author, Sept. 2011.
25. Loder, "Essentials."

other contexts. Long ago Søren Kierkegaard wrote about the spiritual condition of sick people who do not want to get well.[26] More recently Karl Menninger analyzed the "death wish" at work in people who choose for self-destruction when more life-enhancing choices are available.[27] Therefore it is important that the prayer relationship be defined by the Lord, who is rich in knowledge and resources and who must guide our praying for other people. "He alone can teach you how to ask" as you pray and intercede for another person.[28]

The third "R" of prayer is *Re-creation*. "You cannot get into a relationship with One who knows you like that, who loves you like that and is defining the relationship like that, without in prayer undergoing re-creation." When you're living in prayer it reconstitutes you. For example, God's promise *I will never leave you* establishes the person in relationship with God. "You get recreated every time you pray."[29] One of the ways we get reconstituted is by being freed from socialization that hinders prayer. Because we want to be seen as intellectual or as professional, we may hesitate to pray in the presence of other people for the healing of their broken lives. We may hesitate to appear unsophisticated and pray honestly like a child, like one "crying from the heart" as it were. This is why we need to be reconstituted, so that we think and pray with the mind of Christ, with the heart and compassion of Christ, which the Spirit can form in us. We may also be freed from the hesitation or unbelief that causes us to fear God will not respond or provide help.

The Nature of Prayer for Healing

Loder's spoke of the "Three R's of Prayer" as an allusion to the old "Three R's of Education," indicating essential aspects of prayer. Yet though he highlighted three, he often spoke of a fourth fundamental: The fourth "R" is the *Radical* nature of prayer. "It's really weird to shut your eyes and talk to someone that nobody else can see, and believe that this invis-

---

26. Kierkegaard, *Sickness*, 71–74.

27. Menninger, *Man Against Himself*. The term is Freudian, but the behaviors described by Menninger present manifest proof of an interior problem regardless of whether we approach human complexity in a Freudian or non–Freudian framework.

28. Loder, *Essentials*.

29. Loder's prime example of this was the experience he had after his father died. See *Transforming*, 87–88, 191. Yet the "reconstituting" work of the Holy Spirit can happen more quietly and subtly through prayer than in Loder's own example.

ible Reality is going to change the visible world."[30] That may seem weird. At the very least it is radical. Radical not only because it seems strange to people outside the most ultimate and loving relationship that can be found anywhere in the universe, but because within that relationship we come into contact with God's dangerous and marvelous power to reconstitute human life.[31]

Prayer for healing is radical in the way all prayer is radical. All prayer is a real event in the life of the human person praying, as well as a real event in God's life. The relationship we honor and attend to in prayer is established by God, and is attended to by God.[32] This bisociation between Creator and creature is incomparable, and has potentialities that are infinite, including the radicalization of space and time. This means there is no inner wound or memory of a past event beyond the reach of God's healing power. Loder maintained that the prayer for healing is eschatological in nature. Healing of body, mind, or spirit, is always an eschatological sign, for healing today is a participation in the resurrection healing that Christ will bring in fullness at his second advent. This means that a prayer for healing is a prayer for God to reach into the future, when God will be all in all, when all that is broken will be restored, and bring that eschatological future into our present.[33] The Christian eschatological hope is cosmic in scope, and includes individual human beings.

The individual's true being is hidden with Christ in God and will not be revealed until the day of resurrection. But in prayer we ask for a "sneak preview," a partial unveiling. We ask for an in-breaking of the future resurrection time into the crisis of the present moment. Chronological time is real but not definitive, and we ask for its ravages to be reversed. This type of prayer is consistent with the practice of the

---

30. Loder, "Essentials."

31. Ibid.

32. "When petitionary prayer dies out of the Christian mind, its place taken by meditation, men shut their eyes to the fact that the believer is called to hold converse with the Father, and that this converse is a reality not for man merely but for God Himself" (Mackintosh, *Highway*, 93).

33. Loder, "Prayer of Healing." In the Sun interview titled "Prayer of Adoration," Loder tells the story of a woman pastor healed of multiple sclerosis as the prayer for healing turned into adoration of God (later verified by her neurologist through testing and by her renewed physical health and restored capabilities). James and Arlene Loder, with one of their daughters, were involved in this prayer session.

apostolic church as portrayed in the long ending of Mark, the book of Acts, and in the letters of Paul and James.[34] Furthermore, prayer for healing, including physical healing, is not inconsistent with the practice and affirmation of major theologians in the history of the Church.[35] The resurrection of Jesus is the initial and fullest in-breaking of the future reality into the present, and is incomparable. Yet there may be other partial in-breakings of God's resurrection power that simultaneously point backwards to the resurrection of Jesus in space-time history and point forwards to the resurrection day when God will be all in all. Healing miracles today in a Christian context are always signs that point away from themselves in these two directions. Each "sign" is a gift from God, given at the wise and righteous discretion of God, and cannot be earned or manipulated by human beings.[36]

Prayers for the healing of memories involve more than a request for restored health, however, for they touch on the Holy Spirit's interaction with the human spirit. John 14 and Romans 8 indicate that the purpose of the Holy Spirit's work is to connect us to Jesus Christ, to assure our spirits that we belong to God's family, and to protect us from all that interferes with our receiving God's love. Every admonition to "be filled with the Spirit" (Eph 5:18) is an invitation to live in relationship with God

---

34. Mark 16:17–18; Acts 3:1–10; 9:36–42; 14:8–10; 1 Cor 12:9–10, 28–30; Jas 5:14–16. These passages are representative, to say nothing of the many references to healing in the Gospels. See Keener, *Miracles*.

35. Great theologians in the East and West have affirmed belief in the reality of healing miracles. In the fourth century Athanasius testified to healings through the prayer ministry of Antony. This is discussed together with other examples in Oden, *Pastoral Care*, 53–56. Augustine cataloged many miracles of healing through the intercessory prayers of Christians, and said he knew of more than he had room to record. Some cases included testimony from physicians who were not Christians. See Augustine, *City of God, Book XXII.8*, 819–31. For openness to the gifts of the Holy Spirit, and specific advice on praying for healing, see Froehlich, "Charismatic," 136–57. The first and second generations of Reformers in Scotland, particularly John Knox's son-in-law John Welch, were known to have received miraculous answers to petitionary and intercessory prayer. These accounts were researched and presented by John Howie in *The Scots Worthies* (1775, 1781). Howie's book went through several editions. Publishers and editors in the 1850s pruned out all references to the miraculous considered "unbelievable" due to the influence of David Hume and skepticism bred from Enlightenment rationalism. These deletions were restored in the 1870 edition, revised by W. H. Carslaw and are currently available. For a response to David Hume's philosophical attack on miracles, see Earman, *Abject Failure* and Geivett and Habermas, *Defense*. Two shorter responses are Craig, *Reasonable Faith*, 127–55, and Montgomery, *Tractatus*, 103–8.

36. A balanced response to extreme teaching about healing is Fee, *Disease*.

and know the fullness of God's love, truth, and grace. Loder, Seamands, and others, prayed for the healing of memories in the confidence they prayed in harmony with God's will, for where the Spirit works the result is new freedom (2 Cor 3:17), love, joy, peace, and more (Gal 5:22–23). Therefore prayer that asks God to heal is more than a means to an end. "Prayer is a way of existing in the very life of God, it is not a means to an end."[37] Prayer for healing is also about being brought into the right perspective with everything that is Holy. When healing takes place in answer to Christian prayer it always points to the transforming power and presence of Christ's Kingdom.[38] It was nothing less than God's holy presence that established healing in the case we will examine now.

Case History of Eric: Background Information

During my senior year as an MDiv student at Princeton Theological Seminary (the academic year 1989–90), Dr. Loder advised my senior project, which included two independent studies (one involving physicist Jim Neidhardt, Loder's close friend). I also took Loder's course on educational ministry. When we met for our private discussions, many of these sessions were recorded with his permission. At the same time I was doing volunteer chaplaincy work at the Lloyd McCorkle Training School for Boys & Girls, located a few miles away in Skillman, New Jersey, under the supervision of Chaplain Joanne Martindale, as an extension of the seminary's Field Education program.[39] One of my duties was to make weekly visits to the different units that housed the boys, called cottages, as well as conduct some of the Sunday worship services. Early in my work at this juvenile prison I was met by an agitated guard who unlocked the door of a cottage. He told me he had been delayed because of a fight. Looking into the meeting room encased in clear fiberglass, where social workers usually met with the inmates, I could see a very agitated young man of fifteen years with tear streaking down his cheeks, stomping around the room and repeatedly pounding objects with his fists. A few times he screamed obscenities as he glared at the guard. The guard allowed me to go into the room with the boy, whom I shall call

37. Loder, "Prayer of Confession".
38. Loder, "Prayer of Healing."
39. Joanne Martindale's career in chaplaincy includes many years of ministry at psychiatric hospitals in New Jersey, as well as military contexts.

Eric (not his real name), in the hopes that I could calm him down. I did not try to calm him down, so much as stay with him and listen to him.

Eric and another boy had been in a fight. Eric had fought like an enraged tiger. When the guard interfered, he knocked Eric's head against the wall in order to stun him. About an hour later I met the boy who had fought with Eric, and he acknowledged that the guard had knocked Eric's head into the wall with force. During the time I spent with Eric that first night, something in our exchange or in the circumstances of the evening helped Eric to lower his guard. He knew I was not a prison official, and that I was there in case people wanted to pray with me. That was the model of ministry my supervisor, Joanne Martindale, practiced, and she had introduced me to the boys as someone who would offer the same type of ministry.

At one point something prompted me to say, "I think you're tired of being hurt." To my surprise, Eric told me that he had been attacked by two men when he was eleven years old. They wanted to violate him sexually. When he resisted they beat his head without mercy to subdue him. He did not describe that assault any further, merely making reference to its brutality. But it was so wounding and revolting to him that he said, "I'll never let anyone hurt me like that again." He said it with intensity while fresh tears flowed. A few minutes later he allowed me to pray with him.

That was our first meeting. In subsequent visits I spoke with other inmates as well, but when Eric saw me he would usually find a moment when I was free and come for a brief conversation. He wanted some kind of prayer for God to help him, and may have thought that prayer was a good luck charm to ward off evil or provide protection. His vocabulary and forms of expression were simple, and I tried to teach him to pray by praying very short and simply worded prayers. A few times I asked him to repeat prayers after me.

While Eric was always respectful towards me, his rage could be easily provoked in a moment by any other prisoner or officer. He was in fights nearly every week, some times more than one a week. I once saw him get attacked in front of Lieutenant Boone's desk, even though he did not provoke a fight. Eric was handcuffed and could not easily defend himself. The other boy who hit him was not handcuffed, and knew the officers would interfere immediately. They did interfere, but it took three grown men to break up the fight, because it took two just to hold

Eric. He had incredible amounts of strength and energy when he was enraged. Why had the other boy hit him? No doubt because Eric, now sixteen, had the reputation for being the toughest fighter in the prison. Thus he was a magnate for other boys, especially new boys, who needed to prove they were tough enough to fight him.

Many incidents of fighting at Lloyd McCorkle required that the boys involved be taken to the nurse's station, and sometimes to a local hospital for stitches (probably a weekly occurrence). Sometimes it was the intervening officers who required medical attention. The prison officials considered Eric a problem prisoner in this regard, because he participated in so many incidents of violence. They asked for him to be transferred. Reverend Martindale informed me of this and I became even more concerned for Eric's future. The wound underlying his inner rage was unhealed, and if he continued to fight viciously every time he was challenged, taunted or threatened, he would never break out of the cycle of renewed violence and pain.

I felt convicted that I should offer prayer specifically for healing the root cause of his rage, and was equally convicted that there was not very much time left to work with him. I had read David Seamands' books that described prayers for the healing of memory, but I had never yet prayed this way with anyone. Seamands approach seemed balanced, but some of the things he said made me pause. First, this type of prayer was not a quick cure–all. Second, counseling might reveal that healing of memories is not always necessary or the right approach.[40] Third, in the cases Seamands described, there were preparatory sessions between counselor and counselee prior to that prayer, where explanations were given about why this kind of prayer might be necessary and helpful. Fourth, there should always be follow-up work, and this would not be possible in this case. Finally, whether in Loder's counseling, or Leanne Payne's[41] or

---

40. Seamands, *Redeeming*, 22–24. "*It should not be used with certain kinds of extremely emotional or hysteric types of people*" (author's italics), 189f.

41. Leanne Payne's works were examined, but I was not sure at that time whether she was a completely reliable guide either in matters of theological anthropology or in what she called "the spiritual realm." I am still doubtful of some things she says, though I recognize she had insights that were sometimes quite apt. Furthermore her work is devoutly Christian and I can accept that numerous people received healing through her counseling and prayer ministry. Regarding Loder's counselling, see Loder and Neidhardt, *Knight's Move*, xiv and 37–38, where Lance Hickerson is credited as a discussion partner. In private conversation we me, Hickerson reported that he was present on one occasion when Loder recommended Leanne Payne's books to another

David Seamands,' they always protected the counselee with complete privacy, because many times the person being prayed for would weep or even wail loudly at some point in the prayer process. At the prison I could never have that kind of privacy with Eric. I feared that too many variables were not working in favor of a positive outcome, even if he did allow me to pray this type of prayer with him. So I wanted to pray this way, but there was a counter–drift in me opposing it.

I did not have an appointment with Loder soon enough to get his immediate counsel, so I went to see Christina Baxter, a Visiting Professor of Theology at Princeton Theological Seminary that term. Her permanent affiliation was with St. John's College, Bramcote, a Church of England seminary in the UK.[42] While I cannot recall all of our discussion, I do know that she encouraged me to pray with Eric for the healing of his memory, in spite of all the difficulties due to the location and circumstances. Even if I had to shorten and modify what I would like to have done in ideal circumstances, I should go ahead and engage in this prayer. Dr. Baxter told me to prepare myself and engage in intercessory prayer for Eric prior to our next meeting, to "bathe everything in prayer." She also strongly encouraged me to be bold and not to hesitate to do this. Furthermore, she promised to pray for both of us consistently during that week, to the end that we would have an opportunity to pray together and that nothing would hinder us. Then she prayed with me at the conclusion of our conversation, that I would be empowered by the Holy Spirit and given boldness, as well as guidance about how to pray with Eric. She also prayed that God would prepare Eric to receive the healing that he so desperately needed. I believe her counsel and her prayer support contributed enormously to the outcome.

---

student, as an example of a spiritual counselor who used "healing prayer" regularly. This recommendation, however, was not a total endorsement, but an example of what the student could read for comparative purposes, in response to the student's request for additional reading. Loder generally looked for points of contact rather than perfect agreement. He was also aware of the books by Agnes Sanford on healing prayer.

42. Canon Dr. Christina Baxter went on to become Principal of St. John's College in 1997, where she served until her recent retirement in March, 2012. She also served as Lay Chairman of the Church of England's General Synod and as a member of the Archbishops' Council.

Prayer with Eric: The Unanticipated Transforming Moment

I went to the prison a short time after talking with Dr. Baxter, either the next day or day and a half, and found Eric in his cottage. We went to a place somewhat removed from the officer and other inmates, where we could be seen but not overheard. Because I had prayed short prayers with five or six of the inmates on a regular basis, I had become somewhat "invisible" and my meeting with Eric was not likely to draw attention. Not unless Eric became agitated, which was one of my fears. First I said, "Let me ask you something. Does God love you?" He answered "Yes." After that I told him what I had heard, that because of his constant fighting he might be transferred to another prison facility. I was afraid for his future, I said, because he could not control himself. I asked him, "Do you want me to pray with you, and ask God to help you gain self-control?" He nodded in affirmation. "Let's both pray together. We should also ask God to heal you so that you are strong on the inside, so you are calm. Can we pray together for God to help you in these ways?" He said, "Okay."

I prayed a very short prayer: "Loving Jesus, thank you for Eric's life. Right now he's in trouble and needs help. Spirit of Jesus, please come and visit Eric. Bring all the help he needs. Enter his deepest wound and heal his most hurtful memory. Heal his life. Visit him in every cell of his body and in the depths of his soul. Make all things new." I prayed earnestly yet very softly because I did not want to be overheard.

The prayer was no longer than that. My hope was that God would initiate a healing process of some kind, but I could not say I expected anything dramatic to happen immediately. I wanted to remind Eric of the need for prayer, so that even as he went to another location he would be receptive to prayer and spiritual counseling with another chaplain. I also hoped that Eric would be able to repeat a similar prayer on his own. I was prepared to follow my prayer by encouraging Eric to keep praying after his transfer. But when I opened my eyes there was a startled look on his face. His eyes were intense with a look of shock and interest.

"What happened?!" Eric demanded.

"What do you mean, 'What happened?'" I asked.

"When you prayed for me it felt like something entered my body."

This is not what I expected. I was stunned and kept silent for a long moment, but knew I had to pray a second prayer with him. "We forgot something. We need to pray again and thank Jesus for the healing he is bringing into your life," I said.

In Search of Guidance: Discussing the Prayer Event with Loder

Loder Verbatim 1

As I drove home my heart was troubled because I did not expect to see Eric again, yet I rejoiced over the Holy Spirit-human spirit interaction that had surprised us in answer to our prayer. Not long after that, on March 13, 1990, I had my scheduled appointment with Dr. Loder. In the course of our conversation we talked about prayer, and I told him about my session with Eric. When I first related what happened to Loder, he rejoiced and said, "That's wonderful." When I honestly acknowledged how little healing I actually expected to see take place, though I hoped for it, he quoted the words of Jesus, "O ye of little faith,"[43] and laughed with a note of rejoicing. Then he raised his eyebrows, as if to ask, "Now do you see what I've been talking about?" He trusted the Holy Spirit to act far more than he trusted any human to be receptive to receiving gifts from the Spirit, or witnessing the actions of the Spirit. So we shared a moment of joy and awe concerning the wonderful moment in prayer, but we could not stop there. It was important to review and reflect on the experience.

Perhaps there would be other people in my pastoral ministry who would need prayer for the healing of memories. Thinking that I had skipped too much due to the prison setting and time constraints, and that he could offer me additional guidance, I asked, "How can I as a pastoral counselor pray with someone for the healing of their memories?"

Loder's answer was, "Just exactly like that." Pause. "But two or three things are very important. One thing is, he trusts you. He comes to you, asking you to pray for him, because he believes that you can help him through prayer. And that's very important. He's open enough to you and he trusts you, and trusts the prayer relationship to do something, which is already remarkable. And you can already take that as a work of grace. Then you pray for him in a very simple but straightforward way, and something happens. And what happens is something enters his body, he

---

43. Loder used the dominical words in Matt 14:31 and 16:8 in the King James Version. I knew the reference immediately but also knew no offense was intended, for Loder meant it as a teaching moment.

says, in response to your prayer that God heal his memories—how did you put it?"

"I asked Jesus to enter his hurtful memories and heal him," I replied.

"*Enter.* You used the word 'enter.' Enter his hurtful memories and heal him. And he said something entered his body, right?"[44]

"Yeah, that's how he put it. His vocabulary is limited."

"Oh, sure, but then . . ."

Loder broke off and wept for a moment. As hundreds of his former students already know, any activity of the Holy Spirit, even when described in conversation, often evoked silent weeping in Loder. He did this in public lectures as well as private conversations, and was not ashamed of his tears. I recapped the conversation with Eric immediately after the prayer, to the point where we prayed a prayer of thanksgiving.

"Right," Loder affirmed. "Because it is important to affirm the thing that has happened. Now see, one way of looking at this is through the pattern that I was talking about in the ED105 class, which is the strange loop pulled out through time with this twist being the image, that is, that bisociation between two otherwise un-associated frames of reference coming together to give you a new frame of meaning. That's the equivalent of the twist in the loop. That's what's taking place here."

Loder's reference to his "educational ministry" lectures ("ED105" in the seminary catalogue) concerned his discussion of the "strange loop" in August Möbius's band, which he enlarged upon in *The Knight's Move*. In Loder and Neidhardt's model, the strange loop's twist represents the act of the imagination in producing new insight through bisociation. He

---

44. Later in our conversation I asked if Eric's experience could be considered an event of "pure feeling," as I put it. Loder reminded me that Eric's words were "It felt like something entered *my body*." He added, "Emotions feel, body senses, see it has shape. It has contours as it enters his body. It has place. And feeling is, as I think of it, shapeless, its amorphous. I don't think our minds will tolerate pure feeling. They have to give them shape. They have to give feelings meaning, then give feelings a name. And he [Eric] talks about it. He puts it into a verbal configuration in addition to a bodily configuration, in response to your words and your presence. There's a lot more going on than just a feeling, it seems to me" (Loder, *Logic*, 55–60). Loder made it clear that prayer for the healing of memories interacts with the physical body as much as the mind and spirit. He also said, "[T]he 'experience' of the Spirit cannot be identified with any particular psychological manifestation, such as an altered state of consciousness, a sensation of warmth, or a tingling in the hands. 'Experience of the Spirit' is distinctly apart from any particular pietistic or spiritualistic manifestation, yet the Spirit *is* experienced. Physical manifestations may accompany the action of the Spirit, as in Luther's famous tower experience" (117).

defined "bisociation" as "The surprising convergence of two incompatible frames of reference to compose an original and meaningful unity. Bisociation is the basic unit of an insight, which may include several bisociations to form a complex new meaning."[45] Hitherto unrelated frames of reference come together "in a new constellation of meaning without reducing one to the other."[46] When bisociation takes place in scientific discovery, the insight that results from the convergence of formerly separate frames of reference often has remarkable explanatory power over a wider range of phenomena than was formerly thought possible. An example is Einstein's formula $E = mc^2$, "where energy is bisociated with mass around a constant, the speed of light." The elegant simplicity of the formula actually masters a vast range of combinations and complexity.[47] Loder also saw bisociation at work in the conversion experience of Søren Kierkegaard.[48] Bisociation in a therapeutic context generally leads to a greater integration of personality that results in wholeness, providing a new sense of coherence as well as freedom.[49]

The Holy Spirit works to bring the human person into the sphere of God's healing and redeeming activity, which includes merging frames of reference that seem to be in extreme opposition and unable to intersect, so that the human person becomes aware of God's reality and presence and love. Loder quoted Karl Barth on the dynamic power that jolts human persons into awareness of God's reality and near presence.

> The jolt by which man is wakened . . . is the will and act of God. God uses human factors, co-efficients and agencies, "setting them in motion as such in the meaning and direction which He has appointed. We are thus forced to say that this awakening is both wholly creaturely and wholly divine. Yet the initial shock comes from God."[50]

Barth's language is apt, because Eric was "jolted" and shocked by the manifestation of the Presence we requested in prayer. Yet he did not turn

---

45. Loder, *Transforming*, 222. Loder borrowed the term "bisociation" from Arthur Koestler, *Act of Creation*, which is replete with examples and analyses of two frames of reference being integrated into one.

46. Loder and Neidhardt, *Knight's Move*, 228.

47. Loder, *Transforming*, 38; cf. Loder and Neidhardt, *Knight's Move*, 176–78.

48. Loder and Neidhardt, *Knight's Move*, 250–53.

49. Ibid., 247–49.

50. Barth, *CD* 4/2, 557, quoted in Loder, *Transforming*, 116.

away from this "awakening" to the Lord's reality. Loder built on what Barth said and added that "What is 'wholly creaturely and wholly divine' represents the extreme in 'habitually incompatible frames of reference' coming together to form a meaningful unity," so that the life of the creature is not separated from the life and activity of our Creator.[51] Thus in a bisociation brought about by the initiation and activity of the Spirit, the human person is made aware of the Spiritual Presence of Christ. This divine activity, Loder affirmed, was at work during the prayer for Eric.

As Loder said in another context, ultimately the relational self must be "transparently centered upon the power that posited it. In its transparency, this state cannot be achieved by the imagination," but must involve the awareness of God's activity which is the initiator and ground of the transformational process. However, "once the transparency of the Spiritual Presence of God is bestowed, the integrative imagination reaches to give it tangible expression." The Spiritual Presence of God can bestow a new meaning on a person's life, which is both integrative and liberating, offering a future-directed, empowering sense of wholeness, and can be responded to with "Hallelujah!" and a prayer of gratitude.[52] We can say the "transparency of the Spiritual Presence of God" was bestowed on Eric. This real encounter did not involve theophany, lacking manifestation in form or image. It was a transparent interaction between Holy Spirit and human spirit. The significance of this will be discussed below, but here it can be said that this transparency accords with God's being as Spirit, existing without image, bodily shape or gender.

Loder Verbatim 2

We continue with the verbatim of our conversation on Eric.

"There is an incommensurability in his own mind, and in anybody's mind to some extent, between the direct act of God's Spirit and my mindset where I am human. And what happens there is, this bisociation takes place, and when it takes place it is a 'mind blowing' kind of experience for him: 'What happened?!' Shocking."

"So then you do what you need to do in the sequence, which is to be relieved and to thank God. 'Hallelujah!' is the theological equivalent of an 'Aha!' 'Praise God!' is 'Aha!': that's the equivalent."

---

51. Loder, *Transforming*, 116.
52. Loder, *Knight's Move*, 249.

Here Loder was referring to the five key parts of the logic of transformation (see above). Thus in our conversation, Loder focused on the moment when Eric was shocked to feel something "come into" his body, in immediate response to the prayer for Jesus Christ to enter his life with healing power. That moment and that shock were equivalent to step 3 in the logic of transformation (reception of an integrating insight). The discovery of the presence of Christ, as a living reality, present and willing to heal, was not something imaginary that was produced by Eric's imagination. Rather it was a real event to which his mind and imagination would have to respond in thought and tangible expression. The appropriate response includes thanksgiving and praise. Thanksgiving involves interpretation of what just occurred and may continue to occur. In Eric's case step 3 did move into step 4 (see the discussion below). Here, as in many cases, God's grace is not limited to the initial event, for grace is also at work in the interpretation of the event.

Loder continued. "But the main point I'm trying to get at is that a memory, a hurt memory, needs to be bisociated with whatever a person can bring in terms of their understanding of faith. So you allow them to enter the memory, and you can do that without any particular psychological understanding" [in terms of clinical training].

At this point I acknowledged I had not done what some of the books by Seamands or Payne described, where the counselor had the counselee recall his or her memory. I had not asked Eric to remember anything in vivid detail, particularly because of the context that did not allow for complete privacy.

Loder said, "Well it's not important right away, but what is important is that he *believe* that Christ entered him and is at work in him. Once that is there and in place, then you can start working on specific memories."

In some cases Loder might work with a person for more than a year, praying together for the Spiritual Presence of Jesus Christ to enter multiple hurtful memories, one at a time, and heal them. The case of Helen reflects the need for on-going work, even after receiving a visitation of the Holy Spirit: "Although God had acted, she had yet to receive inwardly and to appropriate spirit-to-Spirit what had been accomplished."[53] David Seamands also acknowledges that many people, even after receiving a deep spiritual healing, may need to continue in

---

53. Loder, *Logic*, 50.

counseling to work on long-held behavior patterns conditioned by their old frame of understanding.

Loder Verbatim 3

I knew it was possible that Eric might just think something weird happened. I asked, "I can tell him it was Christ that entered him, can't I?"

"Of course," Loder replied. "And you can tell him that 'this happens because you are loved. Because Christ wants you to be healed. It's not just you [who] want it and He's doing you a favor. He wanted it before you do, and He wants it more than you do, and that's why He responds so readily.'"[54]

"The whole point here is to move this bisociation between the act of Christ and his nature, the act of the Spirit, I mean, and his nature, which is a version of the incarnation, to move it into the context of the incarnation as a whole. Which is to say to him, it is because God already loves you, already wants you to be united with Him and His nature, that He is ready to do this."

"Again, I don't know the person so I don't know exactly the language you can use, but the point about this is to affirm the priority of God's love, the readiness and willingness of God to heal him as he is ready to cooperate."

I then said, "Well, I've just asked him, 'Does God love you?' And he said, 'Yes.' That seemed to be significant as something that had to be in place before we could pray about specific memories and recall them."

"That's very significant," Loder affirmed.

"We could not be alone where he could cry and scream as we pray about the abuse, which he might do if we prayed about specific memories of the abuse."

"Well, to some extent he has to be persuaded of the process. But you ask the Lord to bring to mind the memory that He, the Lord, would like us to work on this time, see, because everything you are doing is in the context of the divine initiative.[55] So we are in prayer, and you ask him to pray . . .'"

---

54. For those cases where biblical citations can help the counselee receive this truth, a paraphrase of John 10:10 is apt: "Jesus said, 'I come to give you life, life more abundantly.'"

55. Loder elaborated: "In this relationship you really want the Holy Spirit to do most of the talking." Because God knows the truth of our lives, the Spirit must guide us in

"That's very difficult for him," I interrupted.

"Well, [you can say] Jesus is here, we're going to talk to Him. I'll talk, you talk . . ."

"Can he repeat after me?" I asked.

"Sure," Loder said. "Whatever he wants to do . . . But he needs to be able to say, 'I want to be healed, Jesus.' That's all, right? He needs to say to Jesus the things he says to you. Say [to Eric], 'Just tell Jesus.' Let him talk to Him, to the presence of the Lord."

"And then he says, 'I remember this time when . . .' and he goes on about it, and you say, 'Okay, now just hold on to that, we're going to ask the Lord to come in [to that memory]. You ask Him to come in.' Ask [Eric] to do it first. 'Ask Him to come in.'"

"He [Eric] says, 'Nothing's happening.' [You respond] 'Okay, then I'll ask Him, and we'll talk and pray together.'"

"And [in a case like this] I'll ask, 'Do you see Jesus? More often than not they'll say, 'Yes, I see Him.' [I'll ask] 'What's He doing?' 'Well, He's just standing there. Seems like He doesn't like what's happening.'"

"[Then I'll ask] 'What's He going to do about it?' You move into the memory and it could be . . ." At this point Loder broke off his sentence, and said, "The trouble with this stuff is it can be very manipulative. That's a danger. On the other hand, the thing that keeps it from being manipulative is you're giving as much initiative as you can to him to follow up on this, and you are keeping whatever happens [in counseling] consistent with who you know Christ to be. It's not a mind game, in other words, because Christ really was there when this was happening. All you're doing is letting Christ do in his mind, in this kid's mind, what Christ, were He permitted in that situation to do [would have done] then. But the situation isn't 'back then' now—it's now in his mind. So now Christ has got to come into his mind to do what Christ was not permitted to do in the actual situation. And healing takes place because the event isn't around anymore. It's stored here [in the memory]. So you [work and pray to] change the storage. And that changes the significance

---

these prayer times. For corroboration on this point, see Seamands, *Redeeming*, 25–28. Loder gives three examples about the Spirit's initiative in prayer from his work with "Helen" recorded in *Logic*, 50–52. He reported that the first memory they were guided to pray about appeared trivial on the surface, but "seemed to have almost unfathomable implications." Loder noted that sometimes the memories the Holy Spirit guides counselor and counselee to pray about initially are propaedeutic, offering healing and strengthening hope as preparatory of deeper matters yet to be dealt with by the Spirit.

of the event for the person. It doesn't mean he won't recall the pain. But he can't recall the pain apart from Christ any more. And that's what gives him the possibility of choosing against violence or choosing against re-enacting this crime."[56]

Our conversation got side-tracked when I pressed Loder to discuss what he meant about Christ somehow being permitted or not permitted to work in the past, as though he could have been prevented from helping during the actual attack. Was the presence of Christ restricted in some way from helping Eric? There was no attempt to force Loder to discuss theodicy, so much as clarify what he meant. In his response Loder did not attempt to state what could or could not have happened in the past in any given scenario. Rather he affirmed that events may always be altered when and where the presence of Christ is welcomed, even when called upon in a state of fear or distress. He stressed that the nature of many things can be changed when Christ is invited and asked to be present. The emphasis, however, is not on what did or did not happen in the

---

56. Echols, *First Name*, presents information from court and criminal records tracing the tendency to re-enact the crime of sodomy with minors on the part of men who were raped (or enticed into the act) in their youth by older males. Gartner, in *Betrayed as Boys*, maintains that the overwhelming majority of boys who are abused do not become men who are abusive. Yet he acknowledges that most abusers were themselves abused. Loder's comment touched on this frightful possibility. One significant study reviews clinical literature on the molestation of boys, and notes that adolescents who were sexually molested by men were up to seven times more likely to identify themselves later as homosexual. See Holmes et al., "Sexual Abuse," 1855–62 and Jones and Yarhouse, *Ex-Gays*, who examine a NARTH (National Association for Research and Treatment of Homosexuality) study of 882 persons who answered retrospective questions: "The average age of awareness that they had 'homosexual tendencies' was age 12.4. Interestingly, 520 (almost 60%) reported having had a childhood homosexual contact at an average age of 10.9 years, with the person initiating that contact being an average age of 17.2 years" (82–83). The molestation came first in a majority of cases. While these studies indicate the impact of molestation, which was not always as extreme as sodomization, there is relevance to the problem of rape. For these studies show the ongoing and distorting impact on memory, emotions, fantasy, meaning-making and self-identity which cannot easily be rectified after the event. Loder's concern came from both his knowledge of the clinical literature and his work with people who sought his help for sexual problems. Although he was aware that abused boys may grow up to become abusers, by no means did he see a cause-and-effect determinism that required them to do so. His concern was for the healing of their wounded spirits and memory. For relevant information on this aspect of his counseling, see Koonz, "Matters of the Heart," 196–217.

past; rather the emphasis is placed on the power of Christ to enter the memory of the past event now (in the present) and alter its meaning.[57]

To illustrate what he meant about the presence of Christ either being welcomed during an attack or long after, Loder gave two examples. The first example was of a woman who began praying when a man tried to rape her. Her attacker became suddenly frightened and quickly left. There may have been other cases where attackers did not become frightened when someone prayed for help, but in this case the woman's liberation coincided with her praying to Christ.

The second example was of a woman who came to him for help after her rape occurred. Loder said, "And I know another case, when a girl who did get raped came back and worked on the memories. She got the memory healed rather than the actual event. And [then] she went back and really helped this guy avoid a prison sentence. Because her mind was changed: the whole significance of it was changed. See, Jesus is interested in everything that happens, but he's much more interested in the *meaning* of whatever happens than in what happens . . . It's very important that we get the meaning of what happens, whatever it is . . ."

Anything that bears upon the human spirit impacts the meaning-making process to some degree. Yet Loder's focus was on the way the presence of Christ can change the meaning that is made more than the process, though sometimes the two can be impacted simultaneously by the Holy Spirit's work. Something more directed and acute may happen that actually focuses on the old meaning that was made, altering it forever, so that the person cannot ever think of the memory in the former way. Christ can enter a memory of abuse and revise and transform the meaning connected to that past event.

After the Prayer: Follow-up Information on Eric

Between the time when I prayed with Eric and the time when I saw him again, a full two or three weeks passed. I did not know that his transfer

---

57. Compare Loder's guidance in the case of "Helen": "The intensity of these times is hard to overstate, but in that time of transition, openness to the Spiritual Presence of Christ seemed completely accessible, and Helen asked to be taken back into the past and be shown how Christ (the One who had thrown her to her knees) *was* there and what he would have done to set it right had he been invited into the situation then as he was now. Would he now do this in the events as they still lived in her mind? What needs to be healed now? Take us there, take us there now" (Loder, *Logic*, 50).

had not taken place yet, or I would have made an effort to talk with him sooner. My work at the prison continued, but in other cottages and areas where I was not apt to encounter Eric. An additional impediment was my need to focus more on my studies, papers and preparation for exams, all of which kept me away from the prison for much of the intervening time. Therefore I was surprised when I did meet him outside on the grounds, walking between buildings, because I thought he had been taken away. [This was to be our last encounter, which took place after my March 13th meeting with Loder]. Eric greeted me with a smile and told me that he was leaving soon [I think the next day] to go to a halfway house, where his mother could visit him more regularly. He was preparing to go home on parole, which would follow if he managed well enough at the halfway house. He seemed very happy at the prospect. Then he told me with a smile, "I haven't been in any more fights."

Before I left that day I confirmed this news with prison officials. Plans to transfer Eric to another prison had been changed; he was now redirected to the halfway house. Since the day we prayed together and Eric felt powerfully encountered by the Spirit of Jesus Christ, he had not been in one fight. There was an inner calmness, balance and strength, which gave Eric a new freedom and self-control. The officers and officials noticed the change. To them it was absolutely remarkable. They were mystified about what exactly had changed for Eric, but they wanted to promote this positive development and move him towards a more helpful setting that would better prepare him for parole.

There is no thought here that the convictional experience is valid because everything turns out all right. Rather the presence of Christ has the power to creatively work in a person's life, so that he or she is able to engage in life more fully and live from a meaningful center rather than from the periphery. Eric's new discovery of freedom to turn against a self-destructive behavioral pattern was most encouraging. Loder wrote, concerning people in therapeutic counseling, "that the surest sign that healing has occurred in therapeutic knowing is the freedom of the 'I' to choose for the self and against patterns of self-destruction."[58]

In my last conversation with Eric I encouraged him to keep praying to Jesus, keep asking for help, protection, guidance, and healing. "Do you know that Jesus loves you?" I asked, repeating my question from the time before. "Yes," he grinned as he answered. "Good," I said. "Keep talk-

---

58. Loder, *Transforming*, 63.

ing to him, keep welcoming him in your life. And tell your mother what God did for you when we prayed together." I groped for something that would stick in his mind. My contact with him was at an end, and I had to leave him in God's care that day. I knew my work was inadequate and incomplete, but I had the assurance Christ would never abandon him.

It was noted above that Loder saw Eric's experience as being encountered by Christ's spiritual presence, and that it had convictional force that fit with step 3 of the 5-step process of transformation. The aftermath resulted in inner peace and an outwardly calm behavior in a context that remained grim and unsoftened. The calm demeanor and the new non-aggressive, non–defensive, behavior was noticed by prison officials, which was an additional confirmation to Eric's own testimony that something radical had happened in his life. Eric's initial "What happened!?" was the "aha!" of step 3, and it was followed by a "release of tension" that did not rob him of energy, but manifested its power by producing a great sense of well–being and inner calmness. This was primarily Eric's property, but the reality of a change was witnessed and thereby shared, and the pattern fit Loder's description: "The 'aha!' and release are the surest sign that genuine insight has been attained." In no way could I, in my work as a volunteer chaplain, have effected this release of tension. Yet I could join with Eric in recognizing and affirming the answer to prayer, the healing moment that produced it, "thus solidifying the gain."[59] We can also recognize, with Loder, that Eric's transformational experience is a sign of God's presence which does not belong to Eric alone. It is a sign "for all who have eyes to see. Just as the miracles of the New Testament are designed as a witness for whoever might see them as such, so these accounts are designed to point away from the experience itself and toward the Spiritual Presence of Jesus, the Christ."[60]

Visualizing the Presence of Christ: Random Selection or Purposeful Interaction?

As Loder attested from his work with other counselees, with whom he prayed for the healing of memory, sometimes the presence of Jesus is manifested with a visual image. In these cases Jesus is seen and heard from within the scenes of the person's memory. The person is often sur-

---

59. Ibid., 59.
60. Ibid., 19.

prised or shocked, and attends to the manifestation of Jesus' presence with acute attention, finding in both that moment and in retrospect that the things Jesus says and does there provide deep healing. This experience is not created by the human imagination, but is one to which the human mind must respond and upon which it must reflect.

The possibility of this occurrence during prayer for the healing of memories is not unique to Loder's pastoral care. David Seamands provides several illustrative examples from cases he worked with. Loder had prayed with a number of people, each in his or her own counseling session, who experienced these visual manifestations of Christ. But he did not lay down such experiences as a spiritual law or something to be expected every time. In the case of Eric, he received an initial healing that did not include a visual manifestation of Jesus within his memory, but which was nonetheless deep and transforming. Loder referenced Iulia de Beausobre, who, when she was tormented in Soviet prisons, experienced a profound awareness of God's holy presence without any vision or visual accompaniment.[61] In my subsequent pastoral work I have never expected any prayer for healing to include this type of visual experience, but I have been open to this possibility and it has occurred. As with Eric, I have witnessed other cases where spiritual healings happened without it. Nonetheless it is possible for people to see Christ as present and active within their memory, because the Lord may choose to heal through this means.

The question of why these images happen sometimes but not at other times cannot be answered with certainty, but the narratives in the New Testament provide a clue. In the Gospels we find that Jesus healed in a variety of ways, using differing methods. Some people were healed instantly, while others were healed gradually. Some were healed in close proximity to Jesus, many when he touched them, while others were physically at a great distance from his presence and healed by his command. In an analysis of the healing ministry of Jesus, Hugh Ross Mackintosh wrote that the Lord accommodated the way he healed to the unique personal needs of the sufferer. For example, the narrative in Mark 8:22–26 tells that people brought a blind man to Jesus, and asked Jesus to touch him, in expectation of an immediate cure. Jesus took the man by the hand, led him away from the others, talking with him and holding his hand as they walked into a field, where they could have privacy. Why

61. Ibid., 85–86.

the extended delay before healing the man's sight? Why the long walk and conversation? Why did Jesus spit into the man's eyes and then rub the saliva with his fingertip? Was it necessary for hopeless mystification and despair to change "little by little into dawning expectancy"? Was this demonstration of compassion needed to thaw a frozen heart? Jesus accommodated his method to the needs and capacity of the individual. Mackintosh notes:

> As it has been put, "Salvation is child's play, if you will only be the child." And here Christ was stooping to employ sense and matter, because a sense-bound nature could only be helped that way. He moistened the poor eyes, and fingered the eyelids, perhaps to arrest the wandering thoughts and win attention, but at all events to predispose the man to trust the Healer. Each act of Christ was a rung in the ladder up which the sufferer might climb to faith.[62]

Christ's Spirit, active in providing the healing of wounded memories, also adjusts the way a person is healed in and through prayer. The Spirit graciously accommodates the way of healing to the unique needs of the individual. This is a sign of God's loving grace. Not all persons need to mentally revisit the scenes of trauma in order to be healed. Of those who may visualize it during a time of prayer, not all need to see an image of Jesus in order to be healed. The visual manifestation of the image of Christ, then, is not essential in every case, though certainly is important in some cases. The graphic or detailed recalling of hurtful scenes is also not essential, though it may be helpful to some people. Yet Loder articulated a deeper distinction:

> At the moment in which one enters absolutely into the Divine Presence, there can be no image at all; the actual reality of the Divine Presence cannot be made into an object of our perceptual imagination. For that moment *we* are the objects composed

---

62. Mackintosh, *Highway*, 195–206. Why the spittle and protracted healing? Mackintosh added, "That was patience, insight, love; and it was all very like Jesus Christ. Teachers of the very young know how irksome it may be to have to use an infantile vocabulary to make our meaning clear to the struggling little mind, and how a quick sense of exasperated humiliation may come over us, till we can hardly bear to shape the syllables in what seems their contemptible simplicity. No one knew half so well as Jesus, besides, that His actions at the moment could only symbolize in most inadequate fashion the benefits He was to bestow. Yet He uses them unhesitatingly, because the man before Him could understand nothing else. He wrapped up His great Divine meanings in what we might think poor shabby envelopes quite unworthy of the contents, all to render them such as an enfeebled soul could grasp and hold" (202).

into *his* presence by his initiative. But then the images rush in to fill the otherwise incomprehensible moment of such a pure and transparent awareness. When these images come, they are designed to help us comprehend the incomprehensible.[63]

This may explain why Loder never saw a vision in his two major transforming moments in 1957 and 1970, as well as explain why "Helen" (the aforementioned case recorded in *The Logic of the Spirit*) did not see an image on the night when the Holy Spirit came upon her so decisively, with intensity of healing love that far exceeded her rage. It explains why Eric's first moment of deep healing did not involve an image. Yet later, as Helen prayed through her memories with Loder, the images of Christ came into those memories. This is what Loder hoped I would do with Eric, meet with him and pray through his memories in the weeks ahead, as a way to help him know the intimate love and personal ramifications implicit and eternally present in the moment when Christ's Spirit visited him so decisively. Unfortunately my time with him was cut short by circumstances beyond our control. Yet Jesus Christ is the initiator and finisher of all transformations, and my trust had to be placed in the Lord's willingness to sustain and complete Eric's transformation.

Ultimately the quality and content of the Holy Spirit's visitation, whether invisible and transparent according to the nature of God as Spirit (without image, shape or gender), or a vision with a specific image of Jesus as healing mediator, must be God's determination. We cannot rule out the possibility of Paul's Damascus Road encounter with the resurrected Jesus or his subsequent visions. Yet overall I think Loder is right to point to the necessity of many completely transparent movements of the Holy Spirit. He also affirmed that Jesus and the Spirit work together in a reciprocal relation. Jesus sends the Spirit into the world to create new life and heal what is broken, and where the Spirit works Jesus becomes the focus in our liberation and transformation. Prayer that focuses on Jesus and invites his intervention always involves the Spirit, and may be deeply healing without intervening images or visions of Jesus. Likewise, where the Spirit is presently working a hurtful memory may be altered forever by a visitation of Jesus' presence and image.[64]

---

63. Loder, *Logic*, 59.
64. Ibid., 118, 121–22.

Further Reflections on Praying with Children

Loder emphasized that prayer for the healing of memories is not a "mind game." That is, it is not the product of manipulation, imaginary pretending, or wish-fulfilment.[65] Therefore, in my interpretation of Loder's affirmation, we should be able to state the positive corollary: it is not a mind game because something real is happening. When we pray we are not merely speaking words into thin air, as though we were only talking to ourselves or to an imaginary friend. Prayer for the healing of memories is part of a real converse with God, where prayer is a real event both in the life of human beings and in the life of God. Thus Christ's response to the prayer is an extenuation of the real event of prayer, of human participation in a living relationship with the Triune God.

In Eric's case I prayed with him four (nearly five) years after the most negative and traumatic event in his young life. There will be times, however, when pastors, counselors, or mature friends, have opportunity to pray with a child even sooner after the trauma. Sometimes the opportunity will come within days or hours. These opportunities should not be lost, but should carefully and sensitively be used to offer prayer. Initially we may feel led to cry with them and pray silently a long while before we attempt to pray out loud. Since hurtful events can impact a child's spirit and "live," as it were, within his or her mind via memory, affecting both childhood and adulthood emotions and behavior patterns. Therefore it is important for the pastoral counselor to guide the child to invite the presence of Jesus into the pain and memory as early as possible. This does not mean the child has to visualize the memory, nor that naming the reality in prayer has to be more explicit than saying "when I was hurt." The counselor or pastor is neither a witness of the past event nor a voyeur intruding on the child's privacy. We should explain to the child that we do not have to know the details unless he or she wants to talk about them. Jesus knows the details, and knows what to do with them.

Depending on the child's age, circumstances, and personal wishes, a trusted family member may be present for his or her comfort level

---

65. Seamands affirms the necessity of prayer and sees it as an important protection against mind games. "This prayer time is the very heart of the healing memories. It is in prayer that the healing miracle begins; without it, the whole process may simply be a form of autosuggestion, catharsis, or feeling therapy. This special prayer cannot be bypassed, if there are to be lasting results" (*Redeeming*, 25).

while you pray. Regardless of how young or old the child is, the prayer may be short and unadorned, but needs to speak honestly of the pain the child initially felt and continues to feel. The child needs then, and in every subsequent conversation or prayer, to be able to speak freely about his or her emotions.[66] Both initial and follow-up prayers need to lead the child (without forcing or manipulating the child) to invite the presence of Christ into his or her pain, into memories and felt emotions where healing love is needed. Prayers can and should be adjusted to the age of the child.

A young child can learn to say, "Jesus, help me," or "Jesus, please heal me." "Stay near me always. Love me. I welcome your love," may also be meaningful in some contexts. Adults have also found short prayers like these meaningful in times of great distress. There is no need to weigh troubled people down with long words, formalized prayers, or prayer clichés. One way Loder showed us how to do this was the way he prayed with adults in simple language, with child-like honesty. William Hendricks says, "Many adults in crises have reverted to childhood prayers. That is not bad. Enlarge the prayers of childhood so that they become a solid building block for adult conversation with God."[67] An opportunity to come alongside and guide the child or teenager with a prayer for spiritual healing may seem overwhelming, because ministering to a person in pain is always daunting. We must offer empathy and a loving presence, but not stop there if welcomed to do more. Explicitly showing a child how to communicate and spiritually connect with Jesus provides a gift for a lifetime. It opens up all the possibilities for interac-

---

66. Lester, *Pastoral Care*. Lester writes, "One important goal of caring for children in crisis is that of providing an opportunity for them to express the emotive content of their trauma. We can provide a safe context for feelings to be described, felt, and discussed without fear of disapproval" (62). In agreement with this, it seems that both the memory and emotive content of the trauma should be brought to the Lord in prayer, in search for Christ's gifts of healing and love to be brought to bear upon the child's painful experience. Lester offers many counseling insights, but sadly does not offer a discussion on praying with children in crisis. Prayers with children can be uncomplicated and simply stated, without being trite. Prayers that are thoughtful and apt can help the child or older youth feel loved and supported, as well as teach him or her how to pray and enter into Christ's presence on his or her own. Prayers need to be sensitive to felt shame and inner pain. But some education about the meaning of prayer may have to be included. Whether working with adults or children, the proposal to engage in prayer can raise questions about God that often need to be discussed. See Wright, *Crisis*, 226–28.

67. Hendricks, *Theology*, 198.

tion between the human spirit and the Holy Spirit, a bisociation that has transformational power. Praying together soon after a frightful or traumatic event also inhibits repression of memory, and so it actively counters the emotional damage and behavioral patterns that would accompany repression in his or her adult years.

Initial prayer should be followed up with additional visits: pastoral care requires not assuming that spiritual power works only in a once-for-all way. Caring involves spending time with those who have gone through horrific experiences or difficult struggles. Follow up visits are important because they allow for continuity and affirm God's loving acceptance. A child or teenager should be linked up with people who model dependence on Christ for spiritual help, and who participate in the worship and Eucharistic life of the Church. After a particular trauma has occurred, receptivity to human interaction may be restricted in the child's life, and he or she may only trust or feel safe around one or two close family members. But in the context of on-going pastoral work, eventually the circle of supporting contact should be expanded. Personal redemption, healing, and transformation, always make possible participation in Christian community, and the community may become helpful in affirming transformation.[68]

Conclusion

How did Loder determine there was a need to pray for the healing of a counselee's memories? I think his own perception and intuition as a therapist was involved, but he also looked for signals from the individual he was working with. If the person indicated there was a nightmare, memory, or event that seemed to haunt his or her life, Loder would then ask whether they would want him to explore it with them in prayer. He looked to them for both guidance and permission, as well as to the spiritual guidance he always sought in prayer. There are also the factors David Seamands noted, about emotionally turbulent people and other types of people who would use this as an exercise in narcissism. No doubt Loder discerned when and where to rule out this type of prayer, particularly with adults who seek attention more than healing. In my own practice I have discovered individuals who cannot distinguish between disappointment over a wedding cake and psychologically scar-

68. Seamands, *Redeeming*, 183.

ring events from childhood, with lists of grievances so long it would be impossible to pray with them for the healing of their memories. Clearly discernment is required, and Loder was usually guided by what he heard and observed in his counseling sessions.

When we are careful in using this approach in prayer, and sense we actually do need to use it, we can have confidence that there is no dark, hurtful, or shameful memory that can preclude the presence of the Lord, nor limit the healing range and depth of the Spirit's work. When a human life is open to Christ's Presence, the Spirit-to-spirit interaction is beyond our control, is surprising and powerful, and cannot be manipulated. Sensitivity to the Spirit's guidance is required throughout the process, whereas any human attempt to control or direct what happens circumvents what needs to happen. Christ is free to appear or not appear within any particular scene of memory, and free to speak the words of truth and healing that transform the meaning of a hurtful memory. When this prayer focus is done in harmony with the guidance of the Holy Spirit, it may become a pathway to greater personal wholeness and transformation that grounds the human spirit in fellowship with the Holy Spirit. We may discover afresh that in relationship with God we are known through and through, and always loved.

Works Cited

Augustine, *The City of God, Book XXII.8*. Translated by Marcus Dods. New York: Modern Library, 1950.
Barth, Karl. *Church Dogmatics*, 4/2. Edinburgh: T. & T. Clark, 1958.
Block, David. *Our Universe: Accident or Design?* Edinburgh: Scottish Academic, 1992.
Carlsen, Mary Baird. *Meaning-Making: Therapeutic Processes in Adult Development*. New York: Norton, 1988.
Craig, William Lane. *Reasonable Faith*. Wheaton, IL: Crossway, 1994.
Earman, John. *Hume's Abject Failure: The Argument Against Miracles*. Oxford: Oxford University Press, 2000.
Echols, Mike. *I Know My First Name is Steven*. New York: Pinnacle, 2004.
Fee, Gordon D. *The Disease of the Health and Wealth Gospels*. Vancouver, BC: Regent College Publishing, 2006.
Froelich, Karlfried. "Charismatic Manifestations and the Lutheran Incarnational Stance." In *The Holy Spirit in the Life of the Church: From Biblical Times to the Present*, edited by Paul D. Opsahl, 136–57. Minneapolis: Augsburg, 1978.
Gartner, Richard B. *Betrayed as Boys: Psychodynamic Treatment of Sexually Abused Men*. New York: Guilford, 1999.
Geivett, R. Douglas, and Gary R. Habermas. *In Defense of Miracles*. Downers Grove, IL: InterVarsity, 1997.
Gilbert, Martin. *The Boys: Triumph over Adversity*. London: Weidenfeld & Nicolson, 1996. Published in the United States as *The Boys: The Untold Story of 732 Young Concentration Camp Survivors*. New York: Henry Holt, 1997.
Guinness, Os. "Scars from an Old Wound." In *Doubt: Faith in Two Minds*, 132–44. Tring, UK: Lion, 1987.
Hendricks, William. *A Theology for Children*. Nashville: Broadman, 1980.
Holmes, W. C., et al. "Sexual Abuse of Boys." *Journal of the American Medical Association* 280 (1998) 1855–62.
Howie, John. *The Scots Worthies*. Restored to its original content by Carslaw, W. H. in 1870. Reprinted by Edinburgh: Banner of Truth Trust, 2001.
Immordino-Yang, Mary Helen, and Antonio Damasio. "We Feel, Therefore We Learn: The Relevance of Affective and Social Neuroscience to Education." *Mind, Brain and Education* 1/1 (2007) 3–10.
Johnson, William A. *The Search for Transcendence*. New York: Harper, 1974.
Jones, Stanton L., and Mark A. Yarhouse. *Ex-Gays: A Longitudinal Study of Religiously Mediated Change in Sexual Orientation*. Downers Grove, IL: InterVarsity, 2007.
Jung, Carl. *Jung on Active Imagination*. Edited and with an introduction by Joan Chodorow. Princeton: Princeton University Press, 1997.
Keener, Craig. *Miracles: The Credibility of the New Testament Accounts*. 2 vols. Grand Rapids: Baker Academic, 2011.
Kegan, Robert. *The Evolving Self: The Problems and Process of Human Development*. Cambridge, MA: Harvard University Press, 1982.
———. *In Over Our Heads: The Mental Demands of Modern Life*. Cambridge, MA: Harvard University Press, 1995.
———. "There the Dance Is: Religious Dimensions of Developmental Theory." In *Toward Moral and Religious Maturity*, edited by J. W. Fowler and A. Vergote, 403–40. Morristown, NJ: Silver Burdette, 1980.

Kierkegaard, Soren. *The Sickness Unto Death*. Edited and translated by Howard V. Hong and Edna H. Hong. Princeton: Princeton University Press, 1983.

Koestler, Arthur. *The Act of Creation*. New York: Macmillan, 1964.

Koonz, Mark S. "Matters of the Heart: James E. Loder on Homosexuality and the Possibility of Transformation." In *Embracing Truth: Homosexuality and the Word of God*, edited by David W. Torrance and Jock Stein, 196–217. Edinburgh: Handsel, 2012.

———. "Prayer and the Cure of Souls in James E. Loder's Counseling Ministry." *Edification: The Transdisciplinary Journal of Christian Psychology* 5/2 (2012) 66–74.

Lester, Andrew D. *Pastoral Care with Children in Crisis*. Philadelphia: Westminster, 1985.

Loder, James E., Jr. *The Logic of the Spirit: Human Development in Theological Perspective*. Colorado Springs: Helmers & Howard, 1998.

———. "Prayer Essentials." Title given to a series of taped sessions with James E. Loder by Mark Koonz, privately held. No date.

———. "The Prayer of Adoration." Interview with Angella Pak Sun for the Drew Seminary television program *Mountain Views*, shown on Dec. 22, 2001.

———. "The Prayer of Confession." Interview with Angella Pak Sun for the Drew Seminary television program *Mountain Views*, shown on Nov. 24, 2001.

———. "The Prayer of Healing." Interview with Angella Pak Sun for the Drew Seminary television program *Mountain Views*, shown on Dec. 29, 2001.

Loder, James E., Jr., and Jim Neidhardt. *The Knight's Move: The Relational Logic of the Spirit in Theology and Science*. Colorado Springs: Helmers & Howard, 1992.

Mackintosh, Hugh Ross. *The Highway of God*. Edinburgh: T. & T. Clark, 1931.

———. *Types of Modern Theology: Schleiermacher to Barth*. New York: Charles Scribner & Sons, 1937.

Menninger, Karl. *Man Against Himself*. New York: Harcourt Brace Jovanovich, 1985.

Montgomery, John Warwick. *Tractatus Logico-Theologicus*. Bonn: Kultur und Wissenschaft, 2003.

Payne, Leanne. *The Healing Presence: Curing the Soul through Union with Christ*. Grand Rapids: Baker, 2008.

Oden, Thomas C. *Classical Pastoral Care*, Vol. 4, *Crisis Ministries*. Grand Rapids: Baker, 1994.

Osmer, Richard R. "Forward." In *Redemptive Transformation in Practical Theology: Essays in Honor of James E. Loder, Jr.*, edited by Dana R. Wright and John D. Kuentzel, ix–xi. Grand Rapids: Eerdmans, 2004.

Seamands, David A. *Putting Away Childish Things*. Wheaton, IL: Victor, 1986.

———. *Redeeming the Past: Recovering from the Memories That Cause Our Pain*. [Formerly titled *Healing of Memories*]. Wheaton, IL: Victor, 2002.

Torrance, Thomas F. *Preaching Christ Today: The Gospel and Scientific Thinking*. Grand Rapids: Eerdmans, 1994.

Wright, H. Norman. *Crisis Counseling*. San Bernardino, CA: Here's Life, 1985.

9

Transformation of the Ego

A Study via Sudhir Kakar and James E. Loder

AJIT A. PRASADAM

Moses said, "Show me your glory, I pray"

EXODUS 33:18

Introduction

At the beginning of the twentieth century Sigmund Freud gave us an understanding of the human psyche: id, ego, and superego. He outlined the dynamics of the ego and then along with Anna Freud gave us an understanding of defense mechanisms.[1] In 1981, Sudhir Kakar,[2]

1. Freud, *Ego*.
2. Sudhir Kakar has a BE in mechanical engineering from Gujarat University, a master's degree (Diplom-Kaufmann) in business economics from Mannheim, Germany, and a doctorate in economics from Vienna. Between 1966–67, he was a lecturer in general education and assistant to Erik H. Erikson at Harvard University and subsequently a research fellow in the program for applied psychoanalysis at the graduate school. Under the influence of Erikson, he changed his field from economics to psychoanalysis. He then trained as a post-doctoral student and later as a lecturer at the Sigmund Freud Institute in Frankfurt, 1971–75. In 1975 he returned to India and set up practice as a psychoanalyst in Delhi and at the same time served as head of the department of humanities and social sciences at the prestigious Indian Institute of

in *The Inner World—A Psychoanalytic Study of Childhood and Society in India*,[3] and James E. Loder,[4] in *The Transforming Moment*,[5] outlined the goal of human development as the transformation of the ego, the organizing principle of the personality, which differentiates and mediates between the "I" and "you" and what is "inside" and "outside." Kakar's understanding arises out of his study of human development, Sigmund Freud and especially Erik H. Erikson, in relation to Hindu culture, more particularly, *Advaitic* Hinduism (monism). He sees the goal of human development as *moksha*, ". . . [the] state in which all distinctions between subject and object have been transcended, a direct experience of fundamental unity of a human being with the infinite."[6] The *atman*, which he variously refers to as Spirit—a major animating force,[7] is a dynamic deeper than the ego and is one with *Brahman*. Loder saw transformation of the ego, in response to Carl Jung, "not [as] psychic wholeness

---

Technology. Significant teaching and research experience include: Adjunct Professor of Leadership at INSEAD in Fontainbleau, France (since 1994), Homi Bhaba Senior Fellow (since 2012), Fellow at the Institute of Advanced Study, Princeton (1984) and Berlin (1994–95 and the summer of 1997), University of Chicago (1989–93), University of Hawaii (1988), Melbourne (1981), McGill (1976–77), Vienna (1974–75), Indian Institute of Management, Ahmedabad (1968–71). He has written 17 books on psychology and culture and 4 of fiction. He established a new discipline of cultural psychology. See his autobiography, *Memory*.

3. Kakar, *Inner World*.

4. James E. Loder (1931–2001) attended Carleton College, Princeton Theological Seminary (BD), Harvard Divinity School (STM), and Harvard Graduate School of Arts and Sciences (PhD). His PhD was in the history and philosophy of religion from Harvard's Graduate School of Arts and Sciences. He was a Danforth Fellow in Theology and Psychiatric Theory at the Menninger Foundation and Research Assistant for the Harvard University Project on Religion and Mental Health. He studied with Paul Tillich, Hans Hoffman, David C. McClelland, Richard R. Niebuhr, Paul Pruyser, James Luther Adams, and Talcott Parsons, among others. He was invited to Princeton Seminary to teach in the Practical Theology Department. He did postdoctoral work at Piaget's Institut des Sciences de l'Education in Geneva, and at Oxford University. He became the Mary D. Synott Professor of the Philosophy of Christian Education and remained in that position till his death in 2001. His work reflects the relationship of theology to the soft and hard sciences with implications for congruent forms of Divine-human action in the world.

5. Loder, *Transforming*.

6. Kakar, *Inner World*, 16. In *Memory*, he states that the goal of human development is the quest is for *sat-chit-ananda* (being-consciousness-bliss) (201).

7. Kakar, *Book of Memory*, 298. He draws on St Augustine's phrase "deeper than the deepest recesses of my heart," and "higher than the highest I could reach" to explicate the dynamic of the Spirit or *atman* in relationship to the psychic space.

but holiness brought into our lives, whatever our fragmented condition, by the only One who is truly holy,"[8] where one lives in the imageless Spiritual presence of the Holy as the goal of human development within a theological understanding. Loder showed this on the basis of Christian theology, through engaging the likes of Wolfhart Pannenberg, Karl Barth via T. F. Torrance, George Hendry, Soren Kierkegaard, and others, and the sciences, engaging Pannenberg (who seeks to address science by showing the religious thematic implicit in science), Wilder Penfield (the two essences of the brain, the program and the programmer), and developmental psychologists—Sigmund Freud, Erik H. Erikson, Jean Piaget, Carl Jung, and others. He argued that there is the dynamic of the human spirit in relationship to the Divine Spirit that is deeper than the dynamic of the ego and that has the power to transform ego and its defenses through negation of negation and the outpouring of the Spirit. Loder overcame dualism through a Christological understanding of the divine-human relationality,[9] as depicted in the Mobius band and propounded for us in the Chalcedonian creed: "indissoluble differentiation," "inseparable unity," and "indestructible (asymmetrical) order."[10]

Kakar argues that *moksha* is a possibility for every Indian, whereas in the West he says that it is conceivable only for the elite, comprised of artists, poets, and "God's fools." He continues, "The point is that in India the idea of *moksha* is not deviant, but central to the imagery of the culture. Any psycho-social study of Hindu India must necessarily grapple with this phenomenon, however difficult or professionally disconcerting the attempt may be."[11] Loder, similarly argued that human beings are hard wired for transformation and it is a normal rather than an abnormal phenomenon. "Thus, what appears as psychopathology to the analyst is in a transformational perspective neither disordered nor degenerate; rather, it is a higher order and a regeneration."[12] In acknowledging the place of intuition and imagination to know reality

---

8. Loder, *Logic*, 308.

9. Loder noted: "'Relationality' is similar to but not synonymous with 'relationship.' A connection that is maintained by two polarities is a relationship; when that relationship takes on a life of its own, defining and sustaining the polarities—not the other way around—then we will speak of a relationality" (*Logic*, 16 n. 7). See also Loder and Neidhardt, *Knight's Move*, 56–60.

10. Loder, *Logic*, 38.

11. Kakar, *Inner World*, 17.

12. Loder, *Transforming*, 145.

both Loder and Kakar overcome what Loder called the "eikonic eclipse," which occurs when any assertion of truth does not recognize and accept its primary dependency on a leap of imagination to be later confirmed empirically.[13]

In this paper, I will focus attention on five concerns:

1. I will explore how the transformation of the ego is possible within both a Hindu *Advaitic* understanding and a Christian reformed theological understanding that overcomes dualism.

2. I will seek to show Loder's unique contribution to human development theory lies in his understanding of the dynamics of the spirit in relation to the Divine Spirit, a dynamic that has the power to negate negation in Christ and the Spirit. Negation can be *calculative*—where objectivity is preserved and subjectivity is negated; *functional*—where the psychological functions in intra-psychic and interpersonal relationships are negated; and *existential*—the negation of one's being. The negation of negation can be operative in dealing with all the above negations. The concern in this paper, however, is with functional and existential negation. A child experiences negation of being when s/he experiences the absence of a caregiver or a "No," as when adults try to protect the child from harm. Negation is also experienced in a big "No," as when s/he grows up in poverty, classism, racism, sexism, ageism, and casteism (in the Indian context in a hierarchically organized society where negation is a part of daily life leading to experiences of narcissism, shame, inferiority, limited opportunities leading to despair and hopelessness). Kakar also talks about negation experienced by an infant in the fears of abandonment and absorption and the experience of the void. He also appears to deal implicitly with the negation of negation in the experience of love of family, relatives, and community and in the image of the *Shakti* and *Shakta*, the energy and the inert, with their thighs clasped around each other in eternal embrace. But the existential and cosmic sense of negation of the non-being/void/nothingness[14] is not ad-

---

13. Loder, *Transforming*, 26f. Also see Kakar, "Resurgence," for a discussion on "connected imagination."

14. I am using Paul Tillich's categories of Being-in-Itself and non-being in this paper even though Loder preferred to use the words the Void and the Holy. Loder was

dressed historically as it is in the Christian understanding of the cross and the resurrection.[15] Thus, we see that both Kakar and Loder talk about transformation of the ego within the four dimensions of human existence—self, lived world, void, and the Holy. However, there is a decisive difference in the understanding of transformation according to Loder between the eastern religions and the western Christian context as it pertains to the role of God in history. Eastern religions emphasize the way of "release." This generalization, however, is contestable.

3. So, I will show, via Kakar, that renunciation as connected to *moksha* does not always mean escaping existential reality or inaction in the world (Quietism) but is a surrender of the notion of selfish actions of the "I" and "Mine" (*Gita*).[16] Gandhi, who can only be understood within a Hindu view of life, is a case in point.[17]

4. I will also seek to show the relevance of Loder's concept of the transformation of the ego within a four dimensional understanding of reality, and the significance of the negation of negation and the affirmation of life in the Christ-event in relation to Kakar's understanding of transformation within a Hindu *Advaitic* framework where negation of negation appears to be implicit. Without the negation of negation and affirmation of life, ego and its defenses cannot be transformed. Atonement and repentance appear to be necessary to deal with sin and evil, or else somebody or some group would be made scapegoat, as it

---

influenced by Tillich but he drew the concept of the Void more from Karl Barth's view of evil as the nothingness that haunts us than from Heidegger, Sartre, and others. See Kuentzel, "Heidegger," 347–72. Loder acknowledged, however, that *calculative, functional, existential,* and *transformational* negations draw on many philosophical sources. But his ultimate category for the Void is from theology, which he shared with me. I am using Tillich's categories intentionally as his philosophical theology correlates and resonates with Indian philosophy and the Hindu culture. Loder, as a student at Harvard, had Tillich as his professor. He went beyond Tillich in his understanding of method and was grounded in reformed theology as expounded by Karl Barth and appropriated via T. F. Torrance, who saw the place of science in relation to theology as geometry is to physics.

15. Kakar, *Inner World*, 54.
16. Kakar, "Setting the Stage," 10.
17. Kakar, *Inner World*, 30.

is possible for those who experience negation to hold on to revenge to their own detriment and that of society. A comparison of Robert Mugabe of Zimbabwe, who made the breadbasket of Africa a poor house, with Nelson Mandela of South Africa, who put in place the Truth and Reconciliation Commission to heal the nation, reveals the dangers of revenge and the wisdom of repentance and forgiveness.

5. Finally, after critically appropriating Kakar and Loder, I will go further to show what caregivers, teachers, counselors, liturgists, and preachers need to do to engage the human spirit in relationship to the Divine Spirit in order to break the power of negation and to encourage the transformation of the ego and its defenses, not just lower them.

Transformation of the Ego: Sudhir Kakar and Hindu Culture

Lead me from the asat [untruth] to the sat [truth].
Lead me from darkness to light.
Lead me from death to immortality."
(Brhadaranyaka Upanishad—I.iii.28)

Sudhir Kakar (1938–) embarks on the study of the inner world of the Indian as he wants to understand Indian identity, a passion that has remained with him throughout his life. In *The Inner World—A Psychoanalytic Study of Childhood and Society in India,* he outlines human development within the understanding of *varnashramadharma,* the four stages of life (*brahmacharya* [student], *grahastha* [homemaker], *varnaprastha* [forest dweller who has handed over responsibilities to the next generation], and *sanyasa* [mendicant]). He correlates these stages with *varna* (*brahmin, kshatriya, vaishya,* and *shudra,* the outcaste is beyond the pale of *varnashramadharma*), the hierarchical ordering of *jatis* (diverse "species" of people), and *dharma,* or moral duty/right action (from which arises happiness and final beatitude[18] appropriate to one's *varna* and its goal as *moksha,*[19] the unity of the self and the infinite, the

---

18. Kane, *Dharmashastra,* 3.

19. The term *moksha* variously means "self-realization, transcendence, salvation, a release from worldly involvement, from 'coming' and 'going.'" Yet in Hindu philosophy it is also described as the state in which all distinctions between subject and object have been transcended, a direct experience of the fundamental unity of a human being with

subject and the object). His study is about so-called upper caste Hindus, the twice-born who comprise the *brahmin, kshatriya,* and the *vaishya.* In so doing, Kakar implicitly affirms *karma-samsara* (the cycle of birth and rebirth) and accepts the caste system as not inherently bad. Though he is uncomfortable with the system and protests in his later writings that the caste system is incongruent with modern India, he makes generalizations about what it means to be Indian. He thinks these generalizations are still as important as an "old map" even in a postmodern context, where grand narratives are questioned.[20]

In *The Indians: Portrait of a People,* Kakar identifies Indians as *homo hierarchichus* in a culture that is dominated by *varnashramadharma,* that which has made Indian society the most hierarchical.[21] (He is more forthright on the negative aspects of the caste system in this later work and in his autobiography). Negation is written right across culture and society inflicting human development with hubris, on the one hand, and shame, on the other. The experience of negation, which is felt in the system in a downward spiral, can be most devastating to those at the bottom. Negation gives rise to what Kakar calls the "capital of narcissism" leading to suffering and humiliation for several million through the centuries. Kakar goes on to quote the Marathi poet, Govindaraj: "Hindu society is made up of men 'who bow their heads to the kicks from above and who simultaneously give a kick below, never thinking to resist the one or refrain from the other.' The hierarchy is so fine tuned that even a low caste will always find another caste that is inferior to it, thus mitigating some of the narcissistic injury suffered by it at being seen as inferior."[22]

The suffering of those on the lowest rung of the caste hierarchy has been documented by S. K. Thorat, who gives an account of his personal experience, as well as B. R. Ambedkar, who influenced him. Thorat writes: "An untouchable child, particularly in a village, is subjected to a stigmatized identity from the time he can begin to walk and to touch things and people. When he innocently enters the village temple or a

---

the infinite" (Kakar, *Inner World*, 16). In Brihadaranyaka Upanishad, 4.3.21, *moksha* is the entry into *brahman,* a merging with *brahman,* eating of *brahman,* breathing of *brahman's* spirit. It is the unity of the self and the world.

20. See Kakar, *Inner World,* 212.
21. Kakar and Kakar, *Indians.*
22. Ibid., 27.

caste Hindu household, or touches someone, he is reprimanded either by his parents or by the caste Hindus . . ."[23] Furthermore,

> Any untouchable adult is subject to stigmatized identity. Since this is not an abstract thing but a matter of day-to-day oppression and exploitation, educated adults always try to discard it and to accept another identity based on justice and on right social intercourse. I have described my own experience.[24]

Kakar's works are important for several reasons:

i. his interdisciplinary conversation between the psychoanalytic study of Indian childhood and Hindu *Advaitic* philosophy and culture;

ii. his study in psychology, religion and anthropology, where the integrity of the disciplines are maintained without one negating the other;

iii. his identification of the *atman* as a dynamic deeper than the ego; and

iv. his understanding of the transformation of the ego in *moksha* experienced in *samadhi* as a first step through the process of Raja Yoga

In this section, these points will be explored with a view to how Kakar envisions ego transformation without explicitly showing how negation is negated in history to impact the psychological, social, and cultural dimensions of life.

Kakar is a singular voice in the psychoanalytic study of childhood and society in India. The primary dimension of his study, its organizing principle, is individual development in which he takes Erikson's conceptualization of the epigenetic sequence of stages of psychosocial growth as the model. While he recognizes that there are several developmental lines for almost every aspect of personality—cognitive, moral, and so on—he writes:

> My discussion of human development in India is organized around yet another basic developmental line or sequence, one which describes the arc of growth in terms of the individual's rec-

---

23. Thorat, "Passage," 67.
24. Ibid., 80.

iprocity with his social environment, where, for a long time, the members of his immediate family are the critical counter players. Erik Erikson has given us the model in his conceptualization of an epigenetic sequence of stages of "psycho-social growth," a sequence which leads from the infant's utter dependence on the nurturing care of a mothering person to the young adult's emotional self-reliance and sense of identity.[25]

Thus, he seeks to understand Indian identity through the network of social roles, traditional values, caste customs, and kinship regulations with which "the threads of individual psychological development are interwoven."[26] He has studied, lived and worked in Europe, the US, and India and compares India with the West with deep understanding. He works on the assumption that both Indian and western societies ". . . offer distinctive solutions to universal human dilemmas, that both (in secular psychological terminology) have specific normative conceptions of what constitutes the 'healthy' personality and of how social relations should be organized to achieve this elusive ideal."[27]

He acknowledges the limits of his early work in that he is primarily dealing with Hindu India and more particularly with the cultural traditions and psychosocial identity of so-called caste Hindus. In his recent work, *The Indians*, he engages the caste system and acknowledges its detrimental impact of narcissism within the hierarchy. It is not difficult to intuit how narcissism, shame and doubt, and inferiority are embedded within the Indian psyche depending on where the person is located in the hierarchy. His observations do not purport to be definitive statements about Hindus throughout India but he merely seeks to illustrate ". . . a dominant mode in the wide and variable range of Hindu behavior."[28] Though he uses Hindu and India interchangeably, he is aware of the diversity of India. He seeks to uncover unifying themes while admitting to the dangers that it poses, but defends himself: ". . . I have ventured to do this for at least two reasons: first, hypotheses have to be advanced if they are ever to be tested; and second, I believe that the generalizations that have evolved out of this study possess an underlying truth resonant with

---

25. Kakar, *Inner World*, 2.
26. Ibid.
27. Ibid., 6.
28. Ibid., 8.

the psychological and cultural actualities of upper caste Hindu childhood and society."[29]

Kakar lays out for us an understanding of human development within an Eriksonian framework. Nonetheless, he seeks to understand the Indian by reframing the discussion within a Hindu *Advaitic* framework where the values of *moksha*, *varnashradharma*, and *karma* are predominant. In so doing, he is looking at human development within a Hindu *Advaitic* religious understanding—a distinctive aspect of his work. What is more distinctive is that he endeavors to show that ". . . the *atman* of Vedantic thought whose only counter player is *brahman*"[30] is deeper than the ego. The ultimate aim of existence is *moksha*, which seeks to undo the process of ego development.[31] This is not what Ernst Kris called "regression in the service of the ego" in which one returns to the beginnings to realign the defensive ego functions so that the adult ego is strengthened from such regression. Kakar writes, "Rather, the intention is to effect a complete revolution in man's psychic organization by providing new goals and different modes of perception which radically alter the subjective experiencing of 'reality.'"[32]

Kakar seeks to show how this complete revolution in human psychic organization is possible through the process of Raja Yoga resulting in *samadhi*.

> To live in this state, it seems, does *not* mean to experience the external world as an utterly subjective phenomenon, as in hallucinations or delusions of the schizoid or schizophrenic kind. Rather, *samadhi* seems to be an intensely creative approach to external reality and the world of facts, an apperception in which everything happening outside is felt to be a creative experience of the original artist within each one of us and recognized as such with (what Blake would call) *delight*.[33]

Kakar says that the perfect *samadhi* of yoga as described by the Hindu texts is "a blissful trance of a transitory nature. *Moksha*, on the other hand, is not a temporary surge of oceanic living, but a constant and fully

---

29. Ibid.
30. Ibid., 19.
31. Ibid., 21.
32. Ibid.
33. Ibid., 26. Compare this sense of delight with Søren Kierkegaard's knight of faith in *Fear and Trembling*, 49.

aware living-in-the-ocean."³⁴ In *moksha* the "I," neither the self, for self is the object of "I," nor the ego, a psychic agency, is the *atman* which becomes one with the *Brahman*. "[A] person living in this state has an all-pervasive current of "I." "I" is the center of awareness and existence in all experience situations and in all possible selves." The feeling of "I" in the selves of others is empathy and in the state of *moksha* one has empathy for the generalized other.³⁵

Samadhi is the closest approximation experientially and psychologically, according to Kakar, to what *moksha* conceivably means. So, he takes up the process of Raja Yoga and compares it with psychoanalysis in its three phases:

i. preparation, ethically and physiologically,

ii. integration, the first step in transformation of the *chitta,* and

iii. meditation, leading to *Samadhi*.

In the first phase of preparation the two steps of yoga are *yama* and *niyama,* rules for everyday living: nonviolence, truthfulness, non-stealing, continence, cleanliness, austerity, study, and so forth. The physiological preparation has to do with *asana* and *pranayama,* bodily postures and breathing exercises for a healthy body. One must first learn to control the things that are nearest to him, i.e., the body.³⁶

The practice of yoga proper begins with integration, phase two and the step of *pratyahara,* which has to do with the control of the *chitta*. *Chitta* is similar to the *id* of psychoanalytic model and represents the elemental instinctual drives of a person. The Hindu texts use the word *chitta* at times for all unconscious mental processes. If for Freud *id* is chaos, a cauldron full of seething excitations, for the Hindu the *chitta* is like a monkey, stung by a scorpion with a demon in it. *Chitta* is closer than the body and is bound up with bodily organs and exists in the experiences of pleasure and pain and in the darkening form of human aggression (sexuality). The aim of *chitta,* however, is "I" awareness and the non-duality of the "I" and the "other." The egoistic and the altruistic drives of Freud are comparable to the understanding of the drives of *chitta*. The transformation of the *chitta* is the main task of this stage

34. Kakar, *Inner World*, 17.

35. Ibid., 19.

36. Ibid., 21–22.

through the process of Raja Yoga. Transformation is made possible by allowing the tumultuous and hideous thoughts to come to the fore till one comes to a place of calmness, which may take many days, months, or years. Kakar likens this aspect of Raja Yoga to Freud's free association in psychoanalytic therapy. The guru, like the psychotherapist, monitors the process to calm the *chitta* and see its transformation without the ego being prematurely engulfed or resulting in a psychotic breakdown.[37]

The third and last phase is meditation, *samyama*. Its aim is the final transformation of the *chitta* leading to *samadhi* through *dharana*, unbending concentration of the mind, and *dhyana*, concentration on a point of focus. The intention here is knowing the truth till the object becomes transparent in the experience "'I' am *Brahman*" and "'I' am the world," the unity of the subject and object. This is comparable to the understanding of icons within eastern Christian tradition and in the tradition *Lectio-Divina* where the Word becomes transparent, leading one into the imageless Spiritual presence of God.

Kakar claims that *rasa*, the aesthetic counterpart of *moksha*, in all forms of art is like *pratyahara* to yoga in calming the *chitta* and bringing it nearer to its perfect state of pure calm.[38] The third phase of Raja Yoga cannot be correlated with psychoanalytic method, which is diagnostic.[39]

Kakar also correlates the experience of *moksha* with the experiences of the numinous of St. John of the Cross and Martin Buber in the western tradition.[40] He mulls over the experience of *moksha* in the context of the erotic, which is in search of the Divine or the Spirit as its goal.

> Could St. Augustine be right that human restlessness finds its rest only in God? I do not know. I keep oscillating between doubt and conviction, between suspicion and wonderment. I believe I have had tantalizing glimpses of the invisible but have also wondered if these were not merely some of the profounder illusions of the soul. Perhaps I am too much of my father's son to take a irrevocable step across the line of reason into a wholehearted avowal of the intangible.[41]

---

37. Ibid., 22–25.
38. Ibid., 31.
39. Ibid., 25–27.
40. Ibid., 29.
41. Kakar, *Book of Memory*, 309.

Being a child of the scientific age, Kakar is tentative in his acknowledgement of the Divine. In his much later book, *Mad and Divine*, he freely acknowledges the Divine and develops a discernment of the genuine experience of *moksha* from the spurious through the study of guru Osho Rajneesh and Gandhi, among others.[42] But, in his discussions of *moksha* in his earlier book, true to his scientific tenor, he seeks to ground the experience of *moksha* scientifically via Roland Fisher, by drawing attention to the heightened state of "trophotropic" (TT, the quieting system) arousal, which is qualitatively different from the heightened state of self awareness in "ergotropic" (ET, energy expanding system) arousal. I reiterate that the transformation of the ego within a Hindu *Advaitic* understanding is philosophically grounded in the understanding of reality as One, non-duality, which sees duality as illusion. When one lives in duality one is in *avidya* (ignorance). Thus, the distinction between Being-itself, the Holy, and the human and physical world is blurred. As a consequence physical existence is not taken as seriously as the spiritual and calls for reconsideration of relating human development to *Vishistadvaitic* philosophy[43] rather than *Advaitic* philosophy. The deeper logic for such a reconsideration lies in the *Vishistadvaitic* conception of reality and its congruence with the unity of the subject-object relationality of modern science. In this way of thinking, the problem of dualism is overcome and at the same time physical existence is affirmed. Thereby liberation from the structure of non-being/nothingness/the Void that plagues human existence is possible.

Transformation of the Ego: James E. Loder and Western Christian Culture

> *I have been crucified with Christ; and it is no longer I who live, but it is Christ who lives in me. And the life I now live in the flesh I live by faith in the Son of God, who loved me and gave himself for me."*
>
> Galatians 2:19b–20

James E. Loder (1931–2001) had two significant convictional experiences: the first while he was enrolled as a student at Princeton Theological

---

42. Kakar, *Mad and Divine*, 1–35, 78–98.

43. *Vishishtadvaita* is qualified monism in which the *Brahman* and *atman* are one in the sense of differentiated unity.

Seminary (PTS) and the second as a professor at PTS when he experienced a nearly fatal accident in 1970. The first one spurred him to study Soren Kierkegaard and the second experience made him question his basic assumptions and turn to a four dimensional understanding of reality explained later in this paper. Subsequently, in his ground-breaking work, *The Transforming Moment*, he gave us an understanding of the transformation of persons, cultures, and societies (the neo-Parsonian model). Our concern here is with human development from an interdisciplinary perspective drawing on the human and social sciences and theology. He asked the two-part question, "What is a lifetime?" and "Why do I live it?"[44] Human development is set within a four dimensional understanding of reality: self, lived world, the void, and the Holy. He showed that human development follows stage transitions through periods of conflict resolution as part of the process of transformational logic (conflict-in-context, interlude for scanning, intuitive insight with imaginative force, release of energy and re-patterning, and verification—coherence and congruence) toward a *telos*—the transformation of the ego and its defenses. He discussed, via psycho-neurologist Barbara Lex, how intuitive insight arises from the way the subsystems ergotropic (ET) and trophotropic (TT) move through four phases of intensification to produce the experience of the numinous. In the course of human development, early in infancy, a child experiences the fears of abandonment and absorption which give rise to primary and secondary repression and defense mechanisms.

Loder also showed how the ego is transformed with its defenses in the encounter with the Holy. The ego does not merely undergo the lowering of its defenses, which happens when children hear stories that address fears of abandonment and absorption. Loder demonstrated how negation of negation in the cross and the resurrection and the affirmation of life in the outpouring of the Spirit gives human development a Christomorphic form.[45] He underlined the significance of the role of the mediator as the person undergoing transformation decisively "bears the marks of the mediator."[46]

Loder, in his discussion of human development, brought theology into dialogue with the human and social sciences without losing the in-

---

44. Loder, *Logic*, 4.
45. Loder, *Transforming*, 123–81.
46. Loder, *Logic*, 308. Also see Loder, *Transforming*, 106.

tegrity of the disciplines. Neither does science negate theology nor does theology negate science but each is critically appropriated in the elucidation of the object of study. This method, which takes a Christomorphic shape with the aim of the Divine and human acting in concert as one in the world, overcomes the problem of dualism and the *tertium quid* in the correlation method that requires a third term to keep the disciplines related.[47] This method arises out of a Christian understanding of reality, in which creation is contingent on the Creator. That which is implicit in the Creator-creation relationality is made explicit in the incarnation—the Divine-human relationality in Jesus Christ. Accordingly, Loder drew on the human and social sciences and theology without allowing theology to negate the sciences and vice-versa, and thus brought them into a Christomorphic relationship, which throws light on the experience of human development to answer the two-part question, "What is a lifetime?" and "Why do I live it?"

Loder showed, "from below" so to speak, via Wolfhart Pannenberg (who drew on Max Scheler), that human beings are unique in that they are exo-centrically centered. They are spiritual beings with an openness to the world, free from the environment, in that they are not subject to it. He then drew from Wilder Penfield's research on the two essences of the brain. Penfield showed that science is not able to fully account for the "I" when he probed the brains of epileptic patients under local anesthesia to help him discover where epilepsy was located. When the subjects heard or saw something they said, "You did that. I didn't."[48] Loder thus went on to show that the human spirit is fundamental to what it means to be human and its ". . . most obvious major achievement, short of the knowledge of God, is the creation of selfhood, societies, and culture in the unfolding course of history."[49] In this context, Loder wrote, "Sin is to be understood as the perversion or turning inward of the human spirit, producing internal conflict, anxiety, and self-destructive behavior. The failure of persons to create and compose lived and liveable worlds may be studied in the human sciences as adaptational failures—the disintegration of groups, societies, and cultures."[50] In another place he noted that sin is "the reenacting in our development the inevitable self-alienation

---

47. Loder, *Logic*, 3–15 and 37.
48. Penfield, *Mystery* in Loder, *Logic,* 5; also see *Knight's Move*, 43–44.
49. Loder, *Logic,* 29.
50. Ibid.

from God implicit in ego formation ... Original sin, then, is inevitable, is not necessary since transformation is possible."[51]

Loder related the human spirit to the Divine Spirit after the Divine-human pattern of Jesus Christ. The work of the Holy Spirit as the Creator Spirit is to transform the human spirit after the pattern of Jesus Christ. Thus, he showed that there is an analogy between the human spirit and the Holy Spirit. The similarity in the analogy lies in the relational and self-relatedness of the Holy Spirit and the human spirit and in the transformational pattern as it operates through time and in creativity.[52] The dissimilarity is that "the human spirit is grounded in the human psyche but the Holy Spirit is grounded in God."[53] Loder did not conflate the human spirit with the Divine Spirit but maintained the distinction between the two and at the same time their unity as discussed earlier.

Loder pointed out that the social and human sciences look at human development from a two-dimensional perspective (the self and the lived world) to the detriment of one's being and the destructiveness of others. He wrote:

> Normal development is psychologically constructed, socially supportive, and culturally maintained so that people are drawn out of the full four dimensions of their being. It is preeminently two dimensional, aiming at the comparatively meagre values of survival and satisfaction as determined by socially accepted norms. Restricting the range of human being has severe consequences; most fundamentally, there is a death of conscience and a loss of ultimate concern. When in the relativity and pluralism of personal and social life nothing deeper is known than the two dimensions of human existence, just the self and its "world," then conscience is no stronger than is necessary for successful adaptation, and ultimacy is irrelevant. Where definitive values and the concern for ultimacy disappear, people will deplete their own being and destroy each other, ironically, in the name of survival and satisfaction.[54]

He went on to say that this pervasive and powerful tendency is the opposite of transformation and can be corrected only within a four dimensional understanding of reality where negation is negated by the

---

51. Ibid., 279 n. 17.
52. 1 Cor 2:10–11; Rom 8:16; Phil 2:12.
53. Loder, *Logic*, 35.
54. Loder, *Transforming*, 157–58.

action of the Holy in history in the Christ-Event and life affirmed in the outpouring of the Holy Spirit.[55] With the Divine intersecting the human plane, the dimensions of reality are fourfold: self, lived world, Void, and the Holy, summarized below.[56]

The Self

In terms of the self, Loder identified 4 characteristics:

1. Reflective awareness as the source of freedom, choice, and belief.
2. Conscience felt as the integrity of selfhood.
3. Imagination as the intuitive aspect of self that helps to fantasize and understand things tacitly, even before one can express verbally or explicitly. Imagination helps to tacitly indwell reality and gain insights into life and reality with intuitive force.
4. The spirit as inherently relational, transformational, self-transcending, and the dynamic basis for choice. The spirit is groundless. The self is truly self when it is grounded transparently in the Spiritual Presence of Christ.[57]

The Lived World

The second dimension of human existence designates the universal human tendency to create and compose one's external realities into a coherent and liveable whole.

The Void

Loder's third basic dimension of human existence describes the irrevocable drift toward emptiness experienced from birth to death in the many faces of loneliness, meaninglessness, despair, and death. This Void

---

55. Ibid., 67–122, 157–81.

56. Loder critically draws on Søren Kierkegaard (*Sickness Unto Death*), Merleau Ponty (*Phenomenology of Perception*), Martin Heidegger (*Being and Time*), and Rudolf Otto (*Idea of the Holy*) in the development of his view of Reality as four-dimensional. See *Moment*, 67–91.

57. Loder, *Logic*, xii–xiii and 34–36.

appears to be the nature of evil; one can be tormented by it or engulfed by it when the self and the lived world collapse.

The Holy

The "Holy" refers to God who is separate from the world, human and the profane, and has the quality to draw and, at the same time, to terrify. Mystery is an aspect of the Holy. The Holy, when brought into interaction with the three-dimensional reality—the self, the lived world, and the void—has the power to transform them all. The Holy has a Christocentric focus and is the basis for Trinitarian understanding. The Holy finds concrete expression in the Christ Event. Through the Christ Event, sin and evil are negated and life bestowed on us through the outpouring of the Holy Spirit. However, the Christ Event has not exhausted the mystery of the Holy.

Through the process of human development, stage transitions are more significant than stages because growth takes place through conflict resolution that follows the transformational logic: conflict-in-context, interlude for scanning, intuitive insight felt with imaginative force, release of energy and re-patterning, and verification—coherence and congruence.[58] The imaginative leap and the empirical are both addressed in this epistemology. In the process of human development the ego periodically erupts and gives an opportunity to discover the center of one's existence in God. When this decentering and recentering in God happens one is able to step outside the whole of the lifespan and embrace it as a totality while one is still within it. Transfiguration of the ego takes place all at once as one is grounded in the One who encompasses both the past and the future and fills the present time. Such experiences move one beyond any kind of Jungian psychic balance in the middle years to a transfiguration. This transfiguration is described in church history dramatically by St. Theresa of Avila, St. John of the Cross, Meister Eckhart, and others.[59]

Loder showed the psycho-neurological basis of transformation in intensification through the two subsystems in the brain, the ergotropic

---

58. Loder, *Transforming*, 35–65.
59. Loder, *Logic*, 311–12; Loder and Neidhardt, *Knight's Move*, 273.

(ET) and the trophotropic (TT), interacting through the four phases of intensity:

i. balanced reciprocity between the subsystems—when one system is stimulated the other diminishes proportionately;

ii. passion and reversed reaction—sustained stimulation of one system generates passion but now the other system also gets intensified;

iii. spillover and vision—when phase (ii) is prolonged both systems fire at once resulting in visions, myths, master images, and so on; and

iv. absolute unity of being gives rise to

Loder wrote:

> . . . the numinous, imageless passage into the absolute unity of all things. Here no-thingness (cf. Eckhart's *Ohne bild*) is experienced as *more real* than the reality of the ordinary state, even after self consciousness returns to phase I. Although imageless, its impact most often leaves the after-image of radiant white light, so vivid it cannot be described except perhaps by a kind of via negativa.[60]

Thus, one moves beyond all opposites that are embodied as one in Jesus Christ in whom the great opposition of all is present: the Divine and the human as one in his person.[61]

Loder took pains to show that the understanding of transformation is within the classical spiritual theology of the church. His interpretation of Helen's case in the *Logic of the Spirit* drew on the categories of awakening, purgation, illumination, and unification, a process through which persons with anxiety (a basic human condition of qualitative and quantitative anxiety) move towards peace even as the self moves in the direction of meeting with God.[62] As a Reformed theologian, Loder did not lay much store by the process, as the Spirit can intersect human life at any time and lead one to encounter the Holy, which is by grace alone.

When the ego is transformed, the defenses are not just lowered but they are transformed. Loder argued that as the ego gets more socialized its defenses harden. Primary repression is reinforced and other defense

---

60. Loder and Neidhardt, *Knight's Move*, 273.
61. Loder, *Logic*, 313.
62. Ibid., 46–70. Also see Groeschel, *Spiritual*.

mechanisms of the ego are built on it. The defense mechanisms are isolation, regression, fantasy formation, sublimation, denial, reaction formation, projection, and introjection. He went on to say: "By conversation and lots of storytelling, acceptance, and the lowering of anxiety, the rigidity and even the need for these defenses dissipate. The theological significance of a transformed ego is that these defenses are themselves transformed and they become means of caring."[63]

In the transformation of the ego and its defenses, secondary repression, instead of making the ego rigid and shrinking its boundaries, become patience and self-control. Isolation, built on repression as a systematic way of accomplishing unconscious forgetting in a selective fashion, becomes concentration. All regression is in the service of transcendence. Fantasy formation becomes the vision of God. Sublimation is in the service of God. Denial becomes forgiveness. Reaction formation not only does not desire revenge but returns good for evil. Projection becomes empathy, putting oneself in others shoes. Introjection becomes vicarious suffering.[64]

In this remarkable way Loder showed how the ego is transformed and the "I" is not annihilated but develops a dialectic identity of "*I yet not I, but Christ.*" Thus, a transformed person is thrust into the world with a velocity not one's own.

Kakar and Loder: A Brief Analysis

Nature itself moves human beings towards transformation of the ego. Yet the ego is unable to transform itself because of the alienation from its source, understood as *avidya* in Kakar and as Sin in Loder discussed earlier. The *atman* or the human spirit has to be met by *Brahman*, or the Divine Spirit, resulting in unification. The role of the mediator is crucial as one takes the shape of the mediator.

Both Kakar and Loder have shown us that transformation of the ego is possible within a postmodern understanding of epistemology where the intuitive, imaginative leap of understanding and empirical verification, are held together. Both men have shown that in the process of transformation of the ego one needs to discern the direction of transformation. This can be done by paying attention to pathology and

---

63. Loder, *Logic*, 184.
64. Ibid., 183f. and 197.

wholeness in the psychoanalytical tradition and at the same time discerning true and false visions in the experience of "holiness" and the positive outcomes of the transformation of the ego defenses in the Spirit.

When the ego is transformed the sense of "I" is not lost in both their perspectives, although in Kakar this sense is not evident because his *Advaitic* leanings conflate *Brahman* and *atman*. Kakar quotes Ramana Maharshi, one of the greatest of Indian sages, who is supposed to have attained *moksha*: ". . . this ego is harmless; it is like the skeleton of a burnt rope—though it has a form it is of no use to tie anything with."[65] Loder similarly said that in the experience of the numinous ". . . there is still differentiated self consciousness, but beyond that . . . a reaction of awe as before the Holy who both fascinates and overpowers at the same time."[66]

In the Indian Hindu tradition and in the western Christian tradition there is an emphasis on contemplative action. Gandhi, a man of contemplation and action, primarily followed the *karma marga* (path of action) towards *moksha* (three paths—*gnana*, *bhakti*, and *karma* are accepted as legitimate ways to attain *moksha*). He thereby acted in the world for freedom from colonialism. He also acted to change Indian social reality. The caste hierarchy contradicts the understanding of the *atman* and *brahman* being one when some are degraded and others are elevated based on the notion of *karma-samsara*. Gandhi found untouchability in Hinduism most embarrassing and he worked to abolish it. But he did not go far enough to abolish the caste system itself.[67] He had a romantic view of the caste system as a division of labor.

Loder gave examples of Christian contemplatives—Theresa of Avila, Kierkegaard, Martin Luther, C. S. Lewis, and others—whose encounters with God led to redemptive action in the world. His understanding of reality as relationality correlates with the *Vishishtadvaitic* (qualified monism) understanding of reality rather than with the *Advaitic*. And accordingly *Vishistadvaitic* thought needs to be brought into dialogue with human development because the "I," though united with *Brahman/God*, is not annihilated as explained earlier. Ramanuja, an exponent of *Vishistadvaita* in the early part of the twelfth century CE, in grappling with the question of the one and the many, put forward the view that reality is relational, intrinsically interconnected with *Brahman* as source,

---

65. Kakar, *Inner World*, 17.
66. Loder and Neidhardt, *Knight's Move*, 273.
67. I have discussed this in detail in Prasadam, "James E. Loder's," 41–73.

support and ultimate self, i.e., contingent on *Brahman*. The goal of *moksha* is understood as relationality between the *atman* and the *Brahman*, expressed in "I, yet not I, but Thou in me."[68] Ramanuja's thought helps form a bridge with Christian thought and western philosophy that is grappling with the similar issue of the transformation of the ego.

Transformation in both their perspectives is not a form of escapism but the engagement of the "knight of faith" with the world as described by Søren Kierkegaard in *Fear and Trembling*.

> The "knight of faith" *lives* in the sea-crossing theophany and so is engaged in the quiet passion of believing at every moment. Thus, he is fascinated that every particular is an embodiment of the universal, yet without losing its particularity; every event and interaction is a gift that is unique but embodies eternity; everything is truly possible but nothing is necessary—all "by virtue of the absurd."[69]

In Kakar, we do not encounter the Christ-Event, which is central to Kierkegaard and Loder, but appears to be implicit in the *Advaitic* philosophy and Hindu culture where the Divine love is expressed in the imagery of the *Shakti* and the *Shakta's* eternal embrace. There is a dynamic movement in the *Brahman* and *atman* to eliminate alienation and overcome non-duality. Kakar's understanding of the transformation of the ego is philosophically grounded, whereas Loder's understanding is historically grounded in the Christ-Event. A Christocentric perspective, narrated in the Emmaus event (Luke 4:13–35), which Loder draws on, lends itself to the perspective of the anonymous Christ.[70] Jesus Christ is at work in the world unseen by naked eyes, but discerned by the human spirit in events that are illumined by the Holy Spirit in the world at large. Such illuminations reflect a Christomorphic pattern as proximate forms of ultimate transformation already realized in Jesus Christ.

The spiritual practice of Raja Yoga, with its initial movements in the calming of the *chitta*, has its parallel in the eight deadly thoughts of the Christian tradition.[71] Both these traditions need to be critically appropriated within the practice of the *Lectio-Divina*, keeping in mind that the desire to move toward God to encounter God is a gift of grace.

68. Radhakrishnan, *History*, 305–20.
69. Loder, *Logic*, 334.
70. Loder, *Transforming*, 97–120.
71. Allen, *Spiritual*, 64–79.

Conclusion

The significance of the Christ-event needs to be seen in the death defying work of Jesus Christ in history. The Christ-Event destroys the structures of non-being/the Void/nothingness and annihilates the forces that haunt human beings, deceptively embedded in cultural values, and replaces them with New Being and life-giving values that regenerate persons, cultures, and societies. In the practice of ministry one needs to address the human spirit within a four dimensional understanding of reality to encourage people to encounter God and experience transformation of the ego. In other words, respect and understanding needs to be shown within a context of worship. Imagination needs to be engaged inasmuch as linear thinking is employed, and the simultaneous encouragement of both is needed to move people through the process of intensification. In Christian education, problem-posing education, which I call the lock and key approach, needs to be used in concert with the understanding of the Word of God as a window to the imageless Spiritual presence of God.[72] In counseling one needs to wait for moments when the ego begins to unbuckle itself and is in need of the ground of being to offer opportunities to be centered in God. In preaching, discursive preaching needs to give way to the oral-aural performance of preaching, which imaginatively brings together text and slices of life to encounter God and the world in life-giving ways, exemplified in the African-American tradition.[73] In liturgy and music the use of ritual needs to be done meaningfully so that the focus is on meeting God rather than going through the motions of a liturgy, a religionless Christianity that Bonhoeffer spoke of. The implications of the transformation of the ego in the Spirit will need to be addressed more fully in another paper.

---

72. See India Sunday School Union, *Windows to Encounter*.

73. LaRue, *I Believe*, especially the chapter "Black Preaching and White Homiletics," 19–36.

Works Cited

Allen, Diogenes. *Spiritual Theology: The Theology of Yesterday for Spiritual Help Today*. Boston: Cowley, 1997.

Brihadaranyaka Upanishad. 4.3.21. http://www.holybooks.com/brihadaranyaka-upanishad-sankaracharya/.

Freud, Anna. *The Ego and the Mechanisms of Defense: The Writings of Anna Freud*. Madison, CT: International Universities Press, 1979.

Groeschel, Benedict J. *Spiritual Passages: The Psychology of Spiritual Development*. New York: Crossroad, 1984.

Heidegger, Martin. *Being and Time*. Translated by John Macquarrie and Edward Robinson. San Francisco: HarperCollins, 1962.

India Sunday School Union. *Windows to Encounter* (Including Student Workbooks and Teacher Guides). 11 volumes [Pre-school to Grade 10]. Edited by Elizabeth Frykberg and Ajit Prasadam. Coonoor, India: ISSU, 1996–2000.

Kakar, Sudhir. *A Book of Memory: Confessions and Reflections*. New Dehli: Penguin, 2012.

———. *Identity and Adulthood*. New Delhi: Oxford University Press, 1979.

——— *The Inner World: A Psycho-Analytic Study of Childhood and Society in India* Delhi: Oxford University Press, 1994.

———. *Mad and Divine: Spirit and Psyche in the Modern World*. London: Penguin-Viking, 2008.

———. "The Resurgence of Imagination." *Harvard Divinity Bulletin* 37/1 (Winter 2009) n.p. http://www.hds.harvard.edu/news-events/harvard-divinity-bulletin/articles/the-resurgence-of-imagination.

———. "Setting the Stage: the Traditional Hindu View and the Psychology of Erik H. Erikson." In *Identity and Adulthood*, edited by Sudhir Kakar, 2–12. New Delhi: Oxford University Press, 1979.

Kakar, Sudhir, and Katharina Kakar. *The Indians: Portrait of a People*. New Delhi: Penguin-Viking, 2007.

Kane, Pandurang Vaman. *History of Dharmashastra, Ancient and Medieval Religious and Civil Law in India, Vol. I, Part 3*. Pune, India: Bhandarkar Oriental Research Institute, 1968.

Kierkegaard, Soren. *Fear and Trembling*. Edited and translated by Howard V. Hong and Edna H. Hong. Princeton: Princeton University Press, 1983.

Kuentzel, John D. "The Heidegger in Loder (or How the Nothing Became the Void): Provoking Wonder in Education." In *Redemptive Transformation in Practical Theology: Essays in Honor of James E. Loder, Jr.*, edited by Dana R. Wright and John D. Kuentzel, 347–72. Grand Rapids: Eerdmans, 2004.

LaRue, Cleophus J. *I Believe I'll Testify: The Art of African American Preaching*. Louisville: Westminster John Knox, 2011.

Loder, James E. Jr. *The Logic of the Spirit: Human Development in Theological Perspective*. San Francisco: Jossey–Bass, 1998.

———. *The Transforming Moment*. 2nd ed. Colorado Springs: Helmers & Howard, 1989.

Loder, James E., Jr., and Jim Neidhardt. *The Knight's Move: The Relational Logic of the Spirit in Theology and Science*. Colorado Springs: Helmers & Howard, 1992.

Merleau-Ponty, Maurice. *Phenomenology of Perception*. New York: Routledge Kegan Paul, 1962.
Otto, Rudolf Otto. *The Idea of the Holy: An Inquiry into the Non-Rational Factor in the Idea of the Divine and Its Relation to the Rational*. London: Oxford University Press, 1977.
Penfield, Wilder. *The Mystery of the Mind*. Princeton: Princeton University Press, 1975.
Prasadam, Ajit. "James E. Loder's Transformational Model for Christian Education in the Indian Context and Beyond." PhD diss., Princeton Theological Seminary, 2005.
Sarvapalli, Radhakrishnan. *History of Philosophy: Eastern and Western*. Vol. 1. London: George and Unwin, 1942.
Thorat, S. K. "Passage to Adulthood: Perceptions from Below." In *Identity and Adulthood*, edited by Sudhir Kakar, 65–81. New Delhi: Oxford University Press, 1979.

10

Walking Alongside Children as They Form Compassion

Loder and Lerner in the Role of Relationships and Experience as Interactive Developmental Processes

WENDY HINRICHS SANDERS

Introduction

When I was a young adult, I was fortunate to travel from the United States to many countries of the world as a student and then a teacher. People made me feel they viewed America as a compassionate nation. Perspectives have changed radically over my adult life and my conversations with others show a perception of the U.S. as a consumptive nation. At some times, I felt despair over this change of perception. But I was fortunate to travel to an international conference on economic sustainability in South Africa in 2003 and was inspired to hope again by a young boy from Canada.

When he was six at a local Catholic school, Ryan Hreljac of Kemptville, Ontario, heard that children in Africa were dying for lack of clean, safe drinking water, even though it only cost $70 to build a well.

> I guess it really hit me in Grade One. We were doing our Lenten project and everybody was bringing our Loonies and Toonies and my . . . teacher was going through the list of what we could buy with the money we raised. She said that for $70 we could buy a well in Africa to stop children from dying from unsafe drinking water. I just couldn't let go of the idea. You know, we were thinking from a Grade One perspective, 'How far is it to walk to get to the nearest well?'
>
> She said, "Five kilometers." We had no idea how far that was so she said, "5000 steps."
>
> So, I counted the steps it took me to get from my classroom to a water fountain and it took ten steps. I couldn't help but wonder, "Is it fair?" And the good part was, there was a solution! So, I went home and talked to my mom and dad . . . and started doing chores and stuff. (Ryan Hreljac, personal communication)

Ryan went home that night and told his parents he was going to earn $70 to build a well. He raised the money only to find the cost was really $1,000. Undaunted he earned the full amount (See www.ryanswell.org).

> Ryan often delights in telling the story that we ignored him when he started with the idea but we didn't. I mean, I've been a volunteer since I was a teenager. He was six and we assumed it was something that would pass. I never expected . . . the stick-to-itiveness . . . I think it is important to instill compassion whether it is through faith or whatever . . . I always thought it is a combination of creating the supportive environment and a predisposition to being compassionate. A lot of it was who Ryan was when he came to us. (Susan Hreljac, personal communication)

Ryan Hreljac's thought and deed compelled me to rethink my understanding of human development. His capacity for empathy and abstract thought defied the stage theorists' views of children. I had found from many years of teaching experience that constrained theory did not always resonate with my experience. For example, I began teaching Sunday School again in the mid 1990's and was awestruck by the wisdom of children. Once, sitting around a campfire along the lakeshore at my home, I asked random questions: "If you came to see God, how would you know it was Him?" Without hesitation, a fourth grade girl replied, "You could see the love in His eyes." Another time, I was driving in my car running errands with a teenage friend who had had a brain injury during her preschool years and was left with significant developmental delays. She turned to me and said, "Miss Wendy, I know Jesus loves me, but I wonder why he let this happen to me?"

My cultural background suggested I needed to take a degree to understand what I was missing. First I completed my master's degree in children's and family ministry at Bethel Seminary in St Paul. Then I took my first tutorial in the doctoral program at Fuller Theological Seminary in Pasadena, CA on spiritual formation, where I was guided by adolescent positive development researcher, Dr. Pamela Ebsytne King.[1] Dr. King led me to *The Logic of the Spirit* by James Loder, and it was Loder's writing that fundamentally changed my views of development. As I continued to read emerging research, I came to perceive that Loder contributed far-sighted ideas to the field of human development that have predicted the direction of thought in the fields of developmental psychology, spiritual formation, and cognitive neuroscience today. He valued cross-disciplinary study, a hallmark of child development work today.[2] Loder recognized the developmental dynamic of internal and external influences, including that of the divine presence.[3] While he drew heavily upon classical theorists, including Freud, Erikson and Piaget, his work reflects an emerging recognition of child capacity and of the value of relationship and experience in the unique trajectories of a child's journey across time and contexts[4] He challenged us to think that transformation occurs "when within any given frame of reference hidden orders of meaning and coherence arise to call the axioms of that frame into questions and reorder its elements accordingly."[5] The dynamic process of transformation is at the heart of the concept of child capacity and emerging child development theory.[6] It may seem almost trite, but one way Loder did this was by inviting us to know the childhood and cultural contexts of the developmental theorists upon whom he drew insights.[7] This understanding yields a deeper critique of theo-

---

1. King et al., "Searching," 513–28. See also King and Boyatzis, "Exploring," 2–6 and King and Furrow, "Religion," 703–13.
2. Loder, *Logic*, 36–43.
3. Ibid., 21–22.
4. Ibid., 42.
5. Ibid., 35.
6. Ibid., 75.
7. Ibid., 20–26.

rists' perspectives and is also a fair topic to address in public institutions in the United States to engage our students in those discussions.

Most importantly, in his writing, speaking and the persona he presented in interviews conducted shortly before his untimely death, he acknowledged the potential role of the Holy Spirit to indwell, shape and form, in unpredictable ways, the child's soul.[8] Recent research suggests spiritual formation is the

> process of growing the intrinsic human capacity for self-transcendence, in which the self is embedded in something greater than the self, including the sacred. It is the developmental "engine" that propels the search for connectedness, meaning, purpose and contribution. It is shaped both within and outside of religious traditions, beliefs and practices.[9]

Loder noted human science informs spiritual formation but does not determine its ultimate meaning. He argued that the "theological perspective must transform human science understandings" to better understand both.[10] Further, Loder's view of the indwelling of God in the spirit of the child laid a foundation for the concept of child capacity. Emerging work, such as that of the Search Institute's *Developmental Assets*, augments that voice of capacity for developmentalists within and outside of the Christian faith.[11]

Finally, Loder's perspective that God is ever present in human development validates the views of the emerging field of child theology to the conversation of human development. Loder's perspective suggests both the relationality humanity has with God through Christ and the experiences God inserts that suggest each child's formation is a unique trajectory of relationships and experiences.

Relationships

Richard Lerner's views on developmental systems theory suggest children form through an interactive process, one that is bi-directional between the person and the context in which he or she is forming, including the interactive relationships within that context. Defining features of

8. Ibid., passim.
9. Benson, "Science," 485.
10. Loder, *Logic*, 33.
11. Scales and Leffert, *Developmental Assets*, passim.

development systems theory include integration of nature and nurture and a fusing of biological, cultural and historical levels within the individual. Temporality and plasticity, from the individual to cultural systems, result in individual trajectories of development. The potential for plasticity at all levels is a fundamental strength of human development. This plasticity and unique developmental trajectories drive research on optimization of human development focused on positive development, aligning strengths of the individual.[12]

Neuroscience research emphasizes a brain that constructs itself through increasingly complex social and cultural interactions.[13] One clear example is that of oxytocin, a pleasure-based neurochemical that transfers from mother to infant through breastfeeding.[14] Another is the capacity of mirror neurons to recreate within the brain the goal-directed behavior of another person. Still another is the role emotions play, not in being overcome by the rational thought but instead informing higher order thinking to engender problem-solving and perhaps creativity.[15] Neuroscientists found that injury to emotional structures in the brain resulted in a lost capacity for moral reasoning.[16] And brain injury from early childhood showed children without a moral rudder.[17] Prosocial emotions appear to help a child develop a theory of mind, the perspective-taking element that underlies the experience of empathy.[18] These

---

12. Lerner, *Liberty*, 7–9, 14–15. See also Lerner, "Developmental," 1–17, and Lerner et al, "Positive," 172–80.

13. Quartz and Sejnowski, *Liars*, 51, 101, 129; Immordino-Yang, "Tale," 66.

14. Quartz and Sejnowski, *Liars*, 142–45, 174.

15. Immordino-Yang and Damasio, "We Feel," 7; Immordino-Yang et al., "Neural Correlates," 5.

16. Damasio, *Descarte's*, 90, 126; Immordino-Yang and Damasio, "We Feel," 4–5. See also Damasio, *Feeling and Looking*, and "Neurobiological," 47–56. See also Immordino-Yang, "Tale," 70 and "Neural Correlates," 8022.

17. Immordino-Yang and Damasio, "We Feel," 3. Sensory data enter the brain through emotional structures (except for smell) and are directed simultaneously to thought, emotion and bodily state (autonomic) systems, reaching the emotion center first due to proximity. Data are evaluated and receive an emotional tag of intensity. The stronger or more complex the emotional reaction is, the stronger the power of the emotion to control the response (see Goleman, *Emotional*; Sylwester, *How to Explain*; and LeDoux, *Emotional*). Further, the more meaningful and narrative rather than data oriented the episodic memory, the more likely for young children to remember. See Ghetti and Alexander, "If It Happened," 542–61.

18. Thompson, "Development of the Person," 36.

biological underpinnings suggest social and cultural value for relationships in learning.

Spiritual formation literature has developed a body of knowledge that recognizes children have an acute *relational consciousness* to others, to their soul, to adults and to God. This relational consciousness is awe sensing, mystery sensing, and wonder sensing. Children had an "unusual level of consciousness or perceptiveness, something more than being alert and mentally attentive, a "reflective consciousness" or a sense of the other, separate from themselves, a "meta-cognition."[19] Love is the basis of a *reciprocating relationship* in which as the Trinity does, humanity made in God's image has the potential to become their optimal selves through observation, reflection and feedback with God, with each other, and with the church. This potential leads to strategies that integrate covenant, grace, empowerment and intimacy which lead to an interdependence and, within each soul, a transformation to the best each can be.[20]

Sophia Cavalletti emphasized the importance of Jesus for children.[21] "It came to me that what is primary for the child in front of the Good Shepherd is the relationship. I think relationship is an important element because in the relationship the child shows his great capacity as a partner in the covenant."[22] At the Loder Symposium Jerome Berryman's paper drew astute attention to the fact that young children do not believe in, or trust, language yet. They are watching you, the teacher, to understand what to believe (See Berryman's essay in this book, chapter 4). From a contemplative theological perspective, Henri Nouwen suggests that intimate relationship with God through humanity leads to transformation into a compassionate servant.[23]

---

19. Hay and Nye, *Spirit,* 113–14.

20. Balswick et al., *Reciprocating,* 51.

21. Cavalletti, *Religious Potential,* 10. See also Cavelletti, *Religious Potential . . . 6–12,* passim.

22. Maresca, *Children.*

23. See several of the writings of Henri Nouwen: *Creative*; *Gracias!*; *Solitude*; *Return.* See especially *Return,* 17, 105.

Experience

Loder's experience with near death in an automobile accident led him to see God's insertion into human life.[24] Experience with the nearness of God has been shown in psychological research to be retained in long-term memory. Research in spirituality has shown adults recalled a sense of nearness to God or direct experience with God during childhood that compelled them to act with compassion. The experience of God is reportedly transcendent,[25] personalized or customized,[26] and an illumination of authority.[27] It correlates with a sense of connectedness and unity,[28] having the characteristics of truth-testedness and peace, calm, joy and/or hope.[29] Most importantly, it is significant or transformative,[30] with a long-lasting moral calling.[31]

Recently, neuroscience has recognized the importance of experience in brain development, finding that the richer and more diverse the experiences, the larger the brain.[32] Experiences are defined as the "complex, bi-directional interactions among the environment and the child's brain" and focus upon the problem-solving capacity of cognition.[33] Looping of emotion and thought occurs through nearly simultaneous firing of neurons in emotion and cognitive processing systems of the brain as thought is motivated by emotion.[34] These two systems have been shown to refine each other in a process Immordino-Yang and Damasio

---

24. Loder, *Logic*, 67.

25. Newburg et al., *Why God*, 109, 125–26; Loder, *Logic*, 6, 10–11; Newburg and Newburg, "Neuropsychological," 183–96; D'Aquili and Newburg, "Religious," 191–93, and Farmer, "Religious," 268.

26. Farmer, "Religious," 268 and Robinson, *Original*, 144.

27. Keltner and Haidt, "Approaching Awe," 307; Davidson, "Toward a Biology," 107–30 and "Neural," 87; Robinson, *Original*, 11; and James, *Varieties*.

28. Tamminem, "Religious," 84. See also Loder, *Logic*, 64–67, and D'Aquili and Newburg, "Religious," 177–97.

29. Farmer, "Religious," 259; D'Aquili and Newburg, "Religious," 191–95; Loder, *Logic*, 64–70; and Klingberg, "Study," 214–16.

30. Robinson, *Original*, 16, 75, 102, 133, 161–70; See also Elkind and Elkind, "Varieties," 102; Farmer, "Religious," 263, 267–68; Loder, *Logic*, 10–11, 13.

31. Hay and Nye, *Spirit*, 17; Klingberg, "Study," 215–16; Loder, *Logic*, 64–70; Farmer, "Religious," 268.

32. Diamond and Hopson, *Magic*, passim.

33. Nelson, "Effects," n.p.

34. Immordino-Yang et al., "Neural Correlates," 8024.

label, "emotional thought."[35] They correct previous neuroscience theory: It is not thought over emotion but rather the two systems refine each other in a process that is reminiscent of the spiritual formation concept of reciprocating relationships.[36] Figure 1 presents a diagram of the integrated concept.

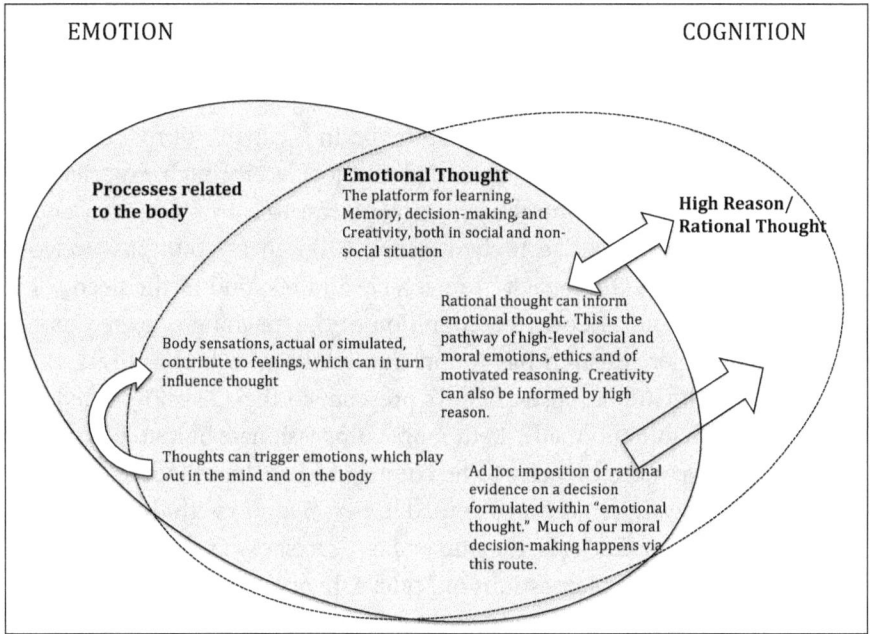

Immordino-Yang and Damasio's Emotional Thought Diagram[37]

This breakthrough fundamentally shifts the focus from emotion or reason to an effort to help children rely upon emotion to problem-solve creatively. Emotional thought is the cornerstone to problem-solving. An integration of emotional responses and rational analysis of the need and opportunities to solve, creates a new idea[38] Higher order thinking may be used to prioritize problem-solving strategies.[39] This attentive state of mindfulness to focus on the problem leads to a spirit of mental force in

35. Immordino-Yang and Damasio, "We Feel," 3, 7–9.
36. Balswick et al., *Reciprocating*, 51.
37. Ibid., 8.
38. Keltner and Haidt, "Approaching Awe," 304.
39. Immordino-Yang, "Tale," 80–81.

which a person can "mindfully direct and focus her attention and willfully actualize the desired behavior."[40]

Child Capacity

Again, Loder's recognition that God may insert himself into the development of humanity opens an understanding of child capacity here and now, not just in the future as an adult.[41] Emerging work supports this view. Neuroscience findings suggest the brain is capable of functioning at birth and the systems are expanded, not formed through experience and relationships.[42] Cultural anthropology research by Warneken and Tomasello suggest that securely attached children as young as twelve months may have the capacity to perceive and respond to the needs of others.[43] Pertinent to Loder's recognition of the meaning of experience with God, other research has found that adults who had a direct experience with God, a sense of God's presence in their lives, reported it was unforgettable and made them more compassionate human beings.[44] Children have more capacity to be compassionate than theorists of the early to mid-twentieth century tended to perceive and with the infusion of God into children's lives, the impact has been shown to be significant. That raises a couple of questions of Loder's theory.

Questions within Loder's Theory

Two questions arise with the foundation of Loder's developmental views. First, does Loder rely on psychoanalytical thesories[45] that have

---

40. Schwartz, "Role," 131.

41. Loder, *Logic*, 173–98 and *Transforming*. See also Balswick et al., *Reciprocating*, 275.

42. Quartz and Sejnowski, *Liars*, 27, 31, 129, 182–86.

43. Tomasello, *Why*, passim; Warneken and Tomasello, "Altruistic," 1301–3.

44. Colby and Damon, *Some Do Care*; Farmer, "Religious," 268; Hardy, *Spiritual Nature*, 271; Klingberg, "Study," 215.

45. At the Loder Symposium, Berryman wrote that while stage theories are explanatory, they are not exhaustive. Loder believed there was another story present. That story is the transcendent insertion of God into the present throughout a trajectory of human development. (See Jerome Berryman's essay in this book, chapter 4).

a deficit approach to development?[46] The concepts of negation and void in Loder's work suggest images of absence and deficit. Yet, in Loder, human spirit is connected to the Spiritus Creator, evidenced by his writing and his deeply passion-filled presentation. While negativity, deficit, void are presented, the hope of the connected life with the Spirit of God is more than enough to overcome the darkness.[47] Loder's writing and words were filled with joy and the asset of Christian connectedness with a loving God.

The second question is the absence of Vygotsky's work (other than his understanding of language.[48] Vygotsky was a forerunner of the concepts of child capacity (peer learning) and the importance of social interaction in development. His work would only have strengthened Loder's theories.[49]

While these questions suggest gaps in Loder's theoretical base, the presentations of others at the seminar make it clear that the personal characteristics of Loder would have led him to this work today. Tom Hastings shared that Loder did not want to retire because there was still so much to learn! Loder's former students describe him as a generative thinker who used the material available to him. They spoke of him as a provocative advocate for high quality spiritual education.

Application in Child Theology and Research

After reviewing the literature which I began with Loder's writings, I considered the theological influences, in this case, a child theology perspective. I then conducted a small, localized study with children in three states in North America in part to understand how morally competent[50]

46. Robert Coles, a psychiatrist, compared research approaches to child development after he listened individually to hundreds of children's stories: "So often our notions of what a child is able to understand are based on the capacity the child has displayed in a structured situation" (a clinical setting). "If the child fails to respond to a researcher's predetermined line of questions, the researcher is likely to comment on a "developmental" inadequacy. If an older child does respond well, he or she is considered developmentally advanced (Coles, *Spiritual*, 40). So much of emerging research today points instead to children as assets with opportunities.

47. Loder, *Logic*, 80–85.

48. Ibid., 173.

49. Vygotsky, *Mind*, 30, 84, 86, 88, 90.

50. This was a conscious decision to focus first upon children who were recognized as compassionate to build an understanding of the capacities within such a child and

children such as Ryan Hreljac developed compassion in the American culture's increasing focus upon consumption.

Child Theology

I first examined from a child theology perspective,[51] the story of feeding the thousands in John 6. I had heard it afresh while participating in a short-term missions trip to Nicaragua when the story was told, not in my native language, by a local pastor for morning devotion. He pointed to the role of the child in offering his or her barley loaves and fish to Andrew when Jesus expressed his desire to feed the throngs. This scene represents the *antimony* of divine sovereignty and human responsibility (also seen in John 6:27–65), the *teaching* aspect of Jesus' ministry, the tool of *irony* (also in John 11:48), and *signs*.[52] While the disciples struggle with the enormity of the task, the child points to Jesus who reigns and who performs miracles.

While throughout the Bible children under twelve are active agents in bringing others to God's Kingdom, the synoptic gospels do not mention the child.[53] In addition many commentaries either ignore the child,[54] dismiss him,[55] or suggest the child simply references John's use of children as new Christians.[56] If the child is insignificant, why is the child present? Why has the gospel placed a child in the midst of this important Eucharistic message?[57]

---

to begin to build a framework. A study of children who were lacking in compassion would have been premature and would have skewed an understanding of the concept at this time.

51. I am indebted to Keith White, the convener of this Loder and Child Theology Symposium, for his suggestions on addressing the often-minimized role of the child in his pericope through the framework of hypothetical questions. The conceptual idea is his but I am accountable for the actual choice of questions.

52. Whitacre, *John*, 37–44; Morris, *Gospel*, 40; Blomberg, *Historical*; Keener, *IVP Bible Background*, 263, 278.

53. Gundry-Volf, "Least," 31–36, and "To Such," 469–80.

54. See commentaries on the *Gospel of John* by Whitacre, Morris, and Bultmann.

55. Blomberg, *Historical*; Tasker, *John*; Haenchen, *John*. Haenchen writes, "How the lad came to be there is not a question to be raised" (271).

56. Thompson, "Children," 195, and idem, *God*.

57. In John 5:49 Jesus invokes the image of Moses as the prophet (Deut 18:15) and the deliverer of bread from heaven (John 6:32) but by the end of this section, Jesus proclaims he is the true bread (John 6:32), the bread of God (John 6:32), the living bread of

At the least, the text invites us to ask questions of the significance of the child. The gift of food, barley loaves and fish, suggest the child is poor.[58] What might have prompted a child living in poverty to offer his or her meal? How did the child know Jesus was seeking food—was she close enough to him to overhear the conversation with the disciples? What led the child to recognize the needs of the hungry? What prompted the child's generosity in response to the physical needs of the people? What part of the child's family relationships might have drawn him or her to act with generous compassion? What role models might have sparked a lifestyle of compassion within the child? What relationship might the child have had with Jesus or Andrew? If not a child, who might have been the assistant to Jesus' lesson? How would the story play out differently if it were an adult who offered? How would it play out differently if the child were well-to-do? Would such a child have been present at such a daytime event? Is the child merely an emotional hook to attract our interest? Where did this child secure the depth of capacity needed to initiate such a bold offer in the midst of such a large group?

Research on Formation of Compassion within Children

To learn children's insights on the formation of compassion, I used a double-layer focus group with 35 children (17 girls, 18 boys) and a semi-structured follow up interviews with three children and an additional two interviews with other children, for a total of 37 children.[59] Each fo-

---

eternal life (6:51). This sign shows Jesus to be the supplier of people's needs (Whitacre, *John*, 142; Morris, *Gospel*, 301). There may be echoes of Elisha's feeding of 100 people with barley loaves from 2 Kgs 4:42–44. (Morris, *Gospel*, 302; Whitacre, *John*, 142). But the analogy to the sacrifice of Isaac (Gen 22) because of the mountain and the lad seems to some scholars to be a stretch (Ruddick, "Feeding," 340–41). Boice notes that the child was insignificant and the offering of food was insufficient but in Jesus' hands it became significant and more than sufficient (Boice, *Gospel of John*, 448).

58. The offering of the barley loaves and fish indicate the small child was poor as barley loaves were the cheapest form of grain, were looked down upon and held in contempt. The Greek term *opsarion*, a diminutive of *opson*, means cooked food, possibly fish used to flavor the bread (Louw and Nida, "Opsarion"). While the term implies a delicacy, the small amount suggests it was not even a substantial meal even for the boy. Only John uses this term in the NT and uses it just five times (see commentaries by Boice, 447, and Morris, 304).

59. The ages of children were as follows: 73.53% were ages 8–10 (with 11.76% at 8 years, 44.12% at age 9 and 17.65% at age ten). Outliers included six 11-year-olds, two 13-year-olds and one 6-year-old. The ethnic distribution of the children included

cus group discussion lasted about one hour.[60] Children were selected in three states through recommendations of children's pastors according to criteria that suggested the children were compassionate.

- a generalized respect for other children;
- a disposition to act with alignment between values and behavior;
- a willingness to take risks for moral or spiritual principles;
- a tendency to inspire others, potentially towards moral action; and
- a sense of humility about one's place in God's world (Colby and Damon 1990: 29).

To validate the children's comments, focus groups with parents (n=13) and church school teachers (n = 13) were recruited.

Children were able to define compassion as sourced in love and containing elements of justice, righteousness/holiness, forgiveness, hope, sometimes sacrifice, and a collective power for the vulnerable. Surprising results included their detailed and longstanding memory of compassion events that suggest the emotional hold within social interactions that involve compassion. Also particularly intriguing was their interaction of sensory input, emotional tags and cognitive problem-solving in recognizing and responding to the needs of others. Emerging from their stories, the following interactive processes arose: receiving, observing, recognizing the need for, responding with, and rehearsing acts of compassion.

RECEIVING. Children spoke of receiving help when they got hurt, being comforted when feeling left out, and the comfort of Jesus watching over them all the time. Of the incidents children reported about receiving compassion, 62% were for physical pain, 19% for social/psychological pain, and 18% for spiritual pain.[61] They received 40.8% of the help from

---

86.84% of European/North American heritage, 10.53% Asian and 2.63% Latino.

60. The complete research protocol is drawn heavily from Pamela King's and Eugene Roehlkepartain's study, with permission, of spiritual exemplars, adapting their protocol, consent forms and interview questions. See Roehlkepartain et al., *With Their Own*, 4–8.

61. King, "Afterword," 12, names spiritual elements of transcendence (awareness of self and connection to others) and fidelity (clarity and conviction of beliefs and ideol-

peers, 33.8% from parents, 18.3% from other adults, and 5.6% from ancillary sources. The contexts for these acts of receipt were most often within their home settings (66.2%), within their communities (19.1%), their playgrounds (5.9%), their church, their school and the spiritual realm (each at 2.9%). Children described acts that included helping (63.2%), comforting (28%), and giving (8.9%).

OBSERVING. Children named compassionate exemplars in their lives: parents (30%), other family members (22.5%), peers (20%), other adults (15%), spiritual leaders and Jesus (7.5%), and others (5%). They observed the following traits within these compassionate people: authenticity/consistency/perseverance, justice, integrity, holiness and hope. The children also reported 29 observed acts of compassion. One boy shared this observation from several years earlier:

> We were going to see our cousins . . . and we stopped for lunch at In 'n Out Burger and this person was like sitting by a tree and . . . she lost her job and she lost her home. She was like very poor and we gave her $20 but like 2 minutes before that Christians who were like on a field trip and they had bags of stuff they might've needed for the trip and they saw her and gave like clothes, food . . . It was really nice because my mom like offered to buy her some more food from the restaurant but she was like, the bags were like full of food and clothes and she already had her lunch . . . Mike, Age 9, CA.

Children also spoke of observing friends help their parents, of a classmate who championed the Operation Shoebox effort. Another children referred to his priest:

> One of our priests at our church, Tom, for like some little homeless kids, they could come in and there would be a tub of free toys for them cause they might be bored at the time. And one night it was hailing and um, these ladies they were walking by and um, they were like really cold and were about to get hypothermia.[62] Tom was about to close his shop but then he saw them and he took out two blankets that were worth like $5 but they were poor and they were broke and they didn't have any money so he just gave them to them. Mike, Age 9, CA.

---

ogy) as spiritual components connected to pro-social behavior and thriving.

62. Children's language authenticity is represented by this example of juxtaposing simple vocabulary with complex words.

Of their reports observing compassion, 48% were related to spiritual pain, 31% to physical pain, and 21% to social/psychological pain. They observed parents (18.5%), spiritual referents (27.6%), peers (24.1%), other adults and ancillary participants, both at (13.8%) and observed the acts at church (34.5%), in their community (24.1%), at home (20.7%), in the broader world (13.8%) and on their school and playground (both at 3.45%). The children observed 34.4% of the acts as helping, 37.9% as comforting and 8.8% as acts of giving. These children were keen observers of the social interactions and experiences of their lives.

Recognizing. Children reported gathering sensory data, specifically auditory and visual data, reacting with an emotion and then adding cognitive processing of the situation. "Well, it kinda seems sad that they don't have stuff like we do. Like right now, actually, like instead of having fun, they really need to actually work. I actually feel like that kid needs help and he needs someone to help him, like to take care of him and to like, ask him to, instead of just walking and walking, to be able to have some fun." (Maria, age 9). Children also used cognitive thinking to discern what made it hard to act with compassion: undesirable recipients (31.6%) who were mean-spirited, bullies or who might misuse the gifts, lack of access to resources (23.7%), letting go of privilege (21.0%), mismatch of the need to their gifts (13.2%), and self-regulation (10.5%).

Responding. Children and parents named 71 acts of compassion with just less than half of them self-reported through indirect questioning. Children named events at church, such as preparing suitcases for the homeless and delivering them, giving up their bedroom for a cousin ousted from her home, taking shoes to Guatemala, raising funds to stop child slavery in Haiti, and giving clothes to younger friends in need. Children's acts were reported 10% of the time with family, 54% at school or church, 14% in their community, and 22% of the time in the broader world. Of the acts, 27.1% were for physical pain, 30.6% for social/psychological pain, and 43% for spiritual pain. Children responded with acts of helping (25%), giving (41.7%), comforting (23.6%), and praying (9.7%).

Rehearsing. Children received the internal rehearsal (strengthening of neural synapses through using the information in repeated and different ways) by the feelings they experienced after helping someone: joy, integrity, satisfaction, hope and self-perpetuation. They also described activities that defined these named interactive developmental processes of receiving, observing, recognizing, responding and rehearsing. Children named observing (30.2%), receiving (12.7%), recognizing the need for compassion (6.4%), responding with acts of compassion (34.9%), and rehearsing (15.9%).

Teachers frequently named engaging children in acts of compassion while parents named serving as role models. Embedded in this parent's story of her daughter's compassion (9 years old), are fundamentals of rehearsal by parents with their child:

> We were going to the funeral and she has a couple of things that Dona made for her and so it touched her that Dona passed away so quickly. Her dad had shared that her husband had had a hard time with it but through it, started reading Dona's Bible and through it came to faith; he changed because of going through all of this. But Elena knew how hard it must be for him. So, on the way to the funeral, she had a um, a crown that she made in Sunday School or something, just construction paper and . . . she got her crown, gave it to him and said, "I wanted to give this to Dona." . . . He sent her a note and thanked her and said he 'Wanted to start coming to church and I haven't been going to church so I don't have anybody to sit with so when I'm ready to start going to church, will you sit with me?' So she's been sitting with him every Sunday since he started coming to church. Parent, WI.

Child Theology and the John 6 Pericope

This research has enabled further questions to arise from the John 6 biblical text. What might God have us see in such a compassionate and generous child? What relationships and experiences might the child have had to lead to acting with compassion? Might the child have received compassion him or herself? From whom? Might Jesus have been such a powerful role model that the child was drawn to climb into his lap to where he heard of the need for food? Where might the child have observed compassionate acts? What emotions were triggered within the child to generate a thoughtful response? What made the child, capable of matching an appropriate solution to a need, offer such a small lunch to feed so many? What emotional, thoughtful insights or experiences might the child have had that led him or her to see Jesus' capacity? What characteristics inherent in this child but not present in the adults allowed the adults to miss Jesus' question? How did the child feel after seeing the baskets of leftovers and a satiated throng? What lessons might the child have learned from this experience and how might it have empowered him or her to act in the future? How might this experience of the presence of God, inserted into the child's life, create a lifestyle of compassion within the child? Was the child transformed by this experience with the presence of God as James Loder was from his own?[63] What did the adults present walk away with from this experience? What do we, as adults take from this child?

Conclusion

What do we have to learn from this child's relationships and experiences? How does it lead us to reflect upon the opportunities we have had to receive compassion from God, to observe God acting with compassion in the world, to recognize the need for our own compassion, to formulate a response and to reflect upon it in prayerful contemplation?

Loder perceived the human spirit is inherently creative but rooted in the human psyche while the Holy Spirit is rooted in God.[64] The pericope in John 6 magnifies the desire of God to come into our daily lives and nurture personal transformation, a metamorphosis. It is this rootedness in relationality and a richness of experience with God that enables transformation through a unique child formation trajectory to occur, and an image of compassion to begin to re-establish, child by child, creatively compassionate people in this struggling nation.

---

63. Loder, *Transforming*, 9–13.
64. Loder, *Logic*, 35.

Works Cited

Balswick, Jack O., et al. *The Reciprocating Self: Human Development in Theological Perspective*. Downers Grove, IL: InterVarsity, 2005.
Benson, Peter L. "The Science of Child and Adolescent Spiritual Development: Definitional, Theoretical, and Field-Building Challenges." In *The Handbook of Spiritual Development in Childhood and Adolescence*, edited by E. C. Roehlkepartain et al., 484–98. Thousand Oaks, CA: Sage, 2006.
Berryman, Jerome. *Godly Play*. Minneapolis: Fortress, 1995.
Blomberg, Craig L. *The Historical Reliability of John's Gospel: Issues and Commentary*. Downer's Grove, IL: InterVarsity, 2001.
Boice, James Montgomery. *The Gospel of John*. Vol. 2. 2nd ed. Grand Rapids: Baker, 1999.
Bultmann, Rudolf. *The Gospel of John: A Commentary*. Translated by G. R. Beasley-Murray et al. Philadelphia: Westminster, 1971.
Cavalletti, Sophia. *The Religious Potential of the Child*. Translated by P. M. Coulter and J. M. Coulter. Chicago: Liturgy Training Publications, 1992.
———. *The Religious Potential of the Child 6–12 Years*. Translated by R. Rojcewicz. Chicago: Archdiocese of Chicago, 2002.
Colby, Anne, and William Damon. *Some Do Care: Contemporary Lives of Moral Commitment*. New York: Free Press, 1992.
Coles, Robert. *The Spiritual Life of Children*. Boston: Houghton Mifflin, 1990.
Damasio, Antonio. *Descartes' Error*. New York: Avon, 1994.
———. *The Feeling of What Happens: Body and Emotion in the Making of Consciousness*. San Diego: Harvest Harcourt, 1999.
———. *Looking for Spinoza: Joy, Sorrow and the Feeling Brain*. New York: Harcourt, 2003.
———. "The Neurobiological Grounding of Human Values." In *Neurobiology of Human Values*, edited by J. P. Changeux et al., 47–56. Berlin: Springer, 2005.
D'Aquili, Eugene G., and Andrew B. Newberg. "Religious and Mystical States: A Neuropyschological Model." *Zygon* 28/2 (1993) 177–97.
Davidson, Richard J. "Neural Substrates of Affective Style and Value." In *Neurobiology of Human Values*, edited by J.-P. Changeux et al., 67–90. Germany: Springer, 2005.
———. "Toward a Biology of Positive Affect and Compassion." In *Visions of Compassion: Western Scientists and Tibetan Buddhists Examine Human Nature*, edited by R. J. Davidson and A. Harrington, 107–30. New York: Oxford University Press, 2002.
Diamond, Marian, and Janet Hopson. *Magic Trees of the Mind: How to Nurture Your Child's Intelligence, Creativity and Healthy Emotions from Birth through Adolescence*. New York: Dutton, 1998.
Elkind, David, and Sally Elkind. "Varieties of Religious Experience in Young Adolescents." *Journal for the Scientific Study of Religion* 2 (1962) 102–12.
Farmer, Lorelei, J. "Religious Experience in Childhood: A Study of Adult Perspectives on Early Spiritual Awareness." *Religious Education* 87/2 (1992) 259–68.
Ghetti, Simona, and Kristen Weede Alexander. "'If It Happened, I Would Remember It': Strategic Use of Event Memorability in the Rejection of False Autobiographical Events." *Child Development* 75/2 (2004) 542–61.
Goleman, Daniel. *Emotional Intelligence*. New York: Bantam, 1995
Gundry-Volf, Judith. "The Least and the Greatest: Children in the New Testament." In *The Child in Christian Thought*, edited by M. J. Bunge, 29–60. Grand Rapids: Eerdmans, 2001.

———. "To Such as These Belong the Kingdom of God." *Theology Today* 56/4 (2000) 469–80.

Haenchen, Ernst. *John*. Vol. 1, *A Commentary on the Gospel of John Chapters 1–6*. Translated by R. W. Funk. Philadelphia: Fortress, 1984.

Hardy, Alistair. *The Spiritual Nature of Man: A Study of Contemporary Religious Experience*. Oxford: Clarendon, 1979.

Hay, David, and Rebecca Nye. *The Spirit of the Child*. London: Fount, 1998.

Immordino-Yang, Mary Helen. "A Tale of Two Cases: Lessons for Education from the Study of Two Boys Living with Half Their Brains." *Mind, Brain and Education* 1/2 (2007) 66–83.

Immordino-Yang, Mary Helen, and Antonio Damasio. "We Feel, Therefore We Learn: The Relevance of Affective and Social Neuroscience to Education." *Mind, Brain and Education* 1/1 (2006) 3–10.

Immordino-Yang, Mary Helen, et al. "Neural Correlates of Admiration and Compassion." *Proceedings of the National Academy of Sciences of the United States of America* 106/19 (2009) 8021–26. http://www.pnas.org/content/106/19/8021.full?sid=e74317c4a9cd-4835-bcc3-e32f54f4e0d0.

James, William. *The Varieties of Religious Experience*. New York: Random House, 1902.

Keener, Craig S. *The IVP Bible Background Commentary: New Testament*. Downers Grove, IL: InterVarsity, 1993.

Keltner, Dacher, and Jonathan Haidt. "Approaching Awe, a Moral, Spiritual and Aesthetic Emotion. *Cognition and Emotion* 17/2 (2003) 297–314.

King, Pamela Ebstyne. "Afterword: Where Do We Go from Here?" In *Thriving and Spirituality among Youth: Research Perspectives and Future Possibilities*, edited by R. M. Lerner et al, 333–42. Hoboken, NJ: Wiley, 2011.

———."Religion and Identity: The Role of Ideological, Social, and Spiritual Contexts." *Applied Developmental Science* 7/3 (2003) 197–204.

King, Pamela Ebstyne, and Chris J. Boyatzis. "Exploring Adolescent Spiritual and Religious Developmnet: Current and Future Theoretical and Empirical Perspectives." *Applied Developmental Science* 8/1 (2004) 2–6.

King, Pamela Ebstyne, and James L. Furrow. "Religion as a Resource for Positive Youth Development: Religion, Social Capital and Moral Outcomes." *Developmental Psychology* 40/5 (2004) 703–13.

King, Pamela Ebstyne, et al. "Searching for the Sacred: Religious and Spiritual Development Among Adolescents." In *APA Handbook of Psychology, Religion and Spirituality*, edited by K. I. Pargament et. al., 1:513–528. Washington, DC: American Psychological Association, 2013.

Klingberg, Gote. "A Study of Religious Experience in Children from 9 to 13 Years of Age." *Religious Education* 57 (1959) 211–16.

LeDoux, Joseph. *The Emotional Brain*. New York: Simon and Schuster, 1996.

Lerner, Richard M. "Developmental Science, Developmental Systems, and Contemporary Theories of Human Development." In *Handbook of Child Psychology: Social, Emotional and Personality Development*, edited by W. Damon et al., 1:1–17. 6th ed. New York: Wiley, 2006.

———. *Liberty: Thriving and Civic Engagement Among America' Youth*. Thousand Oaks, CA: Sage, 2004.

Lerner, Richard M., et al. "Positive Youth Development: Thriving as the Basis of Personhood and Civil Society." *Applied Developmental Science* 7/3 (2003) 172–80.

Loder, James E., Jr. *The Logic of the Spirit: Human Development in Theological Perspective*. San Francisco: Jossey-Bass, 1998.

———. *The Transforming Moment*. 2nd ed. Colorado Springs: Helmers and Howard, 1989.

Louw, J. P., and E. A. Nida. "Opsarion." In *Greek-English Lexicon of the New Testament Based on Semantic Domains*. 2nd ed (electronic source). United Bible Societies, 1996 and 1989.

Maresca, Catherine. *Children and Theology*. Washington, DC: Center for Children and Theology, 2009. http://www.cctheo.org/OP-Children%20and%20Theology.pdf.

Morris, Leon. *The Gospel According to John*. Grand Rapids: Eerdmans, 1995.

Nelson, Charles. "The Effects of Early Adversity on the Development of Brain Architecture." Paper read at Learning and the Brain Conference, Cambridge, MA, November 20, 2009.

Newburg, Andrew and Stephanie K. Newberg. "A Neuropsychological Perspective of Spiritual Development." In *The Handbook of Spiritual Development in Childhood and Adolescence: Moving to the Scientific Mainstream*, edited by E. C. Roehlkepartain et al., 183–96. Thousand Oaks, CA: Sage, 2006.

Newburg, Andrew, et al. *Why God Won't Go Away: Brain Science and the Biology of Belief*. New York: Ballantine, 2001.

Nouwen, Henri J. M. *Creative Ministry*. Garden City, NY: Doubleday, 1971.

———. *Gracias!* San Francisco: Harper and Row, 1983.

———. *Out of Solitude: Three Meditations on Christian Life*. Notre Dame: Ave Maria, 1984.

———. *The Return of the Prodigal Son: A Story of Homecoming*. New York: Doubleday Image, 1992.

Quartz, Stephen R., and Terrence J. Sejnowski. *Liars, Lovers, and Heroes: What the New Brain Science Reveals about How We Become Who We Are*. New York: William Morrow, 2002

Robinson, Edward. *The Original Vision*. New York: Seabury, 1983.

Roehlkepartain, Eugene C., et al. *With Their Own Voices*. Minneapolis: Search Institute Center for Spiritual Development in Childhood and Adolescence, 2008.

Ruddick, C. T., Jr. "Feeding and Sacrifice: The Old Testament Background of the Fourth Gospel." *The Expository Times* 79/11 (1968) 340–41.

Scales, Peter C., and Nancy Leffert. *Developmental Assets: A Synthesis of the Scientific Research on Adolescent Development*. 2nd ed. Minneapolis: Search Institute, 2004.

Schwartz, Jeffrey M. "A Role for Volition and Attention in the Generation of New Brain Circuitry: Toward a Neurobiology of Mental Force." *Journal of Consciousness Studies* (1999) 115–42.

Sylwester, Robert. *How to Explain a Brain: An Educator's Handbook of Brain Terms and Cognitive Processes*. Thousand Oaks, CA: Corwin, 2005

Tasker, R. V. G. *John*. Grand Rapids: Eerdmans, 2000.

Tamminen, Kalevi. *Religious Development in Childhood and Youth: An Empirical Study*. Helsinki: Science Academy, 1991.

———. "Religious Experiences in Childhood and Adolescence: A Viewpoint of Religious Development between Ages 7 and 20." *International Journal for the Psychology of Religion* 4/2 (1994) 61–85.

Thompson, Marianne Meye. "Children in the Gospel of John." In *The Child in the Bible*, edited by Marcia Bunge, 195–214. Grand Rapids: Eerdmans, 2008.

———. *The God of the Gospel of John*. Grand Rapids: Eerdmans, 2001.

Thompson, Ross A. "The Development of the Person: Social Understanding, Relationships, Conscience, Self." In *Handbook of Child Psychology*, edited by Nancy Eisenberg et. al., 3:24–98. 6th ed. Hoboken, NJ: Wiley, 2006.

Tomasello, Michael. *Why We Cooperate*. Boston: Boston Review/MIT, 2009.

Vygotsky, Lev Semonovich. *Mind in Society: The Development of Higher Psychological Processes*. Edited by Michael Cole et al. Translated by A. R. Luria et al. Cambridge, MA: Harvard University Press, 1978.

———. *Thought and Language*. Translated by E. H. and G. Vakar. Cambridge, MA: Massachusetts Institute of Technology, 1962.

Warneken, F., and M. Tomasello. "Altruistic Helping in Human Infants and Young Chimpanzees." *Science* 311 (2006) 1301–3.

Whitacre, Rodney A. *John*. Edited by Grant R. Osborne. InterVarsity New Testament Commentary. Downer's Grove, IL: InterVarsity, 2007.

PART FOUR

James E. Loder and the Transformation of Christian Witness

11

A Tactical Child-Like Way of Being Human Together

Implications from James Loder's Thought for Post-Colonial Christian Witness

DANA R. WRIGHT

Come unto me, all who are heavy burdened . . .
and I will give you rest
Jesus

I have been crucified with Christ,
and it is no longer I who live but Christ who lives in me.
And the life I now live in the flesh I live by the faith of the Son,
who loved me and gave himself for me
Paul

The glory of God is humanity fully alive
Irenaeus, *Against Heresies*

Introduction: The Burden of Being Human and the Hope of Transformation

Robert Penn Warren's epic novel *All the King's Men*, his graphic depiction of human depravity shaping politics in the "Christ-haunted South," arguably becomes explicitly theological only at the very conclusion. Penn Warren's unlikely prophet is the Scholarly Attorney, an old man whom Jack Burden, the novel's narrator, had once wrongly thought was his father. The old man, now an evangelist of sorts, had not taken care of himself and was facing the end. But Burden, a cynical survivor of Willie ("the King") Stark's political machine, took pity on him and brought him to Burden's Landing so he wouldn't die alone. The old man had been working with the down-and-outers living in a decaying section of a southern town, creating and dispensing his gospel tracts. After dictating his latest tract to Jack, the dying man asked him to comment on the following paragraph.

> The creation of man whom God in His foreknowledge knew doomed to sin was the awful index of God's omnipotence. For it would have been a thing of trifling and contemptible ease for Perfection to create mere perfection. To do so would, to speak truth, be not creation but extension. Separateness is identity and the only way for God to create, truly create, man was to make him separate from God Himself, and to be separate from God is to be sinful. The creation of evil is therefore the index of God's glory and His power. That had to be so that the creation of good might be the index of man's glory and power. But by God's help. By His help and in His wisdom.[1]

At first skeptical of the message, Jack later wonders to himself if he just might believe the old man's evangelical musings after all.[2]

How tempting to read this gospel tract as the novelist's own theological convictions secreting into the text, bringing out a hidden dimension of the story that touches the hem of Christ's garment and thereby generates an unexpected hopefulness in the reader.[3] While the force of

---

1. Warren, *All the King's*, 437.

2. In the novel Burden mused: "[B]ut later I was not certain but that in my own way I did believe what [the old man] had said" (ibid., 437). Taking up the burden of the old man is another gesture toward transformation.

3. Whether or not Penn Warren himself was devout, the fact of his birth in Kentucky and his life in the Christ-haunted Bible Belt might be sufficient to account for his im-

the novel as a whole seems ineluctably tragic and hopeless, this theological caveat at the very end raises the possibility that underlying the tragedy of human existence Penn Warren nonetheless recognizes an even deeper truth—the promise, against all odds, of the redemptive transformation of all things becoming visible in intimate gestures of human love! Undergirding the pervasive hopelessness lies a primal hopefulness that every character in the story (and its readers!) longs for even as it appears to elude them all. When Penn Warren places the full tragic force of his novel in surprising tension with this glimmer of theological hope, *All the King's Men* is itself transformed (kicking and screaming perhaps) from unalloyed tragedy into Christian testimony! Human distance from God becomes the index of God's glory, Who brings life out of death and hope out of despair in order that humanity may manifest its own glory as God's image. Burden's act of kindness toward the old man and the hint of his belief in the message of the tract are small but perhaps significant signs of his own tragic life under the spell of "King" Willie becoming slightly but significantly unburdened after all!

The Divine-Human Problematic in Art, Science, and Human Existence

From this theological interpretation we might argue that the creative force of *All the King's Men* arises out of the same "logic of the Spirit" that characterized the redemptive transformation manifest in the life and thought of practical theologian James E. Loder Jr.[4] In the "logic of the Spirit," the mystery of the human condition conveyed tragically as being-unto-death is confronted with the greater mystery of the divine disclosure of the presence of New Being in Christ, manifesting itself as hope amid despair, or as life revealed through death. From this standpoint, *All the King's Men* derives its power from its depiction of the tragedy-hope tension exposed in the tract's theological interpretation of history. Likewise, underlying Loder's life and his creative work was his passionate engagement with what Kierkegaard called the "Qualitative

---

plicit embrace of the biblical categories that inform his description of depravity and the theological hope that becomes explicit in the old man's tract. On this possibility see Brooks, *Hidden*, 103–9, 125.

4. See Wright and Kuentzel, "Are You There?," 401–31, and the introduction to this present volume.

Dialectic" of the God-Man. This Chalcedonian Reality revealed in the Cross places all of human life under question about what it means to be human in this kind of world, opening up the possibility of transformation by the Spirit.[5] Loder lived and died to witness to this Reality at the heart of all things tragic being redeemed by the presence of Christ. He believed that practical theology, the life of the practical theologian, and the health of the theological community only maintained their integrity by engaging over and over again what he called "the core generative problematic." Loder described this "core generative problematic" in a way that resonates with the theology articulated in the old man's witness to the divine presence in the midst of the tragedy that befell "all the King's men" (and women and children!).

> The core generative problematic [for practical theology] . . . require that two ontologically distinct realities, the divine and the human, be brought together in a unified form of action that preserves the integrity of both and yet gives rise to coherent behavior. This paradoxical problematic implies that God's action and human action, although ontologically distinct, are not ultimately dichotomous.[6]

Therefore, the "help" and "wisdom" from God referred to in the old man's tract might be understood as the insights generated when the problematic of God-human relations revealed in the Gospel continues to inspire the intelligence and life responses of believing persons or communities (or the Christ-haunted writer of novels!). Such persons know themselves to be unavoidably implicated in the massive existential conflict the Cross reveals to them about what it means to be human together *corem Deo* in this kind of world. What happens to the "burden" of being human when hope arises in the stricken heart and one is liberated to choose for or against the salvation being offered by sheer grace?[7]

---

5. Ibid., where I have characterized Loder's development of Kierkegaard's philosophical work as "Neo-Chalcedonian" science.

6. Loder, "Place," 2 (pre-publication copy). This essay was published in the *International Journal of Practical Theology*. See my discussion of this concept in chapter 7 of this present volume. What follows is my contention that just as the discipline of practical theology requires repeated engagement with the core generative problematic, so also human life itself and the life of congregations requires the same sustained engagement in order to be creative in a theological sense.

7. Like a good therapist, Penn Warren leaves the "burden" of believing to Jack Burden himself, who is depicted at the end of the novel being brought to the point of choosing for or against hope. Loder taught that one sure mark of the Sprit's work

All of the work of James Loder was generated, either implicitly or explicitly, through his own grappling with the core problematic revealed in Jesus Christ, the One who in his own Person holds together the tensile unity of divine-human relations in its definitive form. Surely for Loder, the core generative problematic of practical theology is nothing less than the core generative problematic of the human condition itself revealed in the Gospel. In Christ, the index of God's glory is revealed in God's movement through the Spirit "inside" the estranged human condition (i.e., Jesus "suffering under Pontius Pilate . . . dead, buried"[8]) to bring about, against all odds and appearances to the contrary, humanity's redemptive transformation in Christ's nature ("But God raised him from the dead . . ."). The index of human glory is our awakening to this divine movement human-ward as an act of sheer grace, revealing the extent of our sin and therefore calling forth the regenerating power of forgiveness.[9] The Presbyterian *Book of Order* affirms this kerygmatic actuality in this striking passage from the "Directory of Worship" that elaborates the Chalcedonian significance of the Christ Event for human transformation, again echoing the gospel tract in *All the King's Men* and Loder's core problematic.

> In Jesus Christ, God entered fully into the human condition in an act of self-revelation, redemption, and forgiveness. Entering the brokenness of the world, God in Jesus Christ atoned for sin and restored human life. By so entering the created world God brought time and space, matter and human life to fulfillment as instruments for knowing and praising their Creator.[10]

The glory of God is humanity fully alive, transformed through God's own self-knowing of us in our sinfulness, which is our own glory re-

---

was the liberation to choose for or against the new life the Spirit made available. See "Fashioning," 194–95.

8. More reflection needs to take place on the "creedal" relevance of this phrase "suffered under Pontius Pilate." I take this confession not as simply a reference to the crucifixion of Christ but to the whole cruciform life of Jesus of Nazareth under Roman domination. Christ identifies fully with the "burden" of being human in this kind of world dominated by imperial forces.

9. For a powerful reflection on human being and creativity as forgiveness see the essay of Haddon Wilmer in this present volume, chapter 2.

10. Presbyterian Church, "Directory of Worship," W-1.1002c. On Loder's own passionate and intelligent witness to the Gospel in a scientific culture see the Introduction to this present volume.

vealed in us through the bestowal of a new identity that participates existentially in the divine-human relationality revealed in Jesus Christ through the Spirit.

Intimacy as the Core Relational Experience for Redeemed Humanity

We must now ask, what lies at the substantive core of our transformation as "instruments for knowing and praising [the] Creator"? For Loder, the answer is "intimacy . . . a quality of relationship in which the relationality itself [between self and the other] takes on a life of its own and overcomes each one's anxiety at being known."[11] This human longing to be known fully without fear is therefore, in Loder's understanding, implicitly the developmental quest for covenant with Christ. However, from the human side "no covenant is ultimately possible in strictly developmental terms because, in such terms, the quest must begin and end in the human ego."[12] Human development toward intimacy requires a theological resolution such that the relational integrity established through the act of God addresses our existential fear of being known at the level of spirit, liberating us for true intimacy. Thus, God's self knowing of us and our becoming alive to God's knowing of us Spirit-to-spirit must be described in terms of the restoration of the intimacy of the holy Creator with the sinful and undeserving creature established through grace. "Holiness acts upon sin as grace," wrote P. T. Forsyth.

Loder understood this gracious act of holiness upon sinfulness Christologically as the restoration of Christo-qualitative relations throughout creation, to which the Church as the first-fruits of the New Creation is called to bear passionate and intelligent witness (*homo testans*). His dependence on Kierkegaard for his analysis of the human spirit under the conditions of despair being restored to intimacy through the Qualitative Dialectic (Kierkegaard's version of the core generative problematic) is discerned throughout Loder's *oeuvres*. Loder noted that Kierkegaard spoke of "the primacy of intimacy" in divine-human relations as our "transparent grounding in the power that posits the self."

---

11. Loder, *Logic*, 254. Loder points out the close etymology between "intimacy" and "intimidation," both being rooted in the Latin *timor*, "fear."

12. Ibid, 254–55.

> The classic discussion of the primacy of intimacy for the healing of human lives, broken in many directions, is found in Kierkegaard, *Sickness unto Death*. A person is "spirit," he claims. Contrary to certain stereotypes, Kierkegaard's view of the self is intensely and irreducibly relational. In his dialectical analysis, the self is constituted by a relation between finite and infinite, necessity and possibility, the temporal and the eternal. This relation between two polar aspects of the self is, however, not yet the self; the relation must become a positive third term. This relation must relate itself to itself, and by this self-relation the self is constituted as an irreducible relationality. The one condition for the dynamic balance of the self is that this high order of relationality be "grounded transparently in the power that posits it." This dynamic interrelational view of the self describes a person as spirit, and it is by the spirit that the inmost core of the person is known (1 Cor 2:10–11).[13]

Unredeemed humanity (described by Penn Warren and countless others in literature, philosophy and theology) naturally, under the effects of sin, lacks this transparent grounding, according to Kierkegaard. Loder accepted Kierkegaard's insights, arguing that if the human spirit is not "grounded transparently in the divine presence, it will collapse or . . . dissipate into despair."[14] Human history is held captive to "a profound failure of intimacy" from which it cannot extricate itself. The result of such despair-unto-death is disrelations on all fronts—a pervasive failure of love. Loder described this despair-unto-disrelations in an essay focused on counseling specifically and practical theology in general, though it no doubt speaks to the human condition as a whole. Here Loder modifies Kierkegaard's formal dialectic to emphasize the reality of personal intimacy in divine-human relations.

> Despair is a disrelationship in the self due to a profound failure of intimacy with the divine presence who creates the appropriate relationality which is the self. If the human spirit is thus grounded, then it testifies with the Holy Spirit that a person is a child of God (Rom 8:16) . . . I am using intimacy with the divine presence in the same way Kierkegaard uses transparency, but with the term intimacy I am attempting to put more flesh on the relationality that Kierkegaard described dialectically. Thus I am attempting to argue that the deep power of this Spirit-to-spirit intimacy to

---

13. Loder, "Great Sex Charade," 84.
14. Ibid.

move persons into the world to "do the works of love" ... should be the most profound focus of our attention on counseling.[15]

In *All the King's Men*, Jack Burden's (possible) transformation from a Willie Stark achiever "burdened" by cynicism and disrelations to a more child-like giver of hopeful care is portrayed in the gestures toward intimacy and reconciliation he enacts at the end of the novel—forgiving and marrying the faithless Ann Stanton and taking the Scholarly Attorney into their hospice. That his "burden" of being the "king's" achiever could be transformed into the bearer of solicitous care ("bear one another in love") is a miracle of grace portrayed here (subtly) in fiction. Loder described this transformative reality in scientific terms, showing how the restoration of intimacy with God through Christ in the power of the Spirit becomes crucial for enabling persons to give and receive love with integrity.[16] For Loder, the Spirit of God fills all of the distorted and disrelational matrices of human experience with the generative power of His presence, so that persons and communities abiding in that presence become the bearers of intimate relations through faith. Loder described this kind of intimacy as "the non-possessive delight in the particularity of the other," his suggestive transposition of the biblical term *agape*. *Agape* is the love with which we are loved for just being there, which is central to our ascriptive worth potential empowering thought and action (We love because God first loved us!). To be fully alive in Christ (Loder uses the word "conviction" to designate this aliveness) is to participate with passion in a non-possessive relational reciprocity that delights in the other (God, self, other human and non-human creation) and that therefore overcomes the distortions of intimacy that mark fallen humanity. In short, the Presence of God revealed in the Gospel should be understood as a Christo-qualitative relational reality interpenetrating all things and filling them with Christ's *agapeic* nature. This actuality in Christ becomes a human possibility through the Spirit of Christ through faith.[17]

---

15. Ibid.

16. For an analysis of redemptive transformation of youth toward intimacy see my essay Wright and Dean, "Passion," 153–88.

17. For Loder, conviction is grounded in an act of God that restores the freedom of the human spirit to choose for or against living out of one's ascriptive worth potential which has been oppressed in an achievement-addicted culture. See "Fashioning," 195.

Loder's neo-Chalcedonian elaboration of the Spirit's transforming work in human experience (in the tradition of Kierkegaard) has enormous implications for the integrity of the Church's witness to Christ in the world, and therefore for the efforts of the Child Theology Movement to influence that witness. That is, if the Child Theology Movement is to have an impact on the Church's witness in the world, it must address the issue of the Spirit's power to transform human experience Christo-relationally by enabling persons and communities to live out of their ascriptive worth potential as the basis for human action and achievement. We will attempt to bring this issue to light in what follows using Loder's insights to contrast two ways of being human that recall the Apostle Paul's contrast between *flesh* (the burden of "king" Stark's achievers) and *spirit* (the way of unburdened, child-like discipleship). On the one hand, the un-redeemed, un-crucified and "adult-like" anthropology of defensiveness-unto-death (the *flesh* as king!) and, on the other hand, the redeemed and cruciform "child-like" anthropology of liberated witness-unto-life (the unburdening call to discipleship). For reasons that should become clear as we proceed, we'll call the way of the flesh "strategic" and the way of the spirit "tactical." Essentially we will argue that in the context of whatever world is emerging in the twenty-first century through the "pains of childbirth," a truly child-like or "tactical" way of being human together must also emerge if we are to thrive. The Church potentially testifies to and embodies such a "tactical" way of being human in her witness within this emerging world, but only if she learns to live "in the Spirit." Apart from the Spirit, the Church conforms herself to the world's "strategic" posture—the way of death and despair—and thereby fundamentally distorts Christ's witness in the world.[18] In other words, *how* we live out our witness to Christ in the emerging world is at least as important as *that* we give witness.[19] Our discussion continues with Loder's understanding of the developmental origins of what we are

---

18 For an elaborate exploration of the way in which Pentecostal movements worldwide are struggling with this "strategic" or "tactical" emergence see Yong, *In the Days*.

19 This concern has weighed on me especially since my involvement in Southern India in the fall of 2011. I was asked by Ajit Prasadam to offer a course on the theology of youth ministry at the India Sunday School Union's St. Andrew's Center in Coonoor. The legacy of colonialism and imperialism and the collaboration of the church's mission with forms of dehumanizing triumphalism weighed heavily on me as I prepared for, and taught, that course.

calling "strategic" anthropology, the way of the Willie Stark's world of the achieving "adult."

The Developmental Origins of "Strategic Defense Initiatives" as the "Adult" Mode of Being Human in the World

Initially I want to describe the "burden" of unredeemed humanity in both personal and public manifestation, large and small, as characterized by "strategic" relations that are "defensive" in nature and therefore, from a theological perspective, ultimately disrelational because they abandon the true human longing for ascriptive intimacy in a tragic effort to exercise autonomy. The core concern of "strategics" is to secure a solid place to stand that is one's own, from which all relations with the other are determined by defensive calculations that secure advantage for the oneself or one's community over and against the other.[20] Loder described the unredeemed creativity and purpose of the human spirit under the condition of sin as a kind of descent into disrelations characterized by what I am calling "strategic defense initiatives" that destroy the possibility for intimacy.[21] He called this "fall" into disrelations "the triumph of negation" in human development, and he argued that this negation of true intimacy permeates the social construction of reality.[22] These defensive disrelations determine every register of human action and infuse every cultural or subcultural expression of that action. More ominously, they can be understood theologically as the human spirit bound in every direction to the entropic powers of sin and death. Loder understood "death" biblically and theologically not as the biological point of the secession of life in a clinical sense but precisely as this disrelational dis-ease woven into human experience, engendering a massive

20. Readers should note here that "strategic" anthropologies are particularly descriptive of the hoped-for fruits of the ideology of capitalism in the late modern period. That so much uncritical support of this free-market ideology comes from churches in the West and beyond betrays, in my judgment, a tragic failure of theological depth.

21. I am counting on the reader's recollection of the Strategic Defense Initiative (SDI) of the Reagan administration, as well as our current anxious defensiveness regarding the terrorist threat as a strategic "war on terror" to emphasize the pervasiveness of strategics as the primary mode of being human in our world.

22. Loder, *Logic*. For Loder, negation might be understood as a kind of spiritual virus that works "disrelation" into every facet of human experience and history until it is itself negated by the Spirit of Christ to serve the relationality revealed in, and empowered through, Jesus Christ by the Holy Spirit.

loss of intimacy (isolation from, or absorption into, the other) at every turn. The human spirit's "burden" is precisely its tragic bondage to "strategic defensive initiatives" that functions as the determinative structure of human meaning-making and creativity. We are bound in disrelations and lack intimacy on every front, from the intra-psychic domain of the ego to the complex negotiations among the competing interests of nation states.[23] And these "strategic defense initiatives" are killing us, just as in the novel all the king's men (and women and children) are destroyed one way or the other.[24] Strategic defense initiatives kill, in fiction and in real life!

We see this evident power of death when the Church's legitimate commitment to the Lordship of Christ takes on the spirit of triumphalism she assumes characterizes "King Jesus." In this false spiritual appropriation of symbols and images our testimony of Christ's Lordship—which in Scripture is presented as a tensile paradox of "all authority" through "vulnerability unto death"—collapses on the side of "all authority." We create "Christ" in our own defensive image of power. In doing so, the tension of the "vulnerable Lordship" of Christ, who manifests his power through suffering service for others, is abandoned through unalloyed attachments to communities that champion domination in the name of "Christ triumphant."[25] The community created in and for creaturely exercise of "power made perfect in weakness" inevitably distorts its witness by communicating an imagined "Christ" who exercises god-like power in the image of executive ego (a sub-Christian iteration of the pathology rendered in *All the King's Men*).[26] Under such distortion, the heart

---

23. Regarding the latter, see the growing literature exposing the "death" rendered through our own country's history of defending our national and economic interests world-wide without consideration of, nor apology to, those who have suffered and died as a result. The works of Howard Zinn, Arundhati Roy, Naomi Klein, Chris Hedges, Andrew Bacevich, Noam Chomsky, Walter Brueggemann, Timothy Gorringe, Daniel Bell Jr., Cynthia Moe-Lobeda, etc., are just a few of the prominent voices warning us of the tragedy of imperial or strategic policies and practices.

24. For example, Tom Stark, Willie's son, becomes a manipulative lout and ends up killing himself, which also destroys Willie's relationship with his wife.

25. This move toward triumphalism is, of course, not limited to Christianity. The present rise of militant forms of Islam, Judaism, and Hinduism around the world indicates the pervasive and deadly nature of the spirit of triumphalism. The question for us is this: Is the Lordship of Christ possible through a non–triumphalist spirit that does not compromise Christ's authority over all things (Matt. 28)?

26. Recall Paul's theology of kenosis: "who thought it not robbery to claim equality

of the Church's embodied witness is prone to be held captive to what Emmanuel Levinas lamented is "a totalizing conceptual framework" that "acknowledges only what conforms to its conceptual scheme" and therefore, "absorbs the 'other' into the 'same.'"[27] This "totalizing" distortion of Christian "witness" leads to forms of Christian living dominated by strategic defensiveness that, in the name of Christ, destroys the possibility of true intimacy with the other. The radical nature of our awakening to the God-Human structure of reality can therefore be easily transposed toward "others" in a way that diminishes or even erases their particularity and humanity. Tragically, we fundamentally distort our witness to the living and *kenotic* mediation of Jesus Christ, who actually loves the other with non-possessive, non-controlling, delight. We reduce the "other" to the status of "it," so that unique and God-loved persons become instead "potential converts," "sinners," "evil axis," or "the white man's burden."[28] Our response to this distorted witness, however, should not be to eliminate or abandon the Lordship of Jesus (as if we had the power to do that!) but to live in the cruciform power of the Spirit that restructures human relationality in conformity to the Chalcedonian Reality itself. But before we can appreciate this impact of the Spirit on the human spirit we must first recall what lies behind our unnecessary but inevitable embodiment of strategic structures of being human that characterize the unredeemed spirit held in thrall to ego.

The developmental origins of our "fall" into "strategic defensive initiatives" was described by Loder in his theological interpretation of Rene Spitz's work on the organizing power of the infant.[29] The problem

---

with God but emptied himself, taking the form of a servant" (Phil 2:5ff).

27. Quoted in Vanhoozer, "Voice," 78. Van Hoozer draws on Emanuel Levinas' theory for his proposal. For another important theological interpretation of Levinas, see Ford, *Self*, esp. 30–44.

28. Perhaps the most extreme examples of this kind of heteropathy are, on the conservative side, the vitriolic actions anti-abortion activists or anti-gay protestors make against their opponents and, on the liberal side, the violent protests green activists or animal-rights or earth-first activists might make against their opponents. Our uncivil and uncompromising political discourse in the U.S. is another pervasive example.

29. See Spitz, *No and Yes*, and *First Years*, and Loder's discussion in "Negation." Loder developed a reinterpretation of the central movement of human development toward the formation of the ego under the power of negation, what he called "the keystone of subsequent ego development" (*Logic*, 89). He defined "negation" existentially as the experience of Nothingness or Void underlying every dimension of the social construction of reality.

Loder confronted here was the self-contradiction that develops within the infant's spirit when, created in the image of God for intimacy with the divine Spirit, she awakens instead to an overpowering experience of absence at the center of her being, fatally undercutting all hope and sponsoring an endless succession of disrelational strategies. Loder wrote:

> Even if it is clear that the dynamics of the human spirit run deeper than the trust created by them [i.e. in the first stage of life], for all of its transformational potential and ingenious capacity to construct and expand human horizons of meaning, the human spirit is by itself without ground and without meaning for itself *as spirit*. By allowing the human spirit to reflect on itself as spirit, we arrive at the intrinsic cry of the human spirit for ground, meaning, and purpose. In itself, it has no answer to the question of why it should create an environment of trust, why it should go on creating the structures of development, or why it should exist at all. This is the cry of the image for reunion with its original.[30]

Loder reinterpreted the programmatic work of Spitz, who had discerned in his study of infancy three propaedeutic developmental foci for the constructive capacities of the infant leading up to a fourth, the construction of ego itself.[31] Loder's work explored the theological meaning of the early search of the human spirit for a Ground, interpreting the dynamic hidden structures of the spirit confronting its own meaninglessness as the negation riven into human development.

The first organizer for the infant is the *Mouth*. As the infant survives the trauma of the birth experience, she engages in an amazingly creative act by bringing the "world" into her mouth. Through this creative and intelligent act, Loder averred, "the mouth begins to do in a primitive way what the ego will eventually do in a much more complex and sophisticated way: serve the drive for survival and satisfaction."[32] What the infant's spirit creates here in primitive form is an embodied connection to the "universe." That is, she relates herself as embodied spirit to a context of ultimacy by bringing all her contact with reality into herself through the mouth. Perhaps we could think of this action as "perichoretic" (i.e., mutually indwelling) in that the infant simultaneously penetrates the external world with her hands and brings the external world inside herself

---

30. Loder, *Logic*, 114.
31. Loder's fullest discussion is found in *Logic*, chapter 4
32. Ibid., 90.

through the mouth. Yet her goal remains survival and satisfaction in response to the trauma of birth.

At about three to six months, a qualitative transformation of the child's relationship to her environment takes place as the child's spirit reconstructs her relationship to a second organizing focus, the *Face*, which is an interpersonal reality. The *face* of the loving other (usually the mother) is for the child both prototypically personal (intimate) and religious (ultimate). In this stage transition, a kind of subject-to-subject relationality emerges to reveal to the child her place in the universe and her reason for being. Indeed, Loder observed: "children seem uniquely endowed with a potential capacity to sum up all the complexity of the nurturing presence in the figure of the face."[33] We never lose this relational sense of intimacy in the context of ultimacy, even when it gets buried (repressed) in the course of "normal" human development and the social construction of reality.[34] When we speak of the "Face phenomenon" we are speaking of a "proto-religious" personal experience of face-to-face relations.[35] Loder noted: "Erikson and others who have no particular theological axe to grind agree that this [experience of the face] has religious significance, so it is consistent with such devel-

---

33. Ibid., 91. David Ford also explores the amazing power of "the face" in our lives in his exquisite book *Self and Salvation*. Ford argues that we live our whole lives before the faces of others, in memory or anticipation, and that "face to face" relations run "deeper than conscious memory" (17). Ford notes how our faces reveal our uniqueness and that this longing for uniqueness lies behind Emmanual Levinas' argument that the cry for human justice grows out of our refusal to be assimilated into another's vision. Our uniqueness or otherness is confirmed in the face of the other who is other. Yet the face is also the bridge to our relation with others. Thus, Ford asserts that faces are "a type of continuity with novelty," an illuminating echo of Loder's transformational logic suggesting that transformation itself is "written on our faces." We "never unravel the dense weave" of our early face-to-face relations. The way people looked at us in our early years stays with us. Ford argues that "the dynamics of such meetings illustrate the contingencies of life as well as anything in nature. A word, a glance, an instantaneous interpretation, a confrontation, a dissimulation, a misconstrual, an indirectly conveyed attitude—these things can be turning points, moments of insight, decision, or shame."

34. Ford, *Self*, 117f. Both Ford and Loder (*Logic*, 90–91) note that the phenomenon of the face was understood in the ancient world. In both Hebrew and Greek, the words for "face" (Heb. *panim*, Gr. *prosopon*) are also the words for "presence."

35. Loder, *Transforming*, 163. This is why the primal wholeness needs to be communicated in personal language. Images of primal wholeness or the "religious thematic" as a "force field" tend to eliminate the personal nature of what is really crucial to the nature and mediation of this wholeness. Even Kierkegaard's emphasis on the human spirit being "transparently grounded" in God tends toward the impersonal.

opmental perspectives to say that this smiling response to the face or the consistent nurturing presence of another is a cosmic ordering, self-confirming presence of a loving other. That is, to be human is implicitly to be religious."[36] Loder argued: "what is established in the original face-to-face interaction is the child's sense of personhood in relation to a universal prototype for the Divine Presence."[37] In other words, these experiences of the face become "the primal prototype of the religious experience in which one is placed with recognition and affirmation in the context of a cosmic order. Universality and particularity, individuality and belonging, deep subjective satisfaction and a sense of ultimate objective order: all combine in a single, living, harmonious presence."[38] The significance for our topic is that this intimate and ultimate sense of relational wholeness is permanently imprinted on the spirit of the mind and remains a tacit apperception throughout the whole of human development and all subsequent social constructions of reality. This "paradise remembered" throughout the life-span provides the underlying structure of intimacy in the context of ultimate meaning and purpose, even though the human spirit's longing for such "relational integrity" inevitably gets distorted and diminished under repression (see below). As Loder reminded us often, "the secret," though buried, "secretes."

Nonetheless, to understand the inevitability of "paradise lost" we must consider the third organizer of the personality according to Spitz, which is *existential Anxiety*. As her powers to objectify her environment continue to develop, the child learns to discern "object permanence," a sign of intelligence in which the child demonstrates intentionality by retaining an object no longer physically present. The obverse side of this advance in intelligence is a knowledge that the *Face* goes away. This awakening to the "presence of an absence" results in a profound existential anxiety at the relational center of the personality, the center which the child now realizes "cannot hold."[39] And this inner sense of absence is confronted at the same time by an outer social restraint

36. Loder, *Logic*, 90. Loder drew in part on Pannenberg, *Anthropology*, 60–74 for his understanding of the "religious thematic."

37. Loder, *Transforming*, 163.

38. Loder, *Logic*, 91.

39. Recall here William Butler Yeats' memorable line in his poem "The Second Coming": "Things fall apart / the center cannot hold / Mere anarchy is loosed upon the world . . ." What Yeats saw falling apart in "the Christian Century" is the cultural extension of what Loder discerns underlies the existential anxiety of the child.

(classically "potty" training) that requires the child herself to "hold" her "contribution" to the social order and deal with it in an "adult" way, or else! The depth of the intimacy revealed in the experience of the *Face* is now transformed negatively into a deep disrelation at the center that is experienced internally as existential anxiety (a sense of profound absence and non-being) and externally as prohibition ("No!"). Here Loder described how the child anticipates her move into the adult world governed by an existential "No."

> ... the six-month old child is learning to understand and anticipate the parental "no". . .to distinguish among faces and anticipate the departure of the most important face. This builds up an internal sense of absence ... a matter of existential significance. At the same time, the external environment is recognizably and forcefully saying "no." ... [N]ow the child hears clearly what the word means. Thus, for the child's psyche, compounding the sense of loss and negation, and the existential impact of these converging forces of negation, leaves no room for the developing child's sense of self. The primary organizer of the personality at this period ... is anxiety.[40]

The absence-generated anxiety that arises in response to this sense of nothingness that now resides at the center of the child's apperception as spirit becomes unbearable for the child. Existentially lost, she will now turn the negation outward in a brilliant but tragic move to secure her life against this sense of absence. She will create the foundations of the "adult" world through the fourth organizer of the personality—the executive *Ego*. In a reaction formation (doing with passion the very opposite of what one wants to do), the child's spiritual sense of abandonment impels a psychic drive to fill the void with her own constructed meanings.[41] Through this "strategic defense initiative" the child thrusts "No!" on the environment before the environment can thrust "No!" on the child. Loder describes this fundamentally tragic disrelational defense initiative as a reaction formation of immense power that now determines the child's will to achieve significance and her own place in the universe.

40. Loder, *Logic*, 92.

41. "The 'I' naturally struggles against 'absence' [sic] as if it were a mortal enemy. It becomes narcissistic, omnipotent, and omniscient, popular, feared, manipulative, 'well-adjusted,' 'grizzly realistic,' etc., in order to fill the 'absence' with some fantastic extension of itself" (Loder, "Fashioning," 196).

> It is as if there were operative during the early years ... of life a reaction formation in which the child learns to do just the opposite of what he wants most. Before the years in which competition becomes important, he wants most the hugs and kisses which ascribe to him an unconditional worth, but they are withheld until he performs well. So he throws himself into performing well and does so with all the passion with which he desires to be affirmed for who he *is*, a child of worth. He eventually learns to repress spontaneous affect and convert that energy into high performance activity and successful competitive ventures. This is the core structure of the achievement-oriented life-style.[42]

Ironically and tragically, the child organizes her life around "No!" in order to preserve her identity and uniqueness against the ubiquitous threat of nothingness she apperceives haunts her being. In so ordering life around "No!," the "triumph of negation," the child accomplishes "a spiritual move of transposing an existential crisis into a functional solution by

> ... establishing the line of repression between conscious and unconscious, inside and outside. This is a magnificent move defensively, since it establishes the basis for primary repression ... "my world" as against "your world," my inner space against unwarranted intrusions from both outside and inside. By means of negation, we construct the nonself, objective world over against and distinct from our human subjective sense of self. No-saying and reactions to no-saying, by translating into the psychic function of primary repression, lay the foundations for the subsequent ego development.[43]

Thus, the ego and every dimension of the social construction of reality based upon ego—even and especially the so-called "positive" constructions—now manifests nothing less than "negation incorporated." Because "Nothingness haunts being" (Qoheleth→Sartre), "strategic defense initiatives" of every kind become the *modus operandi* of the human spirit in its search to overcome the sense of absence pervading its personal, inter-personal, and corporate life. "Negation incorporated"

---

42. Loder, "Fashioning," 188–189. It is important to note that achievement is not the only form negation takes. We also must attend to what we might call anti-achievement related to the traditional recognition of sloth or acedia as a "deadly sin"—i.e., a sin that deadens relationality. See Kruschwitz, *Acedia*.

43. Loder, *Logic*, 93.

becomes the mediating relational center of the adult world into which the child is thrust, repressing most tragically the child's sense of ascriptive worth out of which she was originally created to live and achieve.

In this essay I am using the metaphor of "strategic defense initiatives" to capture the aggressive nature of the power of negation in human experience to infuse disrelations into the fabric of the human life, in essence recapitulating something like the Fall in human development. What will eventually be lost as the child conforms to the adult expectations of her world is the qualitative relational (child-like) intimacy implicit in the *Face* phenomenon, which was created to be the core of human life *corem Deo*. The ego-generated substitutes for that intimacy function defensively on all levels of human intercourse—from one's sense of self, to sexual relations, to the social roles one uses to adapt to the world, to international relations among nations. Because "nothingness haunts being," human development and the whole of human experience emerge as a tragic and burdened longing for a "lost" quality of presence to "overcome our nihilistic uncertainty."[44] We long for "the cosmic ordering, self-confirming impact from the presence of a loving Other" with the power to reaffirm ascriptive worth and to negate the existential negation and restore intimacy in the context of ultimacy.[45] Yet the depth of our fall into disrelational despair becomes determinative in the course of "normal" human development and experience.

Loder nonetheless argues that underlying this existential despair human beings retain a tacit "sense of wholeness" that he understands provides the "enduring context" for human spirit's creative capacities. Deeper than the despair lies a primal sense of hopefulness that underlies every subsequent differentiation and hierarchy human beings construct to find meaning. Loder drew on Pannenberg, who called this implicit hopefulness the "religious thematic."

> In the developmental history of the child, the "exocentric centeredness" with which we are endowed is characterized by universality. The holistic way in which a child enters the world, surrounded and nurtured by the maternal matrix, sets an enduring context within which all other developments take place . . . the sense of universality is never lost. Multiple differentiations and relationalities are constructed in this matrix over the course

---

44. Loder, "Fashioning," 197.
45. Loder, "Negation," 166–91.

of a lifetime, but each sub-part, however delineated, implies the whole . . . the implication of universality runs in and through all differentiations and developments of the personality in that the human spirit—in its creation of language, intelligence, culture and social institutions—is always implicitly the bearer of a "religious thematic."[46]

Thus, human development takes place on the razor's edge between hope and despair. Loder continues, "The human spirit [is constituted by] this relationality between the tacit sense of wholeness and the explicit differentiation of the parts within the whole, from which the parts derive their meaning . . . spirit . . . can be broken or depersonalized if the dynamic interplay between the tacit and explicit dimensions breaks down."[47]

The Good News is that the Fall into disrelational despair has itself been negated through the Death and Resurrection of Jesus Christ. This ultimate "negation of negation" is the central key to the transformation of transformation by the Holy Spirit (the impact of atonement on human personhood[48]). Of this "apocalyptic"[49] transformation of transformation Loder averred:

> . . . the negation of the "experience of Nothingness" [means that] one's potential for nonbeing is ultimately negated . . . Christ crucified and resurrected is taken as a paradigm of the mediator of transformation at the level of existential negation. Christ becomes the adequate "grammar" for existential transformation because in his crucifixion he takes ultimate annihilation into himself and in his resurrection existential negation is negated . . . Christ creates an ontological gain for those whose essential existence is defined by his nature.[50]

46. Loder, "Incisions," 162.

47. Ibid.

48. See Wright and Dean, "Passion," for a description of the impact of atonement in adolescent development.

49. The use of the word "apocalyptic" here is intentionally provocative. The apocalyptic structure of the New Testament—i.e., its stretching of language to the breaking point in order to communicate the ontological impact of Jesus Christ in human history—is being discerned by more and more scholars. See for example, Brown's *Cross*.

50. Loder, "Negation," 169. In another place Loder argued that when Christ effects the transformation of the ego, the re-centered ego liberates the self from the anguish and anxiety at the abandonment and alienation at the root of its defensive propensities. He averred: " . . . human nature is so constituted that built into its ego structure and implicit in its greatest achievements is a cosmic loneliness that longs for a Face that will do all that the mother's face did for the child, but now a Face that will transfigure

The "ontological gain" Christ accomplishes in this atoning Event is a new quality of human life that participates in Trinitarian relations transforming history from the inside out. L. Gregory Jones articulated the "inconceivable self-emptying of God" that made such ontological intimacy with God possible to redeem fallen humanity.

> Our distance from God is itself taken into God, finds a place in God: by the Spirit of adoption we enter the relation between the Father and Son, the relation of exchange and mutuality. In the incarnation, God distances Himself from Himself: the divine, intra-Trinitarian love is enacted and realized in the world by the descent of Christ into Hell. And the separation between Father and Son is bridged by the Spirit, who is the common will and love of Father and Son. The inconceivable self-emptying of God in the events of Good Friday and Holy Saturday is no arbitrary expression of the nature of God: this is what the life of the Trinity is, translated into the world.[51]

The Spirit of Christ communicates this Trinitarian movement human-ward by awakening human beings to the presence of Christ revealed in the Gospel. Christ bestows and mediates a new identity for human beings enlivened through restored intimacy with God, which is actualized through the Holy Spirit, "who testifies to our spirit that we are children of God" (Romans 8). Thus, while the relational essence of the transformation is intimacy with God, the shape of that intimacy is now determined by the Christological and cruciform mediation of the Holy Spirit, which restores radical contingency to human existence in a way that makes non-possessive love possible. In this next section we want to describe this transformation of human experience through the Spirit unto a "tactical-improvisational" way of being human in the world.

---

human existence, inspire worship, and not go away, even in and through the ultimate separation of death" (*Logic*, 119).

51. Jones, *Embodying*, 120.

Tactical Improvisation and the Radical I-yet not I but Christ Structure of Redeemed Christian Existence in the Spirit

Theologian Barry Harvey once described the nature of redeemed Christian existence as "holy insecurity," a "radical vulnerability" set against the ineradicable mystery of God that recalled for him the refrain of Proverbs, *"the fear of the Lord is the beginning of wisdom."*[52]

> Our everyday existence as Christians begins with the acknowledgement of our vulnerability as creatures, or as the Bible refers to it, with the fear of God. This vulnerability is sanctified, made holy, when we learn to embrace and love it as given to us by the creator of all, whom we also learn to love as the one who first loved us. The love of God for creation that is manifested through the incarnation of the Word and communicated in the Spirit, therefore, defines the aim of spirituality as *holy insecurity*. In short, the goal of Christian piety is to keep open the "window of vulnerability," as Dorothee Soelle puts it, for it is the only window toward heaven that we have.[53]

This relation of human vulnerability (holy insecurity) to the awesome mystery of God signifies a true and living relation that cannot be "controlled" or "possessed" from the human side, even as it liberates the human spirit to embody the wisdom of God in all relations. Harvey engaged the work of the Jesuit Michael de Certeau to describe this living faith relation, using de Certeau's metaphor of "tactics" to guide his thinking. Accordingly, de Certeau defined "tactics" as "a calculated action which is specifically determined by the lack of its own place, that is, by its inability to designate a proper locus from which the exteriority of the other is delimited." Without a "place" that allows one to define oneself or one's group over and against the other, identity "lacks a necessary condition for realizing that most cherished of objectives in the modern world—autonomy" (Harvey's word for what we are calling the strategic defense initiatives of ego). Harvey continues:

> Those who follow a tactical course of action do not have the wherewithal to plan a general strategy or to view the adversary

---

52. This refrain captures the Qualitative Dialectic (Kierkegaard à Loder) and the Chalcedonian Ontology (Barth à Loder) in its rudimentary form in the OT Wisdom.

53. Harvey, "Holy Insecurity," 217. Harvey takes the phrase "holy insecurity" from Nicholas Lash, describing the perspective of Martin Buber (ibid., 238 n. 3).

as a whole within a distant space, but must play on and with a terrain imposed on it or organized by a foreign power. A tactic operates in isolated actions, taking advantage of any opportunities which present themselves, but without a place where it can stockpile its winnings for the next encounter. This "nowhere" provides a tactical mobility, but it forgoes the pretense of stability and control, relying instead on the ability to take advantage of the opportunities which present themselves only at particular times and places. The identifying characteristic of a tactic, therefore, is that it has no "place" of its own from which it can define its relations with the "other."[54]

Harvey argues, however, for a "place" beyond the "no place" made available through the logic of conversion, which J. G. Hamann described as "a descent into hell, the hell of self-knowledge which is the only way to being one with God."[55] Human beings enter the "dark gate" (M. Buber) "through which the believer steps forth into the everyday, which is henceforth (and only henceforth) set apart as the *place* in which she must learn to live with the ineradicable mystery" of God—that is, when "our existence between birth and death becomes incomprehensible and uncanny, when all security is shattered through the mystery . . . we call God."[56]

From this description we would argue that for Loder, to live "tactically" in the holy insecurity of the mystery of God describes how the person or community awakened to the Gospel experiences the transformation of the "no place" of human self-securing into the actual, radically contingent relationality revealed in the God-Human Jesus Christ through the power of the Holy Spirit. That is, beyond the "no place" of existential nihilism that infuses human history lies the New Being in Christ who alone authorizes eternal life with human beings as contingent (vulnerable) participation in the Creator Spirit. Thus, we awaken in Christ through the Spirit to a relational quality of existence that recapitulates (imperfectly but really) in vulnerable human experience the perfect relationality between the Father and the Son mediated in the Spirit, which was revealed in human history through the Incarnation.[57]

54. Harvey, "Insanity," 44.

55. Smith, *Hamann*, 40.

56. Harvey, "Insanity," 44 (emphasis added). One of the Jewish names for God is "the Place."

57. Loder argued that convictional experiences gave certitude to human existence

When the Holy Spirit acts upon the human spirit convictionally (Loder's word for conversion) the full theological dimensions of the New Being in Christ that restore contingent creaturehood in human experience are revealed. Loder called these experiences of the Cross in human experience "four fold knowing events" that fully reveal the presence of the "no place" (he called it the Void) permeating all our social constructions of reality engendering the disrelational dis-ease at the heart of our creaturely existence that we have described above. In Christ we face this "hell of self knowledge" as we are encountered by the Face who comes to us from the other side of the Void in the preaching of the Gospel. The Cross exposes the presence of the Void and the negation that is riven into human experience—negation triumphant—as a real but *penultimate* reality. Deeper than the Void is the Presence of a personal quality of Love that holds all things together. Therefore, our disrelational dis-ease (vulnerability unto death) is transformed into "holy insecurity" (faith as contingent vulnerability revealed in Christ) as we find our true Ground in the Love of God, liberating us to live "tactically" in the Spirit in a world burdened by strategic (defensive) initiatives large and small. To live "tactically" in the Spirit is to live in the "holy insecurity" of always being "beggars" (Luther), sinners saved by grace, who never seek ultimate security beyond the intimacy of Spirit-to-spirit relations. Christ calls us to participate existentially in a relational Reality that cannot be "possessed" or "secured" to our own advantage, even as we come to ourselves in that relationality and receive our life over and over again as gift. We live in and through the "no-place" of Face-to-face relationality through which we are "taught of God"—Jeremiah's promise of the New Covenant revealed in Christ and being fulfilled in us who live in the Spirit.[58]

It is crucial for us to remember that because the substance of the New Being (intimacy) is mediated in Christ through the Spirit, the tactical relationality offered to the transformed human spirit bears a

---

but a certitude that manifested itself in openness and mystery and vulnerability. The intimacy of the believer with God through the Spirit enabled one to give up all other false securities and enter courageously into the full contingency of human existence in the world. "The Spirit puts us into the world" was one of Loder's mantras.

58. One way to understand Loder's neo-Chalcedonian practical theology is to see it as a scientific effort to explain the dynamics of the New Covenant for a postmodern world. For an effort to articulate a "covenant epistemology" partly informed by Loder's work see Meek, *Loving*, especially 123–44 and 272–97.

Christological and cruciform structure through which we are called to exercise a radically redeemed agency in the world. In the New Testament Paul articulated this new Christo-anthropological identity structure as a dialectic, *I yet not I, but Christ*. Loder further developed Paul's shorthand in scientific terms to disclose how transparent relationality or imageless, face-to-Face intimacy renders human agency Christo-tactical in the Spirit:

- "*I*" in the Pauline formula is the self, the generative core of human creaturehood created in the image of God for integrity in all relations, as portrayed in the Face-phenomenon, in which human *being* is affirmed beyond measure in every particularity as the focus of divine love;

- "*Yet not I*" in the Pauline formula is the recognition of the triumph of negation in human experience, the acknowledgement that the "I" bears a tacit sense of its own *non-being*, a sense of the negation of ascriptive worth that destroys and distorts relationality;

- "*But Christ*" in the Pauline formula recognizes the redemptive transformation of the self in the image of Christ through convictional experience, grounding human experience and the sense of the absence of being itself in a relational reality stronger than death.

The upshot of this regenerative action of the Holy Spirit is redemptive transformation of the human spirit and all of its creative agency in the service of Christ. *I yet not I but Christ* becomes the "convictional structure" bestowed on human personhood through contingent relations with the Spirit.[59] The nothingness at the center of human experience is now filled with the Presence of Christ, so that the absence underlying "strategic defense initiatives" is acknowledged and accepted as real, yet crucified and transformed to serve the Spirit of Christ. This divine action establishes ontologically in human experience the relational actuality of what the "Face" phenomenon revealed prototypically in the second stage of ego formation described above. Loder elaborated the implications of Karl Barth's generative connection between external creation and the internal covenant that creates and sustains all creation from the "inside

---

59. Loder, "Fashioning," 198.

out." Christ's redemptive transformation transfigures all unredeemed "hierarchies" that bear strategic defense initiatives and restores Christo-qualitative relations in human experience as a manifestation of ascriptive worth restored. The New Being in Christ reconstitutes the structural integrity of created reality.

> The hierarchies of the created order [are turned] inside out [by Christ's nature], revealing that their ground and purpose is hidden in the tacit dynamics that give rise to them. The God-man has redefined history and all its inherent patterns as a created and redeemed order; this order can then be recognized as the external side of an internal covenantal relationship between God and humanity. Thus, all the great antitheses that mark out the created order and give rise to hierarchical accounts of that order get their definition from the relationality of that covenant. Particularity and universality, transcendence and immanence, life and death—indeed, all the classical antitheses that characterize the extremities of human nature, including the contingent relation between the Creator and the creature—are now recast according to the definitive relationship given us in the God-man, Jesus Christ.[60]

We no longer have to maintain those "hierarchies" through our strategic defense initiatives, for they been dethroned as necessarily determinative of relations. The hierarchies (including ego) are not eradicated but reconstituted in the Christomorphic and tactical relationality that now authorizes them to serve the will of the Spirit. Tactical-improvisation shares the non-defensive power of the Spirit of Christ to fund non-possessive delight in the particularity of the other. What Loder sought to articulate, through his neo-Chalcedonian science, was the impact on the generative powers of the human spirit finding its true Ground in the Spirit of Christ. He gave us an explanation of the dynamics and restructuring involved in tactical-improvisational ways of being human generated out of one's existential awakening to God's Presence in Christ through the Spirit.

Furthermore, Loder also emphasized the revolution in human reason or rationality and its semiotic powers under the impact of the Spirit. The *I yet not I but Christ* structure of being in the Spirit requires an analogous structure of thought and language in order to preserve the

---

60. Loder and Neidhardt, *Knight's Move,* 197, quoted with minor alterations in Wright, "Youth Passion," 160–61.

relational integrity of semiotic imagination in conformity to the Spirit's dynamic nature. Conviction requires a "logically odd" linguistic and symbolic universe of discourse to express "the logically odd situation that God has revealed himself."[61] Christianity appropriates ordinary language from unredeemed cultures used to communicate dimensions of human experience that systematically repress the *I yet not I but Christ* dimensions revealed in the Spirit. Ordinary terms like "love," "grace," "god," "lord," "faith," and "redeemed," etc. are affirmed ("*I*"), negated ("*yet not I*") and magnified ("*but Christ*") to communicate the impact of redemptive transformation on meaning-making itself. Indeed, for Loder, all linguistic and culturally symbolic systems bear negation (even Christian language systems!) and lie (i.e. fail to bear truth) until they are continually affirmed, negated, and transformed in the service of the Spirit. This spiritual transformation of language means that in Christ, the spirit of the mind must be liberated from "conceptual rest" to embody a "kinetic mode of reason" that corresponds to the dynamic existence ingredient in the experience of redemptive transformation. Loder drew on Kierkegaard for insight into this integration of thought and being that manifests itself in us when we awaken to, and live in, the dynamic presence of the Spirit.

> What needs to be clear is that . . . Kierkegaard . . . realized that thought about matters of ultimate existential importance cannot be grasped without distortion by an ingenuity of formal or discursive reason, and that if one is to understand the movement of the transcendent into time (as in the incarnation) with the full scope of one's existence (such as faith requires) one must, in contemporary scientific terms, abandon any conceptual point of "absolute rest," such as that which secured the Euclidean space in which Newton constructed the universe. One must instead adopt a kinetic mode of reason; in his language, in "a moment" one must make "the leap of faith," which is just as surely an act of thought as it is an act of choice for radical change in one's whole being. Yet thought and being must never be collapsed either way, for in the tension between them is the velocity and vitality of existence, "the spirit." Thus, his kinetic claim regarding authentic existence: "Man [person] is spirit."[62]

61. Loder, "Fashioning," 199. Loder draws on Ian Ramsey, *Religious*, and Langdon Gilkey, *Naming*, in this essay. On the "odd" nature of Christian language and practice, see also Tanner, *Theories of Culture*, 110–19.

62. Loder and Neidhardt, *Knight's Move*, 185f.

Redeemed "tactical" faithfulness, then, becomes a living improvisation of dynamic relationality, the restoration of our imageless and contingent relation to God in thought and action! To put it cryptically, in Christ through the Spirit we "make life up as we go," but only because God has, through the secular Fact of the Gospel, authorized exactly this kind of "tactical" existence for human creatures. There is no other authentic way to be a human creature or community created in the imageless image of God than living in that dynamic relationality![63]

We may now ask: What does this tactical-improvisational way of being human look like in the context of a world laboring under the throes of the triumph of negation with its embeddedness in strategic postures of life and thought? How might we describe "tactical" personhood or community transparently grounded in the power that posits the self toward the restoration of the kinetic and "imageless" relation to God? What happens to us when the Spirit of Christ negates the double-binding negation of the social construction of reality and we begin to manifest "tactical," Christo-qualitative relational intimacy? A good place to answer these questions may be to consider the evidence of who seem to have been liberated from "strategic defense initiatives" of the adult world to embody a more child-like or improvisational and tactical way of being human. Where might we find scientific descriptions of "tactical" existence to complement Loder's theoretic claims?

Liberation unto Martyrdom: The Substance of Redemptive Transformation in Human Experience as Bearing the Witness of Jesus Christ

I would like to argue in the final section of this essay that what we have characterized as tactical improvisation, humanity grounded in the restored intimacy of imageless Spirit-to-spirit relations and structured Christomorphically (*I yet not I but Christ*) is nothing less than our being

---

63. We note here that the freedom of "tactical improvisation" must be distinguished from distortions of freedom like "protean" modes of being human. The difference is in the mediation of the relation. Protean personalities are self-generated constructions of ego and therefore manifest a particular pervasive form of strategic defense initiatives that resist covenantal modes of commitments for the supposed absolute freedom of self-expression. In Christ, on the other hand, "tactical improvisations" manifest themselves as "works of love" for the sake of the other. Tactical existence in Christ through the Spirit is intrinsically "communion-creating" and "covenant-manifesting."

liberated unto martyrdom—human beings and communities bearing the radical witness of Jesus Christ in their embodied life together to the world.[64] Martyrdom is nothing less than the vocation of the transformed community reflecting the Spirit of Christ and therefore embodying the normative expression of what it means to be human according to the nature of Christ. Ironically, James Fowler's Stage 6 description of mature faith provides us with a good place from which to reflect initially on this claim[65] In *Stages of Faith* Fowler wrote:

> Persons best described by Stage 6 exhibit qualities that shake our usual criteria of normalcy. Their heedlessness to self-preservation and the vividness of their taste and feel for transcendent moral and religious actuality give their actions and words an extraordinary and often unpredictable quality. In their devotion to universalizing compassion they often offend our parochial perceptions of justice. In their penetration through the obsession with survival, security, and significance they threaten our measured standards of righteousness and goodness and prudence. Their enlarged visions of universal community disclose the partialness of our tribes and pseudo-species. And their leadership initiatives, often involving strategies of nonviolent suffering and ultimate respect for being, constitute affronts to our usual notions of relevance. It is little wonder that persons best described by Stage 6 so frequently become martyrs for the visions they incarnate.[66]

This paragraph is pregnant with the tone of liberation unto martyrdom expressed by persons at Stage 6 in Fowler's research. Fowler describes persons liberated from strategic defense initiatives who reflect the buoyancy of tactical improvisation that is difficult to deny. Significantly, Fowler admits that his depiction of Stage 6 faith represents a "radical disjuncture" from outside the course of "normal" development he described in his research. He avers that while "nature" governs "normal human development" through the first 5 stages, universalizing

---

64. I argued in the introduction to this volume that Loder's life and work can be described as *homo testans*, human as witness or martyr. Loder's theories are the logical extension of his person. Thus, we may regard Loder's liberation unto *homo testans* as a case study of martyred Christian existence as normative Christian being in the Spirit.

65. I use the word "ironically" here because Loder criticized Fowler's faith development project for not accounting fully for the work of the Holy Spirit in human transformation. See below.

66. Fowler, *Stages*, 200.

faith "seems to require a disruption or disjunction from the 'natural.'" Persons described in Stage 6 "seem to have undergone an experience of the negation of ties and affections that we generally take to be 'natural' . . . [experiences that] require an explanation based on the initiatives of the Transcendent . . . the work of something like Grace."[67]

Here Fowler reserves for Stage 6 faith what Loder regards as a convictional possibility at any stage, since in the Spirit, the redeemed relational dynamics that now govern stage transitions are stronger and deeper than the constructed stages themselves.[68] The need for Christ to act eschatologically from "outside" the stage sequence pattern to negate the negation riven into unredeemed (i.e., "normal") human development is not fully recognized within Fowler's more Pelagian leanings. From Loder's Reformed, "Christ the transformer of culture" position (influenced by the Lutheran Kierkegaard), the impossibility of moving from nature to Grace is affirmed and the double-bind of the strategic posturing of the ego is revealed. I am awakened to my lostness, to my inability to save myself apart from the Grace that created me, the Grace that now restores me to "child-like" sanity in a world lost to the insanity of strategic posturing.

But beyond human development *per se*, Loder traced how the substance of restored sanity (intimacy in the context of ultimacy) mediated in Christ (*I yet not I but Christ*) could inform our understanding of how the Spirit works tactical improvisations into all four dimensions of human action—organic, psychic, social and cultural. Loder gleaned these categories from Talcott Parsons but interpreted Parsons' action theory theologically in order to bring out the subtleties of the Spirit's creative transformation of human creativity into Christian witness. We can effectively communicate these marturological improvisations using Paul's *I yet not I but Christ* shorthand to guide our discussion.[69]

---

67. Fowler, *Becoming*, 73f. For an excellent discussion of the difference between Fowler and Loder on transformation, see Haitch "Summary," especially the extended footnote 37 on 319f.

68. For Loder's critique of Fowler's understanding see *Logic*, 255–59.

69. For a more thorough elaboration of Loder's use of Parsons, see chapter 7 of this volume. See also Haitch, "Summary."

Organic

The work of the Spirit liberates human beings on the *organic* level from an obsessive and "strategic" preoccupation with survival and safety that tends to bind all human relations (person-to-person, family-to-family, community-to-community, nation-to-nation) in anxiety-ridden competition for advantage or domination over the other.[70] As depicted in Fowler's description of universalizing faith, a disregard for safety and security results from the personality or community gaining confidence that the Presence who comes to us in the midst of death will not only not go away but will also provide for our bodily needs.[71] Concerns for safety and security are affirmed (*"I"*) while the negation manifest in the obsessive preoccupation with securing them or hording them for one's own advantage is negated (*"yet not I"*). The redeemed person or community grounded in intimacy now becomes a grateful recipient of Christ's grace (*"but Christ"*) rather than a demander (Bonhoeffer). Thus, the work of the Spirit negates the strategic defensive initiatives supporting survival-at-all-cost at every level of human intercourse. The Spirit generates a gratitude-expressive and generosity-oriented responsiveness toward God and others that lets the bodily existence of all flourish. The "tactical" confidence in God's care breaks the stranglehold of "territorial" imperatives of every strip, from zero-sum competition in the personal realm to families battling over inheritance rights to a world succumbing under the strains of predatory forms of capitalist greed or oppressive forms of socialist control. Regarding the macroeconomic imagination, much work needs to be done on how we might conceive the Spirit of Christ redemptively transforming *both* the just distribution of wealth *and* the empowerment of entrepreneurial creativity beyond defensive ideologies and hegemonic practices toward the benefit of all God's creation.[72]

---

70. Obsession with security and safety abound, from our anxious fear of terrorist threats feeding defense budgets to the clash of families over inheritances, causing alienation and anger, to the rush by nations to secure mineral and water rights, *ad infinitum*.

71. See the powerful documentary *Mother Teresa* by Petrie, narrated by Richard Attenborough. Mother Teresa is in Lebanon during the war and will not be deterred from seeking out the orphans threatened by a bombing raid. That her life is in danger is beside the point in relation to her concern for the children.

72. The transformation of both capitalism and socialism onto-relationally is crucial for the hope of the world. The negation infecting both socialism and capitalism must be exposed and negated so that they serve the expansive and inclusive generativity of Christ's nature. Both forms of ideology and practice must be redemptively transformed

Psychic

We have already said a great deal about how the Spirit liberates at the *psychic* level. The Spirit first affirms the ego's creative capacities ("*I*") but then negates the strategic defensiveness of its executive obsessions ("*not I*") in order to render the boundaries of ego permeable and reciprocal, depending on circumstances. Transforming ego boundaries is essential in order to promote and generate non-possessive delight in the particularity of others ("*but Christ*").[73] A more "perichoretic" structural intimacy becomes possible as relationality in Christ's non-defensive nature becomes the power generating a non-coercive relational reciprocity between the ego polarities. On the intimacy-restoring power of the Spirit in ego transformation Loder wrote:

> As Carl Jung has pointed out, ego transformation is the key to religious experience and personal wholeness. Ego transformation may then be understood not as destruction to the ego, but as a clear-cut recentering of the personality around a transcendental reality that points to the invisible God. The net effect enhances ego functioning, since the ego has less need to control or limit perceptions or understandings of the self, world, or others. Ordinarily, the autonomous ego would constrict its vision lest the underlying existential negation come into view and the centripetal force of development draw it back through Nothingness toward the true center. However, once the center is invested in God's Presence, the ego's anguish at absence and abandonment is dissipated and its defensive energies can now be poured into its competencies.[74]

The dialectical identity that results from the ego's transformation by the Spirit of Christ is a "reversible" and "reciprocal" ("tactical" and "improvisational") mode of being human that replaces the "irreversibly univocal" ("strategic") identity.

---

in order to reimagine and reconfigure how the world might share together in God's superabundant grace.

73. The identity secured by ego is not eradicated in the Spirit, since a sense of self is needed in order to define one's uniqueness in relation to the other. But the necessity of ego identity manifests negation until the Spirit works to reconstitute the ego non–defensively in Christ's nature.

74. Loder, "Negation," 179.

> Another way of saying this is that a reciprocal relationship between the ego and the Divine center of [the] personality was instituted. By "reciprocity" I mean the figure/ground reversal whereby the ego and the Divine Presence are alternately the center of action, but the center of identification remains the Divine Presence ... "I not I, but Christ ... Recentering the personality means that identity ceases to be irreversibly univocal and becomes instead reversible and reciprocal.[75]

From this standpoint, for Loder, "[s]piritual development consists in increased access between the ego and the Divine center, not in ego development per say."[76] Persons and communities are liberated to create one another in love and therefore to witness to the communion-creating power of Jesus Christ in all interpersonal relations.

Social

The work of the Spirit in the *social* domain is to negate the negation intrinsic to social role constructions (the social analogue to the ego's strategic defense initiatives). Role structures bear a certain kind of functional power to structure social relations and thereby support the social construction of reality and its enduring power. Yet they cannot generate the qualitative relational intimacy that human beings require because of their being created in the *imago Dei*, which the Spirit of Christ seeks to reconstitute. The Spirit of Christ is a "communion-creating Reality" whose work in the world is to restore a Christo-qualitative relationality into the whole of human history. Through the Gospel Christ has filled all reality with His nature, calling all humanity to a revolution in social relations through which non-possessive delight in the particularity of others becomes the norm.[77] And under the power of the Spirit strategic roles structures, generally considered essential for ordering the body politic, are liberated from their defensiveness and become tactically "reversible" and "reciprocal" according to the nature of Christ and the circumstances at hand. That is, static role hierarchies (i.e., parent-over-child, teacher-

---

75. Ibid., 188.

76. Loder and Neidhardt, *Knight's Move*, 284. Counterintuitively, then, "the immature ego of the child may have greater access to the center and be more spiritually mature than an adult ego with less access."

77. For an expression of the fullness of Christ filling the social construction of reality, see my essay "Paradigmatic," 216–51.

over-student, CEO-over-janitor) become reversible as the obsession with maintaining order over intimacy is relativized. Socially constructed role expectations are affirmed ("*I*") for their adaptive function. But now the negation that prevents true intimacy is recognized and negated (the "*not I*" that hardens the self or the community into static role structures that crush intimacy). The longing for a deeper spirit-to-spirit intimacy formerly repressed by the social constructions of reality is liberated ("*but Christ*") to empower a qualitatively different and more dynamic social ordering (parents learn from children, students teach teachers, CEOs listen to janitors!). This transformed communal intimacy is the *koinonia* in which every situation calls for living out "tactical improvisations" that support communal generativity by facilitating a creative interchanging of roles. In this sense, social relations are characterized by the spirit of child-like expectancy and joy rather than the adult-like defensive strategy of expectation and pre-judgment.[78]

Cultural

Finally, the work of the Spirit in the *cultural* domain is to negate the negation riven into the functional use of language, symbols and images so that culture is liberated from its penchant for lying in order to serve the Presence and Reign of God. Culture is affirmed in its generative intention to preserve the symbols of its identity through time ("*I*"). Also affirmed is the revolutionary initiative of even unredeemed cultural visions and movements to overturn the distortions and disrelations that result when dominant cultures turn "demonic" and claim ultimacy (idolatry and blasphemy).[79] When the symbolic capital of a community is "captured" in functionally opaque master images created to maintain that culture's claims of ultimacy, those images inevitably "colonize" consciousness at the behest of those who control the imagination and thereby "subject" persons within idolatrous and inevitably unjust configurations of power

---

78. See Young, *Shack*, for a creative portrayal of this difference between adult-like "expectation" and child-like "expectancy." Indeed, Young's whole novel advocates a kind of "child-like" ontology of divine-human relationality that touched a cord in the Christian community and made it a best seller.

79. I am thinking here of the democracy movements that have sprung up in recent years in the former Soviet Union, in the Arab world, in South American, African and Asian liberation movements, etc.

and meaning.[80] Loder drew attention to the revolutionary movements that sought justice yet ended up perpetuating their own versions of injustice and oppression. He argued that apart from the Spirit of Christ all revolutions inevitably become recaptured by a new symbolic system that, implicitly or explicitly, bears the negation of strategies to confirm their own claims of ultimacy. In the cultural domain, like with Scripture, the "letter" (symbol system) kills and the spirit gives life.

Thus, all cultures as complex symbol systems governed by the unredeemed human spirit must themselves be transformed by the Spirit of Christ and rendered four-dimensional and "transparent." That is, they must derive their meaning and power from the spiritual Presence of Christ to which they bear witness. The Spirit affirms culture ("*I*") but "crucifies" the claims of ultimacy and the promises of intimacy communicated through the system ("*yet not I*") so that symbols no longer bear negation but are liberated to serve God's mercy and justice. In the Spirit culture is rendered servant of a kinetic and imageless relationality characteristic of the mind of Christ ("*but Christ.*"). Even (and especially) symbol systems that are Christian, like doctrinal systems or worship services, must remain transparent to the living power of the Spirit that keeps the relationality to which the symbols bear witness alive and vital. Loder argued that when doctrinal systems become opaque and "complete" in themselves, they ironically and tragically occlude "the self-involvement of God in God's own description" so that "the *sine qua non* factor that makes creeds and doctrines *matter* and makes them expressive of a *living* truth—namely, the involvement of God's self-relatedness—vanishes, leaving creeds and formulas artificial and lifeless."[81]

For example, Barry Harvey describes how the biblical image of "Father" must be transformed in Christo-morphic terms if we are to avoid lying in the name of Christ. He averred: "the ways of God in the world 'can be discerned only in broken configurations of events, not in uni-linear traditions. Accordingly, obedience can never be literal but

---

80. See Manekin et al., *Our Harsh Logic*, experiences compiled by former Israeli soldiers called to keep law and order in occupied Palestine but who "broke silence" about the actual inhumanity and oppressiveness of their actions.

81. Loder and Neidhardt, *Knight's Move*, 25. The same can be said for Loder's own theory as a finished system, complete in itself. See chapter 7 of this present volume, where I argue that it was Loder's intention for his own work on education to be the bearer of the Holy Spirit's transforming logic.

is necessarily paradigmatic."[82] Therefore, how we think imaginatively about obedience affects how we use Scripture, for example. In Scripture the paradigm for obedience is living under the Fatherhood of God, but not in any "domesticated" sense of that image or relation. The image itself must undergo redemptive transformation. Harvey quotes Nicholas Lash:

> . . . before we take this name [i.e., Father] and use it to weave comforting patterns of speculation concerning the "domestic" character of the relation between human beings and the mystery of God, we need to remind ourselves of the context that is paradigmatic for all descriptions of ourselves as "sons" and "daughters" of him whom we call "Father." That context is Gethsemane and Calvary, where we learn what it is truthfully to stand in filial relation to the mystery of God.[83]

Even the transformative Christian language, image, culture must be continually transformed in human experience by the presence of Christ if the community of Christ is to manifest the cruciform nature of Christ in its imagination and thought, not to mention its life and practice.[84]

As we have argued, the overall ontological gain resulting from the Spirit's negation of strategic defense initiatives into transformed tactical-improvisional ways of being human is liberation to love unconditionally according to the nature and witness of Christ. Christ's nature defines and enables ultimate relationality, replicating the kinetic interplay of perichoresis shared in the inner life of God in human contexts. Loder described this Christological nature transforming human relationality as a dynamic and kinetic relational reciprocity that "preserves love's vitality."

> . . . in a positive modality, as love enacts faith in the "works of love," the reciprocal significance of one's existence in faith is given by the God-man. That is, one is repeatedly reaffirmed by the eternal "*dunamis*" (the secret energy of God's love) as the bearer of a particularity (existence) that remains such only as its coinherence with universality (eternity) in love is repeatedly enacted. The relationality in which we live and by which our be-

---

82. Harvey, "Holy Insecurity," 229, quoting from Lehmann, *Ideology*.

83. Ibid., quoting Lash, *Theology*. See also Loder, "Fashioning," 199.

84. See Loder's discussion of Paul Lehmann's understanding of the "central role of imagination" describing how theological language enshrines the parabolic juxtaposition of "the ways of God and the ways of man," an iteration of the "I-yet not but Christ" structure of conviction informing theology, in "Fashioning," 201–3.

ing is constituted is never a fixed and substantive entity. Rather, reciprocity, in existence under the "Governance" of eternity, preserves the kinetic or the dynamic quality of coinherence—and hence preserves love's vitality.[85]

In Christ's Spirit, human embodied existence is liberated from its obsession to find a secure and safe place of absolute (strategic) security and defend it from all intruders, including God. When so liberated, human beings and communities "dynamically rest" in a vital and kinetic passion governed by the relationality intrinsic to the God-Human overcoming the conditions of sin and tragedy and restoring us to sanity. As the Spirit transforms every resister of human action, human agency becomes a "tactical and improvisational" embodiment of "imageless" face-to-Face relations that restores human beings and communities through "the power made perfect in weakness." All of human life becomes a witness to, and an embodiment of, Christ, the True Witness (Revelation 1:2, 5). The glory of God is humanity fully alive to this dynamic and reciprocal relationality indwelling and transforming all things. The vocation of redemptively transformed human beings and communities is to witness to Jesus Christ in the power of the Spirit and thereby to bear Jesus' own witness of Agape redeeming all things, a Trinitarian achievement in the making (Paul Lehmann).

Conclusion: A Parable of Jesus Rock and Roll

The paradigmatic practice of "tactical-improvisational" life in the Spirit before God, our witness, is worship and prayer (*lex orandi, lex credenda*). Martyrdom comes to concrete expression in ordinary liturgical events in which divine and human agency participate together in Christ's mediation through the Spirit.[86] Indeed, beyond these formal services, all of life becomes worship and martyrdom when the Spirit reigns in human communities of faithfulness and transforms all human meaning-making (*homo poeta*) into witness (*homo testans*). Martyrdom is worship and

---

85. Loder and Neidhardt, *Knight's Move*, 109. Loder wrote in "Factor," "the fundamental work of the Holy Spirit of God is to create among his people a koinonia relationality that replicates in creation the inner life of God and thereby reveals the communal unity between the Divine and the human we first saw in [Christ]" (22, pre-publication copy).

86. See Loder, *Educational Ministry*, chapter 10 and my discussion in chapter 7 of this volume.

worship is martyrdom, but only in the Spirit. Moreover, apart from the action of the Spirit, all human practices of worship and prayer (formal or informal, communal or individual) inevitably bear the negation attendant to all unredeemed human experience. These actions must therefore be continually redeemed in order to participate effectively in the Spirit's work of affirmation, crucifixion, and resurrection. Sadly, much Christian liturgical practice expresses the negation triumphant in human history and quenches the cruciform work of the Spirit in order to preserve "positive worship experiences" that retain a sense of power and control in the name of "the triumphant Christ."[87] Being fully alive in worship means we are in constant need to be liberated from the spirit of strategic defense initiatives that pervade our liturgies and that therefore "witness" to a very different "Christ" than the One crucified for our salvation. Let me share a parabolic episode from my own experience to conclude this essay.

A few years ago I attended a rock concert south of Seattle. The joy of the Lord was palpable and the music was . . . well, Christian rock and beyond. I was trying my best to get into the teen/young adult Christian spirit. We watched waves of kids moshing before the Lord and clapped our hands in "awed" appreciation for their radical, child-like witness. And after an hour of celebration we prepared ourselves to receive the Spirit's instruction from various speakers. The second speaker was an evangelist from Atlanta who claimed to preach "in the Spirit." After a couple minutes he got into his rhythm and testified powerfully to the kids about the Lordship of Jesus and making Jesus "real" in the whole of life. "Amen, brother," was heard throughout the excited crowd. "Amen, preach it." And when the gathering was stirred to emotional high pitch, the preacher delivered what became his evangelical punch line: "And when ya'll get your Jesus *thang* together," he pined in Georgian drawl, "in every school and hangout in this here United States of America," he continued, "then we'll all join together under King Jesus and take over this *thang*" (i.e., take over the country for Christians!!!!). And the place erupted. "Jesus Christ is Lord! Amen!"

I have argued in this essay that the spiritual power that shapes human beings and communities in response to the Gospel has nothing to do with "taking over" anything or anyone. Taking over is a "strategic

---

87. For powerful expressions of the idolatrous nature of Christian worship and education and the need for transformation see Bolton, *God* and Farley, "Tragic," 119–29.

defense initiative," an "adult" way of being human decried by the Gospel. Rather, the Gospel has everything to do with taking up the Cross and filling up the sufferings of Christ as a living testimony to another way of being human that shares in the child-like power-made-perfect-in-weakness revealed in the Cross. The marturological anthropology created in Christ can be characterized as "tactical-improvisation" in the intimacy of the Spirit. The Gospel places the human knower awakened to Christ's presence in a qualitative "non-place" of Spirit-to-spirit relations which we have asserted is the vulnerability of primal creaturehood before God (created in the *imago dei*) now restored and transformed into the New Humanity (*imago Christi*)! In the Gospel I am awakened to, through the power of the Holy Spirit, the ontological vulnerability of contingent creaturehood that marks the original goodness of creation. Christ restores creaturehood and the integrity of creaturehood as intimacy with the Creator and with creation. And the only response to the Cross of Christ warranted through the power of the Spirit is the response of being human, fully alive to our contingent vulnerability and reconstituted in intimacy as the people of God who bear confident but humble witness to the Gospel. We are "re-subjected" ontologically to experience cruciform life "in the Spirit." "*I have been crucified with Christ, and it is no longer I who live but Christ who lives in me. And the life I now live in the flesh I live by the faith of the Son, who loved me and gave himself for me.*"[88] In a world burdened by the dehumanizing strategies of "king's men" of every kind, this alternative marturological way of being human is the glory of God manifest in every unburdened person and community that awakens to bear authentic witness to the One who alone possesses all authority in heaven and on earth—the Living Hope of God's groaning creation.

---

88. Gal 2:19b–20, *NRSV Children's Bible*. I have taken the alternative reading suggested in the apparatus, which emphasizes our participation in the faith (life) of Jesus Christ.

Works Cited

Bolton, Michael Myers. *God against Religion: Rethinking Christian Theology through Worship*. Grand Rapids: Eerdmans, 2008.

Brooks, Cleanth. *The Hidden God: Hemingway, Faulkner, Yeats, Eliot, and Warren*. New Haven, CT: Yale University Press, 1963.

Brown, Alexandra. *The Cross in Human Transformation: Paul's Apocalyptic Word in First Corinthians*. Minneapolis: Fortress, 1995.

Farley, Edward. "The Tragic Dilemma of Christian Education." In *Practicing Gospel: Unconventional Thoughts on the Church's Ministry*, 119–29. Louisville: Westminster John Knox, 2003.

Ford, David. *Self and Salvation*. Cambridge: Cambridge University Press, 1999.

Fowler, James. *Becoming Adult, Becoming Christian*. San Francisco: Jossey-Bass, 2000.

———. *Stages of Faith: The Psychology of Human Development and the Quest for Meaning*. San Francisco: Harper and Row, 1981.

Gilkey, Langdon. *Naming the Whirlwind*. Indianapolis: Bobbs-Merrill, 1969.

Haitch, Russell. "A Summary of James E. Loder's Theory of Christian Education." In *Redemptive Transformation in Practical Theology*, edited by Dana R. Wright and John D. Kuentzel, 298–324. Grand Rapids: Eerdmans, 2004.

Harvey, Barry. "Holy Insecurity." In *Ties That Bind: Life Together in the Baptist Vision*, edited by Gary A. Furr et al., 217–42. Macon, GA: Smyth & Helwys, 1994.

———. "Insanity, Theocracy, and the Public Realm: Public Theology, the Church, and the Politics of Liberal Democracy." *Modern Theology* 10/1 (1994) 27–57.

Jones, L. Gregory. *Embodying Forgiveness: A Theological Analysis*. Grand Rapids: Eerdmans, 1995.

Kruschwitz, Robert B., ed. *Acedia*. Christian Reflection in Faith and Ethics. Waco, TX: Baylor University Press, 2013.

Lash, Nicholas. *Theology on the Way to Emmaus*. London: SCM, 1986.

Lehmann, Paul. *Ideology and Incarnation: A Contemporary Ecumenical Risk*. Geneva: John Knox, 1962.

Loder, James E., Jr. "The Fashioning of Power: A Christian Perspective on the Life-Style Phenomenon." In *The Context of Contemporary Theology: Essays in Honor of Paul Lehmann*, edited by Alexander J. McKelway and E. David Willis, 187–208. Atlanta: John Knox, 1974.

———. "The Great Sex Charade and the Loss of Intimacy." *Word and World* 11/1 (2001) 81–87.

———. "Incisions from a Two-Edged Sword: The Incarnation and the Soul/Spirit Relationship." In *The Treasure of Earthen Vessels: Explorations in Theological Anthropology in Honor of James N. Lapsley*, edited by Brian H. Childs and David W. Waanders, 151–73. Louisville: Westminster/John Knox, 1994.

———. *The Logic of the Spirit: Human Development in Theological Perspective*. San Francisco: Jossey-Bass, 1998.

———. "Negation and Transformation: A Study in Theology and Human Development." In *Toward Moral and Religious Maturity*, edited by Christaine Brusselman et al., 166–91. Morristown, NJ: Silver Burdett, 1980.

———. "The Place of Science in Practical Theology: The Human Factor." *International Journal of Practical Theology* 4 (2000) 22–44.

———. *The Transforming Moment*. 2nd ed. Colorado Springs: Helmers and Howard, 1989.

Loder, James E., Jr., and Jim Neidhardt. *The Knight's Move: Relational Logic of the Spirit in Theology and Science*. Colorado Springs: Helmers and Howard, 1992.

Manekin, Mikhael, et al. *Our Harsh Logic: Israeli Soldiers' Testimonies from the Occupied Territories, 2000-2010*. Compiled by Breaking the Silence. New York: Picador/Henry Holt, 2012.

Meek, Esther Lightcap. *Loving to Know: Covenant Epistemology*. Eugene, OR: Cascade, 2011.

Pannenberg, Wolfhart. *Anthropology in Theological Perspective*. Philadelphia: Westminster, 1985.

Petrie, Ann, and Jeanne Petrie. *Mother Teresa*. VHS documentary, narrated by Richard Attenborough, 1986.

Presbyterian Church U.S.A. "Directory of Worship." In *Book of Order*, 2013.

Ramsey, Ian. *Religious Language*. New York: Macmillan, 1963.

Shults, LeRon. "The Philosophical Turn to Relationality and the Responsibility of Practical Theology." In *Redemptive Transformation in Practical Theology*, edited by Dana R. Wright and John D. Kuentzel, 325–46. Grand Rapids: Eerdmans, 2004.

Smith, R. L. *J. G. Hamann*. London: Collins, 1960.

Spitz, Rene. *The First Years of Life*. New York: International Universities Press, 1957.

———. *No and Yes*. New York: International Universities Press, 1965.

Tanner, Kathryn. *Theories of Culture: A New Agenda for Theology*. Minneapolis: Fortress,1997.

Vanhoozer, Kevin. "The Voice and the Actor: A Dramatic Proposal about Ministry and Minstrelsy of Theology." In *Evangelical Futures: A Conversation on Theological Method*, edited by John Stackhouse, 61–106. Grand Rapids: Baker, 2000.

Warren, Robert Penn. *All the King's Men*. New York: Harcourt Brace Jovanovich, 1974.

Wright, Dana R. "Afterword: The Potential Contribution of James E. Loder, Jr. to Practical Theological Science." In *Redemptive Transformation in Practical Theology*, edited by Dana R. Wright and John D. Kuentzel, 401–31. Grand Rapids: Eerdmans, 2004.

———. "Paradigmatic Madness and Redemptive Creativity in Practical Theology: A Biblical Interpretation of the Theological and Methodological Significance of James E. Loder's Neo-Chalcedonian Science for the Postmodern Context." In *Redemptive Transformation in Practical Theology*, edited by Dana R. Wright and John D. Kuentzel, 216–51. Grand Rapids: Eerdmans, 2004.

Wright, Dana R, and John D. Kuentzel. "Are You There? Comedic Interrogation in the Life and Witness of James E. Loder, Jr." In *Redemptive Transformation in Practical Theology*, edited by Dana R. Wright and John D. Kuentzel, 1–42. Grand Rapids: Eerdmans, 2004.

Wright, Dana R., and John D. Kuentzel. *Redemptive Transformation in Practical Theology*. Grand Rapids: Eerdmans, 2004.

Wright, Dana R., and Kenda C. Dean. "Youth, Passion, and Intimacy in the Context of *Koinonia*: James E. Loder's Contribution to a Practical Theology of *Imitatio Christi* for Youth Ministry." In *Redemptive Transformation in Practical Theology*, edited by Dana R. Wright and John D. Kuentzel, 153–88. Grand Rapids: Eerdmans, 2004.

Yeats, William Butler. "The Second Coming." In *The Norton Anthology of English Literature*, edited by M. H. Abrams et al., 2:1880f. 6th ed. New York: Norton, 1994.

Yong, Amos. *In the Days of Caesar: Pentecostalism and Political Theology*. Sacra Doctrina: Theology for a Postmodern Age. Grand Rapids: Eerdmans, 2010.
Young, William P. *The Shack*. Newbury Park, CA: Windblown, 2007.

Loder Bibliography

Archives

Loder, James E., Jr. Papers. Catalogued papers and manuscripts, Luce Library, Princeton Theological Seminary, Princeton, NJ.

Dissertation

Loder, James E., Jr. "The Nature of Religious Consciousness in the Writings of Sigmund Freud and Søren Kierkegaard: A Theoretical Study in the Correlation of Religious and Psychiatric Concepts." PhD diss., Harvard University, 1962.

Books

Loder, James E., Jr. *Religion in the Public Schools*. New York: Association Press, 1965.
———. *Religious Pathology and Christian Faith*. Philadelphia: Westminster, 1966.
———. *Transformation in Christian Education*. Princeton Theological Seminary (from inaugural address delivered December 12, 1979), includes response from James Lapsley, 1979.
———. *The Transforming Moment: Understanding Convictional Experiences*. San Francisco: Harper & Row, 1982.
———. *The Transforming Moment*. Rev. 2nd ed., including two additional chapters and a glossary. Colorado Springs: Helmers & Howard, 1989.
———. *The Holy Spirit and Human Transformation*. Korean translation of *The Transforming Moment*. Seoul: Yonsei University, 1993.
———. *The Logic of the Spirit: Human Development in Theological Perspective*. San Francisco: Jossey-Bass, 1998.
———. *Educational Ministry in the Logic of the Spirit*. Unpublished.
Loder, James E., Jr., and W. Jim Neidhardt. *The Knight's Move: The Relational Logic of the Spirit in Theology and Science*. Colorado Springs, CO: Helmers & Howard, 1992.
Allen, Diogenes, and James E. Loder, Jr., et al. *An Open Letter to Presbyterians: Theological Analysis of Issues Raised by the Re-imagining Conference*. Princeton Theological Seminary, 1994.

Chapters in Edited Volumes

Loder, James E., Jr. "Sociocultural Foundations for Christian Education." In *Introduction to Christian Education*, edited by M. Taylor, 71–84. Nashville: Abingdon, 1966.
———. "The Medium for the Message." In *A Colloquy on Christian Education*, edited by John Westerhoff III, 71–79. New York: Pilgrim, 1972.

———. "The Fashioning of Power: A Christian Perspective on the Life-style Phenomenon." In *The Context of Contemporary Theology: Essays in Honor of Paul Lehmann*, edited by A. J. McKelway and E. D. Willis, 187–208. Atlanta: John Knox, 1974.

———. "Developmental Foundations for Christian Education." In *Foundations for Christian Education in an Era of Change*, edited by M. Taylor, 54–67. Nashville: Abindon, 1976.

———. "Creativity in and beyond Human Development." In *Aesthetic Dimensions of Religious Education*, edited by G. Durka and J. Smith, 219–35. New York: Paulist, 1979.

———. "Negation and Transformation: A Study in Theology and Human Development." In *Toward Moral and Religious Maturity*, edited by Christiane Brusselmans et al., 165–92. Morristown, NJ: Silver Burdett, 1980.

———. "Incisions from a Two-Edged Sword: The Incarnation and the Soul/Spirit Relationship." In *The Treasure of Earthen Vessels: Explorations in Theological Anthropology in Honor of James N. Lapsley*, edited by B. Childs and D. Waanders, 151–73. Louisville: Westminster John Knox, 1994.

———. "Transformation in Christian Education" (reprint of Loder's inaugural address). In *Theological Perspectives on Christian Formation: A Reader on Theology and Christian Education*, edited by J. Astley et al., 270–84. Leominster, UK: Gracewing, 1996.

———. "Normativity and Context in Practical Theology: The 'Interdisciplinary Issue.'" In *Practical Theology: International Perspectives*, edited by F. Schweitzer and J. A. van der Ven, 359–81. New York: Peter Lang, 1999.

Loder, James E., Jr. and Jim Neidhardt. "Barth, Bohr and Dialectic" (followed by a response from Christopher Kaiser). In *Religion and Science: History, Method, Dialogue*, edited by W. Richardson et al., 271–98. New York: Routledge, 1996.

Brochures or Pamphlets

Loder, James E., Jr. *Adults in Crisis*. John Sutherland Bonnell Lecture in Pastoral Psychology. Delivered at the Fifth Ave. Presbyterian Church, New York City, November 9, 1969.

Journal Articles

Loder, James E., Jr. "Conflict Resolution in Christian Education." *The Princeton Seminary Bulletin*, o.s., 57 (1964) 19–36.

———. "The Other Mystique" (reply to M. F. Pierson). *Theology Today* 22 (1965) 283–84.

———. "Dimensions of Real Presence" (sermon). *The Princeton Seminary Bulletin*, o.s., 59 (1966) 29–35.

———. "Acts and Academia" (chapel talk). *The Princeton Seminary Bulletin*, o.s., 60 (1967) 60–62.

———. "Adults in Crisis." *The Princeton Seminary Bulletin*, o.s., 63 (1970) 32–41.

———. "The Corrective: An Educational Mandate" (chapel talk). *The Princeton Seminary Bulletin*, o.s., 68 (1976) 77–79.

———. "Transformation in Christian Education" (text of Loder's inaugural address, December 12, 1979). *The Princeton Seminary Bulletin*, n.s., 3 (1980) 11–25.

———. "Transformation in Christian Education." *Religious Education* 76 (1981) 204–21.

———. "Transformation in Liturgy and Learning." *Liturgy* 4 (1985) 39–41.

———. "The Place of Science in Practical Theology: The Human Factor." *International Journal of Practical Theology* 4 (2000) 22–41.

———. "A Meditation on Evangelism in a Scientific Culture." *The Princeton Theological Review* 8 (2001) 8–12.

———. "The Great Sex Charade and the Loss of Intimacy." *Word & World* 21 (2001) 81–87.

Loder, James E., Jr., and James W. Fowler. "Conversations on Fowler's *Stages of Faith* and Loder's *The Transforming Moment*." *Religious Education* 77 (1982) 133–48.

Loder, James E., Jr., and Mark Laaser. "Authenticating Christian Experience: A Research Request." *The Princeton Seminary Bulletin*, o.s., 66 (1973) 120–24.

Articles in Dictionaries or Encyclopedias

Loder, James E., Jr. "Creativity." In *A Dictionary of Religious Education*, edited by John M. Sutcliffe, 101–2. London: SCM in association with the Christian Education Movement, 1984.

———. "Theology and Psychology." In *The Dictionary of Pastoral Care and Counseling*, edited by Rodney Hunter, 1267–70. Nashville: Abingdon, 1990.

———. "Epistemology." In *Harper's Encyclopedia of Religious Education*, edited by Iris Cully and Kendig Cully, 219–20. San Francisco: Harper & Row, 1990.

———. "Existentialism." In *Harper's Encyclopedia of Religious Education*, edited by Iris Cully and Kendig Cully, 241–42. San Francisco: Harper & Row, 1990.

———. "Interdisciplinary Studies." In *Harper's Encyclopedia of Religious Education*, edited by Iris Cully and Kendig Cully, 327–28. San Francisco: Harper & Row, 1990.

———. "Affekt." In *Religion in Geschichte und Gegenwart*, edited by Hans Dieter Betz et al., vol. 1, col. 135. Tubingen: Mohr Siebeck, 1998–2001.

———. "Allport, Gordon." In *Religion in Geschichte und Gegenwart*, edited by Hans Dieter Betz et al., vol. 1, cols. 321–22. Tubingen: Mohr Siebeck, 1998–2001.

———. "Angst/Furcht." In *Religion in Geschichte und Gegenwart*, edited by Hans Dieter Betz et al., vol. 1, cols. 498–99. Tubingen: Mohr Siebeck, 1998–2001.

———. "Behaviorismus." In *Religion in Geschichte und Gegenwart*, edited by Hans Dieter Betz et al., vol. 1, cols. 1216–18. Tubingen: Mohr Siebeck, 1998–2001.

———. "Erfahrung." In *Religion in Geschichte und Gegenwart*, edited by Hans Dieter Betz et al., vol. 2, cols. 1505–6. Tubingen: Mohr Siebeck, 1998–2001.

———. "Funktionalismus." In *Religion in Geschichte und Gegenwart*, edited by Hans Dieter Betz et al., vol. 3, cols. 438–39. Tubingen: Mohr Siebeck, 1998–2001.

———. "Horney, Karen." In *Religion in Geschichte und Gegenwart*, edited by Hans Dieter Betz et al., vol. 3, col. 1904. Tubingen: Mohr Siebeck, 1998–2001.

———. "Paradox"; "Self-Reference." In *Encyclopedia of Science and Religion*, edited by J. W. van Huyssteen, vol. 2, 648–49; 799. New York: Macmillan, 2003.

Book Reviews

Loder, James E., Jr. *Learning in Theological Perspective*, by Charles Stinnette, Jr. *Religious Education* 61 (1966) 400–402.

———. *Pastoral Care Come of Age*, by William Hulme. *Interpretation* 25 (1971) 248–50.

———. *The Psychology of Religious Doubt*, by Philip Helfaer. *Religious Education* 69 (1974) 511–12.

———. *Origin of the Idea of Chance in Children*, by J. Piaget and B. Inhelder (translated by Lowell Leake et al). *Review of Books and Religion* 5 (1975) 13.

———. *After Therapy, What? Lay Therapeutic Resources in Religious Perspective*, edited by Neil C. Warren. Second John Finch Symposium on Psychology and Religion. *Drew Gateway* 46 (1975–76) 134–36.

———. *Parents and Peers in Social Development: A Sullivan-Piaget Perspective*, by James Youniss. *Religious Education* 76 (1981) 108–10.

———. *Transformation in Faith and Morals*, by Craig R. Dykstra. *Theology Today* 39 (1982) 56–84.

———. *The Human Mind and the Mind of God: Theological Promises in Brain Research*, by James B. Ashbrook. *Religious Education* 81 (1986) 655–56.

———. *Religious Thought and the Modern Psychologies: A Critical Conversation in the Theology of Culture*, by Don Browning. *The Princeton Seminary Bulletin*, n.s., 8 (1987) 76–79.

———. *Otherworld Journeys: Accounts of Near-Death Experiences in Medieval and Modern Times*, by Carol Zaleski. *Theology Today* 44 (1988) 525, 528–29.

———. *An Introduction to Systematic Theology*, by Wolfhart Pannenberg. *Theology Today* 49 (1993) 557–58.

———. *The "Strange Loop" of Complementarity*, by Richard H. Bube. *Perspectives on Science and Christian Faith* 45 (1993) 270–71.

———. *A Fundamental Practical Theology: Descriptions and Strategic Proposals*, by Don Browning. *The Princeton Seminary Bulletin*, n.s., 14 (1993) 327–30.

———. *Between Athens and Berlin: The Theological Education Debate*, by David Kelsey. *The Princeton Seminary Bulletin*, n.s., 16 (1995) 387–90.

———. *To Understand God Truly: What's Theological about a Theological School?*, by David Kelsey. *The Princeton Seminary Bulletin*, n.s., 16 (1995) 387–90.

———. *Kierkegaard as Humanist: Discovering My Self*, by Arnold B. Come. *Theology Today* 54 (1997) 130–34.

———. *Crisis in the Church: The Plight of Theological Education*, by John Haddon Leith. *The Princeton Seminary Bulletin* 19 (1998) 309–11.

———. *Faith of Our Foremothers: Women Changing Religious Education*, edited by Barbara Anne Keely. *Journal of Presbyterian History* 77 (1999) 135–36.

———. *Kierkegaard's Vision of the Incarnation: By Faith Transformed*, by Murray A Rae. *Theology Today* 56 (2000) 638–41.

———. *The Postfoundationalist Task of Theology: Wolfhart Pannenberg and the New Theological Rationality*, by LeRon Shults. *The Princeton Seminary Bulletin*, n.s., 21 (2000) 368–69.

Unpublished Addresses, Sermons, Lectures, etc. (chronological order)

Loder, James E., Jr. Untitled address delivered at the annual spring meeting of the Professors and Researchers in Religious Education, National Council of Churches, 1966.

———. "Adult Education and the Problem of Prejudice." February 20–23, 1967.

———. "The Place of Experience in Theology." September 30–October 3, 1974.

———. "Experiential Theology." February 2–5, 1976.

———. Whitworth Institute Lectures. Summer 1976.

———. "The Place of Experience in Theology." January 31–February 3, 1977.

———. "Relating Theology to Experience." January 9–12, 1978.

———. "Aesthetics and Christian Education" (with D. Campbell Wyckoff and Freda Gardner). November 23–25, 1981.

———. "Christian Learning and Faith Formation." January 11–14, 1982.

———. "The Christian Education of Our Times." Wyckoff colloquium, Princeton Theological Seminary, May 5, 1983.

———. "Human Development and Faith Formation." Lectures in Minneapolis, MN, October 25–28, 1983.

———. "Kierkegaard's Vision of Christian Education." January 16–19, 1984.

———. "Human Development and Faith Formation." Lectures in Winter Park, FL, March 18–22, 1985.

———. "Human Development and Faith Formation." Lectures in Newport Beach, CA, January 5–8, 1987.

———. "Theology and Human Development." January 12–15, 1987.

———. "The Creator Spirit in Faith Formation." Lectures in Seattle, WA, May 3–6, 1988.

———. "Biblical, Spiritual and Communication Growth" (with Patrick Miller and Tom Long). January 30–February 2, 1989.

———. "Christian Education in a Scientific Culture." January 8–10, 1990.

———. "The Journey of Intensification and Christian Education." April 27, 1990.

———. "Christian Education and American Lifestyles: Achievement, Authoritarian, Protean, and Oppressed." Lectures in Tulsa, OK, November 5–7, 1990.

———. "Research in Theology and Human Development." Transcription by Dana Wright of a doctoral seminar PY902, Princeton Theological Seminary, 1992.

———. "Case Study Model." Doctoral seminar PY902, Princeton Theological Seminary, 1992.

———. "Theology and the Human Sciences." Transcription by Dana Wright of a doctoral seminar, Princeton Theological Seminary, 1992.

———. "The Holy Spirit and Human Transformation." Four-part lecture delivered at Yongsei University, Seoul, Korea, summer 1992. Lecture 1, "The Dimensions of Transformation: The Damascus Reality"; Lecture 2, "The Dynamics of Transformation: The Emmaus Vision"; Lecture 3, "The Direction of Transformation: The Golgotha Mirror"; Lecture 4, "Discernment and Transformation: The Eye of God."

———. "The Crux of Christian Education." Faculty seminar paper, Princeton Theological Seminary, 1993.

———. "The Philosophy of Education." Transcription by Dana Wright of a doctoral seminar, Princeton Theological Seminary, 1993.

———. "Pressing Issues Facing Practical Theology in the Twenty-first Century." Lecture given in the Reigner Reading Room, Princeton Theological Seminary, October 21, 1993.

———. "The Educational Ministry." Transcription of ED 105, Princeton Theological Seminary, 1993–2000 (multiple renditions).

———. "Theology of Faith and Human Development." Summer course at Fuller Theological Seminary, 1994.

———. "Christian Education in the Spirit of Christ." Paper delivered at the annual conference of the National Association of the Professors of Christian Education, Chicago, 1995.

———. "Casebook for ED215." Folder of verbatims, 1995.

———. "Theology and Human Development." Transcription by Dana Wright of ED216 lectures, 1999.

———. "The Relevance of Kierkegaard: Attack on Christendom, 1854–1855." 1999.

———. "Training in Christianity." Seven essays by Loder and his students for ED583, Princeton Theological Seminary, 1999.

———. "Christian Spirituality in Christian Education." No date.

———. "Revelation as a Way of Knowing." No date.

———. "Teaching as the Act of Creation." No date.

———. "Transformed Dialectical Hermeneutics: An Outline of a Method of Interpreting Experience in Relation to Christ's Presence." No date.

———. "From Organism to Universe: Nature and the Constructive Capacities of the Human Spirit in Jean Piaget: (A) Piaget, (b) Polanyi." No date.

———. "Transformational Dynamics in Christian Education." Projected book outline, 22 chapters. No date.

Audio Tapes (Princeton Seminary Media Archive)

Loder, James E., Jr. "Meaning in the Middle Years of Life. Current Issues in Ministry." June 6, 1963.

———. "Sex Identification and Education. Presuppositions about Education: Sex in Theological Context." Institute of Theology, July 8, 1968.

———. "Sex Identification and Education. The Problem of Authority: That Which Is Inside a Person." Institute of Theology, July 9, 1968.

———. "Sex Identification and Education. The Issue of Achievement Orientation." Institute of Theology, July 10, 1968.

———. "Sex Identification and Education. Communicating with Adolescents." Institute of Theology, July 11, 1968.

———. "Aggression and Reconciliation: A Psycho-Social Perspective. The Aggression Factor: Its Nature and Role in Reconciliation." Institute of Theology, July 6, 1970.

———. "Aggression and Reconciliation: A Psycho-Social Perspective. Patterns of Socializing Aggression." Institute of Theology, July 7, 1970.

———. "Aggression and Reconciliation: A Psycho-Social Perspective. Ways to Reverse Self-Destructive Socialization Patterns." Institute of Theology, July 8, 1970.

———. "Aggression and Reconciliation: A Psycho-Social Perspective. Teaching the Transformation of Aggression into Creative Patterns of Behavior and Interaction." Institute of Theology, July 9, 1970.

———. "Experiential Theology. The Structure of Convictional Experience." Institute of Theology, July 7, 1975.

———. "Experiential Theology. The Dynamics of Convictional Experience." Institute of Theology, July 8, 1975.

———. "Experiential Theology. The Nature of the Enemy." Institute of Theology, July 9, 1975.

———. "Experiential Theology. Our Fear of Grace." Institute of Theology, July 10, 1975.

———. "God and Psychotherapy." Given to the C. S. Lewis Society of Princeton, April 6, 1979.

———. "Religious Experience in Theology." Theological Forum, November 28, 1979.
———. "Transformation in Christian Education" (inaugural address). December 12, 1979.
———. "Faith and Human Development, Part I." Institute of Theology, July 1, 1980.
———. "Faith and Human Development, Part II." Institute of Theology, July 2, 1980.
———. "Faith and Human Development, Part III." Institute of Theology, July 3, 1980.
———. "Faith and Human Development, Part IV." Institute of Theology, July 4, 1980.
———. "The Holy Spirit vs. the Seminarian." Theological Forum, December 8, 1982.
———. "Sermon" (untitled). Small Church Symposium, September 13, 1983.
———. Lecture I (Alumni/ae reunion), May 30, 1991.
———. Lecture II (Alumni/ae reunion), May 30, 1991.
———. Lecture III (Alumni/ae reunion), May 31, 1991.
———. "The Creator Spirit in Faith Formation." Seminar Series, University Presbyterian Church, Seattle, WA, May 5–7, 1997. Lecture 1, "Dimensions: Damascus Reality"; Lecture 2, "Dynamics: Emmaus Vision"; Lecture 3, "Direction: The Golgotha Mirror"; Lecture 4, "Denouement: Betrayal Betrayed"; Lecture 5, "Discernment: The Eye of God."

Audio Tapes (Academic Technology Center, Fuller Theological Seminary)

Loder, James E., Jr. "Theology of Faith and Human Development" (CN531). No date. Tape one, #2844ab.
———. "Theology of Faith and Human Development" (CN531). No date. Tape two, #2845ab.
———, and David Augsburger. "Interdisciplinary Reflections on Kierkegaard." July 19, 2000. Tape #2943.

Audio Tapes (miscellaneous)

Loder, James E., Jr. "The Creator Spirit and Faith Formation." Five-part course given through Continuing Education, Seattle, WA, 1988. Tapes held by Dana Wright.
———. "The Holy Spirit and Human Transformation" (5 parts). India Sunday School Union. Bangalore, Coonoor, Bombay, Calcutta, and New Delhi, June/July 1997. Lecture 1, "The Dimensions of Transformation"; Lecture 2, "The Dynamics of Transformation"; Lecture 3, "The Direction of Transformation"; Lecture 4, "The Denouement: Betrayal Betrayed"; Lecture 5, "The Discernment: The Eye of God." Held by Ajit A. Prasadam.

Video Tapes

Loder, James E., Jr. "The Transforming Moment" (videocassette, 24 mins.). Interview by Laura Lewis (Austin Theological Seminary) at Presbyterian School of Christian Education, Video Education Center, 1985, #1232. Held in Reigner Reading Room, Princeton Theological Seminary.
———. Christmas Party at the Loder home. December 5, 1998. One copy held at the Reigner Reading Room, Princeton Theological Seminary.

———. "James E. Loder on Prayer." Seven-part series taped for *Mountain Views*, a television program of Drew Seminary, Madison, NJ, with Angela Pak Sun. Held in Reigner Reading Room, Princeton Theological Seminary (n.n). Part 1, "The Prayer of Thanksgiving" (shown November 17, 2001); Part 2, "The Prayer of Confession" (shown November 24, 2001); Part 3, "The Prayer of Covenant" (shown December 1, 2001); Part 4, "The Prayer of Petition" (shown December 8, 2001); Part 5, "The Prayer of Intercession" (shown December 15, 2001); Part 6, "The Prayer of Adoration" (shown December 22, 2001); Part 7, "The Prayer of Healing" (shown December 29, 2001).

Bibliographies

Loder, James E. Jr. "Annotated Bibliography of the Educational Disciplines." Unpublished.
Loder, James E., Jr., and F. LeRon Shults. "Annotated Bibliography for Practical Theology and Interdisciplinary Method." 1999.

Interviews of James E. Loder Jr. (audio or video)

James E. Loder Jr. Audio tape interviews by Dana Wright (approximately 8 hours). April/May 2001. Held by Dana Wright; transcribed.
———. "Seven Types of Prayer." Interview by Angela Pak Sun for the television program *Mountain Views*, Sun Young Joo, Executive Producer. September/October 2001. Seven-part series.

Catechisms

Loder, James E., Jr. "Belonging to God: A First Catechism." No date.

Kierkegaard Research

Loder's considerable research on Kierkegaard is held in the Loder Archive at Princeton Theological Seminary.

Secondary Sources

PhD or DMin Dissertations Discussing James E. Loder's Work (chronological order)

Bateson, C. Daniel. "Creativity and Religious Development: Toward a Structual/Functional Psychology of Religion." ThD diss., Princeton Theological Semianry, 1971.
Nichols, John Randall. "Conflict and Creativity: The Dynamics of the Communication Process in Theological Perspective." PhD diss., Princeton Theological Seminary, 1971.
Conrad, Robert Leroy. "Christian Education and Creative Conflict: Relations between Creative Intra-psychic Conflict as Understood in Luther's Experience and Theology and as Understood in Social Psychological Theories with Conclusions for Christian

Education Principles and Practice." PhD diss., Princeton Theological Seminary, 1975.

Dykstra, Craig R. "Christian Education and the Moral Life: An Evaluation of and Alternative to Kohlberg/Piaget?" PhD diss., Princeton Theological Seminary, 1978.

Schipani, Daniel S. "Conscientization and Creativity: A Reinterpretation of Paulo Freire, Focused on His Epistemological and Theological Foundations with Implications for Christian Education." PhD diss., Princeton Theological Seminary, 1981.

Goldstein, Robert Morris. "On Christian Rhetoric: The Significance of Søren Kierkegaard's 'Dialectic of Ethical and Ethical-Religious Communication' for Philosophical and Theological Pedagogy." PhD diss., Princeton Theological Seminary, 1982.

Tiller, Darryl J. "Pastoral Counseling: A Means through which God Brings Salvation to the Lives of the People." PhD diss., Louisville Presbyterian Theological Seminary (primary advisor David Steere), 1983.

Johnson, Susanne. "Religious Experience as Creative, Revelatory and Transforming Event: The Implications of Intense Christian Experience for the Christian Educational Process." PhD diss., Princeton Theological Seminary, 1984.

Moyer, David Lloyd. "Making Christ Our Head: The Transformation of a Parish Environment." DMin thesis, Princeton Theological Seminary, 1984.

Krych, Margaret Anne. "Communicating Justification to Elementary-Age Children: A Study in Tillich's Correlational Method and Transformational Narrative for Christian Education." PhD diss., Princeton Theological Seminary, 1985.

Harkey, Martin Luther, III. "A Theology for the Ministry of Volunteers: With Reference to Calvin's Doctrine of Vocation, and with Particular Focus on Developing Leadership for Christian Education in the Congregation." PhD diss., Princeton Theological Seminary, 1985.

Heywood, David S. "Revelation and Christian Learning." PhD diss., University of Durham. 1989.

Frykberg, Elizabeth Anne. "Spiritual Transformation and the Creation of Humankind in the Image of God, Male and Female: A Study of Karl Barth's Understanding of the *Analogia Relationis* Correlated with Psychosexual and Psychosocial Developmental Theory." PhD diss., Princeton Theological Seminary, 1990.

Hess, Carol Lakey. "Educating in the Spirit." PhD diss., Princeton Theological Seminary, 1990.

Hess, Ernest P. "Christian Identity and Openness: A Theologically Informed Hermeneutical Approach to Christian Education." PhD diss., Princeton Theological Seminary, 1991.

Rogers, Frank, Jr. "Karl Barth's Faith Epistemology of the Spirit as a Critical Constructive Framework for Christian Education." PhD diss., Princeton Theological Seminary, 1991.

Hancock, Aubrey Perry. "An Investigation of the Element of Conversion in the Faith Development Theories of James Loder and James Fowler with Implications for Adolescent Christian Education." EdD diss., New Orleans Baptist Theological Seminary, 1992.

Barker, Patrick Morgan. "Toward a Model of Pastoral Care and Counseling Based upon the Work of James Loder." PhD diss., School of Theology at Claremont, 1993.

Wigger, James Bradley. "Texture and Trembling: A Theological Inquiry into Perception and Learning." PhD diss., Princeton Theological Seminary, 1992.

Lee, James Douglas. "Petitionary Prayer as Transformation: Finding God's Hidden Presence in the Hospital." DMin thesis, Princeton Theological Seminary, 1993.

Cook, Carol Jean. "Singing a New Song: Relationality as a Context for Identity Development, Growth in Faith, and Christian Education." PhD diss., Princeton Theological Seminary, 1994.

Reader, Jimmy Lee. "Life-Changing Bible Reading: A Model for Transformational Reading of Scripture." DMin thesis, Princeton Theological Seminary, 1994.

Martin, Robert Keith. "The Incarnate Ground of Christian Education: The Integration of Epistemology and Ontology in the Thought of Michael Polanyi and Thomas F. Torrance." PhD diss., Princeton Theological Seminary, 1995.

Reese, Daniel Brian. "The Feast of Wisdom: Thomas Merton's Vision and Practice of a Sapiential Education." PhD diss., Princeton Theological Seminary, 1995.

Balmer, Brice. "Spiritual Transformation in Addicted Men: Spirituality and Addiction." DMin thesis, University of St. Michaels College (Canada), 1996.

Lee, Kyoo-Min. "Koinonia: A Critical Study of Lewis Sherrill's Concept of Koinonia and Jürgen Moltmann's Social Understanding of the Trinity as an Attempt to Provide a Corrective to the Problems of the Korean Church and Its Educational Ministry." PhD diss., Princeton Theological Seminary, 1996.

Pooler, Alfred D. "Images That Move Us: The Power of Metaphor in Spiritual Transformation." PhD diss., Catholic Theological Union (primary advisor Robert Schreiter), 1996.

Spencer, Gary Allen. "A Study of the Founders at Suntree United Methodist Church, Congregation, Florida." DMin thesis, Princeton Theological Seminary, 1996.

Turner, David. "Story and Vision: Shared Praxis in Service to an Institutional Mission." DMin thesis, Princeton Theological Seminary, 1996.

Brown, Sanford Webster. "Creating and Testing a Church Curriculum Resource for the Study of Men's Spirituality Based on the Jacob to Israel Story." DMin thesis, Princeton Theological Seminary, 1997.

Gorsuch, Gregory Scott. "*Analogia Spiritus*—Eternity in Our Hearts: Relational Dynamics and the Logic of the Spirit: An Interdisciplinary Inquiry into the Tripartite Structure and Irreducible Dynamics of *Perichoresis* in Person, Community, and Trinity." PhD diss., University of Edinburgh, 1999.

Kuentzel, John Douglas. "The Ethic of Care and Christian Education: Implications for the Theory and Practice of Christian Education." PhD diss., Princeton Theological Seminary, 1999.

Wright, Dana Rogan. "Ecclesial Theatrics. Toward a Reconstruction of Evangelical Christian Education Theory as Critical Dogmatic Practical Theology: The Relevance of a Second 'Barthian Reckoning' for Reconceiving the Evangelical Protestant Educational Imagination at the Metatheoretical Level." PhD diss., Princeton Theological Seminary, 1999.

Fredrickson, Johnna Lee. "Iconic Christian Education: Pointing to and Participating in the Reality of God." PhD diss., Princeton Theological Seminary, 2000.

Buckles, Susan, M. "The Perichoretic Ministry of the Holy Spirit in Formation and Transformation of Persons in the Thought of James E. Loder and Thomas F. Torrance." PhD diss., Fuller Theological Seminary, 2001.

Fairless, John Patrick. "The Meaning of the Meal." DMin thesis, Princeton Theological Seminary, 2001.

Forster-Smith, Lucy Ann. "A Grammar of Transformation: Language Used by Non-religiously Affiliated College Students in Describing Life-Changing Experiences." DMin thesis, Princeton Theological Seminary, 2001.

Frawley, Matthew J. "Søren Kierkegaard's Christian Anthropology and the Relation between His Pseudonymous and Religious Writings." PhD diss., Princeton Theological Seminary, 2001.

Hess, Lisa Maguire. "Practices in a New Key: Human Knowing in Musical and Practical Theological Perspective." PhD diss., Princeton Theological Seminary, 2001.

Park, Sang-Jin. "A Curriculum Model of Christian Education for Faith as Knowing God: A Critique of the Tylerian Model and a Search for an Alternative on the Basis of New Epistemology." PhD diss., Union Theological Seminary and the Presbyterian School of Christian Education, 2001.

Hastings, Thomas John. "Practical Theology and the One Body of Christ: Toward a Missional-Ecumenical Model." PhD diss., Princeton Theological Seminary, 2003.

Kovacs, Kenneth. "The Relational Phenomenological Pneumatology of James E. Loder: Providing New Frameworks for the Christian Life." PhD diss., St. Andrews University, 2003.

Boyd-MacMillan, Eolene. "Christian Transformation: An Engagement with James Loder, Mystical Spirituality, and James Hillman." PhD diss., Cambridge University, 2004.

Prasadam, Ajit A. "Beyond Conscientization: James E. Loder's Transformational Model for Christian Education in the Indian Context and Beyond." PhD diss., Princeton Theological Seminary, 2005.

Boyd-MacMillan, Ron. "The Transforming Sermon: A Study of the Preaching of St. Augustine with Special Reference to the *Sermons ad Populum* and the Transformation Theory of James Loder." PhD diss., University of Aberdeen, 2009.

Kunz, Sandra Costen. "Sustaining Redemptive Social Action: Intertwining Zen and Ignatian Meditation for Christian Discernment." PhD diss., Princeton Theological Seminary, 2008.

McDowell, Scott A. "Desired Outcomes for College Students' Spiritual Development in Select Church of Christ Universities." PhD diss., Azusa Pacific University, 2009.

So, Tai Young. "Teaching as Creating Harmony Out of Difference: The Role of Imagination in Christian Education." PhD diss., Claremont Graduate School, 2009.

Javore, Barbara B. "In Partnership with God: Recovering Creativity in the Methods and Practices of Christian Education. PhD diss., Garrett-Evangelical Theological Seminary, 2011.

Kim, Brian Byung Joo. "Correlation between Transformative Learning and Cultural Context: A Case Study of Adult Participants in a Korean American Immigrant Congregation." PhD diss., Trinity Evangelical Divinity School, 2011.

Procario-Foley, Carl Boswell. "The Teaching of Solidarity in Catholic Higher Education: Engaging Hearts, Transforming Lives, Changing Society." PhD diss., Fordham University, 2011.

Discussions of Loder's Work in Books and Journals

Adams, Marilyn McCord. "Biting and Chomping Our Salvation: Eucharistic Presence, Radically Reconceived." In *Redemptive Transformation in Practical Theology: Essays in Honor of James E. Loder Jr.*, edited by Dana R. Wright and John D. Kuentzel, 69–94. Grand Rapids: Eerdmans, 2004.

Anderson, Paul. *The Christology of the Fourth Gospel: Its Unity and Disunity in Light of John Six*. Harrisburg, PA: Trinity, 1995. Reissued by Wipf & Stock, 2010.

———. "The Cognitive Origin of John's Christological Unity and Disunity." In *Psychology and the Bible: A New Way to Read the Scriptures*, edited by J. Harold Ellens and Wayne Rollins, 3:127–149. Westport, CT: Praeger, 2004. First published in *Horizons in Biblical Theology* 17 (1995) 1–24.

———. *The Riddle of the Fourth Gospel: An Introduction to John*. Minneapolis: Fortress, 2011.

Anderson, Ray. *The Shape of Practical Theology: Empowering the Ministry of Theological Praxis*. Downers Grove, IL: InterVarsity, 2001.

Balswick, Jack, et al. *The Reciprocating Self: Human Development in Theological Perspective*. Downers Grove, IL: InterVarsity, 2005.

Barker, Patrick. "The Relevance of James Loder's Grammar of Transformation for Pastoral Care and Counseling." *Journal of Pastoral Care* 49 (1995) 158–66.

Batson, C. Daniel, et al. *Commitment without Ideology: The Experience of Christian Growth*. Philadelphia: Pilgrim, 1973 (acknowledgment of authors' debt to Loder only).

———, and Larry Ventis. *The Religious Experience: A Social-Psychological Study*. New York: Oxford University Press, 1982. Reprinted as *Religion and the Individual: A Social-Psychological Perspective*. New York: Oxford University Press, 1993.

Berryman, Jerome. *Godly Play: An Imaginative Approach to Religious Education*. San Francisco: Harper & Row, 1991.

———. *The Spiritual Guidance of Children: Montessori, Godly Play, and the Future*. New York: Morehouse, 2013.

———, et al. "Comments on the Articles by Eugene J. Mischey." In *Character Potential: A Record of Research* 9 (1981) 175–91. Reprinted in *Christian Perspectives on Faith Development: A Reader*, edited by J. Astley and L. Francis, 192–200. Leominster, UK: Gracewing, 1992.

Blevins, Dean G. "Worship, Formation and Discernment: A Wesleyan Dialogue between Worship and Christian Education." *Wesleyan Theological Journal* 33 (1998) 111–27.

Bolt, John. "Theological Abstracts." *Calvin Theological Journal* 32 (1997) 220–30

Borgman, Dean. "Bridging the Gap: From Social Science to Congregations, Researchers to Practitioners." In *The Handbook of Spiritual Development in Childhood and Adolescence*, edited by Eugene C. Roehlkepartain et al., 458–72. Thousand Oaks, CA: SAGE, 2006.

———. *Foundations for Youth Ministry*. Grand Rapids: Baker Academic, 2013.

Boyd-MacMillan, Eolene. "Awkward Relations: Should the Field of Spirituality Distance Itself from Theology?" *Council of Societies for the Study of Religion Bulletin* 33 (2004) 61–68.

———. "Loder and Mystical Spirituality: Particularity, Universality and Intelligence." In *Redemptive Transformation in Practical Theology: Essays in Honor of James E. Loder Jr.*, edited by Dana R. Wright and John D. Kuentzel, 373–400. Grand Rapids: Eerdmans, 2004.

———. "More than Collaboration." *The Way* 43 (2004) 29–40.

———. *Transformation: James E. Loder, Mystical Spirituality, and James Hillman*. Transformation and Discourse Series 31. New York: Peter Lang, 2006.

---. "Vision in the Eye of the Beholder: Translation or Transformation?" In *Dreams and Visions*, edited by N. van Deusen, 299–312. Leiden: Brill, 2010.
Bube, Richard. "The 'Strange Loop' of Complementarity." Review of *The Knight's Move: The Relational Logic of the Spirit in Theology and Science*, by James E. Loder, Jr., and W. Jim Neidhardt. *Perspectives on Science and Christian Faith* 45 (1993) 270–71.
Click, Emily. "Transformative Education Theory in Relation to Supervision and Training in Ministry." *Journal of Supervision and Training in Ministry* 25 (2005) 8–25.
Conde-Frazier, Elizabeth, et al. *A Many-Colored Kingdom: Multicultural Dynamics for Spiritual Formation*. Grand Rapids: Baker Academic, 2004.
Cubie, James. "Both—And? Natural Theology in James Loder: A Response to Michael Langford." In *Koinonia: The Princeton Theological Seminary Graduate Forum* 18, edited by Keith Johnson, 27–34. Princeton: Princeton Seminary, 2006.
Dean, Kenda Creasy. *Almost Christian: What the Faith of Our Teenagers Is Telling the American Church*. New York: Oxford University Press, 2010.
---. *Practicing Passion: Youth and the Quest for a Passionate Church*. Grand Rapids: Eerdmans, 2004.
Demarest, Bruce. *Seasons of the Soul: Stages of Faith Development*. Downers Grove, IL: InterVarsity, 2009.
Duckworth, Jessicah K., and Susan B. Willhauck. "Memory, Identity and Hope: The Exile and Christian Formation." In *Strangers in a Strange Land: A Festschrift in Honor of Bruce C. Birch*, edited by Lucy H. Hogan and D. William Faupel, 51–58. Lexington, KY: Emeth, 2009.
Dykstra, Craig R. *Growing in the Faith: Education and Christian Practices*. Louisville: Geneva, 1999.
---. "Transformation in Faith and Morals." Review of *The Transforming Moment: Understanding Convictional Experiences*, by James E. Loder, Jr. *Theology Today* 39 (1982) 56–64.
---. *Vision and Character: A Christian Educator's Alternative to Kohlberg*. New York: Paulist, 1981
---, and Sharon Parks. *Faith Development and Fowler*. Birmingham, AL: Religious Education Press, 1986.
Engelmann, Kim V. *Running in Circles: How False Spirituality Traps Us in Unhealthy Relationships*. Downers Grove, IL: InterVarsity, 2007.
Engen, Charles E. van, et al. *Footprints of God: A Narrative Theology of Mission*. Pasadena, CA: William Carey Library, 2013.
Erdman, Daniel. "Liberation and Identity: Indo-Hispano Youth." *Religious Education* 78 (1983) 76–89.
Estep, James, et al. *Mapping Out Curriculum in Your Church: A Cartography for Christian Pilgrims*. Nashville: B & H, 2012.
---, and Jonathan Kim, eds. *Christian Formation: Integrating Theology and Human Development*. Nashville: B & H, 2010.
Faber, Heije. "Zicht op de Structuur van de Godsdienstige Ervaring: Twee Boeken (J. E. Loder; J. Scharfenberg and H. Kampfer)." *Nederlands Theolische Tijdschrift* 36 (1982) 311–31.
Frawley, Matthew. "Loder on Kierkegaard." *The Princeton Theological Review* (2000) 8–16.
Frykberg, Elizabeth. "Karl Barth's Theological Anthropology: An Analogical Critique Regarding Gender Relations." *Studies in Reformed Theology and History* 1 (1993) 1–54.

Gaventa, William C. "Singing the Lord's Song in a Foreign Land: A Theoretical Foundation for Growth and Education in the CPE Process." *Journal of Supervision and Training in Ministry* 8 (1986) 21–32.

Gilbert, Kenyatta. "The Prophetic and the Priestly: Reclaiming Preaching in Practical Theology." *Koinonia* 16 (2004) 118–39.

Grannell, Andrew. "The Paradox of Formation and Transformation." *Religious Education* 80 (1985) 384–98.

Groome, Thomas. "Old Task: Urgent Challenge." Response to William Kennedy, "Pursuing Peace and Justice: A Challenge to Religious Educators." *Religious Education* 78 (1983) 492–96.

Gushiken, Kevin M. "Nurturing Spiritual Identity-Formation in Youth Curriculum from the Theological-Psychological Approach of James Loder." *Christian Education Journal* 7 (2010) 319–33.

Haitch, Russell. "A Summary of James E. Loder's Theory of Christian Education." In *Redemptive Transformation in Practical Theology: Essays in Honor of James E. Loder Jr.*, edited by Dana R. Wright and John D. Kuentzel, 298–324. Grand Rapids: Eerdmans, 2004.

———. "Trampling Down Death by Death: Double Negation in Developmental Theory and Baptismal Theology." In *Redemptive Transformation in Practical Theology: Essays in Honor of James E. Loder Jr.*, edited by Dana R. Wright and John D. Kuentzel, 43–68. Grand Rapids: Eerdmans, 2004.

Hampson, P., and Eolene Boyd-MacMillan. "Turning the Telescope Round: Reciprocity in Psychology-Theology Dialogue." *Archive for the International Journal of Psychology and Religion* 30 (2008) 93–113.

Hastings, Thomas J. "Lindbeck and Thomas F. Torrance on Christian Language and the Knowledge of God." In *Redemptive Transformation in Practical Theology: Essays in Honor of James E. Loder* Jr., edited by Dana R. Wright and John D. Kuentzel, 252–78. Grand Rapids: Eerdmans, 2004.

———. *Practical Theology and the One Body of Christ: Toward a Missional-Ecumenical Model.* Grand Rapids: Eerdmans, 2007.

Heywood, David. "Piaget and Faith Development." *British Journal of Religious Education* 8 (1986) 72–78. Reprinted in *Christian Perspectives on Faith Development*, edited by J. Astley and L. Francis, 153–62. Leominster, UK: Gracewing, 1992.

Hess, Carol Lakey. "Abomination and Creativity: Shaking the Order of the Cosmos." *The Princeton Seminary Bulletin*, n.s., 15 (1994) 28–43.

———. "Educating in the Spirit." *Religious Education* 86 (1991) 383–98.

———. "Educating in the Spirit." In *Theological Perspectives on Christian Formation*, edited by J. Astley and J. Crowder. Leominster, UK: Gracewing, 1996.

Heywood, David. *Divine Revelation and Human Learning: A Christian Theory of Knowledge.* London: Ashgate, 2004.

House, Renee R. "An Ecclesiological Hunch." *Koinonia: The Princeton Theological Seminary Graduate Forum* 18, edited by Keith Johnson, 35–40. Princeton: Princeton Seminary, 2006

Jacober, Amy E. *The Adolescent Journey: An Interdisciplinary Approach to Practical Youth Ministry.* Downers Grove, IL: InterVarsity, 2011.

Johnson, Keith. "Editorial: Raising Expectations." In *Koinonia: The Princeton Theological Seminary Graduate Forum* 18, edited by Keith Johnson, i–iv. Princeton: Princeton Seminary, 2006.

Johnson, Susanne. *Christian Spiritual Formation in the Church and Classroom.* Nashville: Abingdon, 1985.

———. "Remembering the Poor: Transforming Christian Practice." In *Redemptive Transformation in Practical Theology: Essays in Honor of James E. Loder Jr.*, edited by Dana R. Wright and John D. Kuentzel, 189–215. Grand Rapids: Eerdmans, 2004.

———. "Subversive Spirituality in Youth Ministry at the Margins." In *Children, Youth and Ministry in a Troubling World*, edited by Mary Elizabeth Moore and Almeda Wright, 153–67. St. Louis: Chalice, 2008.

Jones, Tony. *The Church Is Flat: The Relational Ecclesiology of the Emerging Church Movement.* Minneapolis: JoPa, 2011.

Kaiser, Christopher. "Quantum Complementarity and Christological Dialectic." In *Religion and Science: History, Method, Dialogue*, edited by W. Mark Richardson and Wesley J. Wildman, 291–98. New York: Routledge, 1996.

Keulen, Dirk van, and M. E. Brinkman. *Christian Faith and Violence.* Vol. 1. Zeotermeer: Meinema, 2005.

Koenig, Matthew. "Introduction: Essays in Honor of James E. Loder." *The Princeton Theological Review* (2000) 3.

Koonz, Mark S. "Christian Psychology and the Transformational Logic of James E. Loder: An Overview with a Response to Criticism." *Edification: A Transdisciplinary Journal of Christian Psychology* 5 (2011) 57–65.

———. "Matters of the Heart: James E. Loder on Homosexuality and the Possibility of Transformation." In *Embracing Truth: Homosexuality and the Word of God*, edited by David W. Torrance and Jock Stein, 196–217. Edinburgh: Handsel, 2012.

———. "Prayer and the Cure of Souls in James E. Loder's Counseling Ministry." *Edification: A Transdisciplinary Journal of Christian Psychology* 5 (2011) 66–74.

Kovacs, Ken. *The Relational Theology of James E. Loder: Encounter and Conviction.* New York: Peter Lang, 2011.

Krych, Margaret. *Teaching the Gospel Today: A Guide for Education in the Congregation.* Minneapolis: Augsburg, 1987.

———. "Transformational Narrative in a Non-transformational Tradition." In *Redemptive Transformation in Practical Theology: Essays in Honor of James E. Loder Jr.*, edited by Dana R. Wright and John D. Kuentzel, 279–97. Grand Rapids: Eerdmans, 2004.

Kuentzel, John D. "The Heidegger in Loder (or, How the Nothing Became the Void): Provoking Wonder in Education." In *Redemptive Transformation in Practical Theology: Essays in Honor of James E. Loder Jr.*, edited by Dana R. Wright and John D. Kuentzel, 347–72. Grand Rapids: Eerdmans, 2004.

Kunz, Sandra Costen. "Imagination and the Discernment of Nonviolent Solutions to Problems of Injustice: Possible Applications of the Work of James Loder to Public Peace Education." In *Studies in Reformed Theology: Christian Faith and Violence*, edited by Dick van Keulen and Martien E. Brinkman, 293–308. Zoetermeer: Meinema, 2005.

———. "Reflections on *Koinonia*'s 2006 Forum: Loder and Interdisicplinary Method." In *Koinonia: The Princeton Theological Seminary Graduate Forum* 18, edited by Keith Johnson, 1–4. Princeton: Princeton Seminary, 2006.

———. "Respecting the Boundaries of Knowledge: Teaching Christian Discernment with Humility and Dignity." *Buddhist-Christian Studies* 31 (2011) 175–86.

———. "Teaching Students to Embody Redemptive Social Transformation: Christian Education Theory and Methods for Higher Education." Paper delivered at the

Metanexus Conference, "Science and Religion: Global Perspectives," Philadelphia, PA, June 4–8, 2005.

Lam, Brian K. B. "Transition, Transformation, and True Community: A Spirituality of Mentoring." *Hill Road* 15 (2012) 135–59.

Langford, Michael D. "A Very Present Help: James E. Loder's Trinitarian Soteriology and Adolescent Identity Formation." In *Koinonia: The Princeton Theological Seminary Graduate Forum* 18, edited by Keith Johnson, 5–18. Princeton: Princeton Seminary, 2006.

———. "Response to the Respondents." In *Koinonia: The Princeton Theological Seminary Graduate Forum* 18, edited by Keith Johnson, 41–48. Princeton: Princeton Seminary, 2006.

Lumsden, Scott. "Theology That Matters! James Loder's Significance for Pastoral Ministry." *The Princeton Theological Review* (2000) 4–7.

Martin, Robert K. *The Incarnate Ground of Christian Faith: Toward a Christian Theological Epistemology for the Educational Ministry of the Church*. Lanham, MD: University Press of America, 1998.

———. "Leadership and Serendipitous Discipleship: A Case Study of Congregational Transformation." In *Redemptive Transformation in Practical Theology: Essays in Honor of James E. Loder Jr.*, edited by Dana R. Wright and John D. Kuentzel, 133–52. Grand Rapids: Eerdmans, 2004.

May, Scottie, et al. *Children Matter: Celebrating Their Place in the Church, Family, and Community*. Grand Rapids: Eerdmans, 2005.

May, Scottie, and Don Ratcliff. "Children's Spiritual Experiences and the Brain." In *Children's Spirituality: Christian Perspectives, Research and Applications*, edited by Don Ratcliff et al., 149–65. Eugene, OR: Cascade, 2004.

McClure, John S. *The Four Codes of Preaching: Rhetorical Strategies*. Louisville: Westminster John Knox, 2004.

———. *Mashup Religion: Pop Music and Theological Invention*. Waco: Baylor University Press, 2011.

———. *Preaching Words: 144 Key Terms in Homiletics*. Louisville: Westminster John Knox, 2010.

———. "The Way of Love: Loder, Levinas and Ethical Transformation through Preaching." In *Redemptive Transformation in Practical Theology: Essays in Honor of James E. Loder Jr.*, edited by Dana R. Wright and John D. Kuentzel, 95–115. Grand Rapids: Eerdmans, 2004.

Meek, Esther Lightcap. *A Little Manual for Knowing*. Eugene, OR: Cascade, 2014.

———. *Loving to Know: Covenant Epistemology*. Eugene, OR: Cascade, 2011.

———. "Take Off Your Two-Dimensional Glasses." http://commongroundssonline.typepad.com/common_grounds_online/2007/12/eshter-I-meek-t.html.

Mezirow, Jack. *Transformative Dimensions of Adult Learning*. San Francisco: Jossey-Bass, 1991.

———. *Learning as Transformation: Critical Perspectives on a Theory in Progress*. San Francisco: Jossey-Bass, 2000.

Mikoski, Gordon S. *Baptism and Christian Identity: Teaching in the Triune Name*. Grand Rapids: Eerdmans, 2009.

———. "Educating and Forming Disciples for the Reign of God: Reflections on Youth Pilgrimage to the Holy Land." In *For Life Abundant: Practical Theology, Theological Education and Christian Ministry*, edited by Dorothy Bass and Craig R. Dykstra, 329–52. Grand Rapids: Eerdmans, 2008.

———. "The Flowering of Practical Theology in the McCord and Gillespie Years." In *With Piety and Learning: The History of Practical Theology at Princeton Theological Seminary, 1812–2012*, 133–77 (esp. 148–63). Berlin: LIT, 2011.

———. "Mainline Protestantism." In *The Wiley-Blackwell Companion to Practical Theology*, edited by Bonnie Miller-McLemore, 557–66. Hoboken, NJ: Wiley-Blackwell, 2014.

———, and Richard Osmer. *With Piety and Learning: The History of Practical Theology at Princeton Theological Seminary, 1812–2012*. Berlin: LIT, 2011.

Moorhead, James H. "Princeton and Deepening Pluralism, 1959–2004." In *Princeton Seminary in American Religion and Culture*, 458–502. Grand Rapids: Eerdmans, 2012.

Morton, Nelle. Review of *Religious Pathology and the Christian Faith*, by James E. Loder, Jr. *The Princeton Seminary Bulletin*, o.s., 60 (1967) 74–83.

Nelson, C. Ellis. *How Faith Matures*. Louisville: Westminister John Knox, 1989.

Newell, Edward J. *"Education Has Nothing to Do with Theology": James Michael Lee's Social Science of Religious Instruction*. Eugene, OR: Pickwick, 2006.

Osmer, Richard R. "Foreword." In *Redemptive Transformation in Practical Theology: Essays in Honor of James E. Loder Jr.*, edited by Dana R. Wright and John D. Kuentzel, ix–xi. Grand Rapids: Eerdmans, 2004.

———. "James W. Fowler and the Reformed Tradition: An Exercise in Theological Reflection in Religious Education." *Religious Education* 85 (1990) 51–68.

———. "Practical Theology: A Current International Perspective." *HTS* 67 (2011). http://www.hts.org.za/index.php/HTS/article/view/1058.

———. *Practical Theology: An Introduction*. Grand Rapids: Eerdmans, 2008.

———. "Rationality in Practical Theology: A Map of the Emerging Discussion." *International Journal of Practical Theology* 1 (1997) 11–40.

———. "Toward a Transversal Model of Interdisciplinary Thinking in Practical Theology." In *The Evolution of Rationality: Interdisciplinary Essays in Honor of J. Wentzel van Huyssteen*, edited by F. LeRon Shults, 327–45. Grand Rapids: Eerdmans, 2006.

———. "United States." In *The Wiley-Blackwell Companion to Practical Theology*, edited by Bonnie Miller-McLemore, 495–505. Hoboken, NJ: Wiley-Blackwell, 2014.

———, and Friedrich Schweitzer. *Religious Education between Modernization and Globalization: New Perspectives on the United States and Germany*. Grand Rapids: Eerdmans, 2003.

Parks, Sharon. *Big Questions, Worthy Dreams: Mentoring Young Adults in Their Search for Meaning, Purpose, and Faith*. San Francisco: Jossey-Bass, 2000.

———. *The Critical Years: Young Adults and the Search for Meaning, Faith and Commitment*. San Francisco: Harper & Row, 1986.

———. "Imagination and Spirit in Faith Development: A Way Past the Structure-Content Dichotomy." In *Faith Development and Fowler*, edited by Craig R. Dykstra and Sharon Parks, 137–56. Birmingham, AL: Religious Education Press, 1986.

Pattison, Stephen. *The Challenge of Practical Theology*. London: Kingsley, 2007.

Pazmino, Robert. *Foundational Issues in Christian Education: An Introduction to an Evangelical Perspective*. Grand Rapids: Baker, 2008.

———. *God Our Teacher: Theological Basics in Christian Education*. Grand Rapids: Baker, 2001.

Phillips, Anne. *The Faith of Girls: Explorations in Practical, Pastoral, and Empirical Theology*. London: Ashgate, 2013.

Prasadam, Ajit A. "Education Reimagined in the Logic of the Spirit." In *Christians in the Public Square—Papers from the 2nd SAIACS Consulation*, edited by Varughese John and Nigel A. Kumar, 92–155. Bangalore: SAIACS, 2013.

———. "Imagining Practical Theology Today: Methodology and the 'Margins.'" In *Margins in Conversation: Methodological Discourses in Theological Disciplines*, edited by Joseph Prahbakar Dayam and P. Mohan Larbeer, 322–47. Bangalore: Board of Theological Education of the Senate of the Serampore College, 2012.

———. "Models of Education: Socialization and Transformation (Implications for Seminary Education)." *The Princeton Theological Review* 9 (2005) 13–22.

Ratcliff, Donald. "Qualitative Data Analysis and the Transforming Moment." *Transformation* 25 (2008) 116–33.

———, et al. *Children's Spirituality: Christian Perspectives, Research and Applications*. Eugene, OR: Cascade, 2004.

Rhodes, J. Steve. "Conversion as Crisis and Process: A Comparison of Two Models." *Journal of Psychology and Christianity* 5 (1986) 20–27.

Root, Andrew. *Children of Divorce: The Loss of Family as the Loss of Being*. Grand Rapids: Baker Academic, 2010.

———. *Christopraxis: A Practical Theology of the Cross*. Minneapolis: Fortress, 2014.

———. "Divorce, Young People and Youth Ministry." *Journal of Youth Ministry* 10 (2011) 67–84.

———, with Blair Bertrand. "Postscript: Reflections on Method—Youth Ministry as Practical Theology." In Andrew Root and Kenda Creasy Dean, *The Theological Turn in Youth Ministry*, 218–36. Downers Grove, IL: InterVarsity, 2011

———. *Reflective Pastor: Sharing in Christ by Sharing Ourselves*. Downers Grove, IL: InterVarsity, 2013.

———. *Revisiting Relational Youth Ministry: From a Strategy of Influence to a Theology of Incarnation*. Downers Grove, IL: InterVarsity, 2007.

———. "A Screen-Based World: Finding the Real in the Hyper-Real." *Word & World* 32 (2012) 237–44.

———. *Taking the Cross to Youth Ministry*. Grand Rapids: Zondervan/Youth Specialties, 2012.

Root, Andrew, and Kenda Creasy Dean. *The Theological Turn in Youth Ministry*. Downers Grove, IL: InterVarsity, 2011.

Savage, Sara. *Joseph: Insights for the Spiritual Journey*. Eugene, OR: Cascade, 2013.

———, and Eolene Boyd-MacMillan. *Conflict in Relationships: Understand It, Overcome It: At Home, at Work, in Life*. Oxford: Lion UK, 2010.

———, and Eolene Boyd-MacMillan. *The Human Face of the Church: A Social-Psychology and Pastoral Theology Resource for Pioneer and Traditional Ministry*. York: Federated Church Leadership Press, 2008.

Schipani, Daniel. "Case Study." In *The Wiley-Blackwell Companion to Practical Theology*, edited by Bonnie Miller-McLemore, 92–102. Hoboken, NJ: Wiley-Blackwell, 2014.

———. *Concientization and Creativity: Paulo Freire and Christian Education*. Lanham, MD: University Press of America, 1984.

———. "The Heart of the Matter: Engaging the *Spirit* in Spiritual Care." In *Multifaith Views in Pastoral Care*, edited by Daniel Schipani, 149–66. Kitchener, ON: Pandora, 2013.

———. *Religious Education Encounters Liberation Theology*. Birmingham, AL: Religious Education Press, 1988.

———. "Transforming Encounter in the Borderlands: A Study of Matthew 15:21–28." In *Redemptive Transformation in Practical Theology: Essays in Honor of James E. Loder Jr.*, edited by Dana R. Wright and John D. Kuentzel, 116–32. Grand Rapids: Eerdmans, 2004.

———. *The Way of Wisdom in Pastoral Counseling*. Elkart, IN: Institute for Mennonite Studies, 2003.

———. "A Wisdom Model for Pastoral Counseling." In *Healing Wisdom: Depth Psychology and Pastoral Ministry*, edited by Kathleen J. Greider et al., 94–108. Grand Rapids: Eerdmans, 2010.

Schneider, Stephen. "Eucharistic Knowing." Unpublished paper from Loder's reserve reading list. No date.

Shults, F. LeRon. "Holding onto the Theology-Psychology Relationship: The Underlying Fiduciary Structures of Interdisciplinary Method." *Journal of Psychology and Theology* 25 (1997) 329–40.

———. "One Spirit with the Lord." *Princeton Seminary Review* 7 (2000) 17–26.

———. "Pedagogy of the Repressed: What Keeps Seminarians from Transformational Learning?" *Theological Education* 36 (1999) 157–69.

———. "The Philosophical Turn to Relationality and the Responsibility of Practical Theology." In *Redemptive Transformation in Practical Theology: Essays in Honor of James E. Loder Jr.*, edited by Dana R. Wright and John D. Kuentzel, 325–46. Grand Rapids: Eerdmans, 2004.

———. *The Postfoundationalist Task of Theology: Wolfhart Pannenberg and the New Theological Rationality*. Grand Rapids: Eerdmans, 1999.

———. *Reforming Theological Anthropology: After the Philosophical Turn to Relationality*. Grand Rapids: Eerdmans, 2003.

———. "Structures of Rationality in Science and Theology: Overcoming the Postmodern Dilemma." *Perspectives on Science and Christian Faith* 49 (1997) 228–36.

———. *Transforming Spirituality: Integrating Theology and Psychology*. Grand Rapids: Baker Academic, 2006.

———, and Steven Sandage. *The Faces of Forgiveness: Searching for Wholeness and Salvation*. Grand Rapids: Baker Academic, 2003.

Slemmons, Timothy M. *Groans of the Spirit: Homiletical Dialectics*. Eugene, OR: Pickwick, 2010.

Sponheim, Paul. *The Pulse of Creation: God and the Transformation of the World*. Minneapolis: Fortress, 2000.

———. *Speaking of God: Relational Theology*. St. Louis: Chalice, 2006.

Spooner, Bernard M. *Christian Education Leadership: Making Disciples in the Twenty-first Century Church*. Coppell, TX: CreateSpace, 2012.

Thomas, Harold R. "Conversion Process: James E. Loder in Missiological Perspective." In *Footprints of God: A Narrative Theology of Mission*, edited by C. van Engen et al., 5–18. Monrovia, CA: MARC World Vision, 1999.

Torrance, Thomas F. "Foreword." In James E. Loder and W. Jim Neidhardt, *The Knight's Move: The Relational Logic of the Spirit in Theology and Science*, xi–xii. Colorado Springs, CO: Helmers & Howard, 1994.

Walsh, Albert J. D. *The Eucharist's Biographer: The Liturgical Formation of Christian Identity*. Eugene, OR: Pickwick, 2012.

Webster, Derek. "James Fowler's Theory of Faith Development." *British Journal of Religious Education* 8 (1984) 79–83. Reprinted in *Christian Perspectives on Faith Development*, edited by J. Astley and L. Francis, 77–84. Leominster, UK: Gracewing, 1992.

Welton, Michael. "Seeing the Light: Christian Conversion and Conscientization." In *Adult Education and Theological Interpretations*, edited by Peter Jarvis and Nicholas Walters, 105–23. Malabar, FL: Krieger, 1993.

White, Keith J. "Being Born Again." *Residence* (May 2012). www.childrenwebmag.com.

———. *The Growth of Love.* Oxford: Barnabas, 2008.

———. "Loder." In *Introducing Child Theology: Theological Foundations for HCD*, 166–206. Malaysia: Compassion, 2010.

Wigger, J. Bradley. *The Texture of Mystery: An Interdisciplinary Inquiry into Perception and Learning.* Cranbury, NJ: Associated University Press, 1998.

Willis, E. David. *Notes on the Holiness of God.* Grand Rapids: Eerdmans, 2002.

Wright, Almeda. "What Is Salvation for Adolescents?" In *Koinonia: The Princeton Theological Seminary Graduate Forum* 18, edited by Keith Johnson, 19–26. Princeton: Princeton Seminary, 2006.

Wright, Dana R. "Afterword: The Potential Contribution of James E. Loder Jr. to Practical Theological Science." In *Redemptive Transformation in Practical Theology: Essays in Honor of James E. Loder Jr.*, edited by Dana R. Wright and John D. Kuentzel, 401–31. Grand Rapids: Eerdmans, 2004.

———. "The Contemporary Renaissance in Practical Theology in the United States: The Past, Present and Future of a Discipline in Creative Ferment." *International Journal of Practical Theology* 6 (2000) 289–320.

———, with John Kuentzel. "Introduction: 'Are You There?': Comedic Interrogation in the Life and Witness of James E. Loder, Jr." In *Redemptive Transformation in Practical Theology: Essays in Honor of James E. Loder Jr.*, edited by Dana R. Wright and John D. Kuentzel, 1–42. Grand Rapids: Eerdmans, 2004.

———. "James E. Loder Jr." In *Christian Educators of the Twentieth Century.* Hard copy of the online series *Christian Educators of the Twentieth Century*, edited by Kevin Lawson.

———. "Paradigmatic Madness and Redemptive Creativity in Practical Theology: A Biblical Interpretation of the Theological Significance of James E. Loder's Neo-Chalcedonian Science for the Postmodern Context." In *Redemptive Transformation in Practical Theology: Essays in Honor of James E. Loder Jr.*, edited by Dana R. Wright and John D. Kuentzel, 216–51. Grand Rapids: Eerdmans, 2004.

———, with Kenda Creasy Dean. "Youth, Passion and Intimacy in the Context of Koinonia: James E. Loder's Contribution to a Practical Theology of *Imitatio Christi* for Youth Ministry." In *Redemptive Transformation in Practical Theology: Essays in Honor of James E. Loder Jr.*, edited by Dana R. Wright and John D. Kuentzel, 153–88. Grand Rapids: Eerdmans, 2004.

———, and John Kuentzel, eds. *Redemptive Transformation in Practical Theology: Essays in Honor of James E. Loder Jr.* Grand Rapids: Eerdmans, 2004.

Research Entries (CD Rom)

Wright, Dana R. "James E. Loder Jr." In *Christian Educators of the Twentieth Century*, edited by Kevin Lawson (updated). Online: www.talbot.edu/ce20/.

Reviews of Loder's Books (chronological order)

Stendahl, Krister. Summaries of Doctoral Dissertations. *Harvard Theological Review* 59 (1963) 299–300.

Green, John R. Review of *Religious Pathology and the Christian Faith*. *The Princeton Seminary Bulletin*, o.s., 59 (1966) 66–77.

Rosen, S. Review of *Religion in the Public Schools*. *Journal of Church and State* 8 (1966) 299–300.

Morton, Nelle. Review of *Religious Pathology and the Christian Faith*. *The Princeton Seminary Bulletin*, o.s., 60 (1967) 74–83.

Deconchy, Jean-Pierre. Review of *Religious Pathology and Christian Faith*. *Archives de Sociologie des Religions* 13 (1968) 211–12.

Outler, Albert. Review of *Religious Pathology and the Christian Faith*. *Theology Today* 4 (1968) 540–42.

Smith, J. Review of *The Transforming Moment: Understanding Convictional Experiences*. *Religious Education* 76 (1981) 676–77.

Brownell, T. Review of *The Transforming Moment: Understanding Convictional Experiences*. *Epiphany* 3 (1982) 90–93.

Dykstra, Craig R. Review of *The Transforming Moment: Understanding Convictional Experiences*. *The Princeton Seminary Bulletin*, n.s., 3 (1982) 339–41.

Hunt, R. A. Review of *The Transforming Moment: Understanding Convictional Experiences*. *Pastoral Psychology* 30 (1982) 194–96.

Philibert, P. J. Review of *The Transforming Moment: Understanding Convictional Experiences*. *Horizons* 9 (1982) 390–91.

Russell, J. F. Review of *The Transforming Moment: Understanding Convictional Experiences*. *Theological Studies* 43 (1982) 185.

Faber, H. Review of *The Transforming Moment: Understanding Convictional Experiences*. *Nederlands Theologisch Tijdschrift* 36 (1982) 311–31.

———. Review of *Zicht Op de Structuur van de Godsdienstige Ervaring: Twee Boeken*. *Nederlands Theologisch Tijdschrift* 36 (1982) 311–31.

Dorrien, G. J. Review of *The Transforming Moment: Understanding Convictional Experiences*. *Sojourners* 12 (1983) 36–38.

Dunlap, P. C. Review of *The Transforming Moment: Understanding Convictional Experiences*. *Journal of Supervision and Training in Ministry* 6 (1983) 234–35.

Fuller, R. C. Review of *The Transforming Moment: Understanding Convictional Experiences*. *Zygon* 18 (1983) 463–64.

McClendon, J. W. Review of *The Transforming Moment: Understanding Convictional Experiences*. *Journal of the American Academy of Religion* 51 (1983) 127.

Fiet, Thom. Review of *The Transforming Moment* (2nd ed.). *Reformed Review* 44 (1990) 170.

McKenna, John. Review of *The Transforming Moment* (2nd ed.). *Perspectives on Science and Christian Faith* 43 (1992) 199–201.

Rogers, Frank. Review of *The Transforming Moment* (2nd ed.). *Religious Education* 86 (1991) 323–25.

Wright, Dana R. Review of *The Knight's Move: Relational Logic in Theology and Science*. *Koinonia* 4 (1992) 273–76.

Buis, Harry. Review of *The Knight's Move: Relational Logic in Theology and Science*. *Reformed Review* 47 (1983) 64.

Durbin, William. Review of *The Knight's Move: Relational Logic in Theology and Science. Journal of Interdisciplinary Studies* 5 (1993) 193–95.

Reich, K. Helmut. Review of *The Knight's Move: Relational Logic in Theology and Science. CTNS Bulletin* 13 (1993) 20–23.

Alsford, Mike. Review of *The Knight's Move: Relational Logic in Theology and Science. Science and Christian Belief* 6 (1994) 133–34.

Palmer, Michael. Review of *The Knight's Move: Relational Logic in Theology and Science. Paraclete* 28 (1994) 30–32.

Strawser, Michael J. Review of *The Knight's Move: Relational Logic in Theology and Science. Kierkegaardiana* 17 (1994) 191–94.

Unnamed reviewer. Review of *The Knight's Move: Relational Logic in Theology and Science. Paraclete* 28 (1994) 30–32.

Haught, John F. Review of *The Knight's Move: Relational Logic in Theology and Science. Journal of the American Academy of Religion* 63 (1995) 168–69.

Richardson, W. Mark. Review of *The Knight's Move: Relational Logic in Theology and Science. The Princeton Seminary Bulletin*, n.s., 16 (1995) 345–47.

Torrance, Thomas F. Review of *The Knight's Move: Relational Logic in Theology and Science. The Scottish Journal of Theology* 48 (1995) 139–40.

Ivy, Steven S. Review of *The Logic of the Spirit: Human Development in Theological Perspective. Journal of Pastoral Care* 53 (1999) 495–96.

Torrance, Thomas F. Review of *The Logic of the Spirit: Human Development in Theological Perspective. The Princeton Seminary Bulletin*, n.s., 20 (1999) 316–17.

Carlson, Richard. Review of *The Knight's Move: Relational Logic in Theology and Science. Zygon* 31 (2000) 731–35.

Flett, Eric G. Review of *The Logic of the Spirit: Human Development in Theological Perspective. Christian Scholar's Review* 29 (2000) 622–23.

Frohlich, Mary. Review of *The Logic of the Spirit: Human Development in Theological Perspective. Horizons* 27 (2000) 213–15.

Bregman, Lucy. Review of *The Logic of the Spirit: Human Development in Theological Perspective. Journal of Religion* 80 (2000) 689–91.

Tributes or Memorial Addresses

Alumni News. "Synnott Chair." Announcement of James Loder's appointment to the Mary Synnott Chair in Christian Education, 1981.

———. "Transformation." Announcement of the publication of *The Transforming Moment*, by James E. Loder, Jr., 1981, 4.

Chaapel, Barbara. "A Transforming Life: James Edwin Loder, December 5, 1931–November 9, 2001." *Inspire* 6 (2002) 18.

Crocco, Stephen D. "Windows into the Life of James E. Loder, Jr." *The Princeton Seminary Bulletin*, n.s., 23 (2002) 64–85.

Englemann, Kim (Loder). "Remembering Dr. James Loder as Father: Reflections on the Moments We Shared." *The Princeton Seminary Bulletin*, n.s., 23 (2002) 67–70.

Gardner, Freda. "Memorial Minute" (based on her tribute to James E. Loder, Jr., given at the faculty meeting, February 13, 2002). The Princeton Seminary Bulletin, n.s., 23 (2002) 188–94.

Gaskill, William. "A Work of Love in the Presence of an Absence." *The Princeton Seminary Bulletin*, n.s., 23 (2002) 65–66.

Gillespie, Thomas. "Words of Welcome." *The Princeton Seminary Bulletin*, n.s., 23 (2002) 64.
Hess, Lisa. "A Transforming Life: Apostle of the Living Light." *Inspire* 6 (2002) 19.
Tiss, Tamara (Loder). "James Loder: Our Christlike Father and Gracious Friend." *The Princeton Seminary Bulletin*, n.s., 23 (2002) 71–74.
Wright, Dana. "Prophetic Practical Theology as Testimony: A Loder Legacy?" *Inspire* 6 (2002) 20–21.
———. "Ruination unto Redemption in the Spirit: A Short Biography of a Reformed 'Wise Guy.'" *The Princeton Seminary Bulletin*, n.s., 23 (2002) 75–85.
———. "What Has Athens and Jerusalem to Do with Galilee? A Tribute to James E. Loder." Unpublished paper delivered at the Templeton Foundation/Princeton Seminary workshop on Spirituality and the Adolescent, February 2002.

Dissertations Supervised by James E. Loder (chronological order)

Roberts, William Lloyd. "The Supervisory Alternative to the Custodial Contract in the Educational Ministry." PhD diss., Princeton Theological Seminary, 1970.
Batson, C. Daniel. "Creativity and Religious Development: Toward a Structural/Functional Psychology of Religion." ThD diss., Princeton Theological Seminary, 1971.
Nichols, Randall. "Conflict and Creativity: The Dynamics of the Communication Process in Theological Perspective." PhD diss., Princeton Theological Seminary, 1971.
Conrad, Robert Leroy. "Christian Education and Creative Conflict: Relations between Creative Intra-psychic Conflict as Understood in Luther's Experience and Theology and as Understood in Social Psychological Theories with Conclusions for Christian Education Principles and Practice." PhD diss., Princeton Theological Seminary, 1975.
Dykstra, Craig R. "Christian Education and the Moral Life: An Evaluation of and Alternative to Kohlberg/Piaget?" PhD diss., Princeton Theological Seminary, 1978.
Schipani, Daniel S. "Conscientization and Creativity: A Reinterpretation of Paulo Freire, Focused on His Epistemological and Theological Foundations with Implications for Christian Education." PhD diss., Princeton Theological Seminary, 1981.
Goldstein, Robert Morris. "On Christian Rhetoric: The Significance of Søren Kierkegaard's 'Dialectic of Ethical and Ethical-Religious Communication' for Philosophical and Theological Pedagogy." PhD diss., Princeton Theological Seminary, 1982.
Johnson, Susanne. "Religious Experience as Creative, Revelatory and Transforming Event: The Implications of Intense Christian Experience for the Christian Education Process." PhD diss., Princeton Theological Seminary, 1983.
Cram, Ronald Hugh. "Cultural Pluralism and Christian Education: Laura Thompson's Design for Anthropology and Its Use in Christian Education for Ethnic Groups." PhD diss., Princeton Theological Seminary, 1984.
McClure, John. "Preaching and the Pragmatics of Human/Divine Communication in the Liturgy of the Word in the Western Church: A Semiotic and Practical Theological Study." PhD diss., Princeton Theological Seminary, 1984.
Ford-Grabowsky, Mary E. "The Concept of Christian Faith in the Light of Hildegard of Bingen and C. G. Jung: Critical Alternatives to Fowler." PhD diss., Princeton Theological Seminary, 1985.

Krych, Margaret. "Communicating 'Justification' to Elementary-Age Children: A Study in Tillich's Correlational Method and Transformational Narrative for Christian Education." PhD diss., Princeton Theological Seminary, 1985.

Ruiz, Lester Edwin Jainga. "Toward a Transformative Politics: A Quest for Authentic Political Personhood." PhD diss., Princeton Theological Seminary, 1985.

Croteau-Chonka, Clarisse C. "Intuition: A Paradigm of the Wholeness Necessary for Holiness and Its Relationship to Christian Education." PhD diss., Princeton Theological Seminary, 1987.

Shoberg, Georgia Helen. "Salvation, Sanctification, and Individuation: A Study of the Relationship between Jungian Individuation and New Testament Views of Salvation and Sanctification." PhD diss., Princeton Theological Seminary, 1987.

Frykberg, Elizabeth A. "Spiritual Transformation and the Creation of Humankind in the Image of God, Male and Female: A Study of Karl Barth's Understanding of the 'Analogia Relationis' Correlated with Psychosexual and Psychosocial Development Theory." PhD diss., Princeton Theological Seminary, 1989.

Hess, Carol L. "Educating in the Spirit." PhD diss., Princeton Theological Seminary, 1990.

Proffitt, Anabel C. "The Technological Mindset in Twentieth-Century American Religious Education Curriculum." PhD diss., Princeton Theological Seminary, 1990.

Hess, Ernest P. "Christian Identity and Openness: A Theologically Informed Hermeneutical Approach to Christian Education." PhD diss., Princeton Theological Seminary, 1991.

Rogers, Frank. "Karl Barth's Faith Epistemology of the Spirit as a Critical and Constructive Framework for Christian Education." PhD diss., Princeton Theological Seminary, 1991.

Reese, Daniel Bryan. "The Feast of Wisdom: Thomas Merton's Vision and Practice of a Sapiential Education." PhD diss., Princeton Theological Seminary, 1995.

Martin, Robert K. "The Incarnate Ground of Christian Education: The Integration of Epistemology and Ontology in the Thought of Michael Polanyi and Thomas F. Torrance." PhD diss., Princeton Theological Seminary, 1995.

Lee, Kyoo Min. "Koinonia: A Critical Study of Lewis Sherrill's Concept of Koinonia and Jürgen Moltmann's Social Understanding of the Trinity as an Attempt to Provide a Corrective to the Problems of the Korean Church and Its Educational Ministry." PhD diss., Princeton Theological Seminary, 1996.

Kuentzel, John D. "The Ethic of Care and Christian Education: Implications for the Theory and Practice of Christian Education." PhD diss., Princeton Theological Seminary, 1999.

Wright, Dana. "*Ecclesial Theatrics*: Toward a Reconstruction of Evangelical Christian Education Theory as Critical Dogmatic Practical Theology." PhD diss., Princeton Theological Seminary, 1999.

Fredrickson, Johnna Lee. "Iconic Christian Education: Pointing to and Participating in the Reality of God." PhD diss., Princeton Theological Seminary, 2000.

Frawley, Matthew J. "Søren Kierkegaard's Christian Anthropology and the Relation between His Pseudonymous and Religious Writings." PhD diss., Princeton Theological Seminary, 2001 (special agreement with Diogenes Allen, the actual supervisor).

Haitch, Russell. "Baptizing and Teaching: Three Theological Positions and Their Educational Significance." PhD diss., Princeton Theological Seminary, 2002 (completed under the advisorship of R. Osmer).

Curriculums or Courses Based, in Whole or in Part, upon Loder's Practical Theological Vision

Boyd-MacMillan, Eolene. "Conflict Transformation." Master of Arts course taught annually at Ripon College, Oxford University, 2011 to the present.

———. "Personal Transformation, Spirituality, and Counseling." Unpublished curriculum used in the Department of Counseling and Psychoanalysis, School of Health in Social Science, University of Edinburgh, 2009–2011.

———. "Psychology, Faith and Church Life." Course offered through the Cambridge Theological Federation, 2005–2012.

Frykberg, Elizabeth, and Ajit A. Prasadam. *Windows to Encounter: Workbook and Teacher's Guides for Grades K–10*. 12 vols. Coonoor, India: India Sunday School Union Press, 1994–2001.

India Sunday School Union. "God Revealed in Jesus Christ." In *Windows to Encounter*, vol. 12 [Grade 11]. Edited by Ajit Prasadam. Coonoor, India: ISSU, 2014.

———. *Windows to Encounter* (Including Student Workbooks and Teacher Guides). 11 volumes [Pre-school to Grade 10]. Edited by Elizabeth Frykberg and Ajit Prasadam. Coonoor, India: ISSU, 1996–2000.

Wright, Dana. "The Church Alive with Youth in an Uncertain World." Intensive course taught at the St. Andrews Center, India Sunday School Union, Coonoor, India, October 2011, 2014.

———. "Paradigmatic Madness and Redemptive Creativity in Public Theology: An Imaginative Reading of Ephesians and James E. Loder's Practical Theological Science." Intensive course to be taught at the St. Andrews Center, India Sunday School Union, Coonoor, India, October 2014.

———. "Readings in Christian Education: The Life, Thought, and Contribution of James E. Loder Jr. to Practical Theology and Christian Education Theory and Practice." Doctoral seminar given at Princeton Theological Seminary, Fall 2002.

———. "Readings in Practical Theology: The Holy Spirit in Christian Education." An advanced senior course based on a close reading of *Educational Ministry in the Logic of the Spirit*, given at Trinity Lutheran College, Everett, WA, Spring 2012.

Reviews of Loder Festschrift

Anderson, Ray. Review of *Redemptive Transformation in Practical Theology: Essays in Honor of James E. Loder, Jr.*, edited by Dana R. Wright and John D. Kuentzel. *Journal of Family Ministry* 19 (2005) 94–95.

Fergusson, David. Review of *Redemptive Transformation in Practical Theology: Essays in Honor of James E. Loder, Jr.*, edited by Dana R. Wright and John D. Kuentzel. *Theology Today* 63 (2006) 278.

Yong, Amos. Review of *Redemptive Transformation in Practical Theology: Essays in Honor of James E. Loder, Jr.*, edited by Dana R. Wright and John D. Kuentzel. *Religious Studies Review* 32 (2006) 108.

www.ingramcontent.com/pod-product-compliance
Lightning Source LLC
Chambersburg PA
CBHW071145300426
44113CB00009B/1089